Surviving the Ghetto

Studies in Jewish History and Culture

Edited by

Giuseppe Veltri

Editorial Board

Gad Freudenthal
Alessandro Guetta
Hanna Liss
Ronit Meroz
Reimund Leicht
Judith Olszowy-Schlanger
David Ruderman
Marion Aptroot

VOLUME 65

The titles published in this series are listed at *brill.com/sjhc*

Surviving the Ghetto

Toward a Social History of the Jewish Community in 16th-Century Rome

By

Serena Di Nepi

Translated by

Paul M. Rosenberg

BRILL

LEIDEN | BOSTON

Cover illustration: Giovanni Battista Falda, *Fountain in Piazza Giudea*, Rome 1691 (Private Collection)

This volume was originally published in Italian: Serena Di Nepi, *Sopravvivere al ghetto. Per una storia sociale della comunità ebraica nella Roma del Cinquecentoa*. Rome: Viella, 2013.

Library of Congress Cataloging-in-Publication Data

Names: Di Nepi, Serena, author. | Rosenberg, Paul M., translator.
Title: Surviving the ghetto : toward a social history of the Jewish community in
    16th-century Rome / by Serena Di Nepi ; translated by Paul M. Rosenberg
Other titles: Sopravvivere al ghetto. English | Toward a social history of the Jewish
    community in 16th-century Rome
Description: English edition. | Leiden ; Boston : Brill, [2021] | Series: Studies in Jewish History
    and Culture, 1568-5004 ; Volume 65 | "This volume was originally published in Italian:
    Serena Di Nepi, Sopravvivere al ghetto. Per una storia sociale nella Roma del Cinquecento.
    Rome: Viella, 2013." | Includes bibliographical references and index. |
    Summary: "The expulsion of the Jews from Spain in 1492 and the subsequent expulsion
    from Portugal just four years later mark what is traditionally viewed as a watershed
    moment in Jewish history. Ferdinand and Isabella's strategy of aggressive evangelization -
    conversion or expulsion - had countless consequences from many points of view.
    The resulting wave of refugees transformed the geography of the Jewish presence in the
    Mediterranean basin as well as in central and southern Europe"– Provided by publisher.
Identifiers: LCCN 2020032635 | ISBN 9789004431188 (hardback) |
    ISBN 9789004431195 (ebook)
Subjects: LCSH: Jews–Italy–Rome–History–16th century. | Jews–Italy–Rome– Social
    conditions–16th century. | Jewish ghettos–Italy–Rome. | Rome (Italy)– Ethnic relations.
Classification: LCC DS135.I85 R62513 2021 | DDC 945.3/32004924009031–dc23
LC record available at https://lccn.loc.gov/2020032635

Typeface for the Latin, Greek, and Cyrillic scripts: "Brill". See and download: brill.com/brill-typeface.

ISSN 1568-5004
ISBN 978-90-04-43118-8 (hardback)
ISBN 978-90-04-43119-5 (e-book)

English Edition: Copyright 2021 by Koninklijke Brill NV, Leiden, The Netherlands.
Koninklijke Brill NV incorporates the imprints Brill, Brill Hes & De Graaf, Brill Nijhoff, Brill Rodopi, Brill Sense, Hotei Publishing, mentis Verlag, Verlag Ferdinand Schöningh and Wilhelm Fink Verlag.
All rights reserved. No part of this publication may be reproduced, translated, stored in a retrieval system, or transmitted in any form or by any means, electronic, mechanical, photocopying, recording or otherwise, without prior written permission from the publisher. Requests for re-use and/or translations must be addressed to Koninklijke Brill NV via brill.com or copyright.com.

This book is printed on acid-free paper and produced in a sustainable manner.

Contents

Acknowledgments VII
List of Abbreviations IX

Reframing the Roman Ghetto: Introduction to the English Edition 1

1 Before the Ghetto 26
 1 Rome and the Spanish Refugees 27
 2 A Statute for the Jews of Rome (1524) 35
 3 The Burning of the Talmud and the Anti-Jewish Turn in the First Half of the 16th Century 40
 4 The Avoided Expulsion from the Papal States 45
 5 What If the Emperor Had Won? 55

2 The Birth of the Ghetto and the Dangers Narrowly Escaped in 1555 60
 1 The Sforno Case (1527–1555) 61
 2 Blood Libel in Rome? 66
 3 Imaginary Violence 74

3 A Ruling Class for the Jews of the Ghetto 86
 1 Avoided Reforms 87
 2 Have Faith in the Notary: Pompeo del Borgo 94
 3 Arbitrators and Arbitration in the Selection of the Ruling Class 103
 4 Housing Problems and Issues with Taxes 112
 5 The Discipline of the Rabbis 118
 6 Jewish Identity: a Trial for Crimes and Other Excesses in 1572 124
 7 Religious Belonging in Court? 127

4 Career Bankers 131
 1 A Trial and a Case Study: Salomone Ram (1594) 132
 2 The Ram Family, Moneylenders in the Ghetto Years 139
 3 The Regulation of the Jewish Banks (1590) 144
 4 The Jewish Banks 150
 5 Still Bankers? 153

5 Unexpected Opportunities 159
 1 Valuable *stracci* from the Hospitals 160
 2 Market Spaces: the Jews, Public Space and Real Estate Ownership 174
 3 Business Travel 181

6 The *Camerlengo*, a Protector in the Curia 193
    1   The *inhibitiones ratione foenoris* 193
    2   In the Name and on Behalf of the *Camerlengo* 200
    3   The Story of a Special Relationship 206

7 Separate at Home 214
    1   Christians at the Jewish Notary 214
    2   The Business of Converts 221

Conclusions 230

Bibliography and Reference Works 237
Index of Places 261
General Index 263

Acknowledgments

Seven years have passed since the publication of the Italian edition of this book, during which many important studies on the history of the Jews in the centuries of the ghettos have come out, and are still coming out, of which it was impossible to give a comprehensive accounting. The most interesting results of this renewed season of study are discussed in the new Introduction; in the footnotes, instead, I have referenced only the studies that specifically draw a different and more complex paradigm of this era for Rome and Italy.

This new edition and the reflections that I present here in the *Introduction* and new sections owe a great deal to the international discussion of recent years, and to the opportunity that I have had to be a part of it. From the RSA panels in which I participated in 2014, 2015 and 2017, to the intense months at Hebrew University of Jerusalem under the expert guidance of Yosef Kaplan and the extraordinary group of post-doc researchers that worked with him in 2015; up to *The Rome Lab* program in New York in 2017, supported by the Primo Levi Center and the Jewish Museum of Rome (many thanks to Alessandra Di Castro!). Then there was the work on the PRIN 2015 project *The Long History of Anti-Semitism* (2015NA5XLZ_002), directed at the national level by Germano Maifreda, and by Marina Caffiero for the Rome-Sapienza unit. Of great importance was the debate at the Parisian conference *Non contrarii ma diversi* in 2016, organized by Alessandro Guetta and Pierre Savy (and I thank them both!), which in its discussion of the ghettos ended up defining itself as "a revisionist convention"!. Also of importance was *The Jews in Italy during the Long Renaissance,* the series of international conferences that followed one another during 2019 and 2020, which for the first time allowed us to organically examine the new historiography on Jewish Italy, over the course of three gatherings rich with ideas and questions. Thanks, then, to the dozens of scholars who animated these sessions, and to the friends and colleagues who worked tirelessly to organize them among infinite WhatsApp messages, across three different time zones.

Among the many people whom I wish to thank is Marina Caffiero, who has accompanied me over the years with great generosity, from the Wednesday morning laboratories in long ago 2003 up to today. For the endless chats about Jews, ghettos, Italy and history, my gratitude also goes to Bernard D. Cooperman, Germano Maifreda, Jacopo Mascetti, Mauro Perani, Giacomo Todeschini and Stefano Villani. Thanks to Anna Esposito, who first pushed me to study this subject. Thanks also to Natalia Indrimi, who introduced me to Paul M. Rosenberg, an exceptional translator and now a friend. Last but not least, thanks to

Giuseppe Veltri for accepting my proposal for his series, and to Katelyn Chin, Erika Mandarino and the editorial staff at Brill for staying with this project in spite of the difficulties in getting the paperwork over the Ocean. And finally, thanks to Cecilia Palombelli at Viella for having first supported the original book and now this translation.

The translation of this volume has been generously financed by the Department SARAS (History, Art, Anthropology, Religions and Performance) of Sapienza Università di Roma.

Note on the Criteria for Transcriptions from Hebrew

The different languages in which the documents used in this research are written (Latin, Italian, Hebrew) pose the problem of consistent transcription of names and surnames to facilitate identification of the people who appear in all the sources. In order to facilitate the reading, first names and surnames have been rendered, when possible, in the Italian form that is closest to the contemporaneous wording found in Latin and vernacular, and not in translation; so, for example, *Yosef* or *Ioseph* is Giuseppe and not Ventura, *Aschkenazi* or *Theutonicus* is always Tedeschi, and *Eliezer* remains as is. The same logic has been followed in transcribing the few Hebrew words present in the text, again in order to ease the reading of the work.

Abbreviations

AC	Archivio Capitolino, Roma
ASR	Archivio di Stato di Roma
c./cc.	carta/carte page/pages
DC	ASR, *Camerale I, Diversorum del camerlengo*
f./ff	fascicolo/fascicoli file/files
l. libro	book
NE	Archivio Capitolino, Archivio Urbano, Sezione III, *Notai ebrei*
Processi	ASR, *Tribunale Criminale del Governatore, Processi*
r	*recto*
reg.	registro
v	*verso*

Reframing the Roman Ghetto: Introduction to the English Edition

1 "The Romans know what the Ghetto of Rome is, as do those who have seen it ..."

Every year tens of thousands of tourists make their way down to the basement of the monumental synagogue that overlooks the Lungotevere to visit the Jewish Museum of Rome. Over the course of a couple of hours they are somewhat amazed to discover that the building in which they stand recounts, on its own, part of the history and culture they came to learn about. The Great Temple of Rome, with its imposing structure, its dome set among the cupolas and its location in that part of the city, was only opened, in fact, in 1904. Built little more than thirty years after the annexation of the city by the newly formed Kingdom of Italy (1870), the great synagogue was designed to embody, brick by brick, the inclusive modernity that was supposed to mark the present and the future of the new capital.[1] At the dawn of the new century Rome presented an unprecedented version of itself to the world: a city ready to welcome and recognize all faithful subjects, no longer and not only the holy city of the Pope. After almost twenty-one centuries of uninterrupted presence in the city, the Jewish community finally found its place in the light of the sun. The grand edifice of the synagogue was built as testimony to this moment.

On the other hand, in the new Italy that sought *free Churche in a free State* (according to the famous formulation of Camillo Benso, the count of Cavour), there were no possible alternatives. The process of national unification went hand in hand with equality of rights for the Jews. In February of 1848, the decision by Carlo Alberto, the King of Sardegna, to grant emancipation first to the Waldensians and then to the Jews represented a political manifesto. The Regio Decree was a clear statement by the Savoys, declaring the Piedmont to be the only State in the country governed by a monarchy that was in step with the times. As such, they would take on the task of bringing liberty to all of Italy and all Italians.

It goes without saying that the subject *Dell'emancipazione civile degl'Israeliti* – as the title of the famous pamphlet has it – was hot in the years of the Risorgimento. In 1848, the same year in which Jewish emancipation was declared in Torino, Massimo D'Azeglio, one of the nation's leading thinkers, went so far

---

1 Ascarelli, Di Castro, Migliau, Toscano 2004.

as to plead the case of the wretched Jews of Rome before the Pope. The Piedmont politician's words would fuel an already burning international debate:

> The Romans know what the Ghetto of Rome is, as do those who have seen it. But for those who have not visited it, know that near the bridge of the Four Heads a quarter extends along the Tiber, or rather a formless mass of ill-kept homes and hovels, in poor repair and half collapsed (and which for their owners, due to the low rents, which cannot be changed due to jus Gazaga, are not worth spending anything on unless it is unavoidable) in which are crowded 3900 people, where instead one would not willingly consider half that number. The narrow, dirty streets, the lack of air, the filth that is the inevitable consequence of the forced concentration of too many people, almost all miserable, render this inhabitance sad, smelly and unhealthy. Families live in these disgraces, and more than one per location, piled together without distinction of sex, age, condition, or health, on every floor, in the attics and even in underground holes, which in happier residences function as wine cellars.[2]

The ghettos embodied a past to overcome and forget. The imposition of filth, poverty and ignorance in the name of the faith were ills of the Old Regime, done away with once and for all by the new order. In 1858 the global scandal surrounding the Church's kidnapping of Edgardo Mortara once again shone a spotlight on the violence of the unjust anti-Jewish discrimination that remained in force in Rome and the Papal States.[3] Pius IX's rigid policy of conversion and segregation became a symbol of his resistance to the Savoy advance, and was immediately interpreted as such by all the parties involved. And so, when the Jewish captain Giacomo Segre threatened to open fire on the Porta Pia at dawn on September 20, 1870, bypassing the excommunication that the Pope had ordered for anyone who dared order an assault on the holy city, everyone understood the deeper meaning of this action: Segre unhinged the gates of Rome, opening a path to a new world for the country and for the king. And the Jews were more than ready to play a prominent role in the era that was about to unfold.[4]

Several decades later, after the end of the Risorgimento, the construction of grand synagogues in the biggest cities in the country tangibly closed the circle: at Torino, Florence and then at Rome, the three capitals that succeeded

---

2   D'Azeglio 1848.
3   Kertzer 1996.
4   Ferrara degli Uberti 2017.

one another in leading the Kingdom, the Great Temples replaced the ghetto walls. In Rome the ghetto was swept away; the excavation and construction on the banks of the Tevere and then the fire in the building that housed the *Cinque Scole* erased the old quarter forever. In a short time modern *palazzi* were built, the streets were redesigned, and the call for bids to design the great house of worship was issued. The physical removal of the seraglio made way for the beginning of a new era, leaving the memory of what had happened under the Popes to the imagination, to the watercolors of some artist, and to D'Azeglio's writings.

Understanding what happened under the Popes is the central issue. The ghetto was walled off in the fall of 1555 by order of Paul IV. The newly elected Pope Carafa published the bull *Cum nimis absurdum*, establishing a very restrictive series of rules that, between one thing and another and despite interruptions by revolutions, would remain in force, in fact, until the young captain Segre's decisive actions on that morning in 1870. Three hundred fifteen years passed slowly, and the centuries could not help but have been very different from each other. The way things were at the beginning of the story had little to do with the conditions that marked its conclusion. Over the course of those three centuries a range of phenomena, discontinuous and not progressive, inevitably impacted and transformed the community that had to live there. Yet the traditional image of the ghetto of Rome seems to be built precisely around the misery recorded in the final decades of its existence, almost intentionally disconnecting that image from the ghetto's very long lifespan.

With the English edition of this book I propose to pull together the threads of an extraordinarily productive season of research and discussion around the ghetto. This period culminated in the many events that were built around the symbolic year of 2016, the 500th anniversary (1516–2016) of the founding of the Venice ghetto. The numerous works that have been published in recent years, along with the development of a methodology of archival research that has finally begun to take new sources into consideration in the unearthing of the history of the Jews in the modern era, lead us to critically rethink the interpretive categories which have traditionally explained and defined the ghetto. There are four theoretical premises that are essential for this purpose. In this volume they are applied to the case of Rome in the years immediately following the institution of the ghetto. This English edition also includes considerations that have evolved since the publication of the Italian edition.[5]

---

5 In particular two new subsections: *What if the Emperor had Won?* (Chap. 1.5) and *Religious Belonging in Court?* (Chap. 3.7).

Starting with moving beyond the lachrymose descriptions of ghetto life that are centered on the ideas of absolute poverty and complete isolation, we must first recognize the general complexity of the phenomenon, in each phase and from any perspective one wants to examine it:

- The birth of the ghetto cannot be attributed exclusively to the evolution of violent anti-Jewish thought and practice in the Church. Without denying this evolution's role, the rise of the ghetto must also be placed in the context of the great events of the times: not only the strict ideology that developed as a response to the challenge from Luther, but also the convulsive political panorama in Italy during the decades of the Italian wars, the challenge of the Ottomans and, obviously, the imbalances caused by the formation of the Iberian empires.
- An evaluation of the Jewish response to the decrees of segregation must take into account political and economic trends, and be examined beyond the city walls. The progressive chronology of restrictive provisions and the continuous rise in the number of Italian cities with a ghetto point out the urgency of defining the phenomenon in terms of a national experience, at least for central-northern Italy. The possibility of expulsion is one of the elements to keep in mind, as well as the Jewish "drafting" of clear (and inevitably shared) accounts of what life in the ghetto was and the best way to organize it.
- An investigation of the question of wealth should begin with recognizing the structures of that era's highly stratified society, in which people who practiced a wide variety of professions and came from just as varied conditions coexisted. The study of Jewish ceremonial art objects, for example, strongly confirms the specific role of a small group of wealthy families who had close relations with the local authorities, and who often assumed governing roles in Jewish institutions.
- The persistence and the widening of inter-Jewish networks must be recognized, along with their significance in Jewish cultural dynamics. Italian Jewish culture, which for the whole of the modern age maintained a continuous dialectic as much with international Jewish culture as with the contemporary non-Jewish culture, should be seen as a genuine phenomenon of great relevance. It should therefore be reconstructed as an integral part of the general complexity of the ghetto. A cultural history that looks *over the walls* must also consider linguistic usages; for example the long term persistence of at least double language notarial registries (in Hebrew and Latin/Italian) and often even triple (adding Spanish or Portuguese), as well as the specific and parallel uses for which each combination was consciously employed. Regarding this, as we will see, the choices made by the Jewish notaries of

Rome in the second half of the 16th century point in a direction that is of great interest.

2 An Ancient History

The history of segregation begins well before that fateful year of 1555, far outside the city walls of Rome. The problem which the *claustro* sought to resolve, in fact, was an ancient matter, rooted in the dilemma implicit in the imposition of an unbalanced relationship between State Christianity and religious minorities. Despite countless past efforts, by the mid-1500s a definitive answer had not yet been found to the centuries-old question of what to do with the Jews, and how to convince them to convert in the era of the Church triumphant. The elements of the problem were well known, and they had been reordered and rearranged in many ways, but without arriving at an unequivocal response. On the one hand, there were ideological elements: Augustine's position favoring mediated protection of the Jews; the eschatological wait for the baptism of Israel to seal the theology of substitution; the role of the Jews as witnesses to the historical truth of the Gospels; and a tradition of partial benevolence dating back, though with much discontinuity, to Gregory the Great. On the other hand, there were the local experiences of the Jews, who were spread out across the lands of Europe in countless groups of varying size, more or less organized, and involved in complex relations with the local authorities. It was a pendulum in constant motion, swinging between protections, negotiations, persecution, expulsions and so on.

In this context, the lives of Jews in Italy took on certain characteristics throughout the Middle Ages. The experience of the cities and the great fragmentation of power translated into new dangers and new opportunities for the Jews of the peninsula. Tiny groups of Jews, often built around only one family, would establish themselves in towns where temporary permits for moneylending were granted. As a result, the Jewish presence in Italy was widely dispersed between the 14th and 15th centuries and subject to continual negotiations over their conditions. This led to a very high degree of mobility in the region, along with the formation of constantly overlapping family and business networks. In Christian society, which was being reshaped through progressively more centralized, powerful and oligarchic forms of governance, the role of the Jew became increasingly identified with that of moneylender, with all of the consequences that this could bring. The transformations in economy and finance, coupled with the denial of any form of political representation for the Jews, cleared a path for experimentation with models of exclusionary and marginalized coexistence that were destined to have a profound impact on the future.[6]

In Rome the elements were arranged according to different logic. At the center of the scene was the uninterrupted presence of a stable, numerous and – at times – extraordinarily distinguished Jewish community.[7] The city's Talmudic academies, the migrations to and from the *Urbe*, the complex relationship with the papacy, and the intrinsically ambivalent symbolism of the presence of Jews in the heart of Christianity combined to make the *Universitas* of Rome a unique, model case. With the definitive return of the papal court to Rome in 1417, the Jewish community also began to reorganize itself after the difficult years of Avignon. In the following decades they (re)built a community made up of artisans, important doctors (among whom were many chief physicians to the Popes), and scholars. The Jews lived in a precarious but solid equilibrium with a local scene that was subject to frequent redefinition by the individuality of papal theocracy.[8] The expulsions from Iberia at the end of the century would completely change the rules of the game. In the first half of the 16th century, Italy and Europe were overwhelmed by revolutionary turbulence. For the Jews of Rome, the quiet that followed when the storm finally passed coincided with centuries-long confinement behind the walls of the ghetto and the beginning of a new era, replete with problems and challenges. This era spanned three centuries, which despite everything were each profoundly different from the other.

To orient ourselves in the alleys of the Roman seraglio and recognize its peculiarities, we must precisely define what is hidden within the quite vague rubric of *ghetto*. The inherent contradictions seem to underpin the process of anti-Jewish segregation in the modern age, and historians have attentively highlighted them. The ghetto represented an unsolvable oxymoron; it expelled the Jews at night and partially included them during the day, providing a space of precarious but permanent tolerance (Foa). The 16th century decision to confine the Jews was a symbol of the discriminatory sanctuary granted to them by Christians who hoped for their conversion (Foa; Stow). For this reason the ghetto, while recalling the power of the Church and of its universal eschatological mission, also became the center of Jewish governing autonomy and identity (Caffiero). However, the outside controls, above all in Rome, were so

---

6 Giacomo Todeschini (2018) takes stock of these issues with detailed references to the vast bibliography on the subject.
7 Ariel Toaff's 1996b classic summary remains of value.
8 Regarding this subject, among the many works of Anna Esposito, see at least 1995 and 2007.

invasive and pervasive that they succeeded in cutting off relations between the Jews of the community and the rest of Jewish society, making these Jews extraordinarily courageous, and equally as isolated (Stow).

The nuanced nature of the subject makes the task difficult. The first ghetto was established in Venice in 1516, at the height of the Renaissance but before the explosion of the "Counter-Reformation", as part of *La Serenissima*'s struggle to defend its autonomy; the last ghetto walls were raised in 1781 at Correggio, in Emilia, in the midst of the Enlightenment and while the winds of the American revolution still blew triumphant.[9] The ghetto was canonized by its importation to and rearrangement by Rome in 1555. However, within the Papal States – even without counting Avignon (which was really in a French region) – there coexisted variations on this theme that were quite different from one another. The oppression of Rome stood in contrast to the unexpected opportunities of Ancona's version, where – after the tragedy involving the *marrani* in 1556 – Jewish businesses were explicitly encouraged and protected. The Grand Duke of Tuscany, for his part, ruled over the ghetto walls in Florence alongside the privileges of Pisa, with the *Livornine* just a few kilometers away. In the meantime his lands continued to host Inquisitors and a rather active House of Catechumens.[10] Even the Jews of Livorno, who certainly enjoyed unique liberties in the free harbor just outside the port on the Tyrrhenian Sea, were at the end of the day still Jews, to be managed like all the other Jews in the State.[11]

At the same time, however, the circulation of people, objects, and books (and therefore ideas) maintained constant communication between the Jews of Italy and *others* (whether they were Christians or Jews). From their homes in the ghettos, or while traveling to the fairs, markets and ports of the peninsula, Jews built relationships with those around them, and held leading positions in the great international networks of the western and eastern Sephardic Diasporas.[12] In this sense the phenomenon assumes a national character which deserves to finally be recognized in its entirety, regardless of the fragmentation of the pre-unification States. It should be recalled that the Jewish

---

9   Caffiero 2014.
10   Regarding the ghetto, see Siegmund 2006; regarding the House of Catechumens, see Marconcini 2016.
11   Frattarelli Fisher 2008; Trivellato 2010.
12   Other than the previously cited work by Francesca Trivellato; and specifically regarding the circulation of books from Livorno in the 1700s see: Bregoli 2014. For a historiographical update based on new research on the Sephardic diasporas in Italy, see the essays collected in Kaplan 2019, with particular reference to the works of Cooperman, Dimant, Melcer Padon and the present author.

population faced segregation as a whole, albeit in specific declinations, as has been pointed out in research on particular localities. Jews often found themselves at the center of conflicts that reached well beyond their city walls.[13] New research, still in the earliest phases, is being done on the formation of Jewish libraries, on intercultural commerce in the Mediterranean and beyond, on intellectual production, on mobility, travelers and travel, and on the universities of Padua and Ferrara, which welcomed Jewish students from all of Europe (and, therefore, also from the ghettos in Italy). This work is building a profile of Jewish Italy that cannot be reduced solely to the local scale, as has too often been done.[14]

This diversity and specificity do not mean, however, that we cannot work at reconnecting these communities – and ghettos – given that the organization of the *claustri* was based on a series of generally shared rules. Though each ghetto has its own story and may have been studied as a single and unique case, for Italian Jews segregation represented a common and collective experience which forced them to live according to similar rules, though in different manifestations. If we want to undertake a new and comprehensive history of the ghettos which places them in geographical and chronological context, then the entirety of Italian history, with all of its political and institutional fragmentation, must come into play. It is only within this general framework that, as we will see, the specific case of Rome can and should be read from the beginning of its history, placing it back in its broader context. Without discounting the symbolic and ideological significance of the uncertain and marginalizing acceptance guaranteed to the Jews of Rome with the papal law of 1555, it must be recalled that the decision to set up the ghetto of Rome was a Catholic, proselytizing adaptation (and what else could it have been in the Papal States?) of the two test cases that preceded it: Venice and Ragusa/Dubrovnik. It must also be said that in Spanish Italy, where the Jews were really not wanted, it would have been difficult for the ghetto to succeed as it did, up until the institution of the final ghettos in the Piedmont in the late 1700s, without the blessing and support of Rome.[15]

---

13   Caffiero, Di Nepi 2017.
14   From this point of view, the open questions around the place of the Jews and their culture, obviously including that of the Italian Jews, in the panorama of global interactions and connections of early modernity remain valid and stimulating. A point of departure is the idea of connected histories proposed by Sanjay Subrahmanyam, and the hypotheses regarding the strong circulation of individuals and ideas advanced by David Ruderman in 2010.
15   Cassen 2014.

3   Venice, Rome and the Others: a Collective Experience

An analysis that looks only at the ultimate functions and purposes of the ghetto leaves another series of questions unanswered. Why was Venice first to decide to segregate the Jews, and the others later? For the *Serenissima Repubblica* at least, the answer seems to be simple: during the tragic days of the battle of Agnadello, when defeat seemed to be at the door, the Jews sought refuge *en masse* in the lagoon, as did many others. Venice had traditionally tolerated only the informal presence of a small number of Jewish families that enjoyed close relations to the local oligarchy. Now the rapid growth of a Jewish population living in the city itself forced the Senate to make a clear decision regarding the legitimacy of this settlement. The solution was the concession of a limited space that was surrounded by walls, with gates to the city, in which the Jews could live as long as they returned there to sleep at night.

This response brought together a wide variety of lines of thought: the preceding experience of the formation of predominantly Jewish urban areas in the Iberian *juderias*; the tendency of groups of Jews to settle close to each other of their own accord in nearby streets or quarters for religious needs; the advantage of easier management of public order in tense moments (Easter and Carnevale above all); and general skepticism about the results of the Spanish expulsions. Those considerations undoubtedly had significant reverberations for a city which at that moment had bad relations with Rome and Spain, a complicated relationship with Istanbul, and was worried about the risk of being cut off economically by the opening of new trade routes. The factors that led the *Maggior Consiglio* to invent the ghetto in that March of 1516 are certainly found in the local politics and problems of the moment. However, the religious ferment and eschatological anxieties of a world that was in the throes of war, and which was preparing to reckon with Martin Luther, cannot and should not be underestimated.

Lamenting this new development, the Venetian Jews nevertheless accepted their enclosure. And then they resumed their normal lives among the Venetian *calle*, doing business inside and outside the ghetto confines and returning there at nightfall. And for a while, little attention in general was paid to the Jews. Thirty years later, in the small Adriatic Republic of Ragusa, another seraglio based on the Venetian model was established. Here too the arrival of the Sephardic Jews played a role in the decision. The Ragusa ghetto was created for the purpose of regulating the presence of these families, establishing clear laws that were adapted to sustaining their entrepreneurial activities.[16] Meanwhile, battles continued on the peninsula, the Mediterranean remained

---

16   Ligorio 2017.

infested with Turkish pirates, and the Christians of Europe – the Pope and the Emperor included – began to resign themselves to the idea that things would never return to the way they had been. It was in this climate that Paul IV published his bull, which was released during the negotiations that led to the signing of the Peace of Augsburg, a treaty that was explicitly opposed by Pope Carafa (who was rather perplexed by the very idea of an agreement with heretics).

Thus, at the halfway point of the 16th century, Jews in the Republic of Venice, in Ragusa, and in the Papal States all found themselves living under similar conditions. Over the course of the following two centuries other kings and lords would decide to follow the path that had been laid out in the mid-1500s. Among the diversity of local implementations and the variety of motives that led these rulers to choose to establish a ghetto, there were some elements of the process that were fixed, and these would guide the lives of the Italian Jews throughout this long period. Everywhere a ghetto was built the enclosed space was bounded by a wall, with doors that opened at pre-established hours. The restriction of professional space, control over culture and solid support for Catholic proselytism became the minimum requirements for the process of discrimination. How, to what degree, and according to what logic the States applied themselves to implementing and enforcing these limitations is another story. The multiplicity of local declinations should not, however, obscure the profound similarities among the diverse experiences. While in practice segregation manifested differently from place to place, in the end it still resulted in the construction of the ghettos and the imposition of an *ad hoc* set of laws on the Jews.

4   1555 in Context

This imbalance between synergies and divergences makes it difficult to unravel the term *ghetto*.[17] To sort out such an intricate tangle, it is essential to return to the proposal from the 1500s, recognize its clear affinities with earlier examples, and place them in their historical context. The 500th anniversary of the establishment of the Venice ghetto offered the occasion for a series of important reflections on the birth of the ghettos. These are clearly an indispensable point of departure for beginning to finally connect Rome and Venice to the whole of Italian Jewry in those years.

---

17   Cooperman 2018.

Starting at the end of 2014, in fact, a series of studies published exclusively in Italian have examined the long period of ghettoization from diverse perspectives. I believe it is essential to take these into account, though I will cite only four examples. Donatella Calabi has pulled together years of research with an informative volume, *Venezia e il ghetto*, which was published in the symbolic year of 2016. The work focuses on the peculiar architectural structure of the buildings of the area (much higher than the city average) and reveals the extraordinary vitality of the Jewish group that was confined there.[18] Two important works published prior to Calabi's book investigate the history and modes of ghettoization. Marina Caffiero (2014), places the process of segregation within the history of conversion politics and the progressive definition of new models of antisemitism. Giacomo Todeschini (2016) writes about the economic origins of the ghetto, tracing the strategies of exclusion that defined the ghetto back to the period of complex financial and economic transition in the 15th century. Furthermore, the numerous works of Giuseppe Veltri on Judah Moscato and Simone Luzzato reveal the complexity of Jewish culture in Venice, bringing to light unexplored instances of cultural dialogue – directly within the academies – and finally restoring Jewish intellectuals to their times and milieu.[19] In line with the most recent historiographical publications, all of these works redefine the ghetto around the parameter of continuously negotiated relations between majority and minority.

On the other hand, alongside the essays, conferences, and books about the Italian ghettos in the modern era, produced by the most important scholars in the field, a robust international discussion has sought to focus on the ghetto as a global phenomenon. The working hypothesis underlying this discussion brings together a wide range of phenomena. Beginning with Venice in 1516, it moves to Warsaw during the Holocaust and ends up in the poor and marginalized neighborhoods of contemporary America. The result has been the construction of a unified sociological model which is completely detached from its complex and changing historical roots. Paradoxically, this tendency to uproot the Italian process of ghettoization from its broader context, especially in its initial phases, can also be found in studies by specialists. Here the process is generally viewed exclusively from the perspective of the reshaping of ecclesiastic and counter-reformation policies aimed at the conversion of the Jews. This aspect is undeniably of great importance – the text of *Cum*

---

18 Calabi 2016.
19 Among Giuseppe Veltri's many works, see the collection of Moscato's sermons (with Gianfranco Miletto, 2010–2015); with Evelyn Chayes, 2016; and the historiographical development in (2017).

nimis absurdum confirms this. However, until now insufficient information has emerged regarding how this project to govern an unwanted minority came into being in its particular historical context: during the turbulent period of the Franco-Imperial wars for the conquest of Italy, years in which the very survival of the Papal States was being explicitly called into question by Carlo V and his supporters. The insertion of specific Jewish events into the general history of those years allows us to recognize a line of political meanings and evaluations which are vital subjects for inquiry.

Beginning in the summer of 1492 and increasing in the following years, waves of Jewish refugees, first from Spain and Sicily and then from Portugal, sought refuge in Italian cities. With the arrival of the Sephardim, the communities of the Italian peninsula and the Christian authorities found themselves facing a demanding test. The invasion of Italy by Carlo VIII in 1494 and the opening of the French-Spanish conflict for supremacy on the peninsula made the decision to grant or refuse welcome to the exiles a diplomatic and political issue of great relevance. It is worth summarizing the principal aspects of this issue. On the political level, on one hand, the explicit rejection of Spanish policy regarding the Jews would have displeased Iberian royalty at a time when they were preparing military action for supremacy on the peninsula; on the other hand, taking this position could have been read as a signal of openness towards the French and, therefore, Venice. In their own deliberations the Italian Jews did not underestimate the problem. They well understood the general environment into which the requests of their brethren would enter and the impact that these might have, and they feared the opening of Iberian style investigations into the faith and the identity of the migrants.

Between 1493 and 1494, the Spanish Pope Alessandro VI's decision partially resolved these doubts. The fugitives were admitted to Rome and the Papal States without a formal declaration, and notwithstanding the objections of the ambassadors of the Catholic Kings. The tacit hospitality that was accorded to the Spanish Jews at that juncture clearly demonstrated what Borgia's position was regarding the delicate subjects of the management of minorities, and which proselytizing strategies to employ when dealing with the most recalcitrant among the groups of infidels. At least for the moment, the Pope declared, the Iberian approach would not be replicated elsewhere. Though avoiding open conflict with Spain (while the winds of war blew over half of Italy), Alessandro VI nevertheless reaffirmed that the final word on the Jews and all things Jewish came from Rome, and that the Church would never accept the delegation of any aspect of the subject to others. The coincidental timing between the settlement of the Sephardim in the capital of the Papal States and the drafting of the so-called Bull of Donations raises important questions (which are still overlooked by historiography). In both cases, in fact, different considerations weighed and interacted, related as much to the State, with its borders and its temporal interests, as to the universal mission of the Church itself. On the one hand there was Italian politics, where amongst dynastic quarrels and impossible balances the Pope played a dangerous game through his own son.[20] On the other, there was the ongoing effort to protect the autonomy and universal authority of the Church, and therefore of the States which it governed and the spiritual subjects which it claimed as its own.

From this point of view, the passage from the fifteenth to the sixteenth century in Rome proves to be of great interest for the history of the Jews. Major historical trends compelled the Pope and the Church to have to reckon very quickly with each new manifestation of religious otherness, at the theoretical level as well as in the daily governing of the Pontifical lands. The Jews had to deal with their ancient communities and the Spanish emergency. Muslims were faced with war at sea and the increasingly aggressive policy of the Turks. The discovery of new peoples in the Americas, ignorant and wild, but ready (with a bit of pressure) to welcome the Good News of the Evangelist was obviously another important development. The central issue was the unresolved question of the conversion of infidels, the strategies for which were being modified based on current experiences but also, clearly, on the results achieved up to that time. Thus the Church had to evaluate cases of baptisms, successful and unsuccessful. Almost 1500 years history of relations with the Jews offered these in abundance, and demonstrated how less traumatic options than expulsion or violence could be viable. This expanded perspective clarifies, then, the serious considerations that pushed Alessandro VI to take the path of silent compromise. The result was that the Sephardim settled in the holy city, but without causing disruptive rifts with the Spanish monarchy. Subsequently this model of quiet tolerance became a possible, and perhaps even desirable, model to export to the rest of the peninsula.

The Venetian experiment in 1516, after Agnadello, and during the negotiations at Noyon over a treaty that was destined to remain a dead letter, appeared to suggest that perhaps there was another path that could be taken, one that fell in between the policies of Rome and Madrid. Meanwhile, with the election of Charles V as Emperor in 1518, conflict spread further across Europe. While the voice of Martin Luther rose from Germany and the Church underestimated the problem, the Italian front reopened yet another time. The sack of Rome in 1527 made it clear to the whole world the extent to which the turning point was

---

20   Obviously Cesare Borgia, the Duke Valentino at the center of Machiavelli's *The Prince*.

now irreversible. With the beginning of the long papacy of Paul III Farnese in 1534, the Church closed ranks. The Emperor, committed on at least three fronts (Italy, Germany, and the Mediterranean), had hoped to find an ally in the Pope, but instead he found an indomitable rival, intent on defending the Papal States and, most of all, the ascent of the Farnese. There ensued a decades long struggle between the *Italy of the Pope* and the *Italy of the Emperor* – according to Elena Bonora's useful definition (2014) – which involved the material consideration of the political destiny of the peninsula as much as it did the spiritual consideration of the fate of the Church after the outbreak of Protestantism. In this context the Italian Jews, while not at the center of the authorities' attention (the countering of heresy and political dissent were seen as more urgent), found themselves living in a time of convulsive transition: 1541 saw the final expulsion of Jews from the Kingdom of Naples and the enlarging of the Ghetto of Venice; 1542, the institution of the new Congregation of the Holy Office; 1543, the opening of the House of Catechumens of Rome; then in 1543–1544 there was the imposition of the double tax on the Jews of the Papal States for the war against the Turks, and so on.[21]

Just a few years later, the publication of the Bull *Cum nimis absurdum* and the establishment of Venetian-Ragusan style ghettos in the Papal States seemed to settle the question. Pope Paul IV Carafa decided that the Jews would be accepted, but with limitations and amidst a host of discriminations, while waiting for them to finally present themselves at the baptismal font. There has been a long-standing historiographical debate over the reasons behind this decision. Some insist that the bull is completely in keeping with the theological line of practical discrimination which dates back to Augustine, *adversus Iudeaos,* while others emphasize the growing weight of the pressure to convert the Jews during this period. However one wishes to see it, it is irrefutable that the publication of the Bull served to clarify once and for all what the Pope's position was on the subject, and how that position stood firmly within the Catholic tradition of carefully thought out discrimination: the Jews had a place within Catholic society, but, in the logic of the time, that place could not have been anything other than a space built on humiliation and marginalization.

That Carafa had little love for the Jews is beyond question; that his choices regarding the subject of the Jews oscillated between different positions is also without question. On the one hand – and first of all – the institution of the ghettos, for all their well-known limitations and ambiguities, offered acceptance; on the other hand, the persecution and violence of the 1556 trial

---

21 See, again, the precise chronology reconstructed in Caffiero 2014.

of *marrani* in Ancona instead pointed in a completely different direction. To phrase it differently, there was the way of Venice and Ragusa, and the Iberian approach. These represented two opposing poles, both of which carried precise political significance in Italy at that time and above all during the papacy of Paul IV, the last Pope to make war against the Hapsburgs and to seek, by any means, to thwart Spanish dominance on the Italian peninsula.[22] One wonders if Carafa's choices regarding the Jews, made immediately after his enthroning, can also be read as a message directed at his allies – that is to Venice and to France – and his enemies – which is to say Charles V and Phillip II. Drafted at a Council that was already in session, at the culmination of the final stage of the Franco-Imperial wars and after the peace of Augsburg (1555), of which the Pope greatly disapproved, but before the peace of Cateau Cambresis (1559), that message might have gone something like this: the last word on the governing of faith and the faithful belonged to the one and only Catholic sovereign, the Pope, who ruled based on history and traditions, and because of this, when it came to the hot and always sensitive subject of the Jews, he had explicitly chosen the path of "tolerance." Meanwhile, however, at Ancona there would once again be a reminder of how this tolerance had its clear limits in baptism, always held to be valid however it was performed.

With the birth of the ghettos, this state of familiar otherness regulated by shared rules was reinforced, but without bringing about an absolute separation between Jews and Christians. Moreover, these were years in which the close relationship between space and religion began to emerge as a good solution to problems far more serious than the fate of the Jews. In this sense, from the Peace of Augsburg to the Edict of Nantes, the possibility of a trend in political thought towards combining the ideas of religious and restrictive uses of urban spaces in the age of the ghettos could undoubtedly present an interesting subject for investigation. However, let us return to Italy. From 1555 on, the porosity of the walls of the ghetto, which was indeed fully anticipated by the law that created them, enabled the survival of the same networks of relations between Jews and Christians, and among Jews themselves, that had animated the preceding period. The Sephardic networks certainly played a role in the Papal States and in Italy as well, just as they did in the rest of the Jewish world. The rules of discrimination and humiliation constituted the unspoken foundation around which the interactions between majority and minority would develop. It is also essential to keep in mind the fact that these rules contributed to reshaping the identities of both groups.

---

22 But also a ruler who was attentive to the rebuilding of the State: Brunelli 2011.

5   Towards a New Timeline

If we go beyond the lachrymose 19th century paradigm of the ghetto, a much more interesting and dynamic picture emerges. Even just a careful re-reading of the classic histories of the Roman ghetto reveals that the sequence of legal provisions marks a timeline that must be taken into account, and that until now has not been the subject of a specific study. The list of "subjugating bulls" precisely reconstructed by Attilio Milano, however, is a genuine compass that helps orient us through the evolution of the laws.[23] Furthermore, if we superimpose this list over the events of the community's inner life and its relations with the Christian city, as documented since Berliner's first writings,[24] then by Milano, and now in a period of very lively historiography, a possible line of interpretation begins to take shape. The most recent research regarding Jewish Rome, and more generally regarding the Italian Jewish community in the modern age, finally allows us to think objectively about these subjects. If freeing the history of the ghetto of Rome from the emotional baggage it carries is a complex operation – perhaps even destined for failure – focusing on the milestones is undoubtedly a good place to start. In short, in order to come up with a useful definition of the ghetto of Rome and its status as a successful model for organizing hostile but necessary relations between a majority and a minority – which is the subject of this book – we need to start with the historical context in which this prototype took shape.

The ever-changing combinations of countless factors both external to the "shut-in" community (the Church, major events, the city of Rome itself) as well as within the community allows us to identify at least six distinct phases: gestation (1492–1555); experimentation (1555–1593); consolidation (1593–1681); transition (1681–1720); redefinition (1720 circa -1798); towards emancipation? (1798–1848/1870).

The gestation phase took place in the first half of the 16th century, in the midst of a period of convulsive transformation that overwhelmed Christian society and the political balances both in Europe and beyond its borders. The political climate in those years, and the ambiguous results on the battlefields of Italy also caused serious worries for the Jews. The arrival of the Sephardim then triggered an earthquake in the communities that were called upon to welcome them, followed by an avalanche of questions. How far could and should they extend their solidarity for their persecuted brethren? How would that

---

23   Milano 1984.
24   Berliner 1992.

affect their relationships with power? And if the Spanish had won, what would have happened? Jews also harbored doubts and questions about the faith of the Sephardim: how many of them had relatives who had surrendered and become Christians? How many of them had seriously considered abjuring, or could have done so later? What were the risks for those who helped them? Could these people be trusted? Finally, was there a risk that someone, in order to keep in the good graces of the King of Spain and to control these people, might decide to introduce Spanish style prosecutions in Italy too?

The choices made in Rome in response to this series of questions were charged with specific symbolic significance, both regarding the steps taken by the authorities and, on the other hand, regarding the attitudes of the local community. The initial struggles during the early years of their coexistence with the refugees – which have been convincingly reconstructed in detail by Anna Esposito based on notarial documents – led over time to important solutions that played a fundamental role in the period that followed. The granting of moneylending licenses in 1521 and the enactment of the community's statute in 1524 were milestones of great importance during this long transitional phase. The Pope and the institutions of the Papal States played a major role in both cases. In the first, the decision to legitimize Jewish moneylending, placing it under the sole jurisdiction of the *Camerlengo*, ended up belatedly regulating the unique situation in the Roman marketplace, the only place in Italy which had not yet formally authorized Jewish moneylenders to work in the city. The very significant preponderance of Sephardim among these lenders confirms, from another perspective, the rapidity and success of this group's incorporation into the community, and allows a glimpse of the tensions that must have accompanied the process. The list of beneficiaries who were granted lending licenses testifies to the birth of a new and vital Roman Jewish ruling class, which enjoyed good relations with the pontifical court.[25]

Three years later, the rise of this social group to the top ranks of the *Universitas* was certified by the promulgation, in the name of the Pope, of the *Capitoli* of Daniel da Pisa, which assigned bankers a leading role in governing the community.[26] The institutional architecture established by the *Capitoli* would prove to be extraordinarily resilient. This legal structure survived the test of the difficult months of the Sack and the subsequent rebuilding. It remained intact through the period of diminishing tolerance for Jews that began with the

---

25　Esposito 2002.
26　See the text of the *Capitoli* in Milano 1935 and 1936. I am working with Bernard D. Cooperman and Anna Esposito on a new edition of the *Capitoli* based on unpublished sources.

papacy of Paul III, and persisted through the subsequent decision to erect the ghetto. What's more, as things stood in 1555, with the Pope preparing to reopen the war with the Hapsburgs and pursuing the *marrani* in Ancona, common sense suggested avoiding any changes to a statute that, due solely to the fact that it had been published as an official document (that is as a papal brief), offered important guarantees against expulsion.[27]

The implementation of *Cum nimis absurdum* called for quick decisions, a great capacity for adaptation, and an equal willingness to experiment. Changing the rules of the game led to a recalibration of relations between Jews and Jews, and between Jews and Christians. It did not bring about the isolation of the ghetto, nor did it lead to the sanctification of the ghetto as a private Jewish space, apart from the world. It certainly did not initiate an immediate and unstoppable process of cultural impoverishment in Jewish society. The group's responses to the new condition, through the continuous negotiation of internal positions and the implementation of a network of relations with external decision makers – while remaining within the bounds of the new laws – constitute the heart of this book. The recognition that the walls of the ghetto functioned as an element of passage and connection, not of separation, represents the methodological and theoretical premise of this work. Only by working with both Jewish and Christian sources in parallel is it possible to reflect on the complexity of this experience. Identifying its diverse manifestations permits us to think clearly about the evolution of interactions that were never meant to be completely eradicated.

An inquiry into the organization of the Jewish community in the aftermath of Pope Carafa's decree requires looking closely at who was called upon to guide it and how. This means trying to sketch a reliable portrait of the Jewish ruling class in the early decades of the segregation, and of the radical transformations – social, political, ideological – that Paul IV's revolution provoked within this group. These changes, however, are not immediately evident. In fact, the *Capitoli* of 1524 called for a division of tasks based on a classic top-down pyramid of three groups; *banchieri, ricchi* e *mediocri*. *Cum nimis absurdum* did not address the first group (the Jewish banks were only suppressed later in 1682), but the aim of the bull was clearly to prevent Jews from practicing the lucrative and prestigious professions that allowed an individual to be considered a wealthy man. Once Pope Paul IV's decree was in effect, theoretically the gap between the rules and reality would and could have led to a modification of the Jews' Statute. As mentioned earlier, this did not happen. It is

---

[27] Regarding this, allow me to refer again to my paper Di Nepi 2019.

therefore interesting to ask how Jewish society adapted to the ghetto, and how the institutional life of the community was organized during this early phase.

Jewish society responded creatively to the many challenges presented by *Cum nimis absurdum*. Jewish merchants and bankers worked to find spaces for economic activity wherever possible. In doing so they built opportunities for social mobility through the unconventional use of companies, expansion of the scope of their businesses, and ownership of traditional lending licenses. The most interesting result of these first decades of segregation, though, was the reconfiguration of the ruling class. The unexpected appearance of rabbis (at the time this could mean ordained rabbis, but also men recognized as having training in *halakha*) in the trios of *Fattori*, as well as these same rabbis' membership in the circle of the most influential families was an essential aspect of this change. In this sense, an essential key to this work is Roberto Bonfil's proposal that when looking at the ghetto, we should recognize the challenge that it represented, as reflected in the complexity of the mechanism of partial isolation that sustained it.

Two names speak for themselves, and both should be considered important symbols of a long term process that involved all the Jews of Rome. The first is Lazzaro da Viterbo, about whom Alessandro Guetta has dedicated important pages in his writing. He was a *Fattore* during the second half of the 16th century, the same years in which he too wrote important pages directed at the Pope, reaffirming the centrality of the Jewish-Christian relationship and of Hebrew scripture.[28] The other name is that of the celebrated Tranquillo Vita Corcos, who was a leader in the life of the community between the 1600s and 1700s, and who appears at the center of a recent monograph by Marina Caffiero.[29] Both men lived at a time in which society was completely structured by the choice of religion and the formal adherence to rules of religious behavior. In this context, it is not surprising that, in the height of the "age of religion," the Jewish capacity to adopt innovations and influences from the surrounding majority and adjust them to their own schemes led to a decisive re-evaluation of the role of Jewish culture and of its most learned exponents.[30]

From the perspective of rules that were imposed from outside the ghetto, one of the most important steps in the experimentation phase was, without a doubt, the publication of the bull *Hebraeroum gens* in 1569. With this document Pius V redefined the geography of the Jewish presence in the Papal

---

28 Guetta 2014, in part. pp. 62–78.
29 Caffiero 2019.
30 The works of Robert Bonfil remain exemplary. I cite two here, now classics, as examples: 1990, 1991 and 1996.

States, limiting it to only the cities of Rome and Ancona. Then there were the turbulent years under Sixtus V, which moved between partial openings in practice and equally significant closures in ideology. In 1593 Clement VIII granted the Jews the right to live in the French enclave of Avignon, bringing to a close the uncertain phase of experimentation with ghettoization that had been underway up to that time. This book concentrates specifically on that first period, bringing to light the evolution of a society that was highly stratified and contentious, but also capable of developing pragmatic solutions to the problems of the day. This clear ability to react allowed Jews to build a body of structures of identity and organization that were capable of supporting the community's determined survival over three long centuries of segregation.

The age of the ghetto, despite its many discontinuities, represented a phase of particularly aggressive evangelization directed at the Jews. In every moment of their lives Jews were confronted with the infinite range of possibilities that conversion offered. The doors of the Houses of the Catechumens were always open wide for Jews in search of a different life; emigration towards more welcoming shores was always a possibility. In a climate in which baptisms that were performed with imposing ceremonies followed one another at the pace of dozens a year, living in the ghetto and submitting to its rules implied a continuous reaffirmation of the will to remain Jewish.[31]

The papacy of Clement VIII definitively resolved any doubts about what fate the Church of Rome had in mind for the Jews of the Papal States. The geographical reorganization he ordered swept aside any ideas about the ghetto being temporary, and confirmed that it would, in fact, be the model applied everywhere Jews still lived. From that moment – until 1682 and the repeal of Jewish banking licenses – the system would be consolidated. While the Inquisition, the Apostolic Chamber and the *Vicariato* all claimed jurisdiction over the Jews in their institutional roles (though often pursuing different objectives), the community carried on with its life. The close relations that the richest and most visible families had with the Curia and Roman nobility remained a constant, as did their orientation towards an increasing diversification of economic investments and professional activities while remaining within the limits set by the current laws. The abolition of the Jewish banks in 1682 signaled an important turning point that would impact the restricted group of elites who, at least professionally, had not been affected by the bull of 1555.[32] This transition

---

31   Marina Caffiero 2004.
32   Procaccia, C. 2012.

coincided with the years when Tranquillo Vita Corcos governed, and therefore with a period of particularly intense institutional dialog and equally significant cultural production.

While lacking in-depth and wide ranging studies on the specific manifestations of the social transformations that followed this proclamation, certain facts lead us to consider the phase of displacement and resettlement as having basically ended by the 1720s. The papal decree issued by Clement XI on January 30, 1720 ushered in a new phase, which began with the decision to restrict the borders of the ghetto, leaving out unoccupied stores and rooms (for which the *Università* was still required to pay rent). Furthermore, rental rates were reduced, the salaries for the sentries were divided differently, and the supply of meat and bread was reorganized.[33] This alteration of spaces went hand in hand with a redefinition of social structures, which we still know little about, but which cannot and should not be seen in terms of absolute cultural and economic impoverishment. On the one hand, the group's strong management of Benedict XIV's aggressive conversion policy, while they adjusted their own institutional organization to the modernizing reforms imposed by the same Pontiff,[34] once again confirms the Jewish system's resilience in meeting challenges. On the other hand, the fact that a large number of donations of valuable and luxury objects were made to the synagogues of the ghetto throughout the 18th century indicates the survival of a nucleus of wealthy families who were rich enough to allow them to invest money in this way, and who were animated by a sensibility and a culture that encouraged such choices.[35]

The practice of donating ceremonial art to the *Scole* was a constant during the centuries of the age of the ghetto, and was in large part the product of the rules of segregation set down by Paul IV in 1555. Following the institution of the ghetto, in fact, several factors played a role in determining the success of this custom, beginning with logistical difficulties. The restricted living space granted to the Jews – with the attendant problems of overcrowding and resulting widespread conflicts over housing – meant that Jewish homes were poorly suited for storing private collections of precious objects. For the wealthiest families in particular, this spatial impediment was not accompanied by similar economic problems: in many cases Jews had money available for acquiring luxury goods, as well as the taste and cultural inclination to invest in art. Purchases of this nature were actually frequent, as demonstrated with indisputable

---

33   Milano 1984, p. 99.
34   Caffiero 2004.
35   Di Castro 1994; 2010; and more recently Davanzo Poli, Melasecchi, Spagnoletto 2016.

clarity in studies by Daniela Di Castro. The objects acquired, however, were regularly offered as donations to the *Scole* by their members rather than used for the beautification of homes that did not have sufficient space available to display them.

The choice to donate precious objects, then, was likely based on both a realistic vision of the housing situation in the ghetto and on the traditional ties between Jews and their synagogues. However, two other possible motivations, both related to the organization of the ghetto itself, should be added. First of all, there were the sumptuary laws that were continuously issued by the *Fattori* and by the *Consiglio*. These laws were meant to prevent the ostentation of luxury in every instance of Jewish daily life (including marriages, funerals, honors), with the sole exception, of course, of dressing for synagogue. Second of all, it should also be recalled that the tax computation system excluded donations from the final calculation of the tax share assigned to each head of family. In short, in an internal and external legislative context that rotated around an explicit prohibition on any economic well-being for the Jews, the synagogues represented an exception (one that was acknowledged and recognized by the tax system). Thus the collections of the *Scole* became the only permissible spaces for the expression of a social and cultural dialectic that was impossible elsewhere.[36]

Revolutions, republics, being "forced in and forced out" of the ghettos,[37] and the years spent with and without a Pope overwhelmed the lives of Jews across all of Europe. The long road towards emancipation, with its infinite contradictions that were elaborated in new and even more slippery categories of otherness, began in the Jacobin period. At that moment history would take an unprecedented turn, in which the politics, ambivalence, and modernity of the new century played according to rules that were capable of upsetting the world as it had never been before.[38] If life in the ghetto really was as bereft as it is too often uncritically imagined to have been – moving solely between poverty, ignorance and baptisms – then it must have been with extraordinary difficulty that the Jews of Rome managed to remain Jewish and numerous in such an era. The goal of this book's focus on the first decades of the ghetto's history is to bring to light the anxieties, the questions, and the answers that allowed this community to remain true to itself and survive three centuries of segregation.

---

36 Regarding this, see by the present author: Di Nepi 2015 and 2018.
37 Milano 1984; Caffiero 2014.
38 Kertzer 1996.

6 Culture across the Walls

Precisely reconstructing the life of the Jewish community in the 1500s requires crossing traditional archival boundaries and searching for information through an immense *corpus* of sources; those produced by the Jews as well as the great number of sources produced by the institutions that interacted with them. The fact that it was methodologically necessary to cross-reference information found in different sources confirms, even intuitively, the key importance of an investigative approach that moves across the walls without preference for either side of the barricade.

From these documents the portrait of a well-articulated ruling class emerges at the center of this reconstruction. A variety of sources were examined in order to retrace the general lines of this picture: the administrative registries of the *Camerlengo* of the Reverend Apostolic Chamber (the magistrate who had exclusive jurisdiction over the Jewish bankers), the records of Jewish and Christian notaries, the institutional archives of hospitals, judicial sources, and the legislative production of the period. The inevitable challenge is placing such variegated documents in context with each other, and reattaching the threads that connect people, institutions, negotiations, regulations and therefore models and practices.

The deeds drawn up by Jewish notaries – already identified as a primary source by Kenneth Stow in his essential works on the community during this period – represent an exceptional source from many points of view, and are a qualitatively and quantitatively unique example of testimony from the internal life of a Jewish group.[39] Examination of these registries has revealed a wide variety of aspects of Jewish daily life (in which Christians appear with relative frequency) and has provided a guide line – almost a red thread to follow – for pursuing research in other directions.[40] The systematic collection of this recorded information, in fact, has shed light on aspects which would have otherwise been difficult to notice. Important examples of such discoveries, which are reconstructed here for the first time, are the contracts for the monopoly trade of used clothing from hospitals – *fardelli* – as well as the ownership of management contracts for market spaces. Both of these types of business, as we will see, were keys to the system of professions and careers in the years of the ghetto. In fact, it was only thanks to the information first found in the records of the Jewish notaries that it was possible to continue and deepen the

---

39 See at least, Stow 2001
40 For the period immediately preceding this, see the important collection of annotated summaries of the documents edited by Kenneth R. Stow (1995–1996).

investigation in the direction of archival sources produced by Christian institutions that are not normally included in research about Jews and the modern age, specifically the hospital registries.

The formal structure of this documentation turns out to be of equal interest, and opens up new paths for research. From 1578 until 1590 registries of deeds began to be drafted by the new notary Pompeo Del Borgo in Italian as well as Hebrew, in a series that is apparently parallel to those drawn up exclusively in Hebrew by Isacco delle Piattelle.[41] The linguistic transformation sanctioned by this step was not accidental, and could be interpreted as the most obvious sign of a progressive cultural impoverishment in the Roman community, for which it has been reproached many times in classical historiography. From this point of view, such cultural impoverishment would have materialized precisely in the 1580s, with the progressive loss of the Hebrew language as a known and shared system of communication. Instead, a comparison of the protocols compiled by these two notaries during the decade in which they worked contemporaneously describes a completely different reality. What emerges from these records is the image of a Jewish world that was capable, time after time, of working consciously and flexibly with the cultural and organizational choices that were seen to be most advantageous for its own needs, and doing so without relinquishing its identity. As it happens, Isacco delle Piatelle and Pompeo Del Borgo provided notarial certifications that served different needs; the first for those of a religious nature, and the second for those that were "professional." These specific purposes explain the difference between the languages used in their registries.

The survival of Hebrew as a language of culture and identity is one of the most interesting research subjects regarding the history of Italian Judaism in the modern age. Studies that are currently underway on different communities clearly reveal the parallel and convergent use of Hebrew and Italian in this period.[42] The gradual substitution of Italian as the language for internal administration came about in response to specific regulations handed down by the State. It was also, perhaps, common sense to use a language that was definitely understandable by everyone in the governance of the community. Yet for all of the 17th century the great majority of the registries of the *Università* were drafted in Hebrew; only at the end of the century did the prevalence of Italian become a significant phenomenon, aligning Jewish documentary practices with

---

41   Golan 1985; see also the description of the archival source in http://www.archiviocapitolino.it/files/archivio/archivio_generale_urbano_-_sezione_iii.pdf.
42   For an initial survey of the use of Hebrew in the registries of Italian Jewish communities in the Early Modern Era, see Perani 2020.

the progressive substitution of Italian for Latin in public institutions. However, the use of Hebrew in the composition of poetry, essays, *responsa* and homilies remained constant throughout the entire period. So did the attentive acquisition of books that were printed in Hebrew from all over Europe, many of which remain part of the book collections of the Italian community to this day. The dedication with which Italian Jewish society applied itself to the circulation of books that were subject to censorship and constant control once again confirms the existence of people who were interested in reading works in Hebrew, informed about the latest trends and news in publishing, and participants in national and international book markets.

The disappearance of the Roman Jewish library, which unfortunately was never cataloged, after the Nazi looting in 1943 makes further research on the cultural evolution in Rome during the age of the ghetto impossible. We can only offer hypotheses, which can be tested against the rich notes made by Isaiah Sonne, who visited the collection between 1934 and 1936.[43] But the fact that even later registries compiled in Hebrew are preserved in the community archive, and the enthusiasm of the Alsatian rabbi for the wonderful book collection that he found in his hands, allows us to glimpse traces of a lively Jewish culture, in continuous ferment and never marginal, and yet to be fully revealed.

The point is really this: while the ghetto was synonymous with marginalization and permanence – a closed space in which the tolerated minority was segregated – the implementation of that model of static acceptance led to a period of powerful change and activity for the group that was forced behind the walls. The resulting upheavals profoundly affected the lives of individuals, and as a consequence, the fortunes, careers, emotions, identities, and the rise or fall of illustrious or aspiring families, along with the very institutional structure of the community, its culture, and its relations with the authorities of the Papal States. These were turbulent waters to navigate; however, the Jews of Rome knew how to find practical ways to meet their own needs.

Rome, May 2020

---

[43] Regarding this story, see the final report of the Anselmi-Tedeschi commission (http://presidenza.governo.it/USRI/confessioni/rapporto/rapporto_finale_attivita_Commissione2.pdf) and the complete appendices attached to it (http://presidenza.governo.it/USRI/confessioni/appendice.html). I am preparing a complete study on the history of this library.

CHAPTER 1

Before the Ghetto

The expulsion of the Jews from Spain in 1492 and the subsequent expulsion from Portugal just four years later mark what is traditionally viewed as a watershed moment in Jewish history. Ferdinand and Isabella's strategy of aggressive evangelization – conversion or expulsion – had countless consequences from many points of view. The resulting wave of refugees transformed the geography of the Jewish presence in the Mediterranean basin as well as in central and southern Europe. In the following decades the refugees spread into areas outside the Old Continent, eventually reaching the recently discovered lands across the Atlantic Ocean as well as the coast of the Indian Ocean.[1]

These large migrations in the early 16th century also had an influence on Jewish culture. Jews everywhere were obliged to contend with the different intellectual and ritual points of reference that animated the cultural world which the Spanish exiles naturally brought with them. The best known example of this is the great debate surrounding the reception of Kabbalah, its context and its problems –as well as its connection to Christian humanists' fascination with Jewish esotericism.[2] The forced encounter between groups of Jews that were so different affected every aspect of life. Anything could set off clashes between them, engaged as they were in a slow process of transforming religion and identity, in large part yet to be rebuilt. The refugees' culture and history diverged in many ways from that of their coreligionists; from the pronunciation of Hebrew to the organization of liturgies and management of the synagogues, from superstitious practices to cultured thought at the highest level, from the types of professions they pursued to the memories of the persecution they had suffered, up to the experiences they had dealing with Christian institutions (or Muslim, depending on the case).Those institutions, in turn, established different practices in the governance of Jewish institutions and in the definition of the forms of their autonomy.[3]

---

[1] A broad bibliography exists on this subject; for an initial overview, see at least: Israel 1991; Trivellato 2010; Ruderman 2010 and in particular the first chapter (*Jews on the Move*); Kaplan 2019.

[2] A broad bibliography exists on this subject; for an initial overview, see at least: Yates 1979; Garin 1996; Bonfil 1996; Idel 2007; Dweck 2011; Guetta 2014; Bartolucci 2017.

[3] There are countless studies on this subject, conducted from different points of view, sources and problems according to the context being examined. Interesting summaries, other than Salo W. Baron's classic are the work of Jonathan J. Israel on social and economic aspects

Rome and Italy were directly affected by the massive exodus from the Iberian Peninsula. In Italy, as elsewhere, it created unexpected problems, took on political and diplomatic connotations of great importance, and brought overwhelming change to the local Jewish community. In order to reconstruct an accurate picture of the community which found itself closed in the ghetto in 1555, and to understand its reactions – which are the heart of this book – we must begin with the convulsive changes brought about by the forced addition of the Spanish Jews to the Roman community. The appearance of this group of fugitives on the scene was a trauma, and thus it is crucial to examine the reactions of their coreligionists and of the city authorities; the successes, the failures and the mechanisms with which they began a slow process, first of accepting the new arrivals and then of their integration into the original core group. The choices made by the Roman community in 1555 in response to the anti-Jewish restrictions imposed by Paul IV have their roots in past events. As we will see, the events of 1492, with all their consequences, can serve as a valid point of departure for an investigation of the Roman Jewish experience in the 16th century from within, in a period of transition and upheaval.

1   Rome and the Spanish Refugees

Among the thousands of exiles fleeing Spain (reported numbers range from 100,000 to 200,000 and are all unreliable),[4] some traveled to the Italian peninsula. A significant group of them (a low estimate is around 400 people)[5] arrived at the gates of the Eternal City in the summer of 1493. As the celebrated diarist Stefano Infessura reports, the refugees camped on *via Appia*, outside the city walls, and waited for the Pope to decide their destiny.

> At first most of the Marranos camped outside the wall, on the *via Appia*, near [the tower] of *Capo di Bove*; some of them occasionally came in to the city secretly and, for this reason, many Spanish soldiers were charged with guarding the gates, who many believe are also [*marrani*]. Because of this behavior an unstoppable disease invaded the City, and there were

---

(1985), Anna Foa's general reconstruction (1992) and, in more recent times, the reflection in terms of cultural history proposed by David Ruderman (2010).

4 Beinart 2005.

5 Esposito 2007, p. 180, with particular reference to notes 9 and 10. As this scholar relates, some of these refugees found refuge in the small cities near Rome (Esposito 2004). Also, on the subject of the Sicilian refugees, see again Esposito 2005.

many deaths among the said *marrani* both from the disease and from infection; on the other hand, the City is now full of these *marrani* and, as one can see, this did not happen without approval and permission from the Pope.[6]

Before reconstructing Alexander VI's decision and the reasons that would lead him to informally allow the Sephardim to enter Rome, it is worth pointing out a peculiarity in Infessura's account. His use of the word *marrani* in this text, when referring to professing Jews who had been forced to abandon their much beloved birthplace in order to remain faithful to the religion of their Fathers, shows us the extent to which this group was perceived as a foreign body by their contemporaries (and even by the original nucleus of Roman Jews). The cruel persecution of the Spanish *conversos* happened in plain sight of everyone. The choice to use this deprecating term when referring to the exiled Jews demonstrates, on one hand, how the Spanish distinction between official Jews and suspected Judaizing Christians was not immediately comprehensible in Italy, and on the other hand, how any Spanish Jew might automatically be considered suspicious.[7]

The Spanish Jews on *via Appia*, who perhaps had hoped to receive some assistance from their coreligionists in the city, would meet with bitter disappointment. For the Jews of Rome, who were traditionally protected by the Curia, the arrival of these unwanted guests represented a potential danger, and was treated as such. Centuries of legendary quiet living now risked ruin – they feared – from the tragedies of the Spanish, who bore with them suspicion,

---

6 "In un primo tempo, la maggior parte dei marrani si accampò fuori dalle mura, sulla via Appia, presso [*la torre*] di Capo di Bove; alcuni, di tanto in tanto, entravano in città segretamente e, per questa ragione, della custodia delle porte furono incaricati dei soldati spagnoli, molti, come in tanti credono, [*marrani*] anche loro. A causa di tali comportamenti la peste, irrefrenabile, invase l'Urbe e vi furono numerosi morti tra i detti marrani tanto per la peste quanto per il contagio; dei quali [*marrani*], peraltro, ormai, tutta l'Urbe è piena e, come si può vedere, ciò è avvenuto non senza la volontà e il permesso del papa." Infessura 1890, p. 290.

7 The introduction of the term *marrano* in the Roman vocabulary, in fact, arouses curiosity, confirming, as Anna Foa (2003) has demonstrated, the pervasiveness of the Spanish approach to the question of bloodlines even in contexts quite different and far away: in the eyes of a non-Jew, for whom this mysterious society remained foreign, the Spanish refugees were a separate world, marked by their geographical origins, and could not be assimilated into the well-known group of the Jews living under the Pope. Regarding the problem of bloodlines in Spain, refer to the classic by Yerushalmi 2010. On the ambiguous use of the term *marrano* in sources and in historiography, and its many meanings, of particular interest is the examination offered by Akman 2013.

loss, perhaps contagious diseases – the illness cited by Infessura, or more likely syphilis[8] – and the baggage of a recent past marked by continuing accusations from and bad relations with Christian institutions.[9] All of this had culminated in expulsion. Now Roman Jews feared that the Iberian expulsion would have repercussions in Italy as well, especially at time when, to make matters worse, the newly elected Pope was Spanish. In such an environment it is hard to imagine that the high anxiety among the Jews went unnoticed by those around them.

Shortly afterwards, the confusion, if not open hostility, with which the community regarded the poor immigrants knocking on their door was explicitly documented by the famous historian Shelomoh Ibn Verga, himself a Spanish Jew. The writer, who was the author of a collection of stories about over sixty painful events involving Jews in different times and places, included the sad business in Rome in his saga of endless disasters:

> Some of the [Iberian] Jews, who had reached the port of Genoa, were forced to leave due to the pervasive hunger, and they turned from there to Rome. But the Jews of Rome gathered and took counsel to prevent the strangers from mixing in among them and bringing serious harm to their economic activities. They then immediately put together a thousand *fiorini*, which they offered as a gift to the Pope by way of a request for him to deny welcome to the exiles in his lands. When this was reported to the Pope, he reacted by saying: "For me this is something really new. Until now I knew that it was typical for the Jews to close ranks around each other, and instead for these they act without compassion! I have therefore decided that these too [*that is the Roman Jews*] are expelled from my lands and it is no longer legal for them to live here." Then the Jews of Rome were forced to collect another two thousand *scudi* to offer to the Pope so that he would leave them in peace, and at the same time they resigned themselves to the arrival of the foreigners [*that is the Iberian Jews*] in the city. Thus the poor refugees could partake of the good of this land.[10]

---

8 Foa 1984.
9 Foa 1992.
10 Ibn Verga, *The Vale of the Tears* (in Hebrew, cited here from the translation by Ariel Toaff 1996b). This famous and widely discussed piece has been examined, from different perspectives, within the broad historiographical debate about the arrival of the Spanish refugees. The author's bias is unquestionable, but, in the words of Ariel Toaff (1996b, p. 148), just as evident is "the mixture of sentiments and psychology" that this shows. Bonfil also says that "the fictionalized presentation of the persecution of the Jews, as put forward

The darkly shaded picture drawn by Ibn Verga does not bear much resemblance to actual events. While the Jewish community did have good relations with the Curia, and despite the fact that Alexander VI did not enjoy a reputation for integrity (and neither had he in the past), it is still hard to believe that such a brazen attempt by a group of Jews to bribe a Pope could have been carried out so publicly, in that form and with those words. Rather, the vitriolic dialog reported by Ibn Verga is an indication, in the tones of literary myth, of the tension that existed between these two factions of the Roman Jewish community for most of the 16th century. In this text, the initial profound mistrust shown by the "indigenous" Jews towards the new arrivals is transposed to a mythological and heroic form, for consumption by an exclusively Jewish public who doubtless would have recognized these narrative allusions.

Stefano Infessura's diary is a much more credible source. The diary confirms the same climate of nervousness that is so heavily transfigured by Ibn Verga, though it does so between the lines and completely involuntarily. The Romans' anxieties were not unjustified, and according what the Senate Secretary relates, Spanish Ambassador Lopez de Haro gave them good reason to worry. In fact, right in the middle of a meeting that had been called to obtain an alliance with the Pope against France, the Ambassador presented a formal protest from Spain to Alexander VI regarding the Jews, making it known that

> The King [*Ferdinand of Spain*] expelled the *marrani* from his kingdom, considering them enemies of the Christian faith, and found it astonishing that the Pope, who is the leader of said faith, would welcome them in the Urbe: he thus called on him to expel them from the lands held by the Church.[11]

---

by Ibn Verga, cannot be considered as genuine history, although his work is important for the analysis of the perception of suffering by the Jews following the expulsion from Spain" (2010, p. 85). For a completely different interpretation of the piece, considered as ultimately being a *topos* read in from a very "literary" perspective, cfr. Schwarzfuchs 1970. See also the numerous works of Anna Esposito on the subject and in particular the essays published in 1995 and 2007. For a opposite interpretation of the piece see Stow 1992a/b and 2001: 24–25.

11 "l re [*Ferdinando di Spagna*] aveva espulso i marrani dal suo regno, considerandoli nemici della fede cristiana, trovava stupefacente che il papa, che è il capo della detta fede, li avesse accolti nell'Urbe: e per questo lo invitò ad espellerli dalle terre soggette alla Chiesa."Infessura 1890, p. 288. For the identification of the Spanish Ambassador and for a complete analysis of the relations between the Papacy and Spain regarding the Jews and the permanent settlement of a community of Jews in Rome, see Foa 2001, with particular reference to p.513 for the quote just cited. On the Portuguese side of this story, see Novoa 2014.

According to the recorder's notes, not only did the Pope decline to reply at that moment to the severe remonstrance he had just received, but in the following months, while avoiding the grant of licenses and *condotte*, he quietly authorized the "*marrani*" to move into the city. After all, as all pontifical policy regarding Spain would seek to demonstrate in the following crucial decades, it certainly did not fall to a king (or an ambassador) to dictate to Peter's successor how he was to exercise his ministry.[12] The fact that these were professing Jews – and not "*marrani*," as Lopez de Haro would continue to inaccurately refer them – mattered little in the conduct of a tense dialog aimed at clarifying the terms and limits of the relationship between the Church of Rome and the newly unified Spain. The repeated use of the term "*marrani*," once again employed to describe professing Jews, and not Christians accused of crypto-Judaism, attests to a cultural short circuit in the complex web of institutional and political relationships that was continuously woven between Rome and Madrid in the first half of the 16th century. In this context, the insistence with which the diplomat repeats such an inaccurate term reminds us that when it came to religious issues, Spain intended to continue defending its own opinions, notwithstanding the open hostility of the Pope.[13]

The Borgia papacy made the definition of balances and reciprocal influences with the Catholic Kings a priority matter, one which was raised to the level of urgency by the presence of opposing military forces in Italy, as well as by the pressing questions about Christian universalism raised by the discovery of the West Indies. The responsibilities for governing the lands of the newly discovered continent were divided up geographically by Alexander VI himself with a series of provisions – the bulls *Inter Coetera* and *Eximiae Devotionis* of May 4, 1493 and then the short *Dudum siquidem* on September 25 of the same year. It was with this last bull, in fact, that the Pope sent a reminder to the enterprising Iberian royalty about to whom the spiritual and material sovereignty of the world ultimately belonged.[14] The Roman concession, other than clarifying the source of legitimacy for all human authority, reiterates that the handling of infidels and their evangelization are ecclesiastical matters, to be pursued according to the strategies employed in the capital of Christianity, and not those practiced in the palaces of other European cities. That such a precise definition would appear in writing while the Pope's choices regarding the fate of the Sephardic refugees were still being discussed is a fact that merits attention and that, until now, has been overlooked.

---

12   Foa 2003.
13   For a summary of Papal policy in this period, cfr. the essays in Visceglia 2013.
14   Prodi 1979; Prosperi 1999; Cantù 2007; Schwartz 2008

Accepting the Spanish Jews in Rome was another part, albeit one of extraordinary symbolic relevance, of the long struggle that Alexander VI and his successors faced against the Spanish powers. Politically speaking, Rome's position in 1493 was not easy. On the one hand Spanish pressure and the Italian wars favored the seemingly pragmatic refusal of entry to the refugees; on the other hand there were the Pope's ambitions, as well as a juridical and theological tradition regarding the Jews that had always been characterized by the practice of moderate tolerance aimed at long-awaited conversions.[15] Halted at the gates of the Rome and living in a tent city guarded by Spanish soldiers, the refugees did not lose heart. With the help of a few soldiers who were *conversos* themselves, they entered the city in order to negotiate with the ecclesiastical authorities regarding the mechanism and time frame for an official entrance to the capital of Christianity. It was an extremely difficult mission, further complicated by the outbreak of disease, but in spite of everything the task was successfully completed. The fact that, despite being caught in the diplomatic whirlwind described above, Pope Borgia granted asylum to the Spanish refugees in the end is beyond doubt; how he arrived at such a decision and what it entailed is a rather more complicated matter, from whatever point of view we look at the question.

In the months that followed– starting, therefore, with Alexander VI's tacit consent in the fall of 1493 – the presence of the Spanish Jews in Rome became permanent. The ecclesiastical authorities and the Jewish world were now forced to confront the actual existence of a community of refugees living in the ghetto and the consequences of their settlement. The inheritance that the Sephardim brought with them to Rome represented a heavy burden. The new arrivals were weighed down by a past of tragedies and persecution, and even more so by the implications that accompanied their status as an expelled minority, as the objections made by the Spanish ambassador immediately made clear.

In the eyes of many, as we have seen, the Sephardim were not Jews but rather *"marrani,"* converts to Christianity secretly practicing Judaism. This required direct action of control and repression, which up to that time Rome had never felt the need to organize regarding converted Jews, whose baptism had always been encouraged and supported in every way. The silent decision to accept the exiles put the Pope in a difficult position. Alexander VI found himself poised between a central requirement of Catholic theology, that of promoting the

---

15   Regarding the eschatological centrality of converting the Jews, see the complete discussion offered by Piero Stefani 2004, with particular reference to pp. 163–196 for developments in the 16th century.

conversion of the Jews by any means available, while ensuring the validity of those conversions, and the equally urgent necessity of propping up the alliance with Spain in the Italian wars, while at the same time emphasizing both the independence and primacy of the papacy, as well as pontifical supremacy in Iberia over the Bishops and Inquisition in Madrid. The ferocity with which Torquemada and his closest collaborators and successors pursued the objective of cleansing Spain from any Jewish contamination – and with it Sicily, Sardegna, and then later Portugal – was thus another element in a broader political and strategic game, in which the structure of the Iberian Church and its submission to the authority of Rome were being called into question.[16]

In this context, the only possible choice for a Spanish Pope, ambitious and only recently elected, was to open the gates of the city to the refugees (though without proclamations), and to prepare for a long dispute with Spanish Inquisition, which had to painfully abandon its effort to verify the real religious allegiances professed by the refugees, whom they considered a priori to be suspected Judaizers and not full Jews. The Spanish blurring of identities between Jews and new Christians was not part of the Roman tradition. In Rome the sincere attachment of neophytes to Christ and the Church was, in fact, kept under continuous observation, but this constant monitoring had to be aimed at protecting and caring for the convert more than at frightening him or his family. With the institution of the House of Catechumens in the 1540s and the subsequent erection of the ghettos, the pressure of proselytism grew increasingly intense and the actions of preachers became increasingly aggressive, up to the explosion of anti-Jewish violence of the 18th century. Nevertheless, the axiom that conversion = material benefits remained the pillar around which all of the Church of Rome's conversion propaganda revolved.[17]

Internally, the absorption of this group of foreign Jews was not a painless process, even beyond the major issues of international politics that their tragic story revealed. The sense of otherness that the Spanish brought with them involved every aspect of their lives as Jews, which differed from that of their Roman brothers in ritual, dress, language, culture and professions.[18] It would take decades (and the Sack of 1527 and institution of the ghetto) before the revolution provoked by their arrival could be called complete. The initial isolation of the Sephardim within the community that had to welcome them, willingly or otherwise depending on the circumstances, became a problem in

---

16 Foa 2003. For a general overview of Rome and the Iberians at the time, now also Novoa 2014.
17 Caffiero 2004 and 2008.
18 This question is developed in the following section of this chapter.

the following years. On one hand, as we have already seen, their presence in Rome was at first opposed by the Jews of the city; on the other hand, having been accepted due to the mysterious yet undeniable wishes of the Pope, the recent arrivals were settling in the Urbe, notwithstanding the mutual antipathy between the groups. This led the group of foreigners, faced with such an uncertain situation, to quickly begin organizing themselves, limiting, as much as possible, further opportunities for friction with the local Jews.

Thanks to studies by Anna Esposito we have a complete picture of the events of this period. In 1496 a *Communitas hebreorum hispanorum in Urbe commorantium* appeared on the scene. Within five years this was divided into three distinct communities – *Castigliani*, *Catalani* and *Aragonesi* – following the traditional division of nations in Spanish culture. By 1505 a *Communitas hebreorum forensium teutonicorum et gallorum* was organized, also destined to be quickly split into two distinct organizations in 1509, following national divisions. In the meantime, on March 1, 1506, all the non-Italian Jews decided to join together in a united *Universitas Hebreorum forensium et Ultramontanorum in Urbe existentium*. This congregation, which brought together representatives of each national group, was set up to better organize the collection of funds and aid for the poor, and aimed to be seen as a counterpart to the official *Universitas* for the allocation of taxes and the designation of delegates who would represent the Roman Jews in front of the Christian authorities.[19] In 1511, with the situation having become less fluid, the *Aragonesi* created their own regulatory statute and, in the same year, the *Castigliani* further divided into two *Scole*: one for *Castigliani Novi* and the other for *Castigliani Vecchi*. All these groups were part of the *Universitas Hebreorum forensium et Ultramontanorum in Urbe existentium*, which, together with the pre-existing *Universitas hebreorum romanorum*, formed the actual *Universitas hebreorum romanorum et forensium ac ultramontanorum in Urbe commorantium*, which was the only body officially recognized by the public authorities.[20]

The unique form of the Jewish delegations for relations with the papacy and fiscal institutions would cause a flood of controversies over the following thirty years, primarily related to the equitable division of taxes. Another work of literature, written several decades later in the aftermath of the Sack of 1527 by Spanish priest Francisco Delicado (who was probably a *converso*), confirms the perception of a continued climate of mutual distrust. Using the device of narrative dialog, Delicado relates the story of a brilliant and brazen Spanish

---

19   Esposito 2007: p. 180.
20   All of the documents cited are mentioned and discussed by Esposito 1995 and 2007.

prostitute's education in the slums of Rome during the papacy of Leo X. The lively description of the city's Jewish synagogues given by Rampino, the unusual guide found by the girl, says a lot about what its author thought about the subject, and how much the practice of conversion for convenience continued to weigh on the community. Not by chance, here the accusation is directed at Roman Jews:

> Lozana: "But tell me, what is in that house which so many people are entering?" Rampino: "We'll go there and see. It's the synagogue of the *Catalani*; this one farther down is the one for the women. Here are the *Tedeschi*, the others are *Francesi*, and this is for the Romans and Italians, who are the most foolish of Jews of all the other nations because they don't understand the Law and they tend to convert. Our Spanish are the most learned, because there are rich and cultured people among them, and they are very full of themselves. Here is where they are. How does it seem to you? This synagogue is the best of them all."[21]

It would take thirty years of furious disputes, which too often ended up before the ordinary Christian magistracy, until the Jews of Rome – with the explicit support of the Pope – finally decided in 1524 to confront the question of their community's organization. In order to succeed it was necessary to resolve the Sephardic problem, through a long and disjointed process of assimilation with the Italian Jews. This process was marked by some important milestones both inside and outside the Roman Jewish community, which, along with the trauma of the Protestant Reformation, figured among the conditions that allowed the Jews to confront the challenge from Paul IV in 1555.

2 A Statute for the Jews of Rome (1524)

With the papal decision to accept the Spanish refugees in 1492, the city's Jewish society would face profound changes. There ensued a painful process of transformation which lasted at least three decades, and which would continue to

---

21 "*Lozana*: «Ma ditemi, che c'è in quella casa dove entra tanta gente?». *Rampino*: «Andiamo lì e vedrete. È la sinagoga dei catalani, questa più giù è quella delle donne. Lì sono tedeschi, l'altra è dei francesi, questa dei romani e degli italiani, che sono gli ebrei più sciocchi di tutte le altre nazioni perché tendono a convertirsi e non conoscono la legge. I più istruiti sono i nostri, gli spagnoli, perché fra loro c'è gente ricca e colta e sono molto pieni di sé. Ecco dove sono. Che ve sembra? Questa sinagoga è il fior fiore»." Delicado 1998.

have an impact during the period immediately following the institution of the ghetto. The contemporaneous presence of so many Jewish congregations, all of them eager for legitimization from the Christian authorities, was accompanied by a drastic social and cultural metamorphosis of the entire community. The need for a unique interlocutor at the institutional level, who could represent the interests of the whole group, became progressively more urgent. However, during this initial period it was not possible to find a solution that was acceptable to all. Resolving the injustices incurred by the forced entry of the new group into the small nucleus of Roman Jewry would require more than three decades. The drafting of a shared statute, destined to endure overtime, only happened in 1524, under the rule of Pope Clement VII de' Medici, shortly after the concession of the first licenses for lending to Jewish bankers recorded in Rome (1521), and just before the great tragedy of the Sack of Rome (1527).

During the first quarter of the 16th century, the Jewish population of the city, fragmented among the numerous Italian synagogues and various institutions with origins in the diverse panorama of the *ultramontani* (that is, of the non-Italian families), was riven by numerous conflicts. While there was no lack of disputes related to the diversity of the *minagim* of each *edah*, the most serious controversies revolved around the proper management of the community taxes and the different demands that each social group made regarding the conduct of the community institutions. The tensions surrounding these issues were exacerbated by the Apostolic Chamber's requirement that the allocation of taxes be centralized through the one and only *Universitas* that it recognized, and that was the old *Universitas Iudaeorum de Urbe*, which excluded the *ultramontani*.

Jewish banking represented a second divisive element in these years, also destined to influence the future of the group. After a long wait, in 1521 Leo X finally granted the Jews of Rome authorization for moneylending, issuing a limited number of licenses to the most important businessmen in the sector. A significant percentage of these came from the Spanish and other *ultramontani* groups, which were not yet fully integrated in the community's institutions.[22] Such a situation was anomalous for Jewish society, in which the task of governing traditionally fell to the exponents of the emerging classes (bankers, doctors, and often rabbis). Thus a stalemate resulted, where on one hand the public magistrates granted a prominent role to the immigrants and awarded them privileges, while on the other hand, this ratification was still lacking in

---

22   Esposito 2002.

the community. The rules of 1524 would intelligently resolve both of these problems.[23]

Until the approval of the *Capitula, reformationes et ordinationes Universitatis Hebraeorum tam Romanorum quam Ultramontanorum seu Forentium in Alma Urbe commorantium* of 1524, the *Universitas Iudaeorum Urbis*, the only official entity recognized by the Papal authorities, was governed on the basis of some simple administrative customs. These were thrown irreparably into crisis with the appearance of the *ultramontani*.[24] Up to that time the center of meeting and discussion had been a general assembly of adult Jews which from time to time provided, with a two-thirds majority of participants, the nominations necessary to form the various governing bodies: a *camerlengo* who was elected for a year and delegated to bookkeeping, and the three *Fattori* who held office for four months and wielded executive powers.[25] Under special circumstances, or for particularly delicate assignments – for example, the collection of payments for the tax of 1,130 *fiorini*, which involved the other Jewish communities in the Papal States, who were always late with their payments[26] – other officials would be created *ad hoc*, often as members of a council of "7 good Jews," and assigned to work alongside the *Fattori*.[27] The *Fattori*, or one of these temporary commissions, were responsible for dividing the taxes that had to be paid by the entire community (the *Vigesima*, the *Sussidio Triennale* and the *Tassa del Carnevale*) amongst the Jews of the *Universitas*. Whoever held seats in the administration, therefore, managed the allocation of taxes.

The distribution of tax collections was also a very good reason for the new arrivals to try in any way possible to occupy public roles in the community institutions, and the local Jews did their best to prevent them from succeeding. This was the core of the problem. While the different *ultramontani* groups had set up autonomous *Scole* with national roots, it was not possible for them to establish another true Jewish *Universitas* that was empowered with the same prerogatives as the preexisting one. Thus both groups had to resign themselves to a coexistence that remained without written laws, however, at least when it came to relations with the public authorities.[28] It was a non-solution that was bad for everyone. In the end, in 1524 the urgency of regulating the life of the *Universitas* with a new and more modern device was such that it could no

---

23   Cooperman 2015.
24   Esposito 1995, p. 279.
25   Esposito 1995, pp. 162 sgg.
26   Toaff 1996b.
27   Esposito 1995, p. 163.
28   Esposito 1995.

longer be delayed. The task of settling the tangled mess was given to Daniel da Pisa, who was selected because he did not belong to the Roman community, through an agreement between representatives of the Jews and the Pope (for whom da Pisa was a trustee banker).

In hopes of pre-empting any causes for dispute, Daniel took care to select a commission that included equal membership of *italiani* and *ultramontani* to assist him in the compilation of the new laws. The Roman Jewish community, other than being a mixture of people of different nationalities who were grouped accordingly – by *Scole* actually – also included members of the wealthy social classes, which had been revolutionized by the arrival of the refugees. Aware that he had to take these and many other factors into account, da Pisa asked each socio-economic group, represented by twenty delegates each, to put forth four names, two for each one of the different national groupings, to collaborate with him on the drafting of the new *Capitoli*.[29] The joint structure of *banchieri*, *ricchi* and *mediocri* was Daniel's first success. The hierarchical pyramid established then would be replicated later, and end up supporting the entire structure of the reformed *Universitas*.

At the center of the structure was the Congregation of Sixty. The number of sixty deputies was reached through the lifetime appointment of twenty representatives from each class group; these representatives had to organize committees established to advocate for the needs of each class. The logic of equal participation of *italiani* and *ultramontani* remained in force.[30] From time to time a third of the Congregation members would be nominated as members of the *Consiglio Ristretto* (*vaad*), serving in rotating shifts. Following tradition, executive power continued to be reserved for the three *Fattori*, two *italiani* and one *ultramontano*, who held office for one year. The *Fattori* were assisted with financial accounting by two *camerlenghi* (*parnassim*), one taking the role of treasurer and the other of accountant. They were replaced every six months, always by one member from each of the two main groups. Four *Tassatori*, all members of the Congregation, would collect the taxes. Two of them were

---

29 This version of the *Capitoli* is based on the source edited by Attilio Milano in 1935 and 1936. Recently three previously unknown copies of the Statute have been found – the first in a private collection, the second at the Houghton Library at Harvard University and discovered by Prof. Bernard Cooperman (see the article of 2015), and the third in the State Archive of Rome. I am working with Bernard Cooperman and Anna Esposito to prepare a new edition of these three documents, which offer differing versions and reveal different stages of the development of the text. Regarding the Harvard text, see Cooperman 2006, p. 124, n. 10 and 2015, n. 36.

30 When one of the members died, the group to which he belonged would conduct an internal election for the successor. Cfr. Milano 1935, p. 331.

required to be bankers, and the nominees, as usual, had to be equally divided by nation. Committees made up of two members (who were, as usual, selected based on nation) were charged with collecting the charity donations for the poor from the different *Scole*, and were entrusted with the enforcement of *kasherut*. for the meats being slaughtered by Jewish butchers, an absolutely vital function for a Jewish community. Finally, there were the five *Difensori dei Capitoli*, composed of three *italiani* and two *ultramontani*, who oversaw the correct application of all the laws, and were endowed with an account of 200 gold ducats. Nobody was allowed to refuse an appointment by the Congregation, on pain of excommunication *more hebraeorum*[31] and the payment of a hefty fine to the *Difensori*. However, the various *Scole* within the *Universitas*–as found in eleven items from Christian notarial documentation just before the Sack[32]- were guaranteed the greatest freedom in their liturgy and in the conduct of their own affairs, confirming the permanence of the individual and powerful sub-communities.[33]

The careful- and substantially equitable – division of roles and prerogatives between the nations and social groupings therefore constitutes the guiding principle of the proposal drawn up in the *Capitoli*. The goal was to defuse any cause for conflict and protect all members of the group through the rigorous application of a model of the equal distribution of posts. The main reason for the success of the 1524 project is clearly the intelligence behind this framework. Severely put to the test first by the Sack, and then again thirty years later by the turning point of the ghetto, the law demonstrated just how efficiently it worked.[34]

The solution developed by Daniel da Pisa in better times would guide the fortunes of the *Universitas* with a firm hand during the hard years of the ghetto. It was then that the Jewish ruling class made careful use of their legacy, adapting the systems of cooptation that had been spelled out in 1524 with great skill, but without ever changing the text of the statute. One small modification that was made in 1571 was simply a different balance in the composition of the Congregation; with the assent of Cardinal Savelli, the Vicar of Rome, the number of *italiani* was raised to 35 and that of the *ultramontani*, as a result, was reduced

---

31   Regarding this announcement as a "prop for Jewish internal discipline," see Simonsohn 1996 p. 118, with concrete examples in Ibid. 1988–1991 7, pp. 444 et seq.
32   Esposito 1995.
33   Milano 1935. An institutional discussion of the mechanism chosen in parallel with the ordinances of other Italian communities is found in Lattes 1998.
34   Regarding the application of the *Capitoli* in the 1600s, see Lattes forthcoming. I thank the author for having made a manuscript copy of this work available to me.

to 25. The amendments that were approved in 1698 – following the cancellation of Jewish banking licenses in 1682 – instead produced a significant expansion of responsibilities for the members of the assembly, who were called upon to personally manage an ever expanding range of services and responsibilities, while subject to legal liability and *in solido* (that is, subject to penalties against their private wealth). These included some roles not at all sought after; superintendent of prisoners and of sermons.[35]

3   The Burning of the Talmud and the Anti-Jewish Turn in the First Half of the 16th Century

During the years between the arrival of the Spanish refugees (1493) and the publication of the *Capitoli* (1524), much water passed under the bridges. The ancient Jewish community of Rome experienced major transformations which resulted in a society that was more complex and stratified, but also more contrasted and combative. After a very long gestational phase, and thanks to the specific wishes of Clement VII, the Jews of Rome were given a rational, well-balanced and generally shared statute. This statute was destined to remain unchanged for more than three centuries, and served as a model for other Italian Jewish institutions. In the meantime, in 1521 the banks and their owners had obtained public recognition with the formal authorization to work in the financial sector of the capital city of Christianity.

Throughout this period, Christian thought regarding the Jews – which must be taken into account when we study the history of this minority –also produced important conceptual developments based on the critical evaluation of the Spanish experience. The ghetto represented a radical reversal of conditions for the Jews of Rome and the Papal States, but it was not really an unexpected disruption. The decision to impose segregation was the culmination of a broader process which, spurred by the controversies resulting from the expulsion of 1492, manifested a clear and pragmatic understanding of the problems raised by the subject of the Jews (who were to be converted and instructed like heretics and infidels), but also by the recent geographical discoveries across the ocean, the explosion of the Protestant Reform, and finally, the permanent state of partial war with the Turks. After a brief reconstruction of the institutional events that led the Jews of Rome to create the *Capitoli* – which was so important for the future of the community – this section is dedicated to a

---

35   Milano 1984, pp. 181–182.

concise examination of the anti-Jewish turn that occurred just before the creation of the ghettos, and which actually laid their foundation.

The first stage of this renewed interest in the Jewish condition was the papacy of Paul III (1534–1545), the first to have a wide-ranging program after Luther's attack and the assault on the city during the Sack of 1527. Committed to the work of transforming and controlling the Church and its State, Pope Farnese included the conversion of the Jews in his project of comprehensive reform.[36] Along with the baptism of infidels and reconciliation of heretics, converting Jews was once again a top priority to be pursued with great zeal, but within the boundaries of Roman tradition, which was opposed to forcing the sacraments at the point of a sword. The key to the project was the granting of exceptional rewards and benefits (and not punitive surveillance, as happened in Spain and Portugal) to converts who left Judaism. This ideological framework was embodied, on the one hand, by the House of Catechumens and its associated system of incentives, and on the other hand by the progressive restriction of Jewish culture, culminating with the famous burning of the Talmud in 1553.

Let's look at the first aspect, which concerns the management of conversions and converts. In the space of two years at the beginning of the 1540s, Pope Paul III, with the promulgation of the bull *Cupientes,* first established the definition of a broader range of privileges for converts from Judaism, and then the formation of institutions charged with welcoming those who had already been baptized, as well as converts who had decided to accept the gift of faith and thus required dedicated instruction.[37] The creation of the House of Catechumens in 1543, ordered by the bull *Illius*, represented a fundamental step in the development of the policy of aggressive proselytizing carried out by Rome in the modern age. According to the papal plan, the House was created to offer a "neutral" and protected space for reflection and education, hosting those who had undertaken the road to baptism, willingly or otherwise. Within a short time, however, this center of peaceful introspection was transformed into a space of sometimes violent propaganda and tremendous pressure, deployed by zealous preachers, intent on bringing souls to God by any legitimate means.[38]

The opening of the House of Catechumens can be seen as the first concrete action initiating the strategy of inclusive exclusion that saw its definitive sanction with the opening of the ghettos in 1555. Although its purpose was to assimilate the Jews through the imposition of baptism, it should be recalled that

---

36 Caffiero 2004, pp. 13–26.
37 The complete texts of the two bulls are in *Cupientes Iudaeos* and *Illius*.
38 Caffiero 2004. Regarding the politics of conversion in this period, Segre 1996a, pp. 753–766.

by its very nature the *Casa* proclaimed the necessity of the physical presence of the Jews within Christian society. The unacceptable otherness of the Jews would be eliminated by offering them every opportunity to be educated and persuaded; not by eradication through expulsion, but by recourse to every possible form of evangelization *in loco*. During years in which, however, the debate regarding the significance and validity of accepting the Jews remained intense, the position that Rome began to express yet again emphasized their conversion as the priority and not, as perhaps some would have wished, their removal by exile following the Iberian model. The Pope's choice, in line with a centuries' old tradition, was to offer the stubborn Jews yet another opportunity for salvation. The inevitable consequence of this policy was the decision to make this opportunity increasingly attractive: with the invention of the Houses of Catechumens, access to the process of conversion was made clear and simple, at the same time fully emphasizing the advantages and material benefits that accompanied baptism. On the other hand, in an era in which the Church was engaged in a fierce battle for its own survival against rampant heresy, the conversion of all infidels and Christian heretics was an absolute priority, and this naturally included the Jews.[39]

Thus the papacy of Paul III officially ushered in a difficult period for the Jews of Rome. On the one hand, the system of institutions for conversion represented a constant and annoying prod that reminded Jews of the insecurity of their position; on the other hand, the monitoring and controls became increasingly severe, and ended up attacking the very heart of Jewish identity.[40] Here too we can single out an event that is symbolic of a wider process and which would spur future developments. The burning of the Talmud in Piazza Campo de' Fiori in 1553 was the most traumatic, wrenching event of this phase. The lighting of those flames represented the apex of a period of worsening antisemitism, which began with the opening of the House of Cathecumens in 1543 and was now embodied in more blatant forms. The suspicion harbored against the Talmud was a constant in Christian doctrine, which furthermore had always regarded the rabbis' entire cultural production outside the canon of the Old Testament with suspicion. Notwithstanding this, over the centuries the Jews continued to study, write and comment on the Talmud. Midway into the 16th century the Talmud once again became the center of controversy. In

---

39   Caffiero 2012, pp. XI and 269–296.
40   Segre 1996a, pp. 714–715. More generally it should be recalled that it was under Paul III that, finally and with great delay, the Church laid out a series of strategies and tools for addressing the Protestant offensive: see at least the summary by Bonora 2001, pp. 9–35 and Del Col 2006, pp. 284–342.

1550, the flare-up of a very bitter commercial dispute between two Venetian printers, involving the almost simultaneous publication of two editions of Rambam's *Mishnè Torà,* was the pretext upon which the question of the Talmud and its contents returned to the agenda in Rome. One of the parties filed a complaint and accused the other of having printed blasphemous texts.[41] The burning of the Talmud in Campo de' Fiori in 1553, on the day of *Rosh Hashana* in front of a stunned community, in tears and fasting, was the first in a series of pyres that were lit shortly thereafter throughout the Papal States. The attack on the Talmud halfway through the century represented the most dramatic expression yet of Catholic policy, a policy that was now intent on securing the conversion of Jews by any means; the Jews interpreted it as such, witnessing these events with fear.[42]

The reaction was immediate. Faced with the endless flaring of fires, the leaders of all the Italian Jewish communities gathered at Ferrara on June 21, 1554. Fearing that the burning of the Talmud could be a prelude to the introduction of restrictive rules against all Jewish cultural production, if not even an attack on the people,[43] the group established a policy that from then on, no book could be published without prior approval from a commission of rabbis.[44] This decision to adopt a procedure of self-censorship represents an important step towards the definition of the rules Jews would use as they prepared to respond to the ever more insistent challenge that the Church had launched against their culture, identity and religion.[45] The congress of Ferrara was a declaration that Italian Judaism, though called upon to live in difficult times, would not remain helpless and wait for the searches and seizures. Instead they would seek, where possible, to prevent them.[46] In fact, as Marina Caffiero has recently written, while the obsessive control over what Jews read would never let up from that moment on, for the Jews this control also involved ongoing efforts to continue studying the forbidden texts.[47]

---

41 Parente 1996, pp. 583–584.
42 Stow 1972 and 1977; now also Caffiero 2012, pp. 5–43, in particular, pp. 5–19.
43 Parente 1996 (p. 587) cites a letter in which, on 16 August 1555, more than a month after the publication of *Cum nimis absurdum,* the Jews expressed their fear of being expelled from all the Papal States within three months.
44 Parente 1996, p. 594; Finkelstein 1924, pp. 300 et seq.; Simonsohn 1977; Bonfil 1996, p. 448.
45 Segre 1996a, pp. 762–764.
46 Berliner refers to the abortive attempt to organize a Jewish public demonstration to stop the search for books triggered by the burning, which would have had to involved all of the Italian communities and for which Rome, in 1558, would have named a representative to send to the Marche (Berliner 1992, p. 177).
47 Caffiero 2012 pp. 78–119.

So, it's no surprise to discover that for centuries, every time the police would enter the ghetto they would, playing a perhaps predictable role, leave with their carts full of books to be examined by the Inquisition. The hated Talmud never failed to appear among the suspect volumes. Notwithstanding the fact that it had been placed in the Index of Prohibited Books in 1596, Jews persisted in buying and reading the Talmud, hiding the precious books behind covers citing fake publishers, misleading titles, and permitted authors.[48] This is an important fact which is not always sufficiently emphasized. In a culture like that of the Jews, who had always been accustomed to the transmission of oral knowledge alongside the reading of texts, the choice of self-censorship did not really mean renouncing the defense of their religious belonging and doctrinal foundations. Rather it represented the best, if not the only practical solution in an extreme situation. Editing words, phrases or content did not signify willingly forgetting them, and neither did it constitute surrender to external pressure. Jewish self-censorship was not an agreement, so to speak, to limit their knowledge of Judaism to the mere execution of rites and liturgy, rendered incomprehensible by the absence of interpretive vehicles to explain and support them. Put more simply, the conservation and implementation of the *halakha* and of rabbinic exegesis was entrusted as much to the permitted pages of these controversial books (where often blank spaces were left to indicate a censored phrase to the attentive reader) as it was to the authority of the teachers and to the ancient and very reliable mnemonic systems of instruction.[49] From generation to generation, as tradition dictated. From this perspective, the fact that such a radical decision was made in a plenary meeting of representatives from all of the Italian Jewish communities clearly demonstrates a collective perception of the seriousness of the moment and its attendant risks, as well as the resolve to confront such serious problems together. The Jews did not remain helpless but rather, with the means at their disposal and strengthened by a solid centuries-old cultural tradition, fought a battle for their survival as a minority group. As we will see, the rabbis play a fundamental role in this struggle.

After the autumn of 1553, the Jews of Rome grew increasingly aware of the vulnerability of their situation: the recent trauma of the Iberian expulsions, the tragic experience of the occupation by the Lanzi during the months of the Sack, then the appearance of the House of Catechumens and the book burning in Campo de' Fiori – all were alarm bells that were difficult to ignore.

---

48   Ibid.
49   On this subject, interesting examples of rabbinic sermons are cited by Bonfil 1996, pp. 430–433 and in the papers brought together by David B. Ruderman 1992.

Meanwhile, wars raged all around, and it was becoming clear that the schism with the Protestants was irreparable. The Church Council, with its erratic meetings, seemed incapable of finding solutions and restoring peace among Christians. At the mid-point of the 16th century nobody in the capital of Catholic Christianity could look to the future with confidence. Even less so could the Jews. In the summer of 1554 a black sky spread its clouds over their worried heads. In less than a year's time, the ascent of Cardinal Carafa (with his past at the Holy Office) to the papal throne seemed to confirm all of their anxieties.[50]

4 The Avoided Expulsion from the Papal States

The election of Cardinal Gian Pietro Carafa, known to be an intransigent enemy of the Jews, to the papal throne in 1555, so soon after the attack on the Talmud, was cause for concern among the Jews. The course set with the opening of the Houses of Catechumens was an indication of Rome's preference for a form of proselytism that, by its very nature, excluded the idea of expulsion. This evangelizing was at times extremely violent (as in the case of the burning of the Talmud in 1553), or to the contrary, donned the more traditional garb of preaching and propaganda. Both of these approaches required maintaining contact with the subjects to be instructed. The decision to gather the Jews in specific areas of the city and ramp up the restrictions and pressures on them in order to facilitate their conversion was, therefore, the culmination of a process that had been initiated earlier, and which had progressed cautiously and uncertainly pointing towards the implementation of the most drastic idea- expulsion. Such an outcome was considered a serious possibility, and the anxiety with which the Jews feared reliving the drama of 1492 appears clearly in internal sources, as demonstrated by the legend of a ritual killing in Rome that is reconstructed in the next chapter of this book. For now, it is interesting to recall how on the one hand, the opening of the ghettos constituted the most recent element of a much broader and older strategy of proselytism, and how on the other hand, the lasting memories of the exile from Spain and recollections of the tragic experience of taking in the refugees had not receded at all from the Jewish consciousness in the second half of the century, and thus were destined to influence future choices.

A detailed analysis of Jewish life in the age of the ghettos must begin with an examination of the law that inaugurated it, the bull *Cum Nimis Absurdum*,

---

50   Stow 2001, pp. 40–43; see also Caravale, Caracciolo 1963, pp. 285–288; Mampieri 2020

promulgated on July 14, 1555. It was on that date and with that law, in fact, that the newly elected Paul IV decreed that Jews in every city of the Papal States would be required to live in just one section of the city, or in the case of small towns with equally small Jewish populations, along only one street. These quarters or streets were required to be surrounded by high walls, with only one gate to the city, to be closed an hour before sundown and reopened after sunrise. The Jews and the magistrates responsible for enforcing these rules were granted six months to comply with the Papal decree, after which the new system was to be fully implemented.[51] In a short time the walls were erected, the gatekeepers were hired, real estate assets were liquidated, and the relocation was completed. This happened quietly, without any public attempt by the Jews to protest or negotiate delays or modifications to the decree.[52] The experience of the segregated quarter in Venice, established in 1516, in the midst of a very difficult war for the survival of the *Serenissima Repubblica*, had demonstrated that these types of decrees, while troublesome, did not cause irreparable damages. Despite the physical separation enforced by the ghetto wall, the battles, the treaties, the complex tangle of the era's political affairs and the familial and commercial lines of communication between the Jews of the Lagoon and their coreligionists in Italy and outside it had not been interrupted. In fact Venice, with its port, flourishing commerce, press and traditional tolerance, continued to be one of the key hubs between Christian Europe and the Ottoman Empire for the network of Sephardic refugees.[53]

The regulatory restrictions should not have taken the Jews by surprise, especially and above all in light of the still fresh memories of the book burnings just two years earlier. The ascent to the throne of Peter of Cardinal Gian Pietro Carafa, an exponent of the strictest wing of the conclave, could only be a harbinger of misfortune for the Jews. Like his predecessors, this Pope had been elected to restore order in the chaotic ranks of the Church through the imposition of a rigid program of social and doctrinal purification, continuing the work begun by Paul III – it was not by chance that Carafa kept that name with

---

51   Milano 1984, pp. 71–73. For the text of the Bull, *Cum nimis absurdum*.
52   As Renata Segre writes, "The Jews constantly sought to avoid expulsion with petitions, emissaries, and appeals to the courts and governments, but they did not show an equal opposition to the enclosure in the ghetto: it was always and only the ways in which it was implemented that were opposed or disputed. And although there could have been many reasons for this, there was perhaps above all the awareness that the implementation of this urban system represented protection, and the most certain antidote to expulsion" (Segre 1996a, pp. 776–777).
53   Segre 1996a, pp. 711–713; Calimani 2001; Davis, Ravid 2001.

the next number in sequence.[54] Now, in the middle of the 16th century, the objective was clear and was to be kept front and center at any price: stop rampant heresy from gaining a definitive foothold in Italy.[55] During the decades of the Farnese papacy, the restructuring of the ancient Tribunal of Faith into the now aggressive Congregation of the Holy Office, and the discussion underway at the Council regarding the cornerstones of orthodoxy, as much as these fluctuated, represented two faces of a coin: on one side there was the introduction of increasingly strict means of ideological control, and on the other there was a redefinition of the rules that these means of control were meant to protect and reinforce.

The Jewish world also played a role in this picture, however marginal. The imposition of Catholic Reform turned out, in fact, to be a long and arduous process. To win the battle it was vital to launch specific programs of propaganda and repression against the Protestants.[56] From this point of view, the invention of the Houses of Catechumens responded to a clear priority (to educate infidels and Jews), while at the same time concretely and publicly demonstrating the Pope's resolve to contain the spread of heresy, albeit from a lateral perspective. The burning of the Talmud similarly represented the embodiment of the Church's refusal to accept within its lands the spread of superstition and anti-Christian propaganda that detractors of the Talmud claimed was communicated by the great collection of Jewish wisdom; according to them the Talmud should be condemned just like every other dangerous text. In both cases, the Jews' uncomfortable status as an undesirable, but nevertheless accepted presence in the heart of Catholic society put them first in line for any attempt at social regulation.

The news of Cardinal Carafa's election in the aftermath of the book burnings of 1553 must have been greeted by the Jews with a healthy dose of justifiable anxiety. Thus while they feared that the newly elected Pope would launch an Iberian style expulsion, his promulgation of a law which did not, however, order an immediate expulsion did not cause much alarm. One Pope dies and another is named, and centuries of experience had demonstrated that every change at the papal throne brought periods that were more or less happy for the Jews, but still transitory; in the end, notwithstanding all the edicts,

---

54 Bonora 2001, pp. 9–35; Po-chia Hsia 2001, pp. 28–29. A summary of the election of Paul IV, the climate in the city and some of his foreign policy choices and strategies in the Curia can be found in Bonora 2011, pp. 50–56.
55 Del Col 2006, pp. 395–476.
56 Regarding the (at least apparent) secondary nature of the Jewish question in this phase, Segre 1996a, p. 709.

proclamations and recollections of the pious work of predecessors, the Jews thought that it would be difficult for Paul IV's decision to last very long. So, although Pastor, based on secondary sources, refers to an attempt at convincing the Pope to step back from his decisions (which, in his obvious formulation seems almost like a literary *topos*), in fact there are no other attestations of public and strong protests against *Cum Nimis Absurdum* advanced by Jews. In comparison, the seizure and then the burning of the Talmud only two years previous had elicited vigorous public reactions.[57]

In the dogmatic introduction of the bull, in the lines which presented the ideological framework and its context in current problems, Paul IV simply repeated the rhetoric about waiting for conversion, the ungrateful arrogance of the Jews, and the lack of respect for any of the proper rules regarding the servitude of the Jews and their required separation from Christians. The themes are well known and have long been used in anti-Jewish rhetoric:

> Thus it is absurd and improper that the Jews, who by their own fault are condemned to perpetual servitude, can, given that they are protected by Christian mercy and tolerated in their cohabitation with Christians, be so ungrateful towards Christians as to transform the grace shown to them into an insult and to turn even their servitude, which is their condition, into an opportunity to dominate. We have been informed of the fact that in the heart of our Urbe and in other cities, villages and lands subject to the Holy Roman Church, the insolence of these Jews has reached the point that not only are they living mixed among Christians but also close to churches, without any distinctive marks on their clothing, and that, further, they are renting homes in the main streets and plazas, hiring nannies, housemaids and other Christian servants, and this allows them to pursue their misdeeds and offenses with contempt for the name of Christian. We consider that the Roman Church tolerates these Jews inasmuch as they are testimony to the truth of the Christian faith, and so that they will finally recognize their errors, pushed along by the mercy and benevolence of the Holy See, and make every effort to come to the true light of the Catholic faith and thus recognize that they have been reduced

---

57 Pastor refers to the attempt to pay off the Pope with 40,000 *scudi* (VI, p. 488), based on secondary sources cited by Berliner (1992, p. 174 and nn. 10–15, p. 363) and by Rodocanachi (1891, p. 40). On the basis of these same attestations, Milano gives credit to the proposal to send the Pope a "sizable emolument" (1984, pp. 73–74 and p. 124, n. 4). More recent historiography reports new documents and confirms the fear of expulsion. Cfr. Parente 1996, pp. 587–588; Segre 1996a, pp. 776–777; Foa 2003; Stow 2001, p. 64.

to slavery due to their persistent errors, while Christians have been freed thanks to Jesus Christ.[58]

The motivations put forward here openly echo a solid Christian tradition that, at least since the Council of 1215,[59] had repeatedly emphasized the status of *perpetua servitudo* as the only possible condition for the Jews. The juxtapositions of *pietas/ingratitudo*, *gratia/contumelia* and *libertas/servitudo* represented the supporting (and immediately identifiable) axes of a traditional ideology that was charged with eschatological tensions, given the centrality of the conversion of the Jews to the coming of the new messianic era. For centuries, every action directed at this minority was steeped in this ideology. Notwithstanding this, as Paul IV himself pointed out, the ungrateful Jews had scoffed at all attempts to return them to their just, humiliating and degraded condition. The situation had become unsustainable, and the time for a remedy had arrived. In response, for the health and salvation of the Christian faithful, the Pope intervened, returning to the classical set of economic and social discriminations to which Jews must be subjected, and combining them for the first time within one set of rules.[60] The goal – as always, to obtain the voluntary and conscious conversion of the Jews – would be reached by applying the many and varied rules regarding their separation from Christians, which had been issued randomly, and up to then had been applied with little commitment.

To prevent excessive closeness and any form of mingling or sharing with Christians, the law revived the obligation for Jews to wear a distinctive sign that would unequivocally identify them.[61] A series of old restrictions on Jews were then set down in black and white: it was forbidden to hire Christian servants or domestics,[62] to have friendly relations with Christians or even to just converse with them,[63] to be addressed with the title 'Sir' by the poor,[64] to work in public on Sunday or any other holiday,[65] for Jewish doctors to cure non-Jewish patients[66] and for merchants to deal in new merchandise.[67] The provisions

---

58 *Cum nimis absurdum*, Introduction.
59 Milano 1984, pp. 36–37; Stefani 2004, pp. 156–157. A detailed examination of the legal situation and literature on the subject can be found in Quaglioni 1996.
60 *Cum nimis absurdum*, § 1.
61 Ibid., § 3. See also Moretti 2011; and for a general overview, Cassen 2017.
62 *Cum nimis absurdum*, § 4.
63 Ibid., § 7.
64 Ibid., § 11.
65 Ibid., § 5 and 6.
66 Ibid., § 10.
67 Ibid., § 9.

dealing with moneylenders were also important, but not revolutionary: it was established that the bankers' account books were to be kept in Latin or Italian and not drawn up in Hebrew characters,[68] the approved interest rate for loans was lowered to twelve percent (from the previous rates of eighteen or twenty four percent, depending on the case), and further limitations were imposed on the calculation of interest and the redemption of pawned items.[69]

This whole range of provisions closely followed (and rationalized)an ancient writing which dated mainly back to the Lateran Council of 1215, though with certain amplifications: the mark on clothing, the ban on hiring wet nurses and domestics, the condition of servitude, and limits on the practice of medicine were not new. Each could boast endless precedents of famous failures, between forgetfulness of the rules and the concession of privileges. The provisions concerning moneylending did not present particular cause for worry either; rather, it should be noted that while the law reiterated the prohibition on doctors offering their services to Christians, and restricted Jewish businessmen only to trade in second hand merchandise, it was not by chance that the only prestigious and profitable profession that remained legal was banking.[70] This came with all the accompanying ambivalence: it is easier to become fond of a doctor who saves your life than of a banker, who is often accused of ruining your life. Even within the tight net of prohibitions and obstacles, spaces for Jewish business were not completely suppressed, and a range of possibilities remained open and available to the most willing. In the following years, the ability to take advantage of these openings went a long way towards maintaining solid connections and opportunities for encounter and exchange with the Christian world, as well as in building careers and clientele within the ghetto of Rome.[71]

The coerced living space, the walls that surrounded it and the restriction allowing only one active synagogue were the true innovations introduced by *Cum nimis absurdum*.[72] Among these, the last probably represented the most effective obstacle, difficult to apply in a society made up of such varied rites, traditions and liturgies.[73] The obligation for all Jews to live together within a restricted perimeter, as trying as it was, only codified an already existing reality. This was especially true in small towns, where Jews already lived close together

---

68   Ibid., § 8.
69   Ibid., § 12.
70   A detailed discussion of the bull can be found in Segre 1996a, pp. 714–717.
71   *Infra*, chapters 4 and 5.
72   *Cum nimis absurdum*, § 2.
73   Schwarzfuchs 1970.

due to religious needs and the need for collective security, often on just one street.[74] The area of *Sant'Angelo*, which Rome chose as the location for the ghetto walls, had for years been the preferred area of the city for Jews to reside (there was a butcher, an oven for matzah and a variety of synagogues).[75] Certainly it had been necessary to very quickly sell off real estate located outside the walls and accept forced relocation. However, the Jews silently complied, convinced that the situation was temporary, destined to be set aside upon the death of the hated Pope Carafa.[76] Only in Ancona was the reaction different. Most likely thanks to their greater proximity to Venice, which afforded the clearer understanding of the results of that experiment, by February of 1556 Ancona's Jews had already issued a set of *Capitoli* regarding the management of housing in the ghetto, which was immediately ratified by the local bishop.[77]

Finding a solution to the problem of the synagogues represented a more arduous challenge: the diversity of liturgies, pronunciations and customs among the Italians, the Spanish of varying provenance, the French, the Germans, the Sicilians and the "indigenous" Romans made it impossible for these groups to pray together without asking someone to renounce their traditions. The famous response formulated by the Jews in Rome in the following years, and accepted by Pio V in 1566, was to split up the one building in use as a synagogue. The synagogue's rooms were divided among the five principal *Scole*, following the scheme of memberships already in use during the tragic months of the Sack of Rome: the *Scola Tempio* for Romans of ancient lineage, the *Nova* for all the other Italians, and the *Siciliana*, the *Catalana* and the *Castigliana* for the three other major regional groups.[78]

Paul IV's decree was a return to the emphasis on reorganizing the society of the faithful that had been part of the Christian milieu for a long time, beginning at least with the appeals made in the *Libellus ad Leonem X* of 1513, which some forty years earlier had already proposed the idea of total separation of the Jews.[79] After then, but before the explosion of the Reformation, a critical

---

74 Ferrara 2011, p. 87; Bonfil 1996 pp. 47–55.
75 Esposito 2008.
76 Milano 1984, p. 76.
77 I consulted a copy of this document in Jerusalem, from the sources at the National Archives for the History of the Jewish People, IT/An, 94a. Another has been identified by Luca Andreoni (who I thank for informing me and who is editing it for publication) in the notarial sources of the Archivio di Stato of Ancona. See references to this document in Di Nepi 2017 and 2019.
78 Milano 1984, pp. 216–217; Spizzichino 2011.
79 The *Libellus* was published in 1733 by Giovanni Benedetto Mittarelli and Anselmo Costadoni, in the ninth volume of the *Annales Camadulenses*, columns 612–719. See this for the Latin text, in particular the section dedicated to "infidels" in columns 621–630. For

evaluation of the results achieved after the expulsions and forced conversions on the Iberian peninsula led Vincenzo Querini and Pietro Giustiniani to ask, somewhat idealistically, if it was possible to explore other avenues. Crypto-Judaism and the spread of forms of resistance to baptism represented a high margin of risk, which it was preferable to avoid, above all in a period – such as the one in which the two authors were composing their text – that was filled with a new missionary spirit. That spirit resulted from military confrontation with the Muslims, and also from the discovery of idolatrous populations in the Americas who were unaware of the evangelists' message but ready to welcome it.[80] The strategy regarding the Jews and the tools best suited to lead them to conversion had been suggested many years earlier. Now, influenced by the critical evaluation of the Iberian outcomes, and by the inspiration for universal evangelization (separation, humiliation, preaching, but never expulsion),[81] that strategy was translated into practice and placed within a legal framework based on the organized reintroduction of old principles which over time had been largely disregarded and negated by the concession of privileges to individuals, as well as by the inconsistent political approach to the issue.[82]

---

a detailed description and apologetics of the work for Querini and Giustiniani, see Massa 2005. More generally, for a reconstruction of the significance of the *Libellus* among the premises of the Council of Trent, see Prosperi 2001 pp. 18–20 and 78–80; Stow was the first one to point out this aspect on the Jewish side of the pamphlet (1977, pp. 217–220).

80   Massa 2005 pp. 17–20. Regarding the anti-Jewish pressures present in the Curia, for which the *Libellus* served as a spokesman, see Luzzati 1996, p. 234 and the introduction by Diego Quaglioni in Battista de' Giudici, *Apologia Iudaeorum*, pp. 20–24. A detailed analysis of the anti-Jewish positions of the *Libellus* can be found in Stow 1977, pp. 217–220 and in Prosperi 2001 pp. 174–176. For a discussion on the general ideas of *otherness* and of the comparison among "Heretics", "Savages," Muslims and Jews as attested in the *Libellus*, see Di Nepi 2015.

81   As Stow (1977) rightly pointed out, this is a very ambiguous passage in the original Latin (Mittarelli, Costadoni, *Annales Camaldulenses*, IX, col. 625), which must be put in context in light of the reflection developed just a few lines afterwards which asserts that: "nothing, in all of this business concerning the Jews, would appear less convenient and less appropriate than expelling them completely from all the regions ruled by Christians, with the introduction of the death penalty as well" (from the translation offered in the Italian edition in Massa 2005, p. 20). Adriano Prosperi has come back to this passage many times (2001, p. 20), giving it close attention in the Introduction to the edition edited by Adelisa Malena of *Degli ebrei e delle loro menzogne* by Martin Luther (2000, pp. XLIX–LI. In both cases Prosperi's interpretation links the idea of definitive expulsion. The contextualization proposed by Piero Stefani (2004, in particular pp. 178–195) is different, and closer to my reading of the text.

82   Di Sivo 2012 offers an interesting discussion on the literature of the period.

In compiling his legal framework for the Jews, Paul IV hoped to pin down a matter that was as old as it was unresolved. This is the provision's great innovation, inspired by the proselytizing strategy proposed by two *Camaldolese* monks in 1513, and probably one of the reasons for its centuries-long success. At least on paper, the old rules are presented as articles of one unique law, to be applied equally for all Jews who were subject to the temporal sovereignty of the Church. No Jew could be exempted from the law by way of privileges granted either by magistrates or courts of inferior rank. In July of 1555, for the first time, these ancient discriminatory rules were reprised as a unified whole, and as part of a clearly recognizable project of discrimination. The violation of these rules led to the definition of new types of crimes (leaving the ghetto during prohibited hours, for example), which required, from that moment on, new and different methods of adjudication for Jews, destined to have an impact on the future.[83]

Paul IV's successors, also committed to the anti-heresy campaign, merely refused to repudiate his decisions. Pius V's bull of expulsion in 1569,[84] retracted by Sixtux V in 1586[85] and then reinstated by Clement VIII five years later, further restricted Jewish living space to only the ghettos of Rome and Ancona (and later on Avignon). This represented the corollary to an already formulated theorem: if the Jews were only permitted to live in the Papal States as unwelcome guests who were to be controlled, there was no reason to allow them the pleasure of choosing their city of residence, and it was preferable from every point of view that they be concentrated exclusively in the biggest and most important cities, in order to facilitate both surveillance and evangelizing.[86]

The promulgation of *Cum nimis absurdum*, however, was a true watershed moment. For more than three centuries, until the annexation of Rome into the Kingdom of Italy in 1870, the Jews of the city remained confined to the ghetto, forced to live uncomfortable, perhaps miserable lives, though still living within the city and its society. The path taken by Paul IV represented the alternative to permanent expulsion: the ghetto did not completely sever relations between Jews and Christians, but it certainly had a great impact on them, changing their

---

83　Segre 1996a, pp. 716–717; Di Sivo 2012.
84　This refers to the constitution *Hebraeorum gens* of February 26, 1569. About this document see Milano 1984, pp. 76–78.
85　This refers to *motu proprio Christiana pietas* of October 6, 1586, about which cfr. Milano 1984, pp. 79–80 and Segre 1996a, pp. 736–738.
86　This refers to the bull *Caeca et obdurata* of February 25, 1593, about which see Milano 1984 pp. 80–81, and Segre 1996a, pp. 737–738. A detailed reconstruction of the anti-Jewish policy of Clement VIII can be found now in Caffiero, 2011, pp. 45–47 and pp. 78–86.

dynamics and meanings. In order for them to accept conversion it was essential that the Jews understood the error of their ways, and the Iberian example had demonstrated beyond any doubt that the imposition of mass baptisms did not resolve the problem. At best it was a superficial gesture, one which made it impossible to verify the sincerity of the converts' faith, and which had wrought disastrous consequences for all to see. The Jews, therefore, required instruction, and should be helped to understand where salvation came from and how to achieve it. The ghetto played a role in this system of partial inclusion and incomplete exclusion, and Christians willfully set themselves to the task of revealing the way of the faith to the Jews, using the concrete comparison between the good fortune and happiness given to Christians by the grace of God, and the endless misfortunes to which the Jews willingly condemned themselves.[87]

The raising of the ghetto walls was one element of a more complex construction. Just one year after the institution of the ghettos Pope Carafa raised the stakes, reaching levels of anti-Jewish violence never before seen in the Papal States. The condemnation to death by fire of twenty-four Sephardim in Ancona, under investigation on the extremely serious charge of being crypto-Jews (the first and only investigation of its kind actually conducted in the Papal States), was an event that their contemporaries saw as considerably more serious and dangerous than the decision to make Jews live crowded into one area, as cramped and subject to intrusive surveillance as that area could be.[88]

The turning point was the culmination of a series of steps which, starting with the Papal bull *Illius* in 1542, then the burning of the Talmud in 1553, and finally the release of *Cum nimis absurdum*, ended up delineating the ambiguous polarity between the ghetto and the House of Cathecumens, between servile confinement and liberating conversion, that was destined to embody the new approach to the old problem of Jewish obstinacy. The result was that for a period of time, at least until the 1580s, the issue of the Jews was actually set aside, with the exception of the continued attention reserved for the Talmud and other books. At night the Jews were closed in the ghettos, and during the day they worked in the streets of the city and outside the city at fairs and markets. For the moment the Church had more important business to tend to. The spotlight would return to the Jews in 1581, when a new law by another Pope, the *Antiqua Iudaeorum Improbitas*, would yet again change the rules of the game

---

[87] Regarding the ghetto as a mediated solution between expulsion and occupation, naturally the reference is to Foa 1992, pp. 155–161.

[88] Regarding these issues, cfr. Toaff 1974; Segre 1985; Muzzarelli 1991. Regarding the Jews in the March at the middle of the 1500s, see Andreoni 2013.

by subjecting the thoughts, beliefs and conduct of the Jews to the scrutiny of the Inquisition.[89] From then on the Holy Office's attention to the group would never wane, and the deployment of forces for the conversion of the Jews would become, from Pope to Pope and year to year, increasingly stringent.[90]

5   What If the Emperor Had Won?

There is no doubt that the first half of the 16th century in Italy opened a new phase in the history of relations between Jews and Christians.[91] There is also no doubt that this era paved the way for an increasingly strict and discriminatory redefinition of the rules of coexistence.[92] During this period the questions of the salvation and the destiny of infidels were central topics, and the decisions that were made had a great deal to do with the millennium of experience that Christian society had accumulated around the conversion of Jews. As we have seen, this profound hardening of doctrine was the driving force behind important decisions which appeared in rapid succession, and which had disruptive consequences: the expulsions from the Spanish territories and from Naples, the forced baptisms in Portugal, the ghetto in Venice and then Ragusa, the Houses of Catechumens, the burning of the Talmud, and the ghetto in the Papal States. Recent studies have for good reasons concentrated on these aspects, reconstructing the legal and ideological genealogy of these measures in detail, considering their ancient roots and the turning points that, over a long time, somehow prepared the way. Innovative studies at an international level – one immediately thinks of Jonathan Israel (1985), John Tolan (2015), Joseph Kaplan (2007) and Nicholas Terpstra (2015) – have begun to place specific events that involve European Jewry within the broader context of the necessity of experimenting with tools for governing religious minorities and practices of coexistence that developed in response to geographical discoveries, the Reformation, sectarian dissent and the complex system of relations with the Islamic world. The stories of the Jews of Italy clearly should be inserted in this picture. However, we should add one further element for consideration.

The fate of the Jews of the peninsula (Rome included, obviously) was decided during precisely the years in which a new political scenario was

---

89   Regarding the bull *Antiqua Iudaeorum Improbitas*, Di Nepi 2008, and the detailed discussion in Caffiero 2011, pp. 102–106.
90   Segre 1996a, pp. 765–766.
91   Todeschini 2016 and 2018.
92   Stow 1977; Caffiero 2014.

developing in Italy itself. While the Sephardim sought refuge in the prosperous Italian cities and negotiated with princes over the terms of their possible acceptance, those same princes found themselves being dragged into another conflict. Charles VIII of France's invasion of Italy in 1494 initiated a long period of wars between France and Spain for dominance in Italy. This long dispute was divided into nine consecutive conflicts that, beginning with the ascent of Charles V to the throne (1516) and his election as Emperor (1518), became a fierce confrontation involving all of Europe. Italy was at the center of Hapsburg imperial policy, the focal point of the conflict between the Pope and the Emperor, closely tied to events in Germany and the anti-Ottoman wars, and the theater of a violent struggle that saw the participation, in varying alliances, of all the Italian States, France, Spain, England, and on two occasions even the Sultan.

The peace signed at Cateau Cambresis in 1559 established a new order that would remain substantially unchanged until the middle of the 1700s, and the territorial-dynastic exchanges between the Hapsburgs and the Bourbons. With this agreement, reached after 60 years of war, the peninsula found itself subject to major Spanish influence: the Kingdom of Naples, Sicily, Sardegna and Milan were directly ruled by the Spanish Crown, which was backed by a significant garrison of troops on the Tuscan coast. Then there were the independent States: the Republics of Venice and Genoa, the Duchies of Savoy, Parma, Mantua, Ferrara and Modena, and of course the Papal States, all of which were inevitably concerned with maintaining good relations with their powerful neighbor. In this context, the fate of the Jews was closely tied to that of whichever State hosted them. The Spanish territories followed the rules of the mother country and began expelling their Jews, the last expulsion being from Milan in 1596. The rest of Italy progressively adjusted to the ghetto model, up until the final, anachronistic seraglio established at Correggio in 1782, at a time when powerful winds of revolution and emancipation were blowing elsewhere around the world.

This Spanish peace was one among many other possible outcomes. In fact, things could have turned out much differently, with other combatants emerging victorious: Venice, France, and Rome each had their chances to prevail, and could have ended the game on much different terms, imposing different decisions on the Jewish communities. And while history is certainly not written with "ifs," in reconstructing the genesis of the ghettos, along with the reasons and goals that led the Pope to canonize the Venetian experiment, questioning what political significance this decision might have had – or if it had one at all – can help deepen our understanding of that decision. For example, the decision to allow the expelled Spanish Jews into Rome at the end of the

15th century strongly suggests that there were political factors at work in the Church's decisions about Jews, challenging the common premise that such decisions were strictly theological in nature. After all, as we have seen, it was the Spanish Ambassador himself who explained the incomprehensible decision of Alexander VI regarding the *marrani* camped outside Rome in these terms: the Catholic King was upset, and could not really understand how the Pope could have insulted him in this way. But Borgia knew how to move shrewdly, avoiding official proclamations, and strongly defending the traditional position of Rome on the subject of the Jews. In doing so he provided an important precedent that could be replicated elsewhere.

What, therefore, was the significance of a ruler like the Duke of Ferrara allowing the settlement of Jews in his lands? Could this have complicated relations with the Spanish? What would the Pope's opinion of such a choice have been? Was this political and diplomatic knot addressed in court, or did the Pope act alone, without concerning himself about the opinion of councilors or the reactions of ambassadors[93]?

Questions of this type should also be asked about the birth of the ghettos. The addition of such inquiries brings shades and nuances to the traditional reading of the process of segregation and discrimination as occurring completely within the context of Catholic thought, and allows us to finally fully insert the Jews into history, and history into the specific Jewish events of those years. The ghetto of Venice is, in this sense, a case in point.

The battle of Agnadello (1509) contributed to determining the fate of the Venetian Jews, who at the time lived across the lagoon on the *terraferma*. As the enemy armies advanced, people from the mainland, including the Jews, fled to Venice for shelter. In the first decade of the 1500s Venice had not yet issued a *condotta* allowing Jews to live in the city, as was the practice across Italy throughout the Middle Ages and the early Modern era. Thus hundreds of Jews were suddenly living in the city "illegally," an unusual situation that elicited protest from some quarters. Some even called for following the path of Spain, Portugal and Sicily, and completely expelling the Jews. There were others, though, who saw economic advantages to keeping the Jews in Venice, while at the same time preventing them from living wherever they chose in the city. The solution was the establishment of the ghetto. Not fully expulsion, not fully tolerance, the ghetto was a strategic compromise that allowed the Jews to stay in the city, but in a contained and controlled environment.

---

93   There is no general bibliography on Italian Jews during the Italian Wars. For Ferrara and the Este family, now see Herzig 2019.

In the years that followed, the Spanish authorities in Italy would face the same question. Until 1541, the Kingdom of Naples – a Spanish kingdom – was home to many Jews, who had been negotiating for permanent residence in the area since 1520. After a period of relative inaction the decision was made, and in 1541 the Jews were expelled from Naples.

Meanwhile, however, war raged in the Mediterranean, the Balkans, and in Germany. The Emperor found himself faced with enormous difficulties on every front. The always tense relations between Charles V and Paul III made the search for solutions even more unattainable: every time the Emperor needed to concentrate his forces in Germany, the Pope would sabotage imperial plans on the peninsula, and Venice would try and launch new strikes in defense of its autonomy. There undoubtedly were others who worked towards the goal of a united Italy firmly in Hapsburg hands, from which Charles or his descendants could have built a Catholic alliance and put Europe back on track. The main opponent to such an idea was obviously the Pope himself, who in his role as an Italian sovereign worked to keep Spain weak but who, as head of the Church, would have benefitted from a strong Spain – but only if it accepted Papal rule. In short, it was a big mess, in which plans continually intersected and which was (and is) difficult to untangle with any certainty.

We can be sure that Italian Jews watched the upheavals in progress with attention and concern, just like any other contemporary observer. The events in Naples demonstrated that there was no, nor could there be any place for Jews in lands under Spanish rule, and that in desperate times they should be willing to accept other solutions (such as the ghetto). This also held true for the Church, which had to recognize that there were other ways to manage the problem. The decades that followed contributed to identifying these and to establishing rules of conduct, which inevitably seemed to be responses to the Hapsburgs, and to the centrality that their governing strategies wanted to give this subject. It is likely that Paul IV, in his own way, would also have put the problem in these terms. Also in this case, Carafa's career, famous for his hostility towards the Jews and his strictness as an Inquisitor, spoke for itself: Paul IV, a Neapolitan, was considered a bitter enemy of the Hapsburgs, who had devastated and divided his family property, and signed the Peace of Augsburg in Germany over his objections. Seeking revenge, Paul IV launched a war after having just been elected. The effort had little chance of success, and was ended, in fact, with the signing of the Peace of 1559. The promulgation of the bull *Cum nimis absurdum* needs to be placed within this broader picture: not only from the obvious perspective of converting Jews (and what else should a Pope do?) but also, and this is the main point, from the perspective of canonizing an alternative model of governing a minority, based on the Venetian example and in line with Catholic tradition, whose ancient rules of discrimination were revived and systematized.

In this context we can see that in establishing ghettos based on the model of Venice, the Pope made a clear statement regarding his exclusive prerogative in matters of faith. As the reigning Catholic sovereign, ruling based on history and tradition, the Pope had explicitly chosen the path of "tolerance" regarding the ever-burning question of the Jews.

Meanwhile, the violence against the *marrani* in Ancona served as a reminder that this tolerance had limits. While the presence of Jews was accepted under the regime of the ghetto, those who had accepted baptism and then continued to practice Judaism were elements that had to be forcibly removed from Christian society. The Jews, reading quite clearly between these lines, continued living their lives in the Papal States. Meanwhile, the peace of Cateau Cambresis in 1559 ratified Spanish dominance on the peninsula. Then in 1563 the conclusion of the Council of Trent would officially usher in a new era of strict Catholic cultural and social hegemony. This affected the Jews in many ways, but allowed a form of repressive tolerance that lasted for centuries, in which the strategies for survival brought to bear in Rome played an active role.

CHAPTER 2

The Birth of the Ghetto and the Dangers Narrowly Escaped in 1555

The tightening of regulations that culminated with the burning of the Talmud in 1553 prepared the way for the final stage sanctioned two years later by Paul IV with the publication of the bull *Cum nimis absurdum*. The deployment of tools for controlling the Jewish minority was one aspect of a more general process of social and religious redefinition underway in the Catholic world during this period in response to the schism brought about by Protestant Reform. The question of how the Jews, faced with an increasingly difficult situation and with the memory of the recent Iberian persecutions still fresh, chose to interpret this turning point is of great interest. In the absence of correspondence, memoirs, news or diaries written by the Jews of Rome as participants or even as just spectators in the ongoing upheavals, evidence about how the group interpreted this moment can be found only in secondary sources. For example, Anna Foa has brought to light a paradoxical story about a serious blood libel, recorded in Rome in the weeks immediately preceding the rise of Pope Carafa to the papal throne. This case gives us a sense, albeit indirectly, of the climate of anxiety which must have pervaded the Roman community in those days. This in turn helps us to frame the positions taken by the Jews of the city after the publication of the bull.[1]

We will get right to the point: this is a sensational story, referred to exclusively in Hebrew texts and not found in contemporaneous Christian documentation. Going through the trial records from the beginning of 1555, in fact, one does not find any evidence for an investigation of ritual homicide. Rather we discover that the story was the result of an incredible superimposition of facts, which itself was a product of the difficult phase the Jews were living through. This invented story was the result of the chaotic overlapping of details, all by Jews, between two separate trials that were heard in Rome by the *Tribunale Criminale del Governatore* [Criminal Court of the Governor of Rome] in the spring of that year. The first, the Sforno case, concerned the revival of a thirty year long dispute between Jews from different cities, and a controversy over the restitution of a dowry. The precise date of a Jewish boy's death in 1527 assumed

---

[1] Foa 1988. And now Mampieri 2020, pp. 65–68.

decisive significance in this case. The second, the Solis case, was a trial for the crime of infanticide, in which the accused was executed for murder in 1555. A parallel reading of these two cases allows us to both reconstruct the terms that produced this confusion, and from another point of view, to think about the impact of the pervasive force of the new campaign to convert the Jews that had begun with the papacy of Paul III, and which now, with the ascent of Paul IV to the papal throne between the spring and summer of 1555, was about to see the imposition of major changes.

1   The Sforno Case (1527–1555)

On October 8, 1555, just a few months after the publication of the restrictive bull, and during the struggle to put it into practice, "Donna Floruccia hebrea" was interrogated in the prisons of Corte Savelli. After having sworn "*tacto calmo more hebraeorum*," she testified about an incident from many years earlier. Far back in 1527, during the months of the Sack and the plague that followed it, all the inhabitants of Rome experienced unspeakable suffering. Devastation and disease overwhelmed the city; thousands of people died, and the Jews were not spared. As the Provencal Rabbi Isacco Lattes reported some time later, it was the gravest of trials:

> Unfortunately, however, when God wished to allow Rome to be put to the sack, the Jews of the city were also stripped of all their belongings, and the various communities were reduced in number. Few have survived and most were lost to either violent death or hunger. Many, due to the extreme hardship of the war, abandoned the city and went off wandering elsewhere. In the Scole that remained intact (many were destroyed in those days) they couldn't muster the ten members required for religious functions. It was then that the different ethnic groups found themselves forced to pray together in common synagogues: the Aragonesi decided to associate with the Catalani, while the Castigliani have gotten together with the French.[2]

Among the victims in the confusion of those days was a family of *Romani-Bolognesi* Jews. In the span of just a few years the deaths in this family would include Benenata (written as Bononata elsewhere), her husband Moyses, son

---

2 This text appears in Italian translation in Toaff 1996b, p. 152, from which it is cited.

of the famous Rabbi Ovadia Sforno of Bologna, and little Samuele, the couple's child. Years later in 1547, Paolo Manilio (or Manlilio), the woman's brother and a recent convert, filed a suit for the restitution of his sister's dowry. Manilio maintained that she had died after the child had, and that therefore the money belonged to him according to the law. It was thus essential to reconstruct the order of the deaths with certainty, establishing if the mother or the child died first. In the first case Paolo Manilio would be wrong and the money would remain with the Sforno family; in the second case the woman would have died without direct heirs, and the Sforno family would be obliged to restore the dowry to the closest living relative, that is, to the convert. Between 1548 and 1553 the case moved through different legal stages, and was discussed in the *Rota* of the Papal Curia as well as before the *Tribunale Criminale Goveratore di Roma*, and was then reopened in the autumn of 1555. The Sforno family, rich, cultured, foreign and influential, were not particularly well-liked by their Roman coreligionists. However, up to that moment the evidence that the Jews had collected and prepared so promptly after Paolo's conversion, thanks in part to the work of Jewish notaries, managed to make the difference.[3] The first trial ended in 1553 with a *nulla di fatto*, leaving the convert brother's demands unresolved and unsatisfied.

A new series of back and forth accusations concerning bribing witnesses to commit perjury and the falsification of documents would re-open the case on October 3, 1555. At almost thirty years' distance from the events in question the reliability of the few remaining living witnesses was in question. Therefore, following the same procedure as two years earlier, the judges patiently and repeatedly interrogated the witnesses in order to determine who could be trusted and who could not. At a certain point during questioning on the morning of October 8, Floruccia, the key witness for the Jews, who up to that moment had claimed to have "*aver dato la zinna*," [nursed] Moyses Sforno's son after he was orphaned from his mother, recanted all of her previous testimony and declared that she had been lying.[4]

Floruccia's reversal cast doubt on whether the child had survived the mother, and therefore offered support to the claim requesting the return of the woman's dowry on the grounds that she had no direct heirs. However, not even Floruccia's revision of her testimony could settle the outcome of the case. The Jews' subsequent questioning of Paolo – who had also filed a case against his relatives – instead worsened the neophyte brother's position, and brought to light an ambiguous business of falsified documents and erased papers.

---

3 Procaccia M. 1995, pp. 87–93.
4 *Processi*, b. 20, n. 12, c. 21r.

Questions were also raised regarding a book of death records that would have supported the Sforno's claim regarding the order of deaths (first the mother, then the child), but which had conveniently vanished.[5]

Floruccia was questioned again on October 11. Although for several days she had clearly expressed her desire to convert, Floruccia took the Jewish oath as before. She confirmed, for the second time, the revised version of her testimony, albeit with some further adjustments. According to this new testimony, she had nursed a child, but was certain that it had not been Benenata's:

> Everything I have said and testified before concerning having nursed Benenata's son was the enemy of God who tempted me into telling this lie and I always speak [the page is ripped here] the truth so I can discard all my sins.[6]

Apart from the outcome of the trial, Floruccia's story reveals other important aspects. In the attempt to open a window on the successes achieved by militant proselytism towards the Jews as pursued by the Church at least since the burning of the Talmud in 1553, the choice to convert, the rhetorical forms with which it was promoted and the reactions it caused cannot be ignored. Since all her children had been baptized, and she was once again entangled in a long trial that was costly and unpredictable, Floruccia decided to follow the path of her loved ones and become a Christian.

The woman's decision was a bolt of lightning in a clear sky. A long series of interrogations, begun on July 15 (that is, the day after the publication of *Cum nimis absurdum*), was carried out before the re-opening of the trial, with all the available witnesses testifying in more hearings at Corte Savelli.[7] During this long preparatory phase Floruccia put forward her original claim without doubts or inconsistencies in two consecutive examinations on July 28[8] and August 2.[9] She told the same story on October 4, while being subjected to a slew of

---

5 *Processi*, b. 20, n. 12, c. 28r.
6 "Tutto quello che io havevo detto et testificato prima de havere allattato quello figlio di Benenata era il nimico de Dio che mi tentava che io dicessi la busia et diro sempre [...] la verità per spogliarmi di tutti i miei peccati." *Processi*, b. 20, n. 12, c. 31r.
7 ASR, *Tribunale Criminale del Governatore, Costituti*, b. 49. The folder contains ten loose sheets of paper, restored but often incomplete due to previous tears. These are divided into subsets based on the old numbering and on the dates of the interrogations; records of the testimony given in this trial are found starting from 15 July and end before the initiation of the final phase of the proceeding.
8 ASR, *Tribunale Criminale del Governatore, Costituti*, b. 49, f. 46 bis II, cc. 53r-55v.
9 ASR, *Tribunale Criminale del Governatore, Costituti*, b. 49, f. 46 bis II, cc. 62v-63r.

questions regarding her movements in those years, and her relations with the illustrious Sforno family and their staff.[10] Then, suddenly, on October 8 Floruccia's mind was "illuminated" and the story changed. Now, though confirming that she had indeed nursed someone's "infant as though it was my son" during those terrible days long ago, the woman claimed to not recall who the newborn was or where he had ended up. Floruccia blamed her false testimony on pressure from Leone, *factotum* for the Sfornos family:

> Leone was around me a great deal and every day he came to me five or six times to talk, saying and explaining to me that he wanted me to be questioned and to testify as I have said and that I had no choice but to do this, and that these Jacobbe and their family from Bologna were rich and that they could always get their way with me and I would eventually have to do this, and there was so much pressure on me that I promised to be questioned and give this testimony[...].[11]

Among all the intricate business of real or presumed corruption of witnesses, there are striking aspects in Floruccia's case: the jealousy of the *"richi"* from Bologna, as well as that family's efforts to produce a credible *dossier* (Floruccia had actually nursed a stranger's baby, so her story would not have been completely false). Those efforts, on the other hand, continued for years – confirming the Jews' capacity for expending themselves in order to offer protection to those who were in trouble. Floruccia's initial statements were not only the result of an exchange of money; they also testify to the strength of a network of relationships among Jews, reinforced by reciprocal trust in the fact that assistance and solidarity would never fail.

The sequence of questioning that ends with her repentant about face seems to indicate that her detention in the summer of 1555 had served its purpose. We cannot know what the woman's most intimate reasons were, but it's certain that something suddenly snapped – maybe it was the isolation, maybe the fear – and in that instant the stubborn Floruccia abruptly changed her stance.

---

10   *Processi*, b. 20, c. 12, cc. 7v-10r.

11   "Leone mi fu tanto intorno et ogni giorno mi veniva cinque o sei volte a parlare, dice et spiegandomi che mi volesse esaminare et testimoniare come ho detto et che facendolo non mi mancheria mai e che questi Jacobbe et suoi da Bologna erano richi et che mi potrebbono raggiustare sempre et non mi mancharebbono mai et tanto mi fu addosso che io gli promisi che io mi examinassi et che farii questa testimonianza [...]." *Processi*, b. 20, c. 12, c. 22r.

The language used by the woman to recount the moment of illumination, confirming it several times, is indicative:

> God does everything for the best, if I had not endured what happened to me perhaps my mind would not have been illuminated to come to the Christian faith and tell the truth about this thing which has always troubled me for having said something that wasn't true [...] I have told the simple truth to honor my conscience because God touches the heart and because I want to be shed of all these evil thoughts.[12]

The Devil, divine intervention, the interpretation of suffering and hardship in terms of salvation, the desire to clear the conscience: the key points of the sermon *ad convertendum judaeos* had accomplished their goal, and Floruccia repeated them all, perhaps hoping to end her involvement in the case with a quick baptism and a return to the embrace of her convert sons.[13] However, things did not go this way. Three days later she had not yet set foot in the House of Catechumens, and when called upon to respond to a new series of questions, she swore "*tacto calamo more hebreorum.*" In a few years' time a similar expression of the desire to convert would not be left unanswered for so long, but would rather be seen as a success to crown with a solemn and public baptism as quickly as possible. However, in the contradictory early phase of the history of the ghettos, despite the fact that the first results of the Church's aggressive strategy were there for all to see in the unhappy person of "Floruccia hebrea," the judges, perhaps fearful of further contradictory developments in a story that looked like it would never end, accepted even this statement with great caution.[14]

Despite Floruccia's new story, (which was contradicted by the other witnesses) the case was once again left unresolved. At that point, according to what is reported in the documentation that has come down to us, the Governor's lieutenants decided not to waste any more time on Paolo Manilo's grievances. Another possibility is that the suspicion which had been quietly advanced

---

12 "Dio fa ogni cosa per il meglio, si io non havessi patito questo che mi è intervenuto forsi non mi saria alluminata la mente di venire alla fede cristiana et dire la verita di questa cosa che sempre mi ha dato fastidio per aver detto una cosa che non era vera [...] ho detto la mera verità per honoratione della coscientia mia perche Dio tocco il core et perche mi voglio spogliare de tutti questi mali pensieri." *Processi*, b. 20, c. 12, c. 22r-v.

13 Anna Foa discusses Jews and devils in Rome in 1554, regarding a case of suspected possession in a convent (1988, pp. 160–164).

14 Caffiero 2004 and 2008.

that the convert had falsified documents led authorities to forgo any further investigation into such a complicated case, if only to keep the convert out of trouble. In the summer of 1555, therefore, the case was reopened, only to be closed once again without a resolution, despite the fact that during the course of the hearing clues to dubious behavior on the part of the convert emerged, and a key witness retracted her statements and converted. The coincidence of the dates of the interrogations in this case and the chronology of the Papal decree certainly places the decision to not delve further into Paolo Manilio's past in a different light.

On its own, the Sforno case doesn't reveal more than the obscure history of a convert within one illustrious Jewish family, an attitude of prudent and benevolent dismissal from the judiciary to protect its own actions, and the sufferings of a woman who ended up alone. If we turn to the trial against Solis on the charge of infanticide – the second case chosen – sensational because of the horror of the crime and for the paradoxical version of the events given by a pair of Jewish authors, the picture changes, and helps us to recreate the atmosphere of anxiety and fear that Paul IV's rise to power created in the synagogues of Rome and the Papal States.

2   Blood Libel in Rome?

The Sforno case was the only proceeding to be brought before the *Tribunale Criminale del Governatore* by Jews in Rome in the months immediately before and after the establishment of the ghetto. Jews occasionally appear in court records (which, however, are incomplete and fragmentary for these years) as witnesses to various and never very serious crimes – the theft of a horse or a piece of "hardware."[15] For the most part, however, the appearance of Jews in the final phases of a trial, even in just a secondary role, is very sporadic, and does no more than confirm a period of generally tolerant urban familiarity.

The only dispute where Jews were personally involved was a violent stone fight that broke out in the peaceful streets behind the church of *San Giacomo degli Spagnoli*. In the days immediately following Lent, just after the death of Julius III, "Petro de Cordoba," a Spaniard in the service of his country's ambassador, stoned a bricklayer for disturbing his dog. The whole scene had been observed by two Jewish women who lived in the home next to the irascible Spaniard. They had heard the shouting and immediately appeared outside,

---

15   Both in ASR, *Tribunale Criminale del Governatore, Costituti*, b. 49, f. 46 bis II.

fearing that they might find their own children involved in the uproar. Once they established that their kids weren't in danger, they remained at the door and, while not being able to see perfectly, ended up being the only eyewitnesses to the incident. Thus they gave evidence at the beginning of the murder trial (the victim in the meantime having died).[16] This fight's descent to homicide confirms the existence of occasional social interaction between Jews and Christians at the middle of the 16th century. Paul IV did not like this, and would soon try to put to a stop to it. The decision to believe the two women's story, which was considered reliable even though it was a story that came from Jews, is itself an important aspect, useful for reflecting on the complexity of society and its forms of hostility in the modern age. While the Jews were by definition not trustworthy, in some special circumstances even a Jew's word could and should be considered valid – and a fight between neighbors, in which the witnesses closest to the scene happened to be two Jewish women, fell in this category.[17]

However, another story from that same period seems to go in a completely different direction, and paints a scene of brutal and unresolvable contradictions between Jews and Christians, so far from the world of placid urban sociability that comes through in the events surrounding the stoning incident. Josef ha-Cohen, the author of a chronology of age-old Jewish misfortunes, recounts a very serious episode of ritual homicide that took place in Rome in the spring of 1555, centered on the explosion of ancient prejudices and inspired by bloody legends. The case is not referred to directly in the court documentation of the period, and so, excluding the hypothesis that the author's work was a baseless invention, it is interesting to consider what his sources could have been.[18]

We start with ha-Cohen's account, written between the 1560s and 1570s.[19] In the spring of 1555, a few days before the Jewish Passover, the city was rocked by

---

16   *Processi*, b. 20, c. 6, cc. nn.
17   Regarding the untrustworthiness of Jews as witnesses in trials against Christian, see Todeschini 2007, pp. 171–204, in which, however, explicit reference is made to the problem of testimony from "false Jews/false Christians," that is, converts.
18   Regarding ha-Cohen's reliability on the subject of Jewish mobility in that period, see Segre 1996a, pp. 724–733. More generally about the author and his work as a historian, see the numerous works by Bonfil: 1996, pp. 452–453; and 2010: chapters V, X and XI. More recently Bonfil (2012) has returned to this subject: p. 103, n. 9.
19   The chronicle *The Valley of Tears* remained in manuscript form and was revised continually by its author, who updated it until his death (1575). Thus it is difficult to reconstruct with precision the moment in which any specific element was added to the narration. However it should be recalled the ha-Cohen based this work on his main book, *Chronicles of the Kings of France and Turkey*, printed in *editio princeps* at Sabbioneta in 1553 by

the discovery of a horrible murder. The tiny corpse of a child, four years of age, was found tortured and crucified in the *Campo Santo*. The mob at the scene immediately accused the Jews, thinking that the boy was yet another martyr fallen victim to the brutal practice of preparing matzah with the blood of innocent Christian children. Hananel da Foligno, *alias* Alessandro Franceschi, the "true scourge," preacher to the Jews and already a leader in the condemnation of the Talmud, weighed in on the case, arousing passions and immediately accusing his former coreligionists of the terrible crime.[20] The Jews were prepared for the worst, but – continues the chronicler – the farsightedness of Cardinal Alessandro Farnese saved them. The man of the Church immediately had a notice posted across the whole city, announcing that the body would be viewed in public. Crowds of people came to see the small battered corpse, and someone recognized it; thus the truth came to light. The author of the crime was a Spaniard, who had killed the child he was caring for with the help of his lover, who was also Spanish, in order to pocket a substantial inheritance. While putting his plan into action he went to the lengths of staging the crucifixion in order to turn blame for the murder on the Jews. The killer was discovered and condemned to death during the days of the vacant papacy after the death of Marcellus II, once again thanks to the intervention of Cardinal Farnese, who did not intend to leave such a grave crime unpunished, and despite the anti-Jewish attacks of the convert Hananel di Foligno.[21]

Josef ha-Cohen was not the only one to relate this story. As Anna Foa has indicated in her detailed discussion of the impact and significance of the accusation being raised at that moment in the city – as serious as it was false – there is a second source, also Jewish. The source is a handwritten note in the margins of a book, placed there in the 1600s by Salomone Graziano. The note is based on information derived from an unknown Roman *Meghillà* which has not come down to us. Graziano's version differs from the first in several ways: Cardinal Farnese and the accomplice do not appear, Marcello II is the one determined to do good, the death sentence is ordered by Carafa himself, the guilty party has a name (Doctor Sulim), and the date of April 24 is given for the day when the danger of a pogrom erupting was highest, but was, in fact, prevented from developing due to decisive action by the Pope.[22]

    Cornelio Adel Kind. Regarding this author, see Bonfil 1996, pp. 452–453 and the bibliography cited in the previous note.
20   The definition comes from Shlomo Simonsohn 1986, p. 102.
21   Foa 1988, pp. 164–165 and nn. 28–30. And for other Jewish sources and a comparison among them, now see Mampieri 2020, pp. 65–68.
22   Foa 1988, p. 166, nn. 31–33. And again, Mampieri 2020, pp. 65–68.

These subtle divergences matter little in the description of a major event which follows the classic narrative scheme of dangers avoided through the grace of God, starting with the famous model of the Purim story, with its heroes and villains, and the sudden reversal of an already decided nefarious fate. Once again, as Anna Foa wrote, "what emerges with clarity from the narration is the story of a crisis and its dissolution: a crisis which seriously threatened the very existence and life of the Roman Jews; a miraculous resolution, a *release*."[23]

Roman judicial records do not report any direct information about this case, and such a gap merits further investigation. It's impossible, in fact, to imagine that such an extraordinarily serious accusation would not have left any kind of documentary evidence. And, indeed, with patient searching we do find something.

In the period indicated by the Jewish sources – the final days of Marcello II's papacy, with its vacant throne, and the initial phase of the reign of Paul IV (therefore April 30 to early June 1555)[24] – we don't find records of any trials, investigations, hearings or even accusations concerning infanticide (or homicide) perpetrated by Jews. More generally, there are also no records of proceedings for this type of crime in which Jews appear as witnesses, or in which Jews or Jewish things are even mentioned in some way. The archives are certainly partial and fragmentary. However, despite this incompleteness, it is notable that the registries of the *Tribunale Criminale del Governatore*, which had jurisdiction over homicide by ancient tradition, also preserve no record of this event. Furthermore, the case does not appear in any of the surviving documents from the other *in criminalibus* magistracies that were active during that time period.[25] On the other hand, evidence of any accusation of this type is also absent in the Roman Jewish tradition (which does include on its liturgical calendar the remembrance of another wondrous event in 1793, in which the community was saved from a frenzied crowd thanks only to a providential storm),[26] nor is there any evidence in the records of the Holy Office which, for its part, had for centuries keenly followed any developments concerning accusations of ritual homicide. It is hardly likely that it would have allowed a

---

23   Foa 1988, p. 166.
24   Cappelli 1969, p. 275.
25   Regarding the gaps in the Roman judicial sources for the second half of the 1500s, see Fosi 1985, 2002 and 2007.
26   Milano 1984, pp. 253–254; Spizzichino 2008. On the celebration of *Purim* in Rome, see Caffiero 2011, pp. 369–375. Regarding the "revolutionary" *Purim* celebrations in Italy during the 1700s, see the classical essay by Cecil Roth (1935) and more recently Spagnoletto 1999.

case as tempting as this one to pass by.[27] Nevertheless, if we look at the dates, the type of crime prosecuted, the interrogators and those condemned to death in the late spring of 1555, combining names and crimes, something about an infanticide jumps out.

In April of 1555 a child's body actually was found in the *Campo Santo*. On the 23rd of the month, the Governor of Rome (who was responsible according to Paul III's law on the subject) had an announcement posted "in all the customary locations":

> By order of the Most Reverend Monsignor Vescovo di Sagone Governor of Rome, we hereby publish and notify every person that a child of three or four years old has been found dead in Campo Santo, and by what can be seen and judged the child was strangled and very badly treated in many other ways. If you are the father, or the mother, or any other person to whom this child belongs, or if you have lost a child of similar age, a little more or a little less, you must go to the place where the child is, yet unburied, and see if you recognize him when shown to you, and go to his Reverence with information so that we can learn something about the evildoers and criminals. If anyone does not do this, and is then found to be such – mother, father, or other to whom this child probably belonged, or should have belonged, not providing information may turn the presumption and suspicion against you of being the author of, or participant in the cited wickedness, who we wish to find by all possible means. By express commission of His Holiness we notify each and every person of every rank, state, sex, condition or however influential they may be, that whoever has information, or clues of any kind at all of such great impiety, they must make these understood to his Reverence, who will keep all secret, and they will earn a good reward, which will not be less than 100 *scudi* to be paid immediately. It is further declared that not revealing knowledge of the wrongdoers that then comes by other ways or means to his Reverence is subject to the same penalty as for the crime. We also give notification that if someone is found to have committed this crime, and if some of these make this known, and give information about it to the court so that he can pay for the foul deed, they will be absolved, and will earn more than the 100 *scudi* reward. And the same reward will be earned by each person, who with their work and

---

27 Regarding the blood libel, among the vast bibliography available, see the excellent summary found in Taradel 2002 and the sources cited there.

diligence will help us to find those behind the above mentioned crime of such enormity.[28]

A poor child was found dead in the *Campo Santo*, and in the hope of gathering information about the crime and identifying the victim, the Governor (and therefore not Cardinal Farnese), with the agreement of Pope Marcellus II, promised a generous cash reward. A little boy who had been strangled and tortured (but not crucified) cried out for vengeance, and they needed to find the guilty party quickly. Putting the body on display for identification produced the hoped for results, and in a hurry investigators found themselves with names, last names, and addresses in hand. The machinery of justice was put in to action. On April 30, just seven days after the publication of the announcement, while Marcello II breathed his last and Rome fell stunned by a second vacant papacy, investigators in the cells of *Corte Savelli* obtained a full confession from the killer, a certain doctor "Dominicus de Solis hispanus."[29]

Solis was the father of the slain child. The mother, a woman named Margherita, had also died recently, leaving the man, who was ill prepared for the responsibility, to care for their son. The little boy was the product of an

---

[28] "Per ordine del Reverendissimo Monsignor Vescovo di Sagone Governatore di Roma, si pubblica e notifica a ciascuna persona, che essendosi trovato in Campo Santo un putto di tre in quattro anni morto, e per quanto si vede e si può giudicare, strangolato, et in diversi modi molto mal trattato. Et fusse padre, ò madre, ò vero altra persona alla qual s'appartenesse, ò che li fusse perduto putto di simile età, puoco più o puoco meno, debba andar nel detto locho dove è il putto qual non è ancora sepellito e ricognoscerlo che li sarà mostrato, et ricorrendo da sua S. Reverendissima e darneli notitia accio si possa venire à qualche cognitione delli malfattori e delinquenti. Et non facendolo, che ritrovandosi poi quella tal persona, madre, ò padre, o vero, alla qual probabilmente detto putto apparteneva, ò doveva appartenere, non l'haver denunciato sene pigliara presumptione et inditio contra di lei, che sia stato autore, ò ver participe citata seleragine, la quale desiderandosi con tutti i modi possibili di scoprire. Per espressa commissione di Sua Santità si notifica ad ogni e qualche persona di qual si voglia grado, stato, sesso, conditione, ò ver preheminentia se sia, che havesse notitia, ò in qual si voglia modo inditio alcuno di tanta impieta, debba farlo intendere a S. Reverendissima che oltra che sarà tenuto secreto guadagnarà un bon premmio, che non sarà mancodi Cento scudi quali si pagaranno incontinente. Et non rivelandolo dechiara che venendo per altra via o modo a notitia d sua S. Reverendissima che la medesma pena incorrerà, il consapevole del malfattore. Notificando anchora che s'al commettere detto maleficio si fossero trovato qualche d'uno, et che s'alcuno d'essi lo farra intendere, et ne dara notitia alla corte se li dara la remissione del fallo suo, et ne sara assoluto, et di piu guadagnara la mita delli Cento scudi. Et il medemo premio guadagnara ogni persona, che con lopera et deligentia sua sara causa de apparire et che si trovi il sopradetto delitto tanto enorme." ASR, *Bandi*, b. 2, *Bando sopra il ritrovar l'empii e crudeli homicidiali che hanno morto il puttino di tre in quattro anni.*

[29] ASR, *Tribunale Criminale del Governatore, Costituti*, b. 49, f. 46 bis II, cc. 149v–155v.

occasional relationship – Solis and Margherita were not married, and the child was illegitimate. The two had met each other in church. She lived in the area of *San Giacomo degli Spagnoli*, while he had an apartment in *Borgo*. In short order they ended up in bed together. Maybe Margherita was a prostitute, or perhaps she was just a woman who was alone, poor and looking for better luck. It could be that Solis wasn't ready to marry. In any case, the fact is that the two stopped seeing each other after their first encounters. Months later, once sure that she no longer ran the risk of a spontaneous (or voluntary?) abortion, Margherita informed Solis that she was "with child." Taking advantage of her landlady's absence ("an old woman, fat and stupid"), Margherita went to Venice to find relatives, and gathered them together to give them the news, perhaps hoping to arrange a remedial marriage with the father of the baby. However, the man said nothing about this under questioning.[30] Then Solis fell ill, and at the moment of the birth he was still in the hospital, in serious condition: "I was so sick and poorly that I had no breath," he told the judges during questioning about his recollection of that period.[31] The child was baptized in his absence, and as a result he could not recall the name.

In the end Solis healed, took a small house at Rotonda, and began to regularly attend mass in the local parish. However, he was too poor to help Margherita. The two made an agreement and came up with a ploy to resolve all their problems: they would convince another of the woman's lovers, "mastro Francesco Portoghese," that the little boy was his, in the hope that he would assume care of the mother and baby. This is not to say that Solis harbored any doubts about the fact that the child was his: he was in the habit of noting the dates of his romantic encounters, and, as the man himself repeated to the judges, the interval between intercourse and childbirth was quite clear.[32] Solis would have preferred an exclusive relationship with the woman, but given the situation, he had to resign himself to accepting Margherita's idea. Therefore, with his reluctant approval, she set about trying to "have sex with Francesco" and to "win his friendship."

The plan worked, and for a year and half the innocent Portuguese fell for the trick. Then Solis' protests won out (or, more likely, Francesco discovered the scam); the couple made a home together at *Botteghe Oscure* and began living a normal life, he working in his profession as a doctor, and she occupied with the craft of spinning and caring for the boy. Margherita died, though, just seven or eight months later, and Solis once again found himself in trouble. He

---

30   ASR, *Tribunale Criminale del Governatore, Costituti*, b. 49, f. 46 bis II, c. 150r.
31   Ibid., c. 152r.
32   Ibid., c. 152r.

seriously considered turning the child over to public charity and placing him in an orphanage. Then he managed to find a housemaid from Montefiascone and employ her to look after the child. However, things did not work out this time either, and she was dismissed a few days before the crime. Then, one fatal night shortly thereafter, violence broke out; Solis went crazy and slaughtered his son for having soiled the bed:

> I hit him with a large rope such that my aforementioned child doubled over, the devil worked it so I have lost a certain small whip made in the forge of discipline with four leather straps [...] the devil blinded me and I swear that I think I was half drunk as I am so often and with that rope I gave it to him on the head and in his face so much that he bled and seeing him bleed I began to beat him on the neck and all over him such that he turned black with bruises and while I did I picked him up by his little arm and went toward the fireplace then I let the child fall on the wood now hitting his side now stomach and now the back in such a way that between the lashes I had given and between the fall on the wood and for the beating I gave him the child turned black [...] The child had passed out again, I resumed and with great anger took the rope and in the same violent way I took the child by the arm and began once again to beat him on his entire body and this second beating was much worse than the first [...] the child fell on the wood [...] the child died from the excessive beating [...].[33]

The crudeness of this account is chilling: a drunken man, uncontrollable anger, a child whipped and strangled, pushed into the fireplace and made to fall on burning wood, fear, incontinence, and death from beating and burning. Then

---

[33] "Lo battetti con una corda grossa quanto il mio detto piccolo raddoppiate, che il diavolo volsi che io mi haveva perso una certa frusta piccola fatta a forgia de disciplina co quattro strezzi de corame [...] il diavolo mi accecò et poi mi prometto che io penso che ero mezo imbriaco come soleva anchora esser delle altre volte et con quella corda gli detti nella testa e nel viso tanto che gli feci uscir sangue et vedendogli uscir sangue gli cominciai a dar per il collo et per tutta la persona tanto che haveva fatto tutto negro et mentre gli davo lo tenevo per un braccino appresso al camino et secondo che io gli dava quel puttino cascava sopra la legna hor battendoci il fianco hor il ventre et hor la schiena de modo che tra quelle frustate che io gli dava et tra quel cascar che faceva su le legne per le battiture che io gli dava il putto si anegriva [...] Quel putto de novo era andato de corpo, lo repigliai et in mezzo a quel modo con rabia et con stizza pigliai quella corda et al medesimo modo raccoppata pigliai il puttino per il braccio gli cominciai a dar di novo per tutto il corpo et lo battei la seconda assai di piu che fece la prima [...] quel puttino cascava nella legna [...] detto putto per le troppe battiture si mori [...]." Ibid., c. 152r-v.

there was the attempt to hide the crime from the servant who was sleeping unaware in another room, and the silent run to the *Campo Santo* [*the cemetery*] with the corpse hidden under a cloak: "And when I took him to *campo santo* I took him under my cloak so as not to be seen by the one sleeping in my home."[34] But the plan failed, and after the Governor's public announcement it was Solis' own servant who recognized the cadaver and denounced him, as testified to in the trial that began on the following 11th of May by "Antonius magister domus domini Ludovici de Mendoza,"[35] the doctor's renter, who had immediately been suspicious about the sudden disappearance of the youth. The end of the story is almost obvious: Solis was condemned to the death penalty, and after giving his confession to the brothers of *S. Giovanni Decollato* and dictating his final will, he was hung, and died a good Christian.[36]

3   Imaginary Violence

A series of elements leads us to believe that the story of the false accusation of ritual homicide, referenced first by Josef ha-Cohen, and then by Graziano, grew out of this case and the uproar that surely accompanied it. The first point to highlight is that it turns out that the Solis infanticide was the only one committed in Rome in the year 1555. There were two other cases tried for murder that year, both with adult male victims, and for crimes that occurred outside the window of time mentioned in the Jewish sources: the first trial was heard on March 4 against "Christoforum Robuster procurator," concerning the suspicious death of an old man after days of delirium and illness,[37] and the second trial, which involved a killing by firearm, was heard November 16, 1555.[38] Both these cases tell much different stories than the episode reported by ha-Cohen and Graziano. Furthermore, the only announcement I found involving the discovery of children's corpses in the *Campo Santo* is certainly connected with the Solis case: it matches the dates, and squares with the description of the wounds inflicted on the victim, viz., strangled with a large rope and burned. The information found in the Jewish sources, provided that it is evaluated excluding the mention of the child's crucifixion, lines up easily with the facts of

---

34   Ibidem, c. 152v. Di Sivo 2000; on the rituals of social inclusion of the confraternities dedicated to comforting, see Prosperi 2013.
35   *Processi*, b. 20, caso 7, «Romana homicidi contra doctorem Domenicum Solis», cc. nn.
36   ASR, *S. Giovanni Decollato, Testamenti*, b. 15, l. 31, cc. 79v-80r, s.v. «Dottor Solis».
37   *Processi*, b. 21, cc. 1073r-1080v.
38   *Processi*, b. 21, cc. 811r sgg.

the Solis case: the name of the perpetrator, Solis, is similar to the Sulim cited by Graziano, and at the same time both the profession and the nationality of the accused match up. Even the man's anomalous parenthood, in the end, could have been transposed to a ward/guardian relationship. Solis died weighed down by debt, and his will confirms the need for immediate liquidity and the existence of a lover, who was named as his heir. All told, asking if the doctor Sulim of Graziano's note could in fact be our Solis does not seem to be so far off base.

Things also match up in other ways, such as the intervals of time reported by Graziano, which also correspond to the Solis trial. The public announcement is released on April 23, rumors that the crime was committed by a Jew spread on April 24, and the execution took place shortly after Pope Carafa's consecration on May 26. It is certainly possible that, after the spread of this news, some distressed Christian had suspicions about the Jews, and that some worried Jew feared seeing insinuations about such a crime spread around. That year's calendar certainly provided evidence in the Jews' favor: the accusation of ritual homicide traditionally involved crimes committed before the festivals of Passover and Easter, and in 1555 both holidays fell on April 14, and therefore a week before the discovery of the child. However, in years of pervasive fear and widespread uncertainty, it's not a given that such a date discrepancy would have been noticed by everyone. In short, the equation "Jewish Passover + mutilated child = ritual homicide" could have been formulated in people's minds. Furthermore, we can be certain that in mid-16th century Rome, the sight of the poor mangled body as it was described by the Governor's notary would have led some to wonder if they were looking at the product of the dreaded practice of witchcraft. It is legitimate to ask if someone (perhaps in the offices of the city government) knowingly chose not to reinforce such suspicions in order to avoid more serious problems. There were doubts and suspicions, certainly, but no formal investigations.

In reality there is another question to be asked. Whether or not the defamatory accusation had been voiced and formalized, Josef ha-Cohen and later Graziano make it themselves, then turn to narrating the developments that saved the community. And this has significance. Graziano's account, the second, seems to be closer to the reality of what happened. The fact that it does not in any way cite the earlier text could mean that Graziano had not read *Valley of the Tears*. On the other hand, that might reflect the work's limited distribution – for a long time it remained available only through the circulation of manuscripts.[39] What remains to be clarified is how and why this information,

---

39 Bonfil 1996, p. 453 and here note 85.

which was at least partially confused, was heard by both authors, and for what reasons they both accepted the story without further verification.

Josef ha-Cohen wrote in the years immediately following the crime, and his work is considered to be substantially reliable. As a rule, the facts ha-Cohen recounted, while written in a poetic vein that is typical of martyrology, were real events, not legends.[40] This case, though, seems to be different, and part of its specificity is certainly the setting of the story itself. Rome is a special place, symbolic by nature, charged with myth and significance in the history of the Jews. This cannot be overlooked when reading Jewish writing about this still sacred space. Centuries earlier Rome had determined Israel's destiny with the destruction of the Temple. Now the Pope and his Church, also in Rome, continued to control the life of Jews all over the world, and because of this Rome and the Jews who lived within its walls were regarded with special respect and consideration.[41]

The preceding account by Ibn Verga, with its version of the Spanish exiles' entrance to the city in 1492 and the accompanying resentment and resistance of the Roman Jews, illustrates how within the Sephardic culture the memories of this traumatic experience had been amplified, accentuating the tensions and contradictions that marked the group's settlement in the Roman community, while at the same time not denying painful memories and tensions passed down from other contexts. The theatrical scene of the meeting between Jewish leaders and Alexander VI, mentioned only by Ibn Verga, becomes a literary testimony of an event which, via this anecdotal narration, cannot be confirmed and is certainly not denied, and in which the significance of the urban scene in which the event takes place is essential. The events surrounding the accusation of a ritual killing in the symbolic city of Rome, which was immediately retracted despite the plotting of murderers and converts, could also fit into this scheme. For two other writers in different places and times, and in different texts, the story presented an opportunity to give voice to collective sentiments.

We will try to formulate some hypotheses. Our point of departure is the moment at which the crime was discovered, and the reactions to the discovery. The facts are clear: before the morning of April 23, the date on which the public announcement was released, someone reported the discovery of a corpse in the *Campo Santo*, and the authorities immediately took action. The surgeons' exam found that the child had been strangled and repeatedly tortured. The Governor promised financial rewards to anyone who could provide

---

40   Segre 1996a, pp. 724–733.
41   Procaccia, Spagnoletto 2000.

information that might help them identify the victim and bring such a sacrilege to justice. The news was made public, and despite the fact that Passover and Easter had already passed, and that the case had no other elements from the liturgy of ritual homicide, if not strangulation, it is possible that someone began murmuring against the Jews right from the start (perhaps even the convert Hananel da Foligno). However, this was reckless whispering and nothing more. In just a few days the crime was solved, the perpetrator confessed, and the judicial process followed the inexorable path that would lead the accused to face the hangman.

The death of Marcellus II and the second vacant papacy in little more than a month represented another source of trouble. Rome without a Pope meant endless problems with public order, and there was never a happy moment for the Jews. Among other things, Solis' confession was probably, as usual, not made fully public right away and it's possible that the information available about the infanticide would have been limited to descriptions of the Spanish (and therefore *marrano*, according to certain propaganda we've already looked at) milieu in which it developed, the defendant's irregular parental status, and the murky story of sex that was involved. All incomplete gossip, but sufficient to suggest to some that the doctor, eager for money, had created a scene that would implicate the Jews, and that the plan had only been foiled thanks to the intelligence of the magistrates, or of the Pope who had just died. There was enough to provide a solid basis for the story in *Valley of Tears*. Meanwhile a new conclave was convened, and Gian Pietro Carafa emerged triumphant over Alessandro Farnese, who, as an exponent of the wing of the Church considered to be less strict (and therefore less anti-Jewish), had been cause for some hope. As for Solis, like many others he had contacts with the Jewish world, and the outstanding debts to Jewish lenders reported in his will, though not for great sums of money, and recorded within an even longer list of pawn items to redeem, might have lent support to the idea that Solis had developed explicit resentments against the community:

> He said that Salamone the Jew from S. Martinello had in pawn a shirt, a red shirt, and a barretta of sannito greco de pagolo de castro, all pawned for 11 giuli each. He also said that Lione the Jew in the neighborhood of Chiavari had in pawn a shirt and a towel, pawned for six giuli. He also said that the aforementioned Lione had in pawn a satin dress for five giuli. He also said that Il Rosso at Larco di Cenci had in pawn a black cape with decorations around it for fifteen giuli. He said that Gioseppe at Piazza Giudia had in pawn a cape with decorations for eighteen giuli. And all of the aforementioned items had been left to be collected and that those

that if they can no longer be collected are committed and that half of the money should be given to the church of San Geronimo at Corte Savella and the other half to our company and declares that the half to be given to San Geronimo including a shirt, a manipolo and a black robe are so that three masses will be recited at the church for his soul one being a Spirito Sancto, one being the misericordia both with the oration of Santa Caterina and one Requiem Eternam. He declared that the night before he was put in prison he gave one gold scudo to Pietro who with the ambassador to Spain had brought him a dinner and that Pietro should give back the difference and that half of this should be given to our company and the other half to Camilla from Siena the daughter of a nun from Siena who lives at ponte sant'Angelo. He says that he pawned some textiles worth twelve giuli to Vittoria who lives in the house of Caterina who is the innkeeper for Salamone the Jew from san Martinello. He says that he paid the osteria Ciambella with a small precious stone worth five giuli. He says that he also pawned in the aforementioned place a small necklace with ten pearls and twenty silver plates for about two giuli each. He says that he also left as a pawn in the same place a small brass bucket. And all of the things mentioned in the above four Capitoli were left to Camilla so that they could be hers at any time she needs them [...][42]

---

42 "Disse che Salomone ebreo da s. Martinello haveva pegnio una camiscia, una camisciola rossa, una barretta di sannito greco de pagolo de castro, pegnio per giuli XI ogni cosa. Item disse che Lione ebreo sul cantone de Chiavari haveva in pegno una camiscia e uno sciugamano, pegnio per giuli sei. Item disse che il detto Lione haveva in pegno una vesta di rascia per giuli cinque. Item disse che il Rosso a larco de cenci haveva in pegno una cappa nera con uno passamano intorno per giulii quindici. Item disse che Gioseppe in Piazza Giudia haveva in pegno una cappa con uno passamano per giuli disdotto. Et tutte le sopradette robbe lassa che si riscotino et che di quello che sene cava di piu di quello sonno impegniata la mita si dieno alla chiesa di san Geronimo a Corte Savella et l'altra mità alla nostra compagnia et lassa che di quella mita che sa da dare a san Geronimo soppradetto ne comprino un camiscio, manipolo e stola negra con la quale si dichino tre messe per lannima sua una dello Spirito Santo, una della misericordia con loratione de Santa Caterina a tuttte e due e una di Requiem Eternam. Item disse che la sera denanzi che fusse prigione dette uno scudo dor a Pietro co co all'imbasciatore di Spagnia che gli porto da cena lassa che ci dia il resto et la mita siano li nostri et laltra mita si dieno a Camilla senese figliola della balia senese che sta in ponte sant'Agniolo. Item disse che in casa di Caterina albergatrice da Salamone ebreo da san Martinello haver lassato in mano a una che alloggia in casa di detta Caterina che sadomanda Vittoria in pegnio un panno di state e una tovaglia ogni cosa giuli sei. Item disse haver lassato pegnioall'ostaria della Ciambella doro drentovi una granata per giulii cinque. Item disse haver lassato in pegnio in detto luogo un vezo di X perle e 20 pater nostri d'argento, per giulii dua in circa. Item disse haver lassiato in pegno in detto luogo una secchietta de ottone. E tutte le cose che

The man's close relations with Spain and with Iberian diplomats in Rome, recalled in the drafting of the last will of the condemned, further substantiated that opinion; for a Jew, someone who was a Spaniard, even in the service of his country's king, was synonymous with trouble. The reciprocal mistrust between the groups probably played a role in the exaggerated transposition of simple facts, which seem to have reached ha-Cohen in some way or another. He was very sensitive to the subject, and also from a family of Iberian refugees. On the other hand, there had also been a similar case in Asti just a year earlier; a "Spanish individual" had tried to blame the Jews for the murder of a child who was killed "in a strange and cruel way." The immediate protest which the Jews of the Piedmont city sent to Duke Emanuele Filiberto, who was committed on the front, resolved the issue in the community's favor: as local reporters would write, there was no proof of the crime, and thanks to the Duke's clarifying intervention the case ended with a *nulla di fatto*.[43] Once again, here in a case which comes to us from contemporaneous Christian sources, we have a "Spaniard" acting against the Jews, a difficult political and military moment, and salvation by another Christian. Thus we see a recurring scheme.

We return to Rome. Solis' fate was now sealed, and all that remained was to wait for the execution of his sentence. Paul IV was elected and consecrated, and the question of what his first steps would be became increasingly urgent. The reputation for unwavering rigor which accompanied the ascent of the great Inquisitor could not be ignored by dissidents of every denomination, or by the Jews, among whom the fear of forced expulsion from the Papal States returned to anyone who had lived there for more than a couple of years. Shortly after the doctor's death, with or without malicious gossip, some Jews found themselves back at the prison being questioned about the death of a young boy again, now in connection with the aftermath of the Sforno case. It so happened that the first round of questions was recorded on the very day that the new Pope's decisions regarding the Jews, declining to order the feared exile, yet inaugurating a new phase, dispelled any doubts about their fate. Thus the two trials may have given rise to an involuntary overlapping, to which Josef ha-Cohen unknowingly bore witness.

At times destiny plays bad jokes that, when lined up, have unpredictable effects. The first arrests for the reopening of the Sforno dossier preceded the beginning of formal hearings by at least a few days, which, if we count the

---

    si contengono nelli sopradetti quattro Capitoli lassa che la sopradetta Camilla senese le riscuota et che sieno sua et gliene lassa per quel tempo che lei la servito [...]." ASR, S. *Giovanni Decollato, Testamenti*, b. 15, l. 31, cc. 79v-80r.

43 Segre 1996a, pp. 766–767.

concluding phase, continued through December of that year. Months and months in custody; questions about the fate of a child, over which hung, at least since the preceding judicial ruling, a vague suspicion of infanticide;[44] two sensational trials in just a few months with two little boys who died mysteriously; and all of this amidst growing anxiety about Paul IV and his policies. The fact that one child was Jewish and that his death had occurred almost thirty years earlier may have been secondary: the court was hearing a case which involved Jews from all over Italy (including the very well-known Jewish family, Sforno), and had just recently resolved another case regarding an innocent child who had been strangled, beaten and burned. It was only a little, but it was enough to feed a chain of wild gossip in a small world like that of the Jews.

If we accept the hypothesis of a fusion between the Solis and Sforno cases, we also clear up the mystery of why the story that was passed on first by ha-Cohen and later by Graziano does not correspond to any surviving trial records. Marc Bloch's masterful lecture about war and false news demonstrated the unstoppable and uncontrollable power of human anxiety and the words that express it. Looking at them closely, the developments in this accusation of infanticide seem to reflect, though on a small scale, the dynamics evidenced in the trenches of the Great War.[45]

It remains to be understood, however, why Jews would have corroborated and disseminated the suspicion of ritual homicide, the most fantastic and ignominious crime ever attributed to the people of Israel, which rabbis and intellectuals had always fought against with courage and conviction.[46] In the Christian Europe of the Middle Ages and the Modern Age, the possibility that a group of Jews would find themselves having to confront a blood libel was an ever present risk. The real, fake or presumed torture of a Christian little boy could arouse an entire community. In difficult periods this probability grew considerably. A fine thread of fear accompanied Jewish life, and it did not take much for this anxiety to turn into uncontrolled panic. The poisoned fruits of the imbalanced dialog of proselytism grew within Jewish culture via deep and ambivalent pathways, with the result that the alarm provoked by this specific odious accusation became internalized, albeit in unusual ways. The literary model of the salvation story lent itself to the retelling of episodes in which

---

44   Procaccia M. 1995.
45   Bloch 2004.
46   David Bidussa (2008) talks extensively about these issues and the stickiness of the question of ritual homicide in relation to Ariel Toaff's controversial volume *Pasque di sangue* (2007) in his excellent essay. On the same question see also the *Dibattito* edited by Cristiana Facchini in 2007.

Jews miraculously escaped a great danger without harm. The Roman episode fit perfectly into this time tested scheme.[47]

This is exactly what Josef ha-Cohen and Salomone Graziano did: they gave voice to anxiety, each in his own way. In doing so, they testified to the bewilderment with which the Jewish world struggled to comprehend its particularly precarious position, as the battle to purify Christian society raged on in the years following *Cum nimis absurdum*. In fact, from a certain point of view, the imprecise and troubling story these men left to us also represents an after the fact attempt to account for and partially explain the anti-Jewish choices brought out by the Church starting in that crucial year. The precedents for these choices from the previous ten or fifteen years had perhaps been partially forgotten, and this invented story provided Jews a simpler explanation for their enclosure in the ghetto. The role of good Christian assigned to Alessandro Farnese also points in this direction: Cardinal Farnese, a very powerful man in the Curia and all of Italy, who for years had entered conclaves as the presumed next Pope only to leave with the red berretta on his head, was there as evidence of how, again, another way would have been practicable and how, at the end of the day, the love for justice in heaven and on earth would somehow always save the Jews of the Pope.[48]

The faith ha-Cohen placed in the revised and edited version of the Roman crime, which in all probability was a product of the Jewish world itself (perhaps based on some sermon or drawn from contemporary Christian rumors of which, however, there would seem to be no written trace), is not surprising: the biography of the author and his family of refugees – first at Avignon and then

---

47 Foa 1988, p. 33.
48 According to what Girolamo Seripando related on the occasion of the two conclaves held in the spring of 1555, the odds makers in Rome repeatedly gave as certain the election of the powerful Cardinal (Cassese 2002, p. 119). On Alessandro Farnese, see the comprehensive work edited by Stefano Andretta in *Dizionario Biografico degli Italiani* and the bibliography cited within. Of great interest in this discourse is the question put forward by Gigliola Fragnito regarding the spiritual anxieties of many exponents in the "court" of the Farnese family: "But one can't help but ask if the protection which the Farnese benefitted from against the ecclesiastics that the inquisitors held as strongly suspect, beyond political motivations, derived also from the cultural affinities that brought them, if not to share, and even less to understand their profound religious tensions, their restless spirituality. This is a question to which it is not possible to give an answer given the current state of research, but one can't help but call attention to choices that are hard to attribute only to political considerations" (2011, in particular pp. 203–204); it does not seem, therefore, so unusual to ask if this "anxiety" could have been perceived externally, and in particular in the Jewish world, which was always attentive to the workings of the Curia and very worried about the fame and the actions of Carafa.

Genoa and its surroundings – clearly motivate the choice.[49] The tragic memory of the murder trial with no body at La Guardia, the so-called *Niño* – in which neither a corpse nor a missing person complaint ever surfaced, despite a confession extracted from a convert under torture – which was used as a pretext to convince the Iberian Kings to decree the Jews' expulsion (as well as to send a large group of Jews and *conversos* to the pyre), stood as a reminder of just how little the Jews wanted idle chatter to end up in tragedy.[50] Midway through the 16th century, nobody would have had better reason than a Jew of Spanish origin to give credence to unchecked rumors on the lips of their coreligionists about occurrences of violent antisemitism. Even many decades later, it was enough just for the terrible accusation to be voiced in some Jewish community to cause the idea to become a certainty, and a simple doubt to take on the appearance of a concrete fact.

The sharing of mental and physical spaces between different worlds had a powerful influence on the forms of the Jewish imagination.[51] Jews were fully aware of the incompatibility of this specific crime with the inviolable laws of their faith. Nevertheless, by dint of being told that Jewish perfidy had no limits, their fear that words of propaganda might turn in to the presumption of a crime was so deeply engrained that it would take hold even in events in which the charge was probably never even made. As Roberto Bonfil says, the dialectical movement through which the Jews appropriated elements of the other culture, reworking them until they were compatible with Judaism, transpires even in such extreme situations, and offers further points of consideration for those who want to investigate the elusive terms of this undeniable and ambiguous unwanted complicity, also an unpleasant product of proselytism.[52]

In the period immediately following the release of *Cum nimis absurdum*, therefore, among the Jews there are clear signs of a constantly troubled life.[53] Moreover, the outbreak of violence, even though only feared and imagined, served its purpose in the uncertain contemporary Jewish historiography.[54] The myth of continuing persecution could provide an explanation for the processes of transformation taking place, and give voice to the anxieties and fears

---

49 Ha-Cohen was born in Avignone in 1496 to a family of Spanish refugees. Later he moved with his parents to Genoa, where he continued to gravitate until his death (around 1576). Primary information about his experience in Italy is found in Urbani 2002.
50 Taradel 2002, pp. 109–134; Iannuzzi 2009.
51 Toaff 1996c.
52 Bonfil 1991; Foa 1988.
53 According to the apt definition proposed by Michele Luzzati (2004) regarding the truth and the plausible in trials involving Jews in the second half of the 1400s (p. 280).
54 Yerushalmi 2011; Bonfil 1996.

that gripped Jewish society. An accusation of ritual homicide made the events that followed comprehensible; the rise of the ghetto, the veering of the Church between insults and abuse (here embodied in the figure of the convert), and means of protection (personified in the wise cardinal Farnese, who exited the conclave that elected Carafa in defeat). For the Jewish public – who were the sole audience for information contained exclusively in Hebrew literature – all this served to confirm the risks connected with their position as a minority, and on the other hand, the power of salvation, and the reversal of their fates by the divine hand, which was always possible and had frequently happened.[55]

The overlapping of the Sforno trial and the Solis infanticide combined facts to form the legend of a ritual homicide in Rome, which itself offered a somewhat exaggerated rendering of the Roman community's complex situation: at the center of Christianity, perpetually defending their survival as a minority group in the holy city, accustomed to fearing and loving the Popes and their policies, in need of protection and capable, if necessary, of offering forms of defense and means of representation to other and less fortunate Jews across the world.[56] These sources present a complex scenario from which emerges, other than the terrible accusation made and the danger avoided, both the Jews' continuous negotiations with ecclesiastical authorities (or at least with the most available interlocutors from within the hierarchy),[57] as well as an internal snapshot of Jewish events in the final days before the ghetto, and how they were interpreted in the days immediately following. A widespread feeling of apprehension was accompanied by quiet inaction from the Jewish authorities: the sources that relay the story, in fact, highlight Christian protagonists and the perfidy of the convert, but say little about Jewish reactions. There was fear, hardship, and worry, but no concrete actions or protests: it was a kind of paralysis which, in effect, endorsed the Jewish silence in the face of the events of 1555. This stance, which is so different than the strong reactions after the burning of the Talmud, may have been due in part to an underestimation of the Carafa decree's pervasiveness. However, it also indicates a clear interpretation of the new bull as the "mild" choice which would not expel the Jews from the Papal States. From this point of view, the diffusion of this incredible story reinforced the reading of *Cum nimis absurdum* as a lesser evil: in those times, a mere rumor would have sufficed for decisions far more drastic than the institution of the ghetto to become both popular and possible.

---

55 Spagnoletto 2013, pp. 69–70.
56 Regarding this last aspect, the reconstruction offered by Magda Teter in 2011 is of great interest.
57 This reiterates the definition of negotiated relations proposed by Marina Caffiero in 2004.

The success of Christian preaching to the Jews is the last aspect that is worth highlighting from the criminal trial sources we have examined and the episodes they recount. As we have seen, the themes of Christian propaganda were clearly pervasive in the Jewish world, even if in the weakened form of the *topos* of liberating salvation and stories with happy endings.[58] Reading the Sforno and Solis cases also uncovers the existence of another ethereal character become fully part of common life and speech; the devil.[59] The fallen angel lurks in much of the testimony given during the interrogations: it was the enemy of God who made Floruccia lie for such a long time,[60] and it was also him who placed a rope in the hand of Domenico Solis (in place of the punishment whip) and induced him to get blindingly drunk.[61] Other phrases uttered by these two defendants also confirm the triumph of Catholic propaganda in the common language, and therefore in the mental obsessions of ordinary people. In Floruccia's statements, with her illuminated mind and desire to expunge her sins, it is easy to recognize as much of the ancient themes of derision of the blind synagogue, stooped beneath the weight of guilt and the exaltation of the Church Triumphant, as the recent results of the efforts aimed at more intensive preaching to the Jews.[62] Then there is the child killer Solis, guilty of an unspeakable crime, who made sure to clarify that he was not a heretic, and that he had attended mass regularly;[63] absent father, late to start attending masses and baptisms, a crook, inveterate gamer, living with his mistress, and a murderer, yes: out of the Church, no.

While the Inquisitor Carafa prepared to take leadership of the disoriented and divided flock of Christ, the first results of the responses that Rome had finally put in action began to be seen, even in such humble locations and on such secondary occasions: thirty years after the institution of the Holy Inquisition, and with the Council still open, the first effects of the campaign for the control of consciences manifested at the lowest steps of the social ladder, and among the souls for which it was worth fighting such a difficult and uncertain battle, those of the Jews occupied a place in the front row.[64] The problem was serious, and it was time for that place, itself uncomfortable and precarious,

---

58 Foa 1988, pp. 166–169. Regarding the issues and forms of rabbinic homiletics in this period, see also the essays collected by Ruderman in 1992.
59 See also the case of possession by the devil cited again in Foa 1988, pp. 160–164.
60 *Processi*, b. 20, n. 12, c. 31r.
61 ASR, *Tribunale Criminale del Governatore, Costituti*, b. 49, f. 46 bis II, c. 152v.
62 Caffiero 2011, pp. 269–294.
63 ASR, *Tribunale Criminale del Governatore, Costituti*, b. 49, f. 46 bis II, c. 152v.
64 Prosperi 1996b.

to become separate and distinct from all others. The newly elected Pope was surely the right man to also take that difficult mission to heart, and he would prove it in just a few days, inveighing against the immorality of the habits of Jews and Christians living side by side in the capital of Christianity.

CHAPTER 3

A Ruling Class for the Jews of the Ghetto

The range of Jewish reactions to the innovations introduced by Paul IV explains the fictionalized narrative of a ritual homicide in Rome, the product of a paradoxical superimposition of the Solis and Sforno trials from the spring of 1555. On the one hand, the distress of the moment comes through clearly in the story; on the other hand, the choices that were actually implemented and the social practices recorded in the documentation of the period reveal an atmosphere of calm, in an apparent contrast with the very climate of fear attested to by the imagined accusation. If we look carefully at the social restructuring that the group encountered in the second half of the century – which depended on the institutional consolidation established in the *Capitoli* of 1524 – these two conflicting signals end up creating an understandable picture, in which the fear that events could take an even more dramatic turn played a leading role. It was due to this fear, in fact, that the Jews chose not to adapt their institutions to the new context, neither then or later, and were even less willing to produce new regulations for managing the ghetto. The worries of those months, however, appear throughout the story of miraculous salvation reported by Graziano and by ha-Cohen, giving us a palpable sense of the mood that accompanied the birth of the ghetto of Rome.

The Jews' struggle to accept the new reality in the years immediately following 1555 affected the lives of individuals, who were forced to adjust to the restrictions imposed by Paul IV, and, on the institutional level, also affected how the *Universitas Iudaeorum de Urbe* was run. In fact, the community was called upon to manage a long series of transformational processes within a quite complex and multifaceted social and legal context. An analysis of the professional careers of members of the Jewish ruling class, and a reconstruction of the systems of cooptation among the elites demonstrates how these two factors were closely connected to each other. The people who were obliged to live inside the ghetto still carried on business activities outside it; the successes won within the ghetto, as much as those achieved beyond its high walls, naturally had a reciprocal influence in the context of a continuous dialectic between life in the ghetto and events far from it.

The ghetto of Rome opened its doors in the autumn of 1555, and the Jews moved there *en masse*. They did not, however, alter the shared community organizational structure that had been established by Daniel da Pisa just thirty years earlier, at the culmination of a long period of conflict. In all probability it was the memory of the period preceding the drafting of the *Capitoli* that caused the leadership to avoid adopting what would have theoretically been indispensable amendments in such troubled times. The *Capitoli* had been drawn up in 1524 in response to growing problems, which, thirty years later, were not yet completely resolved; in consideration of these, although the conditions of the Jewish presence in Rome were drastically changed, the leadership avoided pursuing an otherwise essential revision.[1] Reforming the statute carried the risk of lighting at least two fuses (the first national and the other social) inside the newly formed seraglio, which would have inflicted incurable wounds within the community. The capacity of the ruling class, whose members were selected based on their class in the new context, represented a key factor in meeting the challenge to the survival of the community and its institutions. Had they failed to firmly maintain their role as an internal and external point of reference, it could have further compromised the group's abilities, as individuals and as a society, to resist such enormous pressures.

1   Avoided Reforms

In order to orient ourselves in this process, we must once again look back to 1521, and the moment in which the authorization of Jewish lending activity in Rome laid the foundations for the emergence of a class of bankers and entrepreneurs that was destined to govern the future of the *Universitas*. This provision brought with it an improvement in work conditions for a restricted group of businessmen, as well as the resounding and definitive confirmation of this group as the Jewish ruling class.[2] This second aspect deserves to be thoroughly investigated: the resilience of the emerging classes, and their capacity to reshape and redefine themselves, intelligently adapting to the model imposed by *Cum nimis absurdum* and by the provisions that followed, was actually one of the most important factors that allowed the small and frightened minority to determinedly confront the violent change taking place.

During the final months of the papacy of Leon X (1513–1521), after centuries of tacit and ambivalent tolerance, Jewish bankers were explicitly authorized to work in the Roman marketplace. At the time of this concession (three years before the drafting of the *Capitoli*), a significant portion of the owners of pontifical licenses were members of the Spanish minority. This situation meant,

---

1   Esposito 2012.
2   On the centrality of bankers in this phase, see Cooperman 2015.

for some, twice the reason for grievances with the traditional management of the community, from which they were excluded as foreigners, notwithstanding their status as distinguished moneylenders who had been licensed by the Pope personally.[3] In 1524, the *Capitoli* were also able to offer an intelligent response to this problem too. In building its institutional structure, in fact, Daniel da Pisa was concerned with carefully balancing honors and obligations, taking the different *edot* into account, but also the needs of the different social groups that made up the Roman Jewish world. Apart from the division of roles between *italiani* and *ultramontani*, a further mechanism for the distribution of obligations was devised by defining four economic classes. The first three of these – *banchieri, ricchi* and *mediocri* – each organized in its own commission, were now formally called upon to take charge of managing the community's affairs.[4]

The *Capitoli* strongly emphasized the special role of the bankers by directly entrusting them with those duties (collection of taxes and the administration and auditing of public accounts) that were most related to their professional skills. The bankers' preeminent position in the conduct of Jewish public life was established by the *Capitoli* in 1524, and was destined to be further reinforced in the following decades.[5] There was a definite trend in this direction just a few years before the institution of the ghetto, between 1550 and 1554. The reconstruction of the profiles of the Jews who were called upon to manage the community's business (who were mostly licensed bankers) testifies to this beyond a doubt.[6]

Pope Carafa's intervention would lead to an acceleration of this process of centralization, redefinition and legitimization which would end up producing unexpected results, thanks precisely to the restrictions imposed by Paul IV. In the summer of 1555 and the months that followed, the Roman community was forced to undertake a rapid reorganization, with a twofold objective; on the one hand, promptly obeying the Papal edict and on the other hand, complying

---

3 Esposito 2002.
4 It should be recalled that the Jewish ruling class generally was made up of the most important families of moneylenders; for an overview, cfr. Bonfil 1991, pp. 164–167. The reciprocal hostilities between the Spanish of different origins, on the other hand, was an experience that the Roman Jews shared with Christians in those same years in the same city; Spaniards from Castillo, Catalan and Aragon were divided in exactly the same way, with those from Catalan and Aragon on one side and those from Castillo on the other, also within the Churches of Iberian origin; cfr. Vaquero Piñeiro 1994.
5 Cooperman 2015.
6 Di Nepi 2004.

with those wishes while avoiding, as much as was possible, a reawakening of ancient controversies in a moment of extreme difficulty.

Life in the newly created ghetto was difficult for thousands of reasons. The very limited living spaces, the urgency of finding a *modus operandi* that guaranteed all the *Scole* – synagogues of different rites the ability to carry on their activities, despite the fact that only one building had been authorized for liturgical use, the requirement to find funds to send to the *Camera* as payment for the raising of the walls and for the salary of the door guards, in addition to the usual taxes: these were the principle issues faced by the leaders of the community in the aftermath of the publication of *Cum nimis absurdum*.[7] The biggest difficulties involved housing and prayer.[8] The papal limitations on synagogues were circumvented by bringing all the old *Scole* together in one building, and by reducing their number to five. This meant the almost immediate disappearance of some of the old *Scole* of the *italiano* rite that were located outside the walls (and which actually merged with the *Scola Tempio*), and the fusion of the others according to already tested schemes (*Catalana-aragonese, Castigliana-francese*).[9] This solution inevitably led to an explosion of disputes over stairs, doors and windows, and, for the congregations that were formed following the consolidation, there were arguments over the division of responsibilities and over the use of furnishings, books and precious objects.[10] The outbreak of

---

[7] In order to pay for the work of constructing the wall and the salaries of the guards it was immediately decided to increase fiscal pressure by exacting new taxes. So, with the first administrative act registered post-ghetto by the Jewish notary Isacco delle Piattelle, the *Fattori* (Mosè Ha Rofè, Prospero di Ceprano, Leone di Murcia), in the presence of all the constituent nations of the Università, ordered the collection of the *propina* on meat, giving the job of collection to a butcher and a banker (NE, f. 12, l. 1, c. 10r). For a comprehensive summary of this document, see Stow 1999, doc. 1728. Equally important was the imposition of second special tax a short time afterwards, with two different resolutions; in January of 1556, in fact, the *Fattori*, in an explicit agreement with the *Congregazione delle Tasse*, established the special impositions of "eight further taxes" (NE, f. 12, l. 1, c. 28v; a summary of this document is in Stow 1999, doc. 1822), and then charged Giacobbe di Lattes with their collection at another meeting and with a separate contract (NE, f. 12, l. 1, c. 30r; the summary of the document is in Stow 1999, doc. 1831).

[8] Examples of these conflicts are in Stow 2001, chapters II–III.

[9] The *Scole* active in the ghetto of Rome at the beginning of the modern era were the *Scola Tempio*, the *Siciliana*, the *Catalana-Aragonese*, the *Castigliana-Francese*, the *Nova* and the *Tedesca*. For more on this subject see Milano 1984, pp. 218–223. In the months following the Sack of 1527, however, some of these unions – foremost the due that involved the Spanish *Scole* – were having trouble gathering the ten men necessary to perform the majority of religious functions (Toaff 1996b, p. 152).

[10] For a description of a long and lively quarrel over these issues between the *Scola Nova*, the *Tedesca* and the *Siciliana* which stretched until the beginning of the 1600s, see Stow 1992b, pp. 67–72.

these conflicts came alongside the equally explosive conflicts that arose within and outside individual households, stemming from the disappearance of housing as well as, on the other hand, the redefinition of economic activity created by the increasingly narrow possibilities for employment permitted to Jews. Jewish institutions, therefore, were faced with the difficult task of preventing all of these factors from reviving old causes for conflict, the eruption of which at such a time would have further aggravated a situation that was already inherently untenable.

The stakes were high, and the Jewish community could not allow itself to make mistakes, since their very survival as a minority was in question. Considering how difficult management of the group was, we can see that modification of the statutory rules at that juncture, only thirty years after their adoption, when it was hoped that the crisis of the ghetto would only be temporary, might have put the entire community statute back in question. Based on a strict division by class and by nation, the *Capitoli* endured the blow and, through its more flexible tools – the *lodo* [a legally binding arbitration settlement] – and the designation of magistrates – would prove to be an excellent shared point of reference for the next three centuries.

Arbitration was a very important legal tool in early modern Italy. The term *lodo* refers to a settlement reached in arbitration that was recorded in writing and formalized by a notary. Until the French Revolution and the reforms instituted by Napoleon, the notary was the only figure in European society whose documents were considered to be publicly and legally valid. Therefore all documents issued by public administrations, chancelleries, treasuries and even courts had to be written by notaries in order to be considered legally binding. The *publica fide* (public trust) was invested exclusively in the notary, and not in the public systems.[11] The *lodo* was binding on the parties involved in the arbitration precisely because it had to be formally recorded by a notary. Thus this type of arbitration settlement could only be challenged in a Court of law. In this book, the term *Jewish lodo* refers to an arbitration settlement that was written by a Jewish notary who was recognized as an expert both in *halakha* (and thus a "rabbi", more or less) and on common law (*Ius comune*). In this case the *lodo* carried a dual legal validity, as it carried the force of both *ius comune* and of *halakhic* jurisprudence. Such a document was therefore equally valid in front of a Christian court or a Jewish tribunal.[12] The existence of Jewish notaries and the *publica*

---

11   On notaries in Rome: Pittella 2012.
12   Cooperman 2015 came to the same conclusion: note 78, p. 274.

fide entrusted to their documents in Christian courts is, as far as is known, unique to Rome.

The flexible application of the *Capitoli* allowed for, as much as was possible, the resolution of conflicts within the community, according to shared rules, reinforced by the personal prestige of the magistrates chosen to ensure that those rules were respected. It was during these years that the process of legitimizing the *Universitas* as a representative and protective body for of the Jewish collective arrived at a turning point. One of the most important factors in this progressive identification of the structure of its institutions was the ability to choose a ruling class. The tasks of representation were entrusted to those who best knew and could defend the rights and interests of the group (without, however, provoking reprisals or unintended effects) thanks to their personal charisma, their public and private roles, their profession, their social status, their level of education and a thousand other skills. This represents one of the most interesting and least investigated aspects of the ruling class, notwithstanding the official duties covered by such extraordinary personalities as Rabbi Tranquillo Vita Corcos in Rome and Rabbi Isacco Lampronti in Ferrara, both of who were teachers of international renown, as well as spiritual and political guides for their communities between the 17th and 18th centuries.[13] From this point of view, the Roman case turns out to be a model, and deserves to be considered as such.

In the system established by the *Capitoli* in 1524, the main body of self-governance of the *Universitas Iudaeorum de Urbe* was identified in the trio of *Fattori*, who were entrusted with the protection of the group's interests and the administration of its general affairs. This was a delicate assignment, and

---

13   See also the profiles of doctors and rabbis sent to study in Padua and Ferrara who were destined to determine the fates of their communities, reconstructed by David B. Ruderman (1992). The same author, in the introduction to his volume on the preachers of the Italian ghetto (1992), emphasized how: «The communities which sent them to study were energized by their return. More than ever before, Jewish communities were led by men who could creatively fuse their medical and rabbinical expertise» (p. 12). Regarding this subject, Gadi Luzzatto Voghera (2011) rightly recalls that: "This was the focal point that characterized the figure of the rabbi in the Jewish communities of the Diaspora in the medieval and modern ages: his legal function, frequently recognized and at times explicitly requested by the public authorities regarding civil Law (marriages, divorces, non-criminal disputes between members of the Jewish community), was an essential factor in assuring social order. This was likely one of the two reasons for which the non-Jewish world always identified the figure of the rabbi as the "head" of the Jewish community, recognizing him as such precisely due to the role of legal regulations invested in him» (pp. 532- 533). On this subject see also the monograph *Rabbini* by the same author. On Rabbi Lampronti, see now at least: Perani 2017; and on Corcos, Caffiero 2019.

although this criterion was not explicitly spelled out in the *Capitoli*, membership in the most important banking families favored receiving an appointment. Selection based on social standing, moreover, constituted, in Rome as elsewhere, a shared rule[14] that was normally followed in the assignment of all the most important roles, whether it concerned the management of the individual *Scole*, or instead, when they were assigning the highest central positions.[15]

Starting from at least the 1520s, the top levels of Jewish institutions, with the obvious exception of the technical roles related to the control of butchery and *kosher* meat, were occupied by members of only one class, bankers. That the Jewish ruling class should in large part overlap with the group that was most culturally and economically dynamic is not, naturally, a particularly significant fact. Rather it places the Roman situation in line with the experience of other Italian communities. This situation had become increasingly entrenched since the early years of the century. The *Capitoli* themselves, as we've seen, contributed to formalizing the bankers' success. It's not by chance, in fact, that in delineating the social pyramid of the *Universitas* (*banchieri, ricchi and mediocri*), the lawmaker made use of the heading '*banchieri*' to indicate its primacy and to properly distinguish the *banchieri* from the simple *ricchi*.[16] This differentiation did not concern the assets amassed by a single head of family, but rather signaled, with indisputable clarity, where the boundaries lay between the first and the second when it came to skill in finance, ensured by the ownership of a lending license. Once again, it is not by chance that for the nomination of the four *tassatori* (tax collectors), one of the most delicate administrative jobs, the *Capitoli* called for at least two members of the commission in question to be bankers, as they were undoubtedly able to keep accounts, were accustomed to administering large sums of money, and to obtaining the cooperation of recalcitrant clients (whether they be debtors or taxpayers).[17]

Bankers, therefore, had guided Jewish public life since the first quarter of the 16th century, and during those years their central role had been unanimously and peacefully recognized, both externally and within the community.

---

14   The preeminent role of moneylenders in Jewish public administration – whatever size the community in question was – is not actually something exceptional; cfr., regarding this subject, Bonfil 1991, pp. 170–176; Luzzati 1996, pp. 217–218; Segre 1996a, p. 768; Siegmund 1996, pp. 868–869; Allegra 1996, exp. pp. 209–248.
15   On this subject, cfr. the examples of bankers in leadership roles in the Spanish *Scole* reported in Di Nepi 2004.
16   Cooperman 2015, pp. 33–4.
17   Milano 1935 and 1936.

This pre-eminence would be definitively consolidated inside the walls of the ghetto.

During those difficult years, the bankers' interactions with the high offices of the Papal States, *in primis* with the *Camerlengo della Reverenda Camera Apostolica* (the Cardinal Chamberlain of the Apostolic Chamber, who exercised sole jurisdiction over their activities),[18] reinforced their position in the Jewish community. For a group such as the Jews, whose presence in the heart of Christian society could easily be subject to review, putting their fate in the hands of people known for enjoying a personal and privileged relationship with the pontifical court represented a good opportunity to try extending to the entire group the benefits of a network of relationships that was strictly individual in origin. The usefulness of this familiarity with the apostolic *palazzi* was demonstrated, year after year, during the resolution of outstanding accounts with the non-Roman *Universitates*, in particular those of Ancona, for the collection of the contributions for *Vigesima* and for the tax of 1,130 *fiorini*, from which the Roman community was exempt. In order to prevent problems from arising, the envoys of the Roman *Universitas*, often young sons of banking families, would present themselves at their sister cities, empowered by the protection of the central authorities, who were ready to act against anyone who might impede the success of their mission.[19] On the other hand, for the public authorities, the certainty that they were discussing Jewish affairs with those who could, with good reason, claim the unconditional trust of the whole group – which was famous for its high degree of contentiousness – meant that they could be assured of resolving disputes quickly, and without running the risk that others would appeal the decisions that were taken. In short, the homogeneity of the ruling class proved to be a positive asset, which was very useful both for the peaceful management of life in *rione Sant'Angelo*, and for the conduct of its relations with the outside world, either Jewish or Christian.

The pre-eminence of the bankers was not called into question by the institution of the ghetto. Their profession was one of the few to remain untouched by *Cum nimis absurdum* and the restrictions it imposed, which did not outlaw Jewish moneylending. The relative professional tranquility that the group enjoyed helped to confirm the pre-eminent role of bankers in Jewish society in the following period as well. Immediately after 1555, as we will see, what significantly changed within the walls of the ghetto was not so much the established hierarchy, made up of a few well-known families, but rather the office

---

18   See *infra*, chapter 5.
19   See, *infra*, chapter 4.

of the *Fattori* and the list of requirements and skills informally requested of those who were candidates to take on this job. Although nobody would formally modify the current statute, daily practice contributed to the modification, at least in part, of the characteristics and functions of this leadership role. The metamorphosis was substantial. Over the next fifty years following the changes imposed by Paul IV, in fact, positions such as the *Fattori* and the administration of the fiscal policy of the *Universitas* slowly began to be entrusted to the most respected and impartial rabbis, who were chosen by their coreligionists to resolve the infinite debates regarding rights and requirements for tenants and, most of all, regarding taxes. Thus, apart from class and nation membership, they also began to look with interest at the *curricula studiorum* of potential leaders.

The cultural and professional profiles of the Jewish notaries who were active in Rome in those years are a good point of departure for observing the ongoing process. Clearly defining what a rabbi was in an Italian community of that period, and what led to the attribution of that title is an uncertain business.[20] Nevertheless, it is evident that notaries, who were all referred to as rabbis, and who were required to certify in writing, *more hebraeorum*, every decision and every discussion, were the protagonists of a minor revolution during those years. These are complex interrelations, the result of the Roman Jewish community's recent past, which involve different aspects of the experience of the first decades of life in the ghetto. In this sense the Jewish notaries represent a compass that can orient us in a labyrinth of names, functions, businesses and families, and help us make sense of the overlapping stories which are hidden within. Once we have seen how and why this office was the scene of important changes, it will be easier to reconstruct the parameters of this significant but silent evolution in other contexts as well.

2   Have Faith in the Notary: Pompeo del Borgo

Rabbi and notary Pompeo del Borgo, the first to draw up documents in Italian and not in Hebrew, was active in Rome in the last quarter of the 16th century, and can be considered as representative of the broad process that overtook the ruling class, composed of administrators who were bankers, important

---

20   Bonfil 2012, exp. pp. 64–94; Luzzatto Voghera 2011. On the application of the *Capitoli* in the 1600s, Lattes forthcoming.

merchants, sometimes doctors, sometimes rabbis – in any case people with notoriety and prestige among both Jews and Christians.

We begin with the professional aspects that concerned both the moneylenders' business and, as a direct consequence of its evolution, the business of their trusted notary. Indeed, Pompeo's story represents a disruptive example of this, worth following attentively. The changes that affected the public offices of the *Universitas* went hand in hand with the profound transformations that affected the banking profession. It was during this period, following the restrictions imposed by *Cum nimis absurdum*, and notwithstanding the fact that these did not directly affect their businesses, that the Roman Jewish bankers began to turn their interests beyond the scope of activity authorized by their lending licenses. This broadening of commercial horizons coincided with a diversification of requests for public documents from Jewish notaries. It is not by chance, then, that during this phase the notaries began to adjust the form and content of their deeds according to the needs of the new commissions. It is here that Pompeo del Borgo and his Jewish registries written in Italian come into play. Jewish notaries guaranteed the correctness and validity of private documents for transactions between Jews (at times in parallel with Christian notaries, other times independent of them). Thus, in order to understand the importance of this evolution in the management of the community, it is essential to investigate the reasons behind this linguistic and cultural change. In short, we need to use the sources as an interpretive tool, going beyond their content.

A review of the registries of Jewish notaries Isacco delle Piattelle and Pompeo del Borgo in the final quarter of the 16th century clearly reveals the transformations that had taken place in the preceding decades. Thirty years and four Popes after the institution of the ghetto the new condition had been fully accepted, and the community's organizational structures accordingly adapted. Not by chance, the role of Jewish notaries emerged significantly strengthened. To give preference to a Jewish professional was not, in fact, a neutral choice – it implied a desire to make conflicts public and to find solutions to controversies that, as much as possible, kept both the first and the second within the group. The career of the notaries falls within the general framework of the pressures on the Jewish ruling class to adapt to the new situation and its demands; after all, these notaries were not only scribes, they were first and foremost rabbis who were experts in *halakha*. This expertise found a concrete application in the documents they wrote up respecting the customs and the laws of the city and State in which the Jews of Rome lived.[21]

---

21 Bonfil 2012; Stow 2001.

The professional experience of Pompeo del Borgo, the youngest exponent of the trade at that time, reflects the phases of the process of evolution and adaptation to the ghetto that is at the center of this research. Pompeo was the first Jewish notary in Rome to draw up deeds that were not in Hebrew. His decision to not use the holy language raises a series of questions regarding the cultural abilities of the professional and of the public who used his services. The answer we are after concerns the reasons that led a rabbi, who was not a son of rabbis, to pursue this career, offering his services to a clientele of coreligionists but abandoning the use of Hebrew in compiling their papers. In short, we need to ask if this choice, made in order to meet the needs of those who requested deeds for business that were Jewishly valid, conceals an irreversible process of acculturation and decay of identity or if instead, this too was one of the expedients elaborated in order to confront an extraordinary situation, making the best use of available resources, specifically, the rabbis and their unquestioned authority. Bankers and rabbis, these are the terms of the problem.

In February of 1578, Rabbi Pompeo del Borgo inaugurated a notebook of 68 pages that was destined to become his first notarial registry,[22] and began to compete with those compiled contemporaneously by Rabbi Isacco delle Piatelle. The practice of a general notary service was one of the common professions for rabbis in the Italian communities of the Middle Ages and the Modern Age. It was also a typical practice for rabbis, hired by a group of Jews to attend to the community's educational and ritual necessities, to be charged with the drawing up of documents that were needed for the life of the community – marriage contracts *in primis*. Rabbis considered this a way to supplement their salaries, as well as, in a certain sense, the performance of a public service.[23] Only in Rome, however, did this occasional role go on to assume more defined characteristics. Starting from at least 1536, the ancient Roman *Universitas* could boast the presence of a genuine notary office in its midst, established to respond to its members' requirements for documentation.[24]

1536, though, was not the year in which the Jews of the city first discovered the possibility of recourse to certification by a notary.[25] It was simply

---

[22] NE, f. 3, l. 1.
[23] Bonfil 2012 and, more succinctly 1996, pp. 170–176.
[24] Here the Jews showed themselves to be in line with the passion for publicly formalizing contractual agreements of every kind that was quite widespread in Italy from the 13th century, about which see Cipolla 1998. Regarding the types of agreements formalized between the Jews of Rome and the Christian notaries of the city in the course of the 1600s, cfr. Ago 1998.
[25] Anna Esposito's studies have clearly demonstrated the confidence that existed between the Jews of Rome and the Christian notaries of the city; cfr. Esposito 1995.

the moment, according to the sources available to us,[26] that marked the first compilation of documents composed in Hebrew and authorized by specialist rabbis, based on a mixed law that combined *halakha, jus comune*, and local customs.[27] Recourse to the services of Christian notaries, naturally, never declined. Rather, according to all the evidence, these were preferred to their Jewish colleagues for the drafting of the most important documents, such as wills, which are hard to find in the registries of the Jewish notaries. The choice of a Christian trusted notary normally depended on an existing relationship between the recorder and the client. For example, the continued success in the Jewish world of the professionals based in the sixteenth office of the *Trenta* notaries, following the footsteps of Belardino Pascasio – a notary who was active between *Arenula* and *Sant' Angelo*, and, from the 1580s, recorded items pawned to Jewish banks and compiled countless other Jewish documents that had nothing to do with moneylending[28] – who continued to write assiduously for the Jews even into the first decades of the 18th century.[29]

Thus when Rabbi Pompeo took his pen in hand, more than forty years after the drafting of the first deed in Hebrew, his career choice should not have surprised anyone. He was not the only rabbi of his community, nor was he the only one of his colleagues in general to offer services as a *sofer*; the new element is that his professional works, though concerned with Jewish things, were composed in Italian. Pompeo del Borgo's choice of language was a success, and from that moment on the notaries who came after him, up to the

---

26   Naturally it is not possible to rule out the existence of deeds that precede this date but which were not collected in the *Archivio Urbano* at the time of its establishment in 1614 (Lori Sanfilippo 1990 and Francescangeli 2012); rather, some notations in the draft text of the *Capitoli* of Daniel di Pisa lead us to suspect that such registries existed at least since the 1520s, but that these were lost (thanks to Prof. Bernard Cooperman for making available a copy of a still unpublished copy of the document he discovered, about which see *infra*). For a chronological order of the registries of the NE, that proposed by Stow, De Benedetti Stow 1986 is useful. The same author has put together useful summaries of the deeds compiled between 1536 and 1557 in Stow 1999. In general, for references to this source, unfortunately often quite scant, in the classic bibliography about the Jews of Rome, cfr. Berliner 1992, p. 153 e pp. 359–340; Vogelstein, Rieger 1895–1896, p. 262; Milano 1984, pp. 52–73. More recently, cfr. Golan 1985; Di Nepi 2004; Francescangeli 2012. For an analysis of the social and anthropological value of this special art of Jewish notaries in Rome, Stow 2001, with particular reference to chapter III, *Social Reconciliation from Within and Without*, pp. 99–126.

27   Di Nepi 2004.

28   ASR, *Trenta notai capitolini, Ufficio 16*, 1579–1599. Thanks to Prof. Anna Esposito for this suggestion.

29   Di Nepi 2015.

final document drafted by Grandilio di Porto,[30] respected that decision and abandoned, perhaps definitively, the use of Hebrew.

Why? It is undoubtedly legitimate to ask whether Pompeo and those who followed in his footsteps renounced Hebrew in favor of a simpler and more comprehensible construction due ignorance, their own or that of their clients. This, however, conflicts with the actual facts. Rabbi Pompeo, as a good rabbi, was perfectly capable of reading and writing fluently in Hebrew, as exemplified by a marriage contract he drew up, found in the final pages of his first registry.[31] Such a contract exhibits an ability that was in no way used only occasionally, but which was destined to be regularly repeated in the production of other contracts of this type, and above all in the drafting of single *sententiae in folio*, which were issued on simple paper and not included in the actual registries.[32] If Hebrew's centrality in Pompeo's cultural world does not alone confirm his knowledge and use of the *alef bet*, a paleographic analysis of his own work tips the scale: the early drafts and broken scribbles found on the covers and frontispieces of Pompeo's books are for the most part in Hebrew and not in Italian, and the rapid and sure *ductus* (that is, lines) of the words drawn in that alphabet is clear evidence of a writer that was capable of and accustomed to working in this traditional form. A comparison between Pompeo's Hebrew handwriting and that in Italian makes it clear that fluid writing came more naturally for him in Hebrew rather than when using the sharp and angular lines of the Latin alphabet. This obvious preference clearly reflects Pompeo's cultural point of reference, in which he learned the art of penmanship at a

---

30 The documentation preserved in the NE source ends with 1640 and with copies of the last deeds drafted by Grandilio di Porto, who passed away, however, just before 1637, as can be seen in the dedication of the cover of the registry; cfr. Stow, De Benedetti Stow 1986, p. 116, n. 14. However, we cannot assume that there were not deeds later than this date that have not survived to this day; even if, in this case, the fate of documents created in an office that possessed such a structured archive but did not end up in it, still may induce us to at least entertain the idea of a temporary interruption or other difficulty happening in the life of the office itself.

31 NE, f. 3, l. 1, cc. 63v-65v.

32 AC, *Archivio Urbano, Sezione I*, voll. 877–887. The discovery of these ten new volumes of papers of Jewish notaries, recently completed by Laura Fancescangeli, who I thank for the information, does not pose, however, at least upon a preliminary examination, problems in the definition of the activity of Jewish notaries in Rome; they are, in effect, loose papers, perhaps released to those directly involved, and for the most part concerning single arbitration rulings edited by the same writers who, in the form of a public deed, recorded the various phases of the same arbitration and which, much the same as Christian judges, rather than recording the final decision in the related "dossier," registered it elsewhere. On this subject see Fracescangeli 2012, p. 276. On Pompeo del Borgo see also Stow 2001, p. 151, n. 82.

young age. Now, as an adult and in his professional life he still felt the same connection with writing: a Jewish connection.

The transition from Hebrew to Italian, brought about by someone who had no difficulty with Hebrew, was determined by different kinds of reasons. The key to the mystery is in the contents of that protocol from 1578. During his first year of activity as a notary, Pompeo worked almost exclusively for Leone Asriglio (who notarized the small, short term loans made to other Jews), and to a much lesser extent for Vito Treves, who availed himself of Pompeo's services in the drafting of contracts for his many young apprentices.[33] During this same period, Isacco delle Piattelle's clients turned to him for a completely different type of document, one that was essentially public in nature, and therefore drafted in Hebrew. Though Isacco's regular clients included individuals renting and selling to each other, the notary's specialty was actually the drafting of reliable, formal reports of the deliberations and discussions of his community, expressed through the legislative and judicial actions of the occasional arbiters, the *Fattori*, the *Consiglio Ristretto* or the *Congrega dei Sessanta*. Deliberations regarding the duties of the *Fattori*, the commitments of the *Scole*, or the phases of a *lodo* – in short, all the different forms in which the activity of governing by the bodies that composed the *Universitas Iudaeorum de Urbe* took place – were all occasions when decisions were made based on the customs and law observed by the Jews of Rome. Therefore, the certification had to comply with essential formal standards: among which was evidently the use of the Hebrew language.

Pompeo del Borgo's work turned in another direction, taking on the provision of reliable and irrefutable private agreements; the economic agreements that were entrusted to Pompeo required a linguistic form that was centered on practical criteria of immediate and unquestionable comprehension, not on needs of a ritual nature, which Rabbi Pompeo nevertheless knew well. The *Universitas Hebreorum* needed documents that were perfectly Jewish; its members, caught up in running their daily lives, wanted functional documents. The difference between Isacco and Pompeo, between the Hebrew used by the first and the Italian preferred by the second, lies in these two different types of documents.

While Isacco delle Piattelle inherited his notary office from his father and predecessor Leone, Pompeo del Borgo was trained in a profoundly different setting, one which he would never completely leave. Pompeo came from one of the many merchant families of the Roman community who were

---

33   Cfr., again, NE, f. 3, l. 1.

not too rich and not too poor. They were not included in the small circle of families that were capable of turning out bankers and businessmen in every generation, but may well have been keen to join it, just as were many others in their position. It is not by chance that in 1579, Pompeo's first year as a professional notary, Prospero del Borgo (Pompeo's father) was awarded the contract to collect the Agone and Testaccio tax, that year to also be collected in Romagna and Lombardia, in partnership with his sons David and Mosè, *alias* Pompeo. This contract, together with the credits the *Universitas de Urbe* claimed from taxpayers who were delinquent on payments from the last collection of contributions for poor and unmarried girls, would have earned Prospero and his family ten *giuli* for every scudo received. Among the responsibilities accepted by Prospero was that of furnishing a precise accounting of income and expenses until the end of the contract.[34] Keeping perfect documentation was among the primary obligations of the agreement which, naturally, had been drawn up in Hebrew by Isacco delle Piattelle. This accuracy, then, became the product that Pompeo began offering to the Jews of Rome.

The opening of Pompeo's studio did not compete directly with the successful office of Isacco delle Piatelle. Rather it was set up to respond to needs which, up to that time, had only been addressed in front of Christian notaries. The economic insecurity connected with life in the ghetto – made harder or easier over time by the succession of different men to the papal throne – and the awareness of the fragility of an institution that was at once well-defined and uncertain, by virtue of being the expression of a compromise between different political and ideological demands, drove Jews to formalize agreements between private parties, be they Jews or Christians, with Jewish notaries. The Christian parties to these agreements, as long as they did not fear facing a less trustworthy counterpart, were satisfied with far lesser guarantees.[35] Pompeo del Borgo's sensibilities gave him common ground with his public and, precisely because he was a member of the same class and experienced the same anxieties, he was able to offer the assurances of reliable and indisputable regulation

---

34   From what we find also in the analytical index of the names of the people cited in the registries collected by Kenneth Stow (1999), this was the first time in which the del Borgo family appeared on the community scene; previously, in 1577, David del Borgo, as the owner of an adjoining market space, declared that he had no *gazagà* on the contiguous space sold by Gemma Bondi, the widow of Isacco di Perugia, to brothers Benedetto and Mosè Fiorentino (NE, f. 9, l. 1, cc. 37v-38r).

35   It seems that Jewish accountants were also counted among the counterparts considered to be unreliable (Ago 1998, p. 75).

A RULING CLASS FOR THE JEWS OF THE GHETTO 101

of contracts between gentlemen that were indispensable to his clients. Such a need would have been hard to satisfy elsewhere.

Pompeo never completely gave up his earlier business initiatives, and continued to look after his affairs as well as those of his family. He duly found a way to place entries for these accounts in the free spaces of his registries, under the heading "*memoria come*" (reminders), typically in Latin characters. So, on the first page of one of the registers he recorded the terms for the rental of one of his family's market spaces by his sister Graziosa del Borgo to her in-laws, at the rate of 5 *scudi* per year;[36] on one of the last pages can be found the terms of the "division of the spaces," drawn up by Bernardino Pascasio, and based upon which he was required to pay 6.80 *scudi*;[37] or again, beginning a new register, he took care to keep in mind developments regarding another location that was registered in his name, sold to him by Leone Marini, and for which he had personally stipulated the contract;[38] at the end of another registry he jotted down a few accounting notes from another company of merchants with which he was associated,[39] and on the last page of still another he transcribed information about the assumption of a debit in his name "from magistrate Foppa to Monte Giordano for 111 *scudi* and 20, notarized by magistrate Diomedi Ricci, notary of the *Auditore della Camera in Banchi*."[40]

One last note: Pompeo's writings demonstrate how Italian – even if pronounced with their particular Judeo-Roman cadence and filled with terms from that special dialect – was the language of daily communication for the Jews of Rome, spoken among family and with friends, and learned from the youngest age. Hebrew remained the language of study and prayer in Rome, as well as the *lingua franca* of communications with foreign Jews, somewhat akin to the role of Latin for Christian intellectuals at the time. Thus it was inevitable that even a rabbi-businessman would resort to ordinary language – that is, Italian – to keep track of his own private accounts.[41]

Moving from the direct conduct of his own affairs to the drafting of binding documents concerning those of others, Pompeo would not lose sight of the family business and his roots. The change of occupation was attributable to

---

36   NE, f. 11, l. 5, c. 1r.
37   The other owners owed, respectively, 6.25 (Angelo), 5 (Michele) e 6.80 (Vito); NE, f. 11, l. 5, c. 130v.
38   NE, f. 6, l. 1, c. 1r.
39   NE, f. 14, l. 1, cc. 181v-190v.
40   NE, f. 6, l. 2, c. 220r.
41   Brief notes about the choice of using Italian, which is not, however, attributed to a differentiation in the requests of the clients, nor to a process of social transformation, are found in Stow 2001, p. 151, n. 82.

ambitions for social climbing, achievable precisely through rabbinic experience and the honors connected to it. For the historian today this demonstrates, though from quite an oblique perspective, the spirit of enterprise and readiness to create opportunity where at first glance opportunity could not exist which is central in the experience of the Italian ghettos.[42] This initiative was common to the members of the Jewish ruling class, whether they were occupied in the monopoly recycling and wholesale of used clothing or, instead, engaged in intellectual careers, of which the position of notary was emblematic, being halfway between a free profession and an artisan of writing.[43]

Pompeo and Isacco's success also tells another story. While their deeds were set up as documents that were valid for all purposes, there remained, however, certain special documents that were drawn up in Hebrew and, for the most part, based on *halakha*. Entrusting a Jewish notary implied, after all, a request for a rabbinical consultation regarding the handling of a business transaction and, consequently, the guarantee that the legal negotiation would be conducted in full compliance with not only civil law, but with *halakha*. These were the strengths and the limits of the Jewish notaries, and the main reason for which there was not a wide variety in the subjects addressed and the documentation produced within their registries, above all for those drawn up in Hebrew. Establishing what those subjects were, and how they had changed compared to the preceding period, or rather clarifying which types of problems were seen as requiring the legally binding opinion of a rabbi, is of unquestionable interest for the purposes of this research, which is aimed at reconstructing the salient characteristics of the Roman Jewish experience in the first decades of life in the ghetto.

Analysis of the issues that were dealt with by Jewish notaries holds no surprises, and reveals how, at a time of difficult physical reorganization, the Jews of Rome were concerned with paying the correct taxes (that is, they would try to get reductions), and ensuring their rights of possession of homes and commercial locations. The fact that really stands out from a quick reading of these Hebrew documents is the increase in the number of cases where the resolution was entrusted to rabbis. This meant a growing influence of the rabbinate in Roman Jewish society, in which, up to that time, rabbis had mainly undertaken roles in the community that were limited by and related to the management of religious life: the instruction of children, editing of books,

---

42   Regarding the social value of the title of rabbi, see Bonfil 1990, 1991 and 2012.
43   Regarding the balance that a notary struck, Berengo 1999, pp. 369–392. For Rome, see Pittella 2012.

administration of the branches of justice relevant to family rights, etc ... What were the consequences of this change?

The incursion of the rabbis revealed in the documentation could have come at the expense of others, specifically the *Fattori* and bankers whose jobs, at first glance, seemed unchanged in the paralysis of the *Capitoli*. In reality, things did not go that way or so simply, and the rabbis, who were often members of the same families as some of the bankers, progressively began to personally manage the *res publica* of the community – starting with the designation of the trio of arbitrators and ending up with the selection of the *Fattori* themselves. In short, not only was the composition of the Jewish ruling class changed, but also, at least in part, their training. The area in which this transformation was most immediately evident was that of the internal administration of justice. Let us look at how.

3   Arbitrators and Arbitration in the Selection of the Ruling Class

Although it appears that a genuine rabbinical tribunal was never assembled in Rome, the Jewish community did not give up autonomous management of its own legal affairs.[44] In fact, when it came to areas where the Jewish law diverged significantly from Christian law (marriage and divorce, inheritance and the protection of minors), the authorities willingly allowed the Jews regulate themselves.[45] During the Middle Ages, the Jews' jurisdiction was confined to civil law; for criminal cases obviously the ordinary criminal courts were responsible. In this context, and notwithstanding the lack of a genuine *Bet Din* in Rome, the practice of regulating the daily life of the community by other means, that is, essentially with the use of arbitration and the *lodo*, was never disputed. Indeed, when it came to a subject of absolute importance like that of taxation, Jewish self-governance was often encouraged by the Pope, or really by the *Camerlengo* of the *Reverenda Camera Apostolica* in his name. The Apostolic Chamber had every interest in seeing that the Jewish communities of the Papal States had sufficient power to successfully collect the taxes imposed on their members. For example, two decades after the institution of the ghetto, in January of 1577, Gregory XIII revisited this subject, and at the explicit request

---

44   Colorni 1945, pp. 319–320. For examples of arbitrations in Livorno, and city in which jurisdictional autonomy in matters between Jews had been guaranteed since the privileges granted by the Grand Duke, see Galasso 2002.
45   Bonfil 2012, pp. 195–248; Esposito 1995, p. 151; Colorni 1945, pp. 181–200.

of the *Cardinal Camerlengo* the Pope reiterating that the broad range of powers granted to the *Fattori* in matters of taxation was not up for discussion.[46]

The apparent contradiction between the taxation policy pursued by the magistracy that had jurisdiction over the Jewish community and the strategy of conversion pursued by the church is yet another element of the intrinsic ambiguity of the ghetto compromise, and of the vision of the workings of the Jewish world that this represented. When it came to the Jews, the aim on one hand was to reinforce the community's authority in order to ease the collection of taxes to be sent to the Apostolic Chamber, while on the other hand the Church more generally worked to slowly and progressively discredit those same Jewish institutions. On one side of the Church a utilitarian representation of the Jews came into play, in the form of able merchants and bankers who were a secure source of revenue for the exchequer – and therefore, from the point of view of those responsible for the papal coffers, figures to protect and assist. On the other side, the Jewish presence was looked upon as though it was a plague to be cured with conversions, to be obtained through material humiliations. Meanwhile the tax burden, which was subject to frequent increases over three centuries in the ghetto, performed a precise function in the policy of proselytism towards the Jews where, as we know, the continued imposition of heavy taxes further complicated the lives of the Jewish subjects and their institutions.[47]

The community's authority, moreover, rested on the possibility, as limited as it was, that they would be able impose compliance with their decisions, including via the application of punitive proceedings against offenders. It is not by chance, then, that we find our Roman Jewish notaries concerned with defining the consequences of violating a newly concluded agreement, setting down penalties in the concluding clauses of their deeds (therefore in the *sanctio*). The contracts invariably called for the impositions of heavy fines, on the order of 100 gold *scudi*, as well as the inevitable religious maledictions. It is hard to believe that these detailed rules concerning infractions were drawn up without any hope that, at need, the threats would translate into actions with real capacity for deterrence.[48] Even admitting that the community's actions

---

46   Cfr. the brief entitled *Che li Fattori possano risquotere li dazii e che nessino possa ricusare di pagarli* (ASR, *Camerale II, Ebrei*, b. 2).

47   Milano 1984, pp. 129–154.

48   The *sanctio* "consists of a formula that has the objective of guaranteeing the observance of the regulation via the threat of penalties against those who do not comply with the obligation, resulting in legal action [...]. The penalty can be spiritual (exclusions, excommunication: from ecclesiastical acts the penalty extends, with clear but understandable abuse, to documents issued by lay authorities and to private papers) or secular (exclusively in

had always been and still were confined to the limits granted by the Christian authorities, and that they simply appeared in the guise of the *longa manus* of those authorities, the fact remains that such deterrent actions must have existed to some degree, however reduced, and that they must have been able to convince those whom they were directed at of their force, even if it was quite weak.[49]

The establishment of arbitration as the accepted forum of the *Universitates* was something more than a mere expedient devised to guarantee a small portion of authority to the Jewish institutions. Created and elaborated in the works of Justinian, over the centuries arbitration proved to be efficacious for the resolution of conflicts, particularly those concerning civil subjects and those with opposing litigants who were business partners or members of the same organization. Much like others, this custom was incorporated into later legislative compilations and became a constant in the practice of law as an institutionalized form of agreement between private citizens, guaranteed by notarial documentation.[50] Arbitration was a practice, therefore, which was in line with the common mentality as well as with clearly established doctrine. As such, arbitration was also used by Jewish communities, for whom this institution allowed them to easily regulate a long list of subjects.

Halfway through the 16th century in Rome the Jewish system of arbitration was already fully defined. A reading of the valuable registries of the Jewish notaries, whose pages mainly deal with conflicts and their solutions, demonstrates this quite clearly. The registries also allow us to extrapolate, from an analysis and chronological ordering of the developments of the different cases, a paradigm for the civil procedure that was followed and applied.

When both parties, or even just one of them, whether they were individuals or business entities, decided to pursue legal avenues (obviously those which were viable while remaining in Jewish institutions), they went to a Jewish notary and filed a formal complaint containing their claims against the other party. The complaint could use one of two distinct formulations: the first was called a *protesta,* and could actually launch a genuine proceeding, and the second was called a *citazione,* which in some sense was less binding than the first, and was essentially used to advise the other party of the existence of a dispute. Thus the

---

the pecuniary in nature, in the form of fines)"; Pratesi 1999, p. 84. In the deeds of Jewish notaries both formulations are normally found (Di Nepi 2004, pp. 56–57).

49   For this interpretation of the value or Jewish legal automony, cfr. Bonfil 2012 and 1991, p. 177.
50   Regarding the legal institution of arbitration and its evolution, cfr. Martone 1984; see also the entry *Arbitrato – Diritto intermedio* (Mortari 1958); Bonfil 2012, pp. 145 et seq.

citazione was used only in the introductory phase of the hearing. The *protesta* could also be employed in other instances, both as a formal means of presenting evidence for or against a claim, and more generally as an instrument via which the parties continued to file motions in the midst of the arbitration.

Once a *protesta* or a *citazione* was received, the defendant was faced with a choice. The first possibility was to respond to the adversary with a second *citazione* or *protesta*, in which they expressed their own opinion, and then wait and see what the other party's next move would be. The second, faster option was to decide to reach an agreement with the plaintiff so they could come to an arrangement that was satisfactory to both parties. In this case both parties had to commit in advance to accepting the ruling, and to this end each side nominated its own arbitrator, who, in agreement with the other party's designated arbitrator, would hand down a ruling within an established time period, often quite short, less than ten days. Such an agreement was given the name *comprimisio*, a word taken from the Latin *compromissum*, with which Christian notaries indicated the drafting of documents that had the identical functions.[51] Therefore, at the time this term referred to the simple joint decision to resolve a problem via Jewish arbitration, and not to the actual solution to the problem given by the arbitrators.

At this point nothing remained but to await the sentence – at least in theory. On occasions when the two arbitrators were unable to reach an agreement, which happened frequently, they could request the presence of a third arbitrator *super partes* as the deciding vote between them. In more delicate and complex cases the litigants would hire *procuratori* (a sort of paralegal) to negotiate with the chosen arbitrators, and to provide them with any documentation or clarifications they requested. In these more detailed cases the arbitrators themselves could make use of the *Inviato della Comunità Santa di Roma*, which, as the official messenger of the arbitration court, informed the parties of developments in the case and acted as an intermediary between them, as well as between the litigants and the court itself. Only rarely did the arbitrators manage to issue rulings within the time allotted to them. In case of a delay they would inform the interested parties that they had decided on an extension, that is, they had declared *foro in cedula*. In the end, once an agreement was reached, often with the decisive assistance of the third arbitrator, it had to be accepted in all aspects by the parties, who declared that they were satisfied with the sentence and were obliged to respect the ruling under the threat of

---

51 Martone 1984, p. 26. Stow, seen here instead as a mechanism to weaken the effects of intervention by the Court of the Vicar (2001, pp. 117–118).

penalties. In a case in which economic restrictions were called for in the terms of the settlement, the notary, to ensure the fulfilment of these commitments, would also note the inclusion of this clause in his registries, and at that point, the affair could effectively be considered closed.

The different procedural phases were documented in the records of the rabbi notary, who, while writing the correct formulations in the correct place, concerned himself with assuring their validity both in terms of Jewish law and the City law. The institution of arbitration was established based on reasonably similar conceptions in both legal systems, each of which stipulated, from its own point of view, that arbitration is not equivalent to a real sentence handed down by a genuine court, as well as the idea that the task of reaching the agreement should be assigned to two arbitrators, each representing one of the parties, who were to be given a precise time limit for deliberations, and the possibility of turning to a third person in the case of irreconcilable differences.[52]

The most important act – the one that certified the validity of the entire arbitration – was the signing of the *compromesso*, through which the parties agreed to make use of this institution. Arbitration was, in fact, an alternative to a ruling by a true court, both from the Talmudic point of view and from the legal point of view (in which case a court meant a decision by a genuine magistracy and certainly not a simple agreement between private citizens). At this point the parties told the witnesses that the decision to take this course had been made "from our personal good will, without any duress or pressure in the world, but only with integrity of heart, a diligent spirit and thoughtful opinions," and that they had placed the problem in need of resolution in the hands of the selected arbitrators, swearing to comply with "everything that they decree or sentence as law or close to the law."[53]

According to the contemporary Jewish legal literature, masterfully examined by Roberto Bonfil, the expression "law or close to the law" (*le-Din o kharov le-Din*) was reserved for use only in those arbitrations that were being overseen

---

52   On the application of the institution called for in common law in the Jewish context cfr. Bonfil 2012, pp. 200-215 and the bibliography cited within, with examples of arbitrations on pp. 307–331; regarding the aspect of Jewish law, see at least the summary by Cohen 1999, pp. 361–363.

53   In this case the formula is taken from NE, f. 2, l. 2, c25*r* (summarized in Stow 1999, doc. 1343) but this phrasing is normally present in all of the *compromessi*. Roberto Bonfil emphasizes how this formulation, which has disappeared by the beginning of the following century, was meant to indicate a kind of initial phase in the evolution of legal arbitration from simple custom to a genuine legal institution (Bonfil 1990, pp. 224–225). It would clearly be interesting to initiate a study in this sense of the documents later preserved in the series *Notai ebrei*.

by titled rabbis: this formulation, in fact, ensured the judge's proper understanding of the law, and informed those involved of the validity of the legal bases that would support the ruling. The absence of this phrase would theoretically have allowed anyone who felt disadvantaged or penalized by a verdict to appeal, based on a flaw in the document that rendered it legally invalid. In a certain sense this implied that only the opinion of rabbis, who were doctors of law, could be considered valid. Any other opinion not backed by the doctrinal certification of the one who pronounced it could easily be challenged, and was thus susceptible to appeal.[54]

Yet this formula is present in all of the *compromessi* recorded by Jewish notaries, whoever the arbitrator was – and it was not always a rabbi. The expression indicated, rather than the exclusive skills of the scholars, the binding force of that type of document, which, being "close to the Law" – supported as it was by the actual principles of the Law or what would we could call common sense – would not have lost its inherent validity despite the fact that it could be weakened by a sort of labeling as semi-official. We find some confirmation of this in the precise choices of terminology made from time to time by the Jewish notaries, who rarely ever referred to the role of arbitrator with the word *daian* ("judge" in Hebrew and in *halakhic* language, in the strict sense of the word), preferring instead the term *berùr* (from the root *brr* = clarify, verify), meaning fact-checker.[55]

All of this once again served as reminder to those who compiled a *compromesso* of what the difference, and the distance was between judgement by arbitration and a rabbinical court. In the first case, in fact, due to this legally sanctioned distance, it was necessary to invoke additional legal force, as expressed precisely by the phrase "close to the Law." Considered this way, this had little to do with the credentials of the arbitrator/fact-checkers, and instead applied in some way to the legal institution itself. During the years prior to the ghetto, the third arbitrator (who for clear reasons of fairness did not have to be approved by the opposing parties) was often an important rabbi who took the role voluntarily, and could thus be called *daian*[56] (the notary Leone delle

---

54   On this subject, see Bonfil 2012, pp. 207–216, with particular attention to the detailed rabbinic responsa on the issue, which, however, confirm the widespread practice of nominating "normal" people as arbitrators and illustrate the fear the rabbis had of losing ground in the delicate question of managing legal affairs.

55   Thanks to Dr. Giacomo Limentani for bringing this linguistic peculiarity to my attention. On the use of this same word, see also Cooperman 2015, note 17: "The terminology seems to have been flexible. *Brurim* here would probably be best translated as 'elected' rather than as 'arbitrators', the most common use for the term in Hebrew legal literature."

56   Regarding cases in which non-rabbinic arbitrators sought the help of a rabbi, cfr. Bonfil 2012, pp. 214–216.

Piattelle himself was often chosen).[57] However, the arbitrators who were normally selected at first, at least in Rome during the first half of the 16th century, were not rabbis at all.[58] Rather, in every case from this period where the dispute involved money – and there were many – the litigants turned to bankers as arbitrators. Perhaps they were considered appropriate for the subject because they were able to untangle accounts and cash, or perhaps this is further proof of this group's importance in the conduct of the community's business. In any case, Jewish law states that "all Israelites are eligible to judge in civil cases,"[59] and considers being a fair person of certain moral and intellectual stature to be sufficient qualification for a judge; the title of rabbi is not required.[60] The direct intervention of the rabbis, at least up to the middle of the 16th century, might have been preferred in more intricate cases – in acknowledgement of the fact that, obviously, those who had studied law the most best knew its subtleties. However, on those occasions they would often be joined, perhaps as *procuratori,* by men who had no doctrinal certification, who if possible were holders of a banking license, but still qualified to deal with complex subjects.[61]

So, in 1550, to untangle a dispute over the formulation of an oath and the correct method of its administration, two rabbis who were experts in legal affairs took charge of the case, Leone delle Piattelle, a notary, and Abramo Scazzocchio, a skilled attorney.[62] A few months later, though, to establish the amount of Benedetto Merizi's taxes, in credit with the *Universitas,*[63] those called upon to decide were Angelo di Venafro, a licensed banker since 1521,[64] and Prospero

---

57 Cfr., for example, the arbitration trios selected in NE, f. 2, l. 2, c. 27r; f. 2, l. 2, c. 38r; f. 2, l. 2, c. 64r-v (recorded respectively in Stow 1999, docs. 1350, 1399 and 1474).

58 Roberto Bonfil proposes a different reconstruction for the other Italian communities of the Renaissance, for which the scholar frequently emphasizes the specific and essential role of the rabbis in the administration of justice. Here this role is not, however, denied but at most, based on what emerges from the example examined for Rome in the years immediately preceding the institution of the ghetto, was proportioned for the community and the period cited; as is demonstrated below in this research, in fact, the "rabbinate" in the years of the ghetto will be an undisputed protagonist in the institutional life of the Roman community. Cfr. Bonfil 2012, pp. 195–249 and 1991, pp. 170–183.

59 Cited from Cohen 1999, which explains the relevant passages in the *Babylonian Talmud, Sanhedrin*, IV, 2.

60 Cohen 1999, pp. 363–368.

61 Cfr., for example, the division of roles between rabbi-arbitrators and moneylender-procurators, in NE, f. 2, l. 2, c. 25r-v (found in Stow 1999, docs. 1343 e 1344).

62 NE, f. 7, l. 1, cc. 158v-163v. For the registries of documents relevant to this case, cfr. Stow 1999, docs. 1028, 1029, 1033, 1038, 1045. On Abramo Scazzocchio, see Stow 2002.

63 NE, f. 7, l. 1, c. 185 r-v (registries in Stow 1999, doc. 1079).

64 Esposito 2002, p. 576.

di Ceprano, a *Fattore* on several occasions, in 1552 and then in 1555.[65] Again in 1552 we find a similar choice was made, this time for bankers Leone di Murcia and Vito di Capua to settle the outstanding accounts between the *Scola Castigliana e Francese* and its former *parnas*.[66]

Things, however, were destined to change. Twenty years later, in 1576, in a now fully functioning ghetto, Servadio Cracolo and Salvatore Corcos requested the intervention of Isacco Gioioso and Israel Provenzale in a dispute over determining the size of a dowry and the interest that had accumulated with it.[67] The first was the descendant of a dynasty of moneylenders and holder of a special privilege for bankers,[68] while the second was instead of much more obscure origins. The appellation *maskil ve navon* is used for both of them, a title that indicated a person who was following rabbinic training, and who could therefore be considered reasonably competent on the subject.[69] The following July, in order to formally establish the boundaries and ownership of some market and butchery stalls, the *Fattori* once again nominated an arbitration trio composed of *maskilim*; Giacobbe Gioioso, Israel Provenzale and Samule di Lattes.[70] Even a controversy over the distribution of the profits obtained from a tax collection contract ended up, in those days, entrusted to rabbi and notary Isacco delle Piattelle, along with Rubino Avdon, an important banker who was shortly thereafter awarded a lending license.[71] Then, in 1590, in an effort to resolve a serious debate over a banking policy, Iechiel Sacerdoti di Viterbo del fu Mechallel and Sabbato Serena di Lustro asked for a binding ruling from Pompeo del Borgo, the commercial notary and rabbi, and Aron di Venafri, who,

---

65   Respectively, NE, f. 7, l. 1, c. 231r (register in Stow 1999, doc. 1226) and NE, f. 2, l. 1, c. 10r and c. 30r (register in Stow 1999, docs. 1728 and 1731).

66   NE, f. 7, l. 1, c. 217r (register in Stow 1999, doc. 1179). On bankers Leone di Murcia and Vito di Capua, cfr. Esposito 2002, pp. 576–580.

67   NE, f. 9, l. 1, c. 1r.

68   DC, r. 392, c. 113v.

69   The same term appears on tombstones in Padua from the 1600s. For an analysis of its use and significance see Malkiel 2014, p. 295, notes 68 and 69: "'Educated' and 'wisest' are written in Hebrew, but 'of the Fellows' is in Aramaic, in a clear allusion to the Talmudic expression 'smallest of the Fellows', used in reference to a *junior student or a colleague in the rabbinical academy*" (italics mine). A similar gradation of rabbinic titles is found in Lugo between the 17th and 18th centuries, as demonstrated in Elena Lolli's rich PhD dissertation (2019).

70   NE, f. 9, l. 1, cc. 3v-4r.

71   NE, f. 9, l. 1. c. 16r. Rubino Avdon will end up among the owners of a license in the concession granted by *Cardinal Camerlengo* in the following February (DC, r. 377, cc. 6v-8v); in June of 1578, in a confirmation of the prestige he had reached, he will also obtain the related *Inhibitio in Curia ratione foenoris* (DC, r. 379, cc. 18v-19r).

like Rubino Avdon in the preceding case, was probably called in the role of expert, as he was member of an important family of moneylenders.[72] Back in 1577, moreover, the same Rubino Avdon, who was a *Fattore* at the time, would enlist the *maskil* Salomone Corcos to resolve an ongoing conflict between the *Universitas* and Mosè Menasci for the restitution of a guarantee made on a community contract.[73]

Therefore a change was underway in the second half of the 16th century, as attested to by the selection of the arbitration trios and the increasingly frequent appearance of *rabbis* in them. Whether it was large or small, it is undeniable that this change should be seen as a powerful sign of the process of adaption to external pressures, which with ever growing force sought to tear Jewish society apart. The problem remains, however, of clearly defining what a rabbi was at that time in Rome. Roberto Bonfil's studies have amply demonstrated that the Jewish community was not guided by rabbis of international prestige and extraordinary culture during this period. Nevertheless it is clear that, for one reason or another, a significant number of the men who took on institutional responsibilities in the community were classified as *maskilim* in the Jewish documentation.[74] Based on the sources that I have examined –documents drawn up by Jewish notaries – it is not possible to clarify exactly what earned this title: it might have meant the partial completion of a genuine rabbinic degree conferred by other, already titled rabbis, or the completion of a less challenging course of study. It's also possible the title was instead considered more simply as a sort of honorific to be obtained by hours of study, but without examinations and the effort connected with the pursuit of ordination.[75]

---

72   NE, f. 9, l. 2, cc. 80v-81r. An Angelo da Venafri appears since the first list of licensed moneylenders (Esposito 2002, p. 576); later both Mosè and Dattilo are awarded two different licenses in 1577 (DC, r. 377, cc. 6v-8v); in the following May Mosè obtains, for himself and his brothers, the *inhibitio* (Ibidem, r. 377, c. 12v), then reconfirmed in 1584 to Dattilo (Ibidem, r. 388, c. 51v) and in 1588 another Mosè *fu* Giacobbe was granted a license, even over the normal number of 55 (Ibidem, r. 394, c. 22r).

73   NE, f. 9, l. 1, c. 30v. Salamone Corcos' rabbinic title is reported, for example, in NE, f. 9, l.1, c. 57r-v. Although it is complicated distinguishing between the many Salomone Corcoses cited in the sources available to me, even more for the variations in language in which these were compiled, it is beyond doubt that moneylending was the family business; two Salomone Corcoses, one the son of the late Elia, the other of Salvatore, appear among the licensees of 1577 (DC, r. 377, cc. 6v-8v). The term *maskil* normally refers to a person that has studied without, however, completing rabbinic ordination.

74   Bonfil 2012, in particular pp. 165–173.

75   A precise discussion of the problems connected to the presence or lack of ordination is in Bonfil 2012, pp. 35–93. An example regarding this terminological confusion is in Cooperman 2015, note 83.

Furthermore, it must be considered that the wording is often confused and does not draw a clear and indisputable boundary between actual rabbis, who can perform the functions of *daian* and *maskilim*, and those who perhaps could not but in reality ended up being qualified as such. In this book, therefore, the titles *maskil* and *rabbi* are used in a general sense. For the purposes of my research it is important to focus on how the title of *maskil* was felt to be necessary for those who were named as arbitrators or administrators, whether because behind the title was the implied trust of their peers, or that, more simply, because it was seen as a guarantee of the good conduct and fear of God of the person chosen. However one wishes to read it, these are dynamics of the minority's self-representation of that cannot be overlooked, and which, not by chance, appear on the scene during the phase of institutional, identity, cultural, and social crisis and redefinition that characterized the second half of the 16th century.[76]

4   Housing Problems and Issues with Taxes

If things had stopped at this point, by all accounts there would have not have been much to be surprised about. The procedure based on *arbitration* remained unchanged, and in certain situations asking legal technicians, the rabbis, to rule on legal questions that involved Jews did not in and of itself represent something exceptional. At most it allowed a significant and inexorable drift compared to the preceding period (during which the rabbis were only involved in particularly intricate judgements, and in the role of third arbitrator *super partes*) and a return, in the Roman community as well, to a strict observance of the law.[77] In short, by the middle of the century, with the era of powerful nation-class disputes brought to an end by the now peaceful installment of bankers, from whatever Scola they came from, in key positions of the *Universitas*' self-government, this alignment with the strictest interpretation of the law could also be considered the sign of a simple readjustment. After all, the tradition specified that the arbitrator/fact-checkers should, in fact, be expert rabbis, capable of making decisions according to

---

76   I am referring to the fitting definition proposed by Carlotta Ferrara degli Uberti for the Risorgimento phase (2017).

77   In effect, from this point of view, in the last quarter of the 1500s the Jewish arbitrators of Rome worked in line with the practices reconstructed by Roberto Bonfil for the other Italian communities from which the Roman experience seems to be significantly different in the preceding period; cfr. Bonfil 2012.

the law by virtue of their learning. An effort to assure the legitimacy of rulings made by those who did not formally have this power never completely failed, and was realized by precisely the notarial legal force guaranteed by Leone and Isacco delle Piattelle in their registries during those years. In this sense, recourse to a protocol in Hebrew can be interpreted as the choice to have a genuine rabbinic consultation available, drafted in the form of a document which was invested with *publica fides*, and which was therefore valid in front of a Christian court.[78] The point, however, is that little by little, due to the external situation and the insecurity it created, this role became significantly broader than what was prescribed by a very solid tradition, going well beyond the certification of the Jewish notaries and participation in arbitration.

As the reality of confinement in the ghetto gradually came to be accepted in all its aspects, certainty about the law became an urgent necessity for the Jews. The main problem was housing, and disputes over property ownership were on the agenda. The issue of the distribution of living spaces was not entirely new. A centuries-old rule, the *takana* of Rabbi Gershom, had firmly regulated the relations between Jewish tenants, other Jews, and Christian owners since the 11th century, preventing coreligionists from taking the few rooms available in the Jewish streets of the city away from one other. Following the institution of the ghetto, the rights of tenants were guaranteed by *jus gazaga*, a special legal principle whose uniqueness is signaled in the choice of wording used to name it (one half in Latin, the other in Hebrew). *Jus gazaga* established a fixed rate for rents, preventing the Christian owners of homes where only Jews were permitted to live from taking excessive advantage of the situation. This legal mechanism ended up granting an unwritten right of possession (similar to that in civil uses) to Jewish tenants, who, both under Rabbi Gershom's provision and on the basis of *jus gazaga*, could not, in fact, be evicted.[79] Because of this, the ownership of *gazagot* was considered to be a very precious commodity. Just as with shares of lending licenses and market spaces, ownership of this privilege was specially protected, divided into personal claims, used as part of dowries, or as an exchange and a guarantee in sales between Jews, and was transferable only through a notary's deed.

---

78 In my interpretation, therefore, this is not the creation of a "virtual" community through the tools of the notary, but rather offering the real community juridical tools that met their needs. It should be recalled that these agreements could be drafted by a Christian notary as well, as demonstrated in the many works of Anna Esposito. On this subject also see Stow 2001, p. 109.
79 On this subject, see still Laras 1968. More recently, on Rome: Gasperoni, Groppi 2018.

The intersection of differing laws regarding a Jew's most important possession – the ownership of an apartment in a world that suffered from an endemic lack of space – meant that decisions about the issue had to be made with caution. In addressing these matters it was crucial to act not only with full respect for the complex legal universe in which they had to be deliberated, but also with an awareness of the social impact that certain decisions could bring with them, both among the individual families involved and among the entire group.[80] This policy of caution went beyond the central question of the ownership of rooms and furniture to include issues that were seemingly unrelated, but all in need of finding shared solutions among the Jews without crossing over to dangerous legal complications. Turning to the outside and appealing to a genuine court, in fact, encouraged the authorities' interference in the business of the ghetto. That meant, first of all, the authority of the Vicar (who had general jurisdiction over the Jews of Rome), who was himself looking for any occasion to complicate the lives of those who lived in the ghetto. The presentation of some actual cases helps to identify the terms of the problem.

In 1576, a dispute arose between Salvatore Corcos, his son Salomone, and the Jewish Community of Rome, represented by the Congregation of Sixty, regarding the amount of taxes allocated to them and some unliquidated collateral. Considering the social stature of the characters entangled in the suit and the good relations that the Corcos family (a dynasty of rabbis, bankers and *Fattori*) enjoyed across the walls of the ghetto, everything possible was done to resolve the issue within the bounds "of obedience to our holy Torah." The "lawyers of the holy and terrible Commission" granted the opposing counsel abundant time for presenting their arguments, agreed to have the case split into two different strands, and presented notice after notice to induce the Corcos men to explain themselves, and to assure that these clarifications would be "heard by all Israel" and fully comply with the dictates of the Law.[81] Even the notary Isacco, who had personally administered the oaths of the three commissioners under the oversight of two other *rabbis*, took care to transcribe into Italian the sentence issued by the tribunal, which presided together with a third colleague

---

80   So, for example, from the moment of stipulating a nine-year rental contract for "a room on the side that faces the opening of that room onto *via di Passatore*" in the home of "Messer Giovanni Maria Cremonesi, carpenter beside the river," through a Hebrew deed by Isacco Delle Piattelle, the Christian owner, by obliging the tenant, Samuele Capellaro, to maintain residence there for the entire agreed upon time period, and prohibiting him from having guests or lodgers of any kind, was guarding against any changes of mind or subletting that would trigger the sanctions related to the takana of Rabbi Gershom (NE, f. 9, l. 1, c. 7r).

81   NE, f. 9, l. 1, cc. 57v-58r.

and consisted of, other than the two *rabbis*, three bankers. To guarantee the formal and legal correctness of the arbitrators' work, the ruling was signed only by the two respected rabbis.[82] Not finding anything to object to regarding the wording of the opinion, the Corcos family attempted to invalidate it by lodging a new complaint with the *Fattori*, meant to demonstrate the bad faith of the entire Congregation in their designation of these judges. The accusation was that the Congregation, made up of incompetent and ignorant people, had conspired to fraudulently select a jury of experts who were known adversaries of one of the parties in the case. Openly exempted from all these charges was the notary, who was repeatedly referred to as "respected," and the only person involved whose behavior did not raise any objections. The accusations against the selected technical trio and the Congregation that chose them were quite serious, and it was only the involvement of the rabbis and the notary in the hearing that prevented the case from leaving Jewish jurisdiction and being presented to the Christian authorities, as would have happened earlier:

> They changed the order and turned the jar [*in which were the black and white balls used for voting*] on its mouth [...] and it was not their will to go and make requests for peace in righteousness and faithfulness because their will was to hurt me with all their strength [...] and I am stunned that they have assembled people to hear this case who are known by all to hate me and due to this as is commonly known I will not discuss or speak with these people in any way or manner because hate destroys the ranks and I am a man who shares a home with a snake and I well know that to your eyes blocking my grievances is the only way [...] but the truth of the earth will bloom and justice will take its course and thus for now know and understand that I am he who is clear in the eyes of the Lord and of Israel and that they demand arguments and allegations and false accusations and the good Lord will bless the good and the upright in their hearts [...].[83]

On a similar occasion, some time prior to the Corcos case, after finding it impossible to reach an agreement with the Congregation of Sixty, the Ceprano family and the three arbitrators who had deliberated over the taxes owed by the family decided unanimously to send the case to two inspectors. However, these

---

[82] In order: the first two rabbis were Prospero Sacerdoti e Giacobbe Gioioso, the third was Beniamino Zadiq; the bankers were Rubino Avdon, Casciano Ram and Durante delli Sestieri (NE, f. 9, l. 1, c. 58v).

[83] NE, f. 9, l. 1, c. 59r.

inspectors would have been bound by the opinion of one or two experts who were surely unfamiliar with the argument and therefore, so that their honesty would not be called in to question, they could have even been Christians.[84] In that particular case, the resounding failure of the hearing commissioned to the rabbis led to the addition of a new group to oversee the case. To keep the matter inside the ghetto, a new strategy was employed: two other Jews, for the moment anonymous, were entrusted with taking charge of a decision that had really been requested of others.

Rabbinic authority was normally more than sufficient for settling differences. In just one year, for example, this authority was invoked, as we have seen, to permanently define the borders of a market space, as well as for a wide range of issues which came in rapid succession in the autumn of 1576, such as the awarding of a tax collection contract to Michele di Palestrina, which was decided by a trio of *Fattori*, among whom was the knowledgeable Salomone Corcos;[85] the equal division of part of the late Giacobbe Rosciello's inheritance between his sons and the *Universitas*, which was entrusted to the "great sages" Giacobbe Gioioso and Samuele Anav:[86] a decision regarding the distribution of the profits from a partnership, assigned to Rubino Avdon with the doctrinal support of the notary Isacco;[87] or, finally, a decision regarding another contested inheritance between one of the three *Fattore*, Durante del Sestier, and the family of the late Gabriele di Tagliacozzo, which was delegated to Elia Corcos and *rabbino* Israel Provenzale at the request of the other two *Fattori*.[88]

At times the precaution was taken to call a rabbi in on a case even when peace reigned supreme. Thus in 1588, for example, the *parnassim* (administrators) of the *Commissione dei Prestatori* (Angelo Capuano and Giacobbe Corcos) requested a pair of rabbis (Salomone Corcos and Beniamino Zadik) to be among the colleagues assigned to the Commission's council for the following year. The rabbinic authority of some of the commission members was meant to temper any future controversy within the group of rich and powerful bankers.[89]

Keeping a group united that was anything but was an urgent task. Reasons for tension arose from the diverse economic and cultural conditions of

---

84   NE, f. 9, l. 1, c. 50r.
85   NE, f. 9, l. 1, cc. 5v-6r.
86   NE, f. 9, l. 1, c. 7r.
87   NE, f. 9, l. 1, c. 16r.
88   NE, f. 9, l. 1, cc. 20r-23v.
89   NE, f. 9, l. 2, c. 75v.

its members, the conflicting groups of far flung nationalities, rivalries, and in the ancient liturgical antagonisms, and these only grew with the institution of the ghetto. The path for resisting these powerful disruptive pressures was found within Jewish society. Though it was impossible to prevent the outbreak of arguments, as we've seen, the community slowly worked to moderate the conflicts, not through the negation of the causes for the conflicts, which was anyway unachievable, but through the reinforcement of the authority of those who from time to time were called upon to resolve them, or at least by creating conditions that would prevent conflicts from spilling over to the outside. In a word, the *curriculum* of those who aspired to be *Fattori* progressively broadened, just as had happened for those who would be arbitrators, and as a way to confront widespread uncertainty, rabbinic training was added to banking expertise as one of the preferred qualifications for the position. Religious learning was considered to be the one and only form of knowledge that could assure the fairness and legitimacy of the decisions made by the highest judiciary, whether that meant adjudicating a contract, settling a dispute, or placing its solution in other hands.[90] So, *maskil* Salomone Corcos was twice one of the three *Fattori* between 1576 and 1578,[91] and *maskil* Giacobbe Gioioso served among them in 1583.[92] In the following years this position was occupied several times by *maskil* Salomone Corcos (in 1579 and 1585)[93] and by his colleagues Eliezer Prospero Coen di Viterbo (1581, 1582 and 1588)[94] and Israel Provenzale (1579 and 1580).[95] The fact that in all of these cases the rabbis were also bankers, or close relatives of bankers, indicates how the qualification of banker was now a title, but no longer the fundamental prerequisite for holding the position. So it was that, thanks to the prestige of rabbinic authority, and despite a lively tradition of fierce conflicts in the community, a quite radical transformation took place in the years of the ghetto without inflicting any damage. It was an excellent solution, devised by a small and combative minority stubbornly defending its very identity.

---

90   Useful reflections in this direction can be traced for the preceding period related to the authority of rabbis of other communities over events in third party communities. In particular the reflections advanced by Cooperman regarding the Bolognese proclamation of 1511 are of great interest: "The issue itself was a longstanding one in European Jewish History and reflects the problem inherent in maintaining discipline and coherence for a group with no central authority" (2004, p. 370).
91   NE, f. 9, l. 1, cc. 5v-6r e f. 9, l. 1, c. 69r.
92   NE, f. 3, l. 2, c. 91v.
93   NE, f. 9, l. 1, c. 75v e f. 9, l. 2, c. 25v.
94   NE, f. 3, l. 2, c. 34v; f. 3, l. 2, c. 41v e f. 9, l. 2, c. 59r.
95   NE, f. 9, l. 1, cc. 114r-115v e f. 9, l. 1, c. 125r.

5   The Discipline of the Rabbis

The ascent of the rabbinate to key roles in community governance was a novelty of the ghetto. If, in fact, as Roberto Bonfil has claimed, having a son who was a rabbi was for the Jews of the Renaissance equivalent to having a son who was a priest for the families of the urban "bourgeoisie," this did not normally imply that scholars were directly involved in the management of Jewish public life. Up to that time the rabbis' role had been to educate the younger generations, fortify consciences, compile and preserve the archives of the *Universitates* in the role of *soferim* and, at most, reinforced by the deterrent of Jewish excommunication, which they alone had the power to execute, resolve disputes over issues that were exclusively Jewish in nature, such as marriages. Up to that time the job of equally dividing taxes between members of a community had not been part of their responsibilities, just as organizing the procedure for awarding the contracts for tax collection had not been either. Before the ghettos became operational, the rabbis of Rome were only occasionally called in to trials in order to establish rights and wrongs based on Jewish law. Sometimes their intervention was requested regarding other questions, but up through the first half of the 16th century nobody would have considered turning to a rabbi to establish the exact physical location and monetary value of commercial properties.

The times had changed, and already by the years 1553–1554 (thus after the burnings of the *Talmud*), the title of rabbi had taken on new importance. Given that access to complete versions of the fundamental texts of Jewish wisdom was impossible, the scholars' knowledge became increasingly central, both during the teaching and memorized repetition of the precepts and commentaries, as well as in the equally essential phase of making decisions and offering responses which had to be consistent with the complex, codified, but continually evolving system of the *halakha*. 1555 represented a second breaking point in a process of revolution that was already underway, which was quickly brought to extreme consequences in the management of the new situation. At a time when the material aspects of every Jew's life were being regulated, they began to seek, beyond only the technical opinion of someone who by occupation had expertise regarding the issue at hand, and who enjoyed good relations with the political powers, the endorsement of someone who could guarantee that the decisions were in line with the teachings of the Fathers.

The desire to soften Jewish resistance to conversion through the imposition of material and spiritual suffering which is summarized in the strategy of the ghetto led, on one hand, to a progressive increase of religious influence in Jewish self-governance and, on the other hand, to a general alignment with the perspective of religious orthodoxy in the Jews' attitudes toward the trials and difficulties of life. Although there have not yet been any treatises investigated that offer a contemporary internal examination the new reality of the ghetto and the changes that it brought about in the Jewish worldview, and data from other communities is not available, a systematic investigation of the registries of the Jewish notaries of Rome – which are witnesses to the ongoing transformation – reveals the growing role of the rabbis with unquestionable clarity, both quantitatively and qualitatively: we find many rabbis involved in a wide range of community issues, from the resolution of arbitrations to procedural and government responsibilities, in numbers and assignments far greater than those recorded in the years immediately preceding the promulgation of *Cum nimis absurdum*.

According to this interpretation, the inclusion of rabbis in the response devised within the closed-off ghetto for resisting the eschatological and anti-Jewish demands aroused by the Reformation, as well as the doctrinal and legal thought that emerged from the Council of Trent, whatever its effectiveness was, inserts the specific affairs of a marginal minority group within a general and widespread trend that included all the many Christian denominations of Europe, though in different forms and with different tools.[96] The dynamics encountered in a specific place and time – the Jewish community of Rome in the years of the Counter-reformation – reveal lines of continuous communication between Jews and Christians that somehow, in spite of the erection of physical and cultural barriers that were accepted by both of the parties involved, continued to function and create occasions for exchange in different environments that were not limited to simple economic subsistence. The institutional processes implemented within the ghetto demonstrate, once again, the persistent manifestation of cultural transmission, which was somehow inevitable even in a society of diverse and unequal groups, deeply and consciously discriminatory towards the other.

In this sense, the rise of the rabbis to positions of power – or really, for Jewish communities, to key roles in the management of the tax policies of the

---

96 For a historiographic discussion of the phenomenon of confessionalization and its relations to that of social regulation, referral to the classical dossier by Paolo Prodi (1994) is required, with particular reference to the essays by Bruckner, Reinhard and Schilling. Moreover, Giovanni Miccoli (1974) had already begun discussing "rigid organizational recovery, harshly disciplined and mercilessly repressive" (p.996), and "strengthening of discipline and thus a restoration of custom and ecclesiastical organization" (p. 1000) towards the end of "greater regulation of the ecclesiastical structure, firmly composed under a Roman authority that is incredibly more powerful and undisputed than before" (p. 1077).

Universitas – could be an indication of a process of progressive "sacralization" of the community institutions. If this idea was confirmed by findings in different sources and places, this would be an interesting process to consider. Inasmuch, therefore, as rabbinic authority rested on the knowledge gained over years of difficult study (and not on a position of special relations with the divine), Jewish society's choice to make direct use of the guarantees which that wisdom could offer in the management of conflicts and ordinary administration may have echoed, albeit in different terms, solutions devised to similar problems in the Christian world.[97] Physical separation from the surrounding society, made even more difficult by continued humiliations and repeated invitations to abandon the religion of their fathers, did not succeed in definitively excluding the Jews from the historical processes that were underway around them. This is a crucial fact that must be taken into consideration in the reconstruction of these phenomena and the success of the models they established. Through the appropriation of external cultural paradigms and their transfiguration into acceptable forms,[98] the Jewish experience, even closed in the ghetto, remained an integral part of society well beyond the happy years of the Renaissance, albeit manifested differently and despite having been explicitly set aside at its borders, and it should be considered as such, to avoid forcing Roman Jewish society into a kind of posthumous and historiographical ghettoization.

The Jews, therefore, to keep from falling into the hands of the preaching fathers, decided to place their trust in those they felt were the strongest and safest: the hands of the rabbis.[99] After the Council of Trent the Church of Rome closed the ranks of the shepherds charged with protecting the flock of Christ and struggled, through confession and propaganda, to defend the souls of believers. In those same years the Jewish world, which had also fallen prey to a new uncertainty, largely caused by the measures they had to adopt in confronting the many and varied demands of Christian purification, also aimed at better strengthening consciences and institutions that were under serious attack.

---

97 Cfr. on this subject see at least the classic work edited by Kellenbenz and Prodi 1989; Reinhard 1989; an obvious reference on the theme is Prodi 1982.
98 For a detailed analysis of these forms of cultural appropriation that were typical of Renaissance Italian Jewry, and of this definition of them, cfr. Bonfil 1991; an interpretation of some phenomena of acculturation, understood, however, as the only way to preserve a form of Jewish culture in Christian society, and not as an element in a continuing dialog between groups and clearly distinct identities, is in Stow 2001.
99 Renata Segre reconstructs, instead, an inverse process based on the Venetian experience in which rabbis were relegated solely to the role of teachers (1996, pp. 770–771).

It was a need felt by all, the clearest signal of which is the professional choice made by the merchant Pompeo del Borgo, the rabbi notary who wrote in Italian.[100] These were the same years in which other rabbis began to collaborate closely with bankers – among whose ranks, moreover, many rabbis, such as Salomone Corcos, counted themselves – in the guidance, material as well as spiritual, of a Jewish community committed to surviving their new and adverse circumstances with the means they had available. In the end, ghetto or no ghetto, the existence of a combative minority in the heart of Catholicism translated into the contemporaneous development of social and cultural processes that were common, or at least similar, between the Jewish world and the Christian world. One group was assailed by the eschatological anxiety of the majority that surrounded it, the other by the fear of heresy and the unexpected discovery of Christianity's fragility. In those years everyone was looking for cultural representatives who could be trusted with the disciplined management of life and institutions.

In the heart of the society of the many Christian denominations in different lands and States the process was certainly not uniform, much less linear. However one wants to interpret it, the period spanning the 1500s and 1600s involved, in a large part of Europe, a prevalent phase of deep and universal attention to faith and orthodoxy, and to the correct behavior of individuals, groups, and institutions, about which States and Churches intervened in defense of their own interests, in various ways and by different means, at times united, at times in conflict with one another. The manifestation of this process in the Jewish realm, as it emerges from the reconstruction of the Roman case, was a phenomenon of another nature. Here, the need to protect the alternative identity of a besieged community, which was being lured by all means available to accept the renunciation of their otherness, could not help but be shared with conviction both by the faithful and by experts in religious matters.

The Jews of Rome, who were proud precisely because they were *giudii romani*, survived three centuries in the ghetto due to a historical capacity to close ranks and keep the group united in the face of hardships, despite the fact that the continued tensions between competing demands, personalities and interests (primarily economic in nature in a world so multifaceted and stratified) often caused disagreements to flare violently. The choice to entrust control over the most critical questions and the management of disputes to the rabbis (and not only the well-known ones) can be read from different perspectives.

---

100   See also the contemporaneous case of Debora Ascarelli reconstructed in Procaccia M. 2007b.

The rise of religious influence in Roman Jewish society could, undoubtedly, represent a symptom of an inevitable Jewish acculturation to the surrounding society, where central cultural elements were lost during the long yet victorious battle they fought to remain Jews. From this perspective, the main victims of this intellectual loss (induced by the unavailability of the Talmud) would therefore have been knowledge of Hebrew and the lack of progress in the study of *halakha*, leading to a general decline of Judaism in the community.

Or, more plausibly, as I have sought to demonstrate, the same phenomenon could be an indication of Italian Jews' traditional ability to remain inside history, even if in adverse conditions. The Jews of Italy reworked the ideas and stimuli currently in play in the surrounding majority society based on their own cultural specificity, ultimately transforming them and making them legitimate for Jews. In this second, and in my opinion more convincing interpretation, the key to success must be looked for in the uninterrupted flow of exchanges between the Jewish world and the Christian world. Due precisely to the unresolved ambivalence of the strategy of inclusion/exclusion that led to its creation in the heart of papal Rome, the ghetto ended up encouraging these exchanges. While negotiating the price of a pawn, the sale of a second hand fabric, playing dice, getting involved in a stoning or a brawl, buying or selling goods of any type, and sometimes even engaging in illicit carnal trade, Jews and Christians ended up meeting in a daily sharing of rituals, spaces and time in the holy city.

The phenomenon of the religious regulation of Jewish society was a result of segregation, and developed through a continuous channel of communication with the majority society, their problems and their solutions. This did not result in the creation of a consecrated space that was separate from the surrounding world, governed by its own rules, unable to function outside the protective walls and thus inevitably misconstrued and isolated. The reality of Jewish society in Rome and in its ghetto was complex, multifaceted, and rich in contrasting aspects, but it was also very much the reality of a Jewish society under siege. Despite this, acting in response to external stresses, and in line with a prevalent development at the time, the choice was made to place their cultural survival in the hands of the rabbis and Jewish law. Thus the importance of the traditions and *halakha* grew, developing in full awareness of the events and developments happening outside the ghetto and through a process of complex social and cultural evolution that occurred in continuous dialogue with the outside, in which, however, there was no possible confusion about the true nature of relations between Jews and Christians. It is good to recall that these rabbis, other than being teachers and scholars, were also merchants, jewelers, antique dealers and bankers, involved in their businesses. Thus they were in continuous contact with the facts of daily life in the city and with Christians: this allowed them to hold the group firm in their otherness without irrevocably removing it from the world and its stories.

This is not to say that this change made it possible to eradicate even just a small part of the internal conflicts within the group.[101] The criminal records in the Italian archives preserve hundreds and hundreds of trials naming Jews, with other Jews in the roles of witnesses, victims and accusers. These records are proof of an ever growing incidence of often violent disputes and arguments. It is useful to review an example of one of these trials, remaining in Rome and in the range of years examined in this book. The case was the result of a series of violations of Jewish law as well as local laws, and gives us the opportunity to ask how, despite the fact that transgressions like this were undeniably frequent (if not daily), the group managed to survive in its otherness and contentiousness.

In the second half of the 1500s, the strengthening of the arbitration procedure and the establishment of the *lodo intra hebraeos* became essential aspects of life in the ghetto, and were accompanied by a redefinition of tasks and perspectives within Jewish society. The transformation of the role of rabbis and their increasing presence in the governing of Jewish institutions is an element of great importance, which has much to do with the ghetto system and with the reshaping of Jewish society it imposed. The distinction between political roles – the *Fattorato* and the *Tesorierato* – and responsibilities which were explicitly rabbinical – for example the control of the closure of shops at the beginning of Shabbat, or the management of conflicts – remained clear, at least on paper. In practice, the title of rabbi began to have importance in the selection of the ruling class and in its processes of self-identification as such. To count for something and be included in the restricted circle of those who

---

101 Although from another point of view, Berliner's considerations on this subject, based on some disputes from 1573, are of interest: "These examples demonstrate how the disciplinary power of the community had strengthened, and how they no longer shrank from the exercise of criminal jurisdiction due to the fear that those who were penalized would seek revenge through apostasy or false accusations. Within the confines in which they could move, the community's government found, when it needed to, sufficient support from the pontifical authorities to which the Jewish collective was subject" (1992, p. 198). An important definition in this direction is that of "traditional society" for medieval Ashkenazim advanced by Jacob Katz (1993), which, however, does not seem to adapt to the Roman case delineated here, precisely due to the evident differences between the two examples, as much for the tensions between Jews and Christians, as for the significance of the dialectic between society and institutions that are internal and external to the Jewish world.

counted for something, one had to come from certain families, practice a high level profession, maintain prestigious contacts with Christian society and also receive a solid training in Judaism, which could result in the attainment of the title of rabbi.

In the midst of the 17th century, the excellent biography of Tranquillo Vita Corcos speaks for itself: an illustrious dynasty, wealth, important relationships, and both Rabbi and *Fattore*. The elaboration of this dual focus model, where cultural and professional successes and confirmations had equal value, sheds light on the processes of construction and reconstruction of religious membership in such a difficult context. If, in fact, at the helm of the Jewish world were those who had completed Jewish studies with such excellence as be called "maestro," this means that, in some sense, excellence in Judaism was attributed a specific value in ghetto society. And it is on this that we must still reflect. The ghetto was encapsulated in Christian society, and the daily interactions between the Jewish group and the Christian group were an inevitable and indispensable part of life. Jews and Christians came into contact day after day, talking, gathering, buying and selling together, arguing, sometimes even coming to blows. However, in the end, despite everything, the vast majority of Jews decided to return to the ghetto. This was true for the *Fattori*, the illustrious rabbis, for the rich and the poor; it was true for those who accepted litigation and negotiation through internal Jewish arbitration and those who, instead, immediately turned to Christian justice.

6 Jewish Identity: a Trial for Crimes and Other Excesses in 1572

In 1572, the Criminal Court of the Governor found itself judging a case involving a series of thefts committed in the ghetto by a group of Jews who had stolen from the wealthiest among their coreligionists, with the cooperation of Christian junk dealers, whose job was to sell off the stolen goods. The thieves had acted with impunity week after week, stealing commonly used objects from the terraces of the homes of the richest Jews. All of the thefts were perpetrated on Friday nights immediately after sundown, at the start of Shabbat, while the families of the ghetto were either in synagogue or around the table for Shabbat dinner. They certainly weren't capable of imagining this kind of violation of the weekly day of sacred rest. As the investigations progressed, beginning with the arrest of the Jew Vituccio di Lanciano, who was surprised outside the ghetto at night, the position of the defendants worsened. Inquiries revealed a past of unpaid gaming debts and a network of acquaintances, friends and relatives that the judges found inextricable. All of the defendants, in fact, admitted to knowing each other on sight, owing to the fact that they were "*giudii.*" Likewise they admitted to knowing something about the burglaries that had been taking place and to maybe having occasionally taken part in one as an innocent observer – and little else.

In an attempt to untangle the mess, the magistrate decided to question another Jew – Sabbato del Corsetto, who had recently been acquitted of an accusation of involuntary homicide. Sabbato had been accused of this crime only because on the evening before the discovery of the corpse he had been seen furiously arguing with his wife in precisely the location where the body of the victim was found the following morning. As such, Sabbato was undoubtedly a witness to manage carefully. Not mincing words, he told of having been framed by the gossipers of the ghetto, who were always ready to make a family discussion into something much more serious, and to sling mud at innocent fellow Jews. As he described to the investigators, the machine of defamatory accusations was well-oiled and always in action within the Jewish enclosure. There were even some who would habitually denounce other Jews to the authorities, even three or four times, only to then retract the accusation and guarantee their release – after having pocketed sufficient payment from the relatives of the imprisoned. In his own case, Sabbato added, he too had been targeted, but the same thing could (and did) happen all the time to many others.[102] The documents that have reached us preserve the outcomes of the two proceedings: Sabbato was exonerated because he was extraneous to the case, while the leaders of the gang of thieves were condemned to permanent exile.[103] However, for the purposes of this reflection on Jewish society in the years of the ghetto, on the pervasiveness of external influences and the attempts to resist them, this aspect is completely secondary.

Beyond the laws and the punishments, the two intertwined cases from 1572 actually present a ranking of transgressions regarded as serious from a Jewish

---

102 The trial against Sabbato del Corsetto is in *Processi*, r. 140, caso 8, cc. 422r- 457r. Interesting considerations regarding the tensions among Jews have been advanced by Michele Luzzati based on a trial held in Lucca between 1471 and 1472, where the author correctly recalls how "Beyond any other consideration about the specific episode in Lucca, it should in any case be emphasized that this shows how very often the difficulties encountered by the Jews in different Italian urban environments traced their origins, obviously in the general context of widespread anti-Jewish prejudice, more from the complexity of interpersonal relations between Jews and Jews, between Jews and Christians, between clerics and lay people and between clerics and clerics, than from a genuine discriminatory "project" of the State or Ecclesiastical authorities" (2004, p. 279).

103 ASR, *Tribunale Criminale del Governatore, Registri di Sentenze*, 4, cc. 151r and 167v.

perspective. Because of this they are interesting in considering the phenomena of religion's growing influences in the society. While it is true, in fact, that the first arrest was carried out for a particular crime (a nighttime trip outside the ghetto walls) only because it was committed by a Jew, and that the investigations proceeded to uncover thefts and intersect with a homicide, the seriousness of Vituccio di Lanciano and company's violations becomes even more evident when examined from the point of view of Jewish traditions and laws. Interpreted this way, the obvious penalties for theft, murder and gambling were accompanied by the kind of infractions that were prosecuted only because they were committed by Jews within Jewish society; starting with, naturally, the endless litany of profanations of the Shabbath rest perpetrated by the gang of thieves. Without going into an in depth examination of the issue, it is easy to recognize elements in the story of a good nights' work for the handful of thieves that are quite far from the observance of Shabbat: theft, stolen goods moved in public places, work, their absence from the festive rituals typical of the day, and so on. In the same way, the picture of slander drawn by Sabbato del Corsetto cannot be overlooked, exactly because it was committed by Jews at the cost of other Jews, according to a system of allegations and accusations explicitly forbidden by Jewish law.

These events, like many others, demonstrate how impossible it is to describe the ghetto using the definition of a sanctified space that was separate and autonomous from the surrounding world.[104] The ghetto and its inhabitants lived the tensions of their era and of the place in which they unfolded, experiencing them, however, in a specific way that was peculiar to being Jewish. The thieves in Vituccio di Lanciano's company chose their targets from inside the group, carefully selecting the homes that were most exposed and the families who were likely to be slowest to notice the disappearance of an object of little value. The cold reasoning that led to the selection of Friday night as the ideal time for their activities was not random, but was, again, the result of a full awareness of the ways and customs of the society they belonged to, of which they had no doubts about wanting to remain a part.

It is difficult finding accurate information about the degree of orthodoxy in Jewish religious practices in such far off times.[105] What is certain is that, notwithstanding the actual infractions described, it is precisely their consciously Jewish nature – expressed by the timing of the thefts, adapted solely for crimes to be committed against Jews by other Jews, and in a strictly Jewish

---

[104] Feci 1998; Fosi 1998; Di Nepi 2007a; Di Sivo 2012.
[105] An interesting attempt for Ferrara in the 1700s is in Malkiel 2005.

space – that reveals, in its own way, the terms of a membership that was perhaps contentious, but certainly not questioned. The crimes are relative: there was a prank, and an unscrupulous use of opportunities, but not an irrevocable decision for conversion, thanks to which, it should be recalled, any problem could be smoothed over. The capacity for keeping the group Jewish was also the product of these types of dynamics; alongside a ruling class in continuous evolution, the commitment to preventing the conflicts that were most dangerous for the autonomy of the institution (such as those regarding taxes) from being resolved outside the community, the effort to educate and inform the Jews of Rome and their rabbis, and the intellectual strain of holding off the aggressive evangelizing, it is possible that these were accompanied by the intelligent management of the "sins" of the Jews. This would be an interesting subject for new studies and research.

It is a relentless game of mirrors, in which it is never easy to fully grasp where the borders lie between that which exclusively outside the ghetto and that which is entirely within it. The gang of Jewish thieves was able to rely on Christian (and convert) accomplices to quickly sell off their stolen goods. The officials of the *Universitas* moved incessantly between the care of their own personal affairs and the oversight of the interests of the group, through a continuous dialectic involving recognition among Jews, individual successes and legitimization by the Christian authorities. The inevitable osmosis between inside and outside did not, however, manage to erode the durable core of religious otherness at the heart of Roman Jewry, despite the fact that, at least in theory, the solicitations and promises of propaganda made the choice to abandon the ancestral faith easier and more reasonable.

7 Religious Belonging in Court?

The past and the future of the gang of thieves from 1572 played out in the ghetto, among intersecting disagreements, jealousies and vendettas. The story of Sabbato del Corsetto and Vituccio di Lanciano is not exceptional, at least from this point of view. Several years later, in 1624, another group of Jews ended up summoning the police to the ghetto to have them search a room owned by a very wealthy merchant who was accused of sodomy. Two people were arrested and put through a lengthy trial that ended with a large fine, and without the merchant in question ever being summoned in front of the court: his business was conducted between Umbria and the Marche (obviously outside the ghetto), the testimonies could be taken even in his absence, and things moved forward, amidst conflicting legal medical assessments, and on this occasion, without any conversions of convenience.[106] There are many more examples, an inexhaustible range of personal affairs in which business and personal ties were inextricably intertwined in a constant coming and going between that which would seem to be take place exclusively within the Jewish group and that which, instead, happened on the outside.

Blurred boundaries were also a part of legal disputes. In 1620, Doralice Petrapauli, a Christian woman, denounced the Jew Salomone Scandriglia and his son-in-law Angelo to the Tribunale Criminale del Governatore, accusing them of cheating her on the sale of a batch of flour. But the two, who had previously had mutual differences, managed to reach a private agreement before they testified and poor Doralice was unable to do anything to get them to contradict each other.[107] Or again, returning to 1563, a furious controversy between two families around an annulled engagement went back and forth between the Christian court and the Jewish arbitrators, with rabbinic decisions and opinions translated into Italian, and great uncertainties for the Christian judges in dealing with a conflict that revolved around Jewish ceremonies and their correct meaning.[108]

Looking only at Jewish sources, there is a risk of recounting the ghetto and its rabbi administrators in a misleading manner, describing it as a sacralized and separate space. The ghetto and its inhabitants were part of the city, and living there they passed through it at any time and in a thousand ways. The limitations imposed on the Jews by extrernal authority contributed to the blurring of those boundaries, which not even the most rigorous internal identity laws were able to completely delineate. So, Vituccio and his group had gone about violating the Shabbat and exploiting this private and separate sacred time for criminal objectives with Christian accomplices; but this did not mean that they had renounced their Judaism.

The impossibility of separating inside and outside strongly distinguishes the three long centuries of segregation, and further explains the choices made in the period immediately following the promulgation of *Cum nimis absurdum*. This brings us back again to the ruling class and its almost impalpable transformations. The process of selecting arbitrators, and the parallel illustrious parables of the notaries Del Borgo and Delle Piattelle offer clues to the paradigm of identity – in which economic and social behavior play a part – which is at the heart of the minority's will to survive in the ghetto. It was necessary to rely on Jews who knew about Jewish things and had the expertise to explain them to

---

106   Di Nepi 2017.
107   Processi, r. 162.
108   I retrace this affair in two articles, to which I allow myself to refer: Di Nepi 2017 and 2019.

Jews, and also to Christians when needed. It was necessary that these Jewish things be incontestable under Jewish law and thus valid in court. In a dangerous world that daily invited crossing borders, the Jews of Rome consciously and individually chose to remain Jews – to not be like the others, and to return to sleep and argue in the ghetto, according to the rules that they stubbornly chose to follow – or violate, but only to a certain point. On May 8, 1848, while the Springtime of the People roiled Europe and the Italian cities rose up dreaming of Unity, in Rome, the *Università degli Ebrei* circulated this peremptory notice:

> In our former *hascama* we thought it appropriate to wait for the long period of time that has passed, and due to some abuses that have been introduced to remind our brothers and enjoin them to the strict observance of the ancient religious provisions concerning differences and the arguments that can arise between scuole and pious Corporations, and so to not spend large sums at the expense of the poor, and with mutual dishonor in sustaining disputes, they should submit the whole thing to arbitration [...] There has been a misunderstanding and some think that this does not concern individuals [...][109]

The word *hascama* (in Hebrew in the document) refers to the rabbinic authority that supports and validates the internal procedure of arbitration. Almost three centuries after the deeds and procedures developed by the Jewish notaries of Rome and two centuries after the official conclusion of this rabbinical notarial experiment (1640), it was formal rabbinic validation that gave force and meaning to a voluntary, internal proceeding. In the meantime the world had changed; Napoleon and his reforms had once and for all buried the common law and its overlapping jurisdictions, the Pope's government faltered as never before, and in Rome the Jews had tasted the thrill of freedom. Yet the basic rules of Jewish life remained the same, and those who day after day confirmed their desire to remain Jewish were asked to accept them, at least in part. And this means that, at least on paper, the first step in any dispute had to be managed internally; if this did not succeed then it was another story.

The uneven development of this process of precarious equilibrium will be examined in the following pages of this book, through a consideration of the professions of the Jewish ruling class and the changes in the organization of the most prestigious occupations brought about by the restrictions imposed in the modern era. Here it is interesting to point out another aspect: the relocation

---

109   ASCER, *Università degli Ebrei di Roma, 209.*

to the ghetto did not resolve the conflicts within the group, and in all probability it actually accentuated them (but, in the absence of a statistical study of the issue, we are not sure about the numbers). Precisely because of this, in the effort to contain the difficulties produced by the lack of living space, by overcrowding, by the anxieties of the moment, by the dread of poverty, and by the fear of conversion, the rabbis often found themselves playing a completely new role in representing the community. That an effort should be made in this direction is not surprising. That this commitment produced partial results is beyond doubt – in the end, generally only the most serious conflicts ended up in the gentile courts, and normally after a failed passage through the arbitration process. The fact that the growing responsibilities of religious authorities in the midst of a segregated society, during a time of serious discrimination, did not translate into the group's definitive alienation from the surrounding world is the most interesting fact to emerge up to this point, and a valuable interpretive lens.

There is a funny adage from the time of the ghetto that Jewish scrap dealers, when responding to a question about the quality of a product they had for sale, would dare to swear on their own son's head in order to guarantee the appropriateness of the deal. Once the child was invoked and the name of God spoken (one hoped not in vain), who could doubt the good faith of the seller? Thus when questioned, Jews would respond "*Morèno 'sto fijo!*," which the Christians understood as "If I have lied to you, may my son be struck dead!" because in Roman dialect *morè* sounds a little like *morté,* that is *morte*, death; and, at this point, their doubts having been resolved they would willingly make the purchase. However, this was a clever *quid pro quo*. With this obscure phrase, in fact, the Jews intended something completely different: "*Morèno 'sto fijo*" or really "If I have lied to you, may my son become our head rabbi!," where, in a game of words and assonances, the word *morèno* is taken to mean our teacher (from the Hebrew *moreh*, teacher, with the possessive suffix –*nu*), the traditional title for the position of head rabbi. Is this acculturation? Is it appropriation and re-elaboration? Or is it, more simply, a strategy for survival within a shared history?

CHAPTER 4

Career Bankers

In the decades following the enclosure of the ghetto, the institutions of the *Universitas* continued to be governed based on the laws established in the *Capitoli* of 1524. Although no formal modifications were made to the statute, the new regime of the ghetto brought about a series of processes of adaptation to the segregation that translated, in the first place, into changes in the criteria for selection of the ruling class: it was no longer only bankers but also rabbis who, on the strength of their learning, took on an unprecedented leadership role in the Roman community. Bankers continued to work alongside them (the title of rabbi often went along with the business of moneylending, among other things). Among the professions that brought honors and privileges, the career of banking was the only one to emerge unscathed by the socio-economic restrictions imposed by *Cum nimis absurdum*.

Now that we have considered, from an internal perspective, the tools with which the community was able to reinforce and legitimize its leaders as qualified representatives by leveraging those leaders' personal prestige, it is necessary to draw, this time from the outside, a social and professional profile of the Jewish ruling class. The importance of rabbinic titles played a decisive role inside the ghetto; outside the ghetto, in the management of relations with the Christian world, other skills were called for. Recognition of the esteem of both individuals and families passed in a bidirectional and porous manner in the intertwined relationships with Jews and with Christians. This chapter focuses on the second aspect, reconstructing the professional lives of the Jewish bankers. As will be recalled, the *Capitoli* entrusted the conduct of the *Universitas* to the moneylenders; thus we must start with them and their businesses in order to understand the concrete changes that were brought about by segregation, and the successes achieved by the policy of anti-Jewish marginalization in the second half of the 16th century.

The bull *Cum nimis absurdum* allowed Jews to work in very few occupations, almost exclusively connected to the sale of used goods. This major reduction of available work opportunities meant a revolution in the Jewish labor market, which in turn influenced the use of different means for the building and consolidation of assets and careers, even for the privileged class of bankers. As was traditional in this period, success in business facilitated acceptance in the ruling class of the community. The discriminations imposed in 1555 changed the strategies for pursuing this success, impacting the profile of the top profession (moneylending) through which those advances were possible, again thanks to a web of relations with the Christian world. A few examples help to summarize this complex story, in which it is not easy to get oriented. A sensational proceeding against Salomone Ram for a scheme involving fake coins pulled off between 1590 and 1594 acts as a guide, and helps us to draw a portrait of a profession – that of banker – that had been profoundly revolutionized.

1   A Trial and a Case Study: Salomone Ram (1594)

On July 25, 1594, in the prisons of Savelli, the Jew Salomone di Casciano Ram, worn down by months of detention, told Tranquillo Ambrosini, a lieutenant *in criminalibus* of the Governor of Rome, the truth about a business in fake coins (*baiocchelle*). It was scheme that had occupied different courts in the cities of the Papal States more than once since at least 1590. At Rimini, and Ancona, and then even in Rome there had been a series of discoveries and seizures of suspicious money. Now, after a long whirlwind of proceedings, things were becoming clear.[1] Salamone's full confession reported events that had occurred in northern Italy, between Venice and Mantua, starting in the closing months of the papacy of Sixtus V and his vacant office (1590).

It all started at the end of the 1580s, in the final period of the reign of Sixtus V, when the Pope ordered that the *baiocchelle* in the mints be checked for weight and quality in order to distinguish between those that were still good and those now too worn, which were to be marked with a stamp.[2] This was a

---

[1] *Processi*, r. 251 (1592–1594). This is a substantial volume of trials, subdivided in dossiers whose page numbering restarts from the beginning in each one, registered to different defendants but all related to the distribution of the false *baiocchelle*; f. 1, for which the cover with the name of the defendant no longer remains, covers the interrogations of employees and clients of the Mint from December 19, 1592 to February 9, 1593; f. 2 is the *Processus in causa baiocchelarum pro Fisco contra Iulium Robertum, Octavium Brancadorum et alios quamplures* and goes from December 27, 1592 to February 18, 1593; f. 3 is the one related to Salamone Ram and covers a chronological arc that spans January 14, 1594 to March 1 1595; f. 4, which is very difficult to read and is also related to the *baiocchelle*, is the case against *Laudadeus Naccomani hebreus, Isach Manzanellus hebreus e Petrus Cuccus de Ravenna* and goes from July 7 to 25 of 1594.; f. 5 is the *Copia processus fabbricati in Civitate Arimini super obolis seu baiocchellis incepti die quarta usque ad diem XV Maii 1593*, followed by copies of the other three trials for the same crime held in Romagna starting in 1590. Tranquillo Ambrosini was the author of a fundamental treatise on the functioning of criminal trials (*Processus informativus, sive De modo formandi processum informatiuum breuis tractatus …*, Venetiis, apud Nicolaum Morettum, 1602); see Bellabarba 2008, pp. 130–158.

[2] I was not able to find the announcement in question, dated in 1590 by witnesses in the first and second dossier of the trial (*Processi*, r. 251, ff. 1–2); the provision, however, concerned a

frequent practice, crucial in regulating finances in an economy where the value of money was closely connected to the effective weight of the precious metal with which the coins had been minted. The work was awarded to men who, in a variety of occupations, managed significant amounts of money: bankers, merchants, small artisans and so on. In just a few days those hired for the work arrived at the mints to perform the requested verifications. Immediately in Rome there were scattered rumors, such as the one reported on December 12, 1592 by Antonio Carpianus, a Florentine and a banker in the Urbe, regarding a trial already underway for fraud perpetrated by the employees of the mint:

> Those ministers who were deputized to receive the *baiocchelle* for stamping and to take out the bad ones committed countless frauds and stole them in quantity [...] and apart from this I have heard it said that those who take out the bad coins also put good ones among the tubes giving the impression that they were bad so that they can steal them for themselves as they did, and the truth is that many people also complain that these *capatori di baiocchelle* and other ministers of the mint, to steal the good *baiocchelle* in a way that people would not notice, would cut a small band in them and then place them among the bad coins that were cut the same way, and then they take them from among the fakes, and they stamp them like other good coins, and I have run across these good *baiocchello* that are cut in this way many times.[3]

The rumors about the trustworthiness of the controls and the controllers certainly could not go unnoticed, and with a few quick discoveries of evidence, the Governor's police were able to confirm the story. A large number of bad *baiocchelle* were circulating in Rome, and they were coming from the mint

---

habitual practice. Cfr., for example, the numerous notices put out on this subject in this period reported in *Regesti di bandi, editti, notificazioni e provvedimenti diversi relativi alla città di Roma e allo Stato pontificio*. On the Mints and the magistracy for money in the Papal States, cfr. De Caro Balbi, Londei 1984; Londei 1987.

3 *Processi*, r. 251, f. 2, c. 1r-v. "Quelli ministri che s'erano deputati a recevere le baiocchelle per farle bollare et a caparle commettevano infinite fraudi e ne rubbavano in quantità [...] et oltre a questo ho sentito dire pubblicamente che quelli che capavano mettevano fra le tube anco delle buone dando ad intendere che fussero triste per rubbarle per loro come facevano, et a la verità anco che molte persone si lamentavano che quelli capatori di baiocchelle et altri ministri della zecca per rubbare le baiocchelle buone che il popolo non se ne accorgesse le tagliavano un poco da una banda et le mettevano fra le triste così tagliate, et poi le capavano tra le triste, et le facevano bollare come l'altre buone, et di queste baiocchelle buone così tagliate et bollate a me ne sono capitate molte."

itself, where they had been fraudulently mixed in with the good coins during examinations of the money. On the solid base of these facts, it did not take much to trace the path back to the officers who were guilty of this fraud, charge them, and send them to trial. However, the problem remained of understanding where these coins came from and how they made their way into the city.

Salomone Ram was arrested in connection with this case at the end of December 1593. Unfortunately, considering the long gap in time between the earlier two trials heard, respectively, for the employees of the mint and the non-Jewish counterfeiters, which were conducted almost simultaneously by Tranquillo Ambrosini, and the trial that opened more than a year later against Salomone Ram, it is not entirely clear what connects them. The fact remains that questioning of the Jew immediately centered on the distribution and provenance of the money. Therefore at the time of the questioning, the Governor's deputy had probably already completed a preliminary (and undocumented) investigation, thanks to which he was able to track down our defendant. The following July, many months and many questions after the first interrogation in January 1594, Salomone found his courage and offered a full and detailed description of the role that he had played in the scheme: in a nutshell, he was the courier, on commission, responsible for collecting the fake coins in Castiglione di Gandolfo and sending them to the Papal States, destined for the Roman market.

This was Salomone's story. Starting in 1590 a rumor had rapidly spread among the Jewish merchants, bankers, and brokers of Venice that the mint of Castiglione di Gandolfo (today Castiglione delle Stiviere) in the duchy of Mantua was producing bad *baiocchelle* for shipment to Rome, and that it was possible to earn 50 to 70 percent profit on each scudo invested in these coins.[4] Giuseppe Ram (Salomone's brother, who hosted him in Venice) asked Salomone to go and verify this in person, and if it was true to make a purchase on behalf of Bartholomeo Errera, a bankrupt convert in Montegiordano. Though with some misgivings (which were repeated at every opportunity for the ears of the judges), Salomone accepted the task and soon left for Castiglione, where he made contact with the contractor at the mint, Francesco Berardini, and with his wife.[5]

Salomone's strategy for the hearing thus began to take shape: maintain that he had harbored doubts about the mission before it even got underway, and

---

4 In general regarding the Jews at Venice, cfr. Cozzi 1986; Concina, Camerino, Calabi 1991; Zorattini 1980–1999 and Calimani 2001; for Mantua see Simonsohn 1982–1986.
5 On the contrary, the first load of *baiocchelle* was in fact given to Salomone by the woman (*Processi*, r. 251, f. 3, c. 22v).

implicate others, with names and surnames, in both the conception and implementation of the plan. These efforts were of course aimed at improving the defendant's position, putting himself in a good light in front of the magistrate, and trying to pin the major responsibilities for the crime on third parties.[6]

According to his testimony, Salomone made two different trips to collect the money for Bartholomeo. Once back in Venice, he sent it to his father in the ghetto of Rome, via Rimini and Florence, where the convert would retrieve the merchandise as agreed upon. Meanwhile, Giuseppe organized a second shipment, this time via Pesaro, talk of which was also heard in Ancona, and which attracted the interest of another two Jews. At the same time in Rome, perhaps to mask the identity of the true recipient, Casciano Ram, Salomone's father, split the money up among several people, giving a small quantity to the Jew Leone Sgrizzaro and to Francesco, son of one "banker" Silvestro in *Piazza Giudea*. An unstoppable swirl of people in which a gang of Jews – the Ram family and their friends – together with a reasonable number of converts and a few Christians (who were conveniently employed at the mint) had crossed half of Italy, skirting by cities and crossing borders.

The Governor's deputy had no other choice but to call the people who Salomone had named to court, with the exception, at least from what is found in the trial dossier, of Francesco, who is not further identified. The choice to hear witnesses who were Jews that lived in the ghetto was motivated by the desire to precisely reconstruct Salomone's movements, and those of his money, about which his coreligionists, for obvious reasons of proximity and familiarity, could and should have been better informed than others.[7] The damage, however, caused by the unhindered circulation of false coins was extensive, and it was vital that the system which had been able to operate unhindered for so long be definitively dismantled. Thus the Governor's deputy was also sure to question the Christians who had carried out the transportation of the coins.[8]

The Jewish witnesses marched in one after the other, at irregular intervals. On September 23 Abram Leonis Sdriglio, *alias* Leone Sgrizzaro, appeared

---

[6] In this sense the prostitute Camilla's behavior described in Cohen E. 1991 is exemplary.

[7] It should be recalled that behind the interrogations' focus on Jews could certainly hide the intent to persecute them, animated by anxieties and fears of an actual plot by the perfidious Jews to damage the pontifical finances. Theories of this type, which do not appear in the trial under examination, precisely for the crime of counterfeit money, have been advanced for the 1600s in Fosi 1998.

[8] *Processi*, r. 251, f. 3, cc. 58v-60r. Regarding the feelings of the Roman judiciary towards Jewish defendants, for the sixteenth century, Procaccia 1998; Stow 1985; Esposito, Procaccia 2011. For the seventeenth century, Fosi 1998; Feci 1998; Di Sivo 2012. For relations with the Holy Office, Caffiero 2000b.

spontaneously and immediately offered the court his apologies for his slow response to the summons; he had been on a business trip with his father to the Fiera di Pistoia since the preceding August 28.[9] Some months later, on December 19, 1594, Alessandro Angelo di Montefiascone appeared for his turn at the court. He was also seriously late, though due to fear, not work. His testimony about the banking company in which he was a partner[10] yielded no result other than the decision to hear from one of his associates. Thus on March 11, 1595, Simone delli Panzieri, having returned from Venice in haste and anger after being informed by his mother of the search and the summons to appear in court, confirmed his colleagues' statements once again,[11] finally closing the Roman front of this very long case. Unfortunately, records of the sentences have not survived.[12]

In the meantime a new proceeding was opened against "Laudadeus Naccomani hebreus, Isach Manzanellum hebreum and Petrum Cuccum de Ravenna,"[13] that is, against the men at whom Salomone had pointed his finger as the ones responsible for the sorting of the bad money. It was this last aspect, actually, that interested Tranquillo Ambrosini. Starting with his first interrogation of Salomone, Ambrosini's questions had concentrated on the operational aspects of the trafficking of the *baiocchelle*. This was quite an understandable line of inquiry, bent as he was on dismantling the network of accomplices that had been able to move fraudulent currency across borders with impunity, eluding all controls. The purpose of these questions, obviously, was to prevent others from taking advantage of that same complicity in the future. At a certain point, in order to orient himself among the many and often contradictory pieces of information he had received – some of which had been obtained from reading

---

9   *Processi*, r. 251, f. 3, cc. 60r-63v. Regarding Sgrizzaro and his father Leone, see *infra* in this same chapter; it should be noted that Sgrizzaro is in all probability Leone Asriglio, the first client of notary Pompeo del Borgo, about whom see above in Chapter 3.

10 *Processi*, r. 251, f. 3, cc. 84r-87r. Alessandro Angelo di Montefiascone was the owner of one of the licenses for moneylending granted with the tolerance of 1577 (DC, r. 377, c. 8v).

11 *Processi*, r. 251, f. 3, cc. 87r-89v.

12 As is known, the series of the *Sentenze* of this court is incomplete, and for the years under examination the deliberations of the judges are missing; a cross-check made against the registries of the *Registrazioni d'atti*, where the penalties handed down are also listed, as well as those of the confraternity of *San Giovanni Decollato*, did not produce any results; despite this, even in the absence of further documentary discoveries, it would seem possible, however, to hypothesize a different penalty than the capital punishment called for in these types of crimes but rarely imposed by Jews. Regarding the functioning of the Criminal Court of Governor of Rome, Barrovecchio San Martini 1981; Pompeo 1991; Di Sivo 2001 and, more recently, Fosi 2007.

13 *Processi*, r. 251, f. 4.

a long trial for the same crime in Rimini in 1594, a copy of which he had sent to him – Ambrosini jotted down a quick note. In a few lines which are very useful for us, the deputy summarized what he had learned during months of work, reconstructing the complex plot of events, people, places and crimes:

> David son of Angelo de Nanna is in Ancona; Isach Lopagio da Pesaro and Moisè Blanis da Pesaro, residents of Ancona; seven or eight horses loaded with certain things for Bartholomeo a banker in Rome; the sons of Silvestro who run a bank in Piazza Giudea which had many in those of Castiglione; these men gave them to certain Jews; Bartolomeo Herrera and Matio his partner: bankers in Rome have done much stockpiling and abuse of the *baioccchi* of Castiglione; when they bring the *baiocchi* to Leone di Mus and to his partner Simone they met up with police who took it from him; the trial was held in Campidoglio; Marco and Giovanni Antonio di Imola in Mantua receive the product of the party with the *baiocchelle* in Castiglione.[14]

The prosecutorial framework reconstructed by this patient investigation sought to shed light on elements beyond the simple guilt of the individuals – which had already been established in a full confession recorded in July 1594 – and attempted to define the organization and the collusion that had enabled the traffic of fake money. The main scene of the crime was identified as being outside Rome and, although those responsible for these actions were not immediately named, he tried to identify the different stages of the system. In summarizing the salient facts for himself Ambrosini focused on the role of the Jews of the Marche more than on what had taken place in the ghetto of Rome, and he did not pay any attention at all to the intolerable continuing commerce between Jews, Christians and converts in the capital of Christianity. After all, thanks to the police searches, among other things, the city's legal system had already issued rulings on some of the events related to the case in Rome, and therefore there was no reason in this context to pursue them further.

---

14   *Processi*, r. 251, f. 4, c. 7r. "David figliolo de Angelo de Nanna sta in Ancona; Isach Lopagio da Pesaro e Moisè Blanis da Pesaro, habitanti in Ancona; sette o otto cavalli carichi de certe cose a Bartholomeo bancherotto in Roma; figli di Silvestro che faceva il banco in Piazza Giudea il quale n'ha avuti assai in quelli de Castiglione; questi messeri ne detteno a certi hebrei; Bartolomeo Herrera e Matio suo compagno: bancherotti in Roma hanno fatto grandi incitta et maltrimento di baiocchi di Castiglione; quando portano li baiocchi a Leone di Mus et à Simone suo compagno s'incontrano nelli sbirri che glieli tolsero; il processo fu fatto in Campidoglio; Marco e Giovanni Antonio di Imola ricevono in Mantua che li frutti il partito delle baiocchelle in Castiglione."

The second aspect, that of the habitual and illicit meetings between Jews, Christian and converts, was solely an issue of conduct and morality, and so by nature would have been the purview of the Holy Office, and would certainly not have been relevant to an ordinary court. We don't know if the issue was actually moved to the Inquisition's court of the conscience. Nevertheless, the fact that the questions in this trial do not show any hint of interest, curiosity, or at least some sense of scandal about these relations between Jews and Christians is itself an indication of the degree to which the sharing of spaces, businesses and confidence was the order of the day, despite the prohibitions and the natural prejudices.[15] Another element should be noted instead. The fact that the source of the *baiocchelle* was in the Po Valley had, after all, been established before the Jew's arrest. Thus, starting with the declaration in January 1594, Salomone Ram had been asked to clarify his movements, with particular focus on his stops in Mantua, Venice and then Pesaro, the occasional hospitality he received, and the official reasons for each of these trips. Beyond the criminal offence being investigated in the hearing, it is precisely these last elements of Salomone Ram's testimony – the trips, the friendships and the organization of work – that are the most significant for us.

We will try and take stock of the facts that have emerged up to now. Close examination of a single trial for the very serious crime of counterfeiting money, as well as the characters that emerge from that trial, provides, as we have seen, a range of information about the Jews of Rome and the Papal States during the first decades of the age of the ghettos, about their business, and about the existing relations within the various Jewish settlements across Italy and between these and the Christian world.[16] The reconstruction of these connections, in turn, allows us to sketch a concrete profile of the economic role of the Roman

---

15   On the Roman Inquisition and the Jews, see Prosperi 1994a; Romeo 2004; Del Col 2006, in particular pp. 442–467, 630–639; Di Nepi 2009; Maifreda 2019. For relations between Jews, Christians and converts, see Caffiero 2004 and 2012 for a theoretical development of a shared, not separate history.

16   The counterfeiting of money was an extremely serious crime, for which the guilty were often condemned to death; see De Luca 1673, pp. 140–143. Counterfeiters had never enjoyed a good image: for example, Dante, for his part, did not hesitate to put them in an immense lazaretto in the final circle of the Inferno, just over the traitors (*Inferno*, XIX). Regarding counterfeiting, Scarlata Fazio 1967; on counterfeiting in the modern age, Grendi 2004; on this crime in Rome in the modern age, cfr. Calzolari 2001, in particular pp. 45–47. This was, however, one of the crimes of which the Jews of Rome were more frequently accused, likely due the type of professions practiced, and at least starting with the beginning of the 1500s, cfr. Esposito, Procaccia 2011. For a case from Verona in the 1400s, see Castaldini 2005.

Jews at the end of the 16th century, as well as to focus on developments in the profession of banking, so important to the life of the group.[17]

The Ram family figured at the center of the whole story. They were spread out across at least three different Italian cities, and involved in dense tangles of relations, friendships and acquaintances. The Ram family's network of relatives and contacts was able to manage very dangerous traffic, securely and privately.

Casciano Ram and his sons were full members of that restricted group of merchant-bankers which the *Capitoli* had put in charge of the *Universitas Iudaeorum de Urbe*, a group that was still fully operational many years later. The trial of 1594, if investigated as a case study, offers a helpful view of the Jewish moneylenders of Rome forty years after the promulgation of *Cum nimis absurdum*. Salomone's statements about his travels, his profession, and his family go beyond the fake *baiocchelle,* revealing important clues concerning the question of the fate of Jewish banking in the aftermath of the institution of the ghetto. His testimony opens a window on this phase, both in terms of normal work practices as well as the mobility of Jews in the age of segregation. These issues are fundamental in sketching the portrait of a minority society that was extraordinarily dynamic in developing tools for self-protection, both culturally and institutionally, and in parallel, building their relations with the hostile majority.

2 The Ram Family, Moneylenders in the Ghetto Years

Who was Salomone Ram? Ambrosini asked this question at the beginning of the first interrogation, as was customary, and the witness responded by saying he was a Roman Jew, son of Casciano. The Ram family had arrived in Rome with the wave of migration that followed the expulsion from Spain; since then they had figured as influential members of the *Scola Catalana*, distinguishing themselves in the public life of the *Universitas* as *Fattori* and taking other high profile assignments. They were a dynasty of bankers with members across Italy, working in public and private roles of great prestige, as their status required.

A very long list of Ram family members appears in the deeds of Jewish notaries from the second half of the 16th century, cited in the performance of

---

17 The working conditions were, however, by all evidence far from the stereotype of the sudden decay and marginality long considered typical of the long chronological arc of the age of the ghettos. On these aspects see Berliner 1992; Milano 1984.

official functions for the Jewish community of Rome.[18] The family business was banking, in which various members of the family had been active since at least the 1540s.[19] A papal license, the seal of full professional and personal prestige – and the *cursus honorum* of the public offices confirmed this – came in 1577. The *tolleranza* granted to 55 bankers by Gregory XIII was, in fact, awarded to both Rosciolo Ram and Donato Ram *alias* Casciano, son of the late Salomone.[20] Casciano's position was then further strengthened in 1585 thanks to the concession of an *inhibitio in Curia ratione foenoris* (a special privilege extended to bankers), granted by the new *Camerlengo*.[21]

The Ram family's success was unstoppable, and the *inhibitio* only sealed it definitively. Still, in spite of everything, the family's fortunes eventually had to fall, perhaps in tandem with the legal troubles of 1594. While it is not possible to reconstruct this family's history and evolution between the 15th and 16th centuries, what is certain is that nobody with this last name appears on the list of moneylenders still active in Rome at the moment of the ban on Jewish banks in 1682.[22] Therefore it is clear that during this period, at least in the arena of work, the Ram family was no longer part of the main group of Jewish companies active in this field. It is possible that this outcome was the consequence of the inevitable loss of trust resulting from their involvement in a trial for counterfeit currency. The story of the Ram family turns out to be an important

---

18 From a very extensive list and as an example, the fortunate careers of the two Ram men in different times attest to the importance of the family: such is the case of David Ram del fu Samuele, listed in the trio of *Fattori* of 1554 (NE, f. 2, l. 2, c. 114r), already nominated as tax collector in 1536 and 1550, even if in the second instance, so long after the first assignment, could actually be someone with the same name, perhaps a younger relative (cfr., respectively, Stow 1999, doc. 48, and NE, f. 7, l. 1, c. 185r-v). Shortly thereafter Casciano Ram, who had taken the first steps in the institutional work in the role of arbiter for the *Universitas* in the resolution of a dispute in 1577 (Ibidem, f. 9, l. 1, c. 22r), was assigned the task of selecting the best candidate for a tax contract (Ibid., f. 9, l. 1, c. 69r), up to taking on, in 1583, the role of Fattore himself (Ibid., f. 3, l. 2, c. 61r).

19 Although, in fact, no Ram is mentioned in the list of Jewish moneylenders authorized by Leone X in 1521 (Esposito 2002, with particular reference to the document reported on p. 576), nor in that of Julius III in 1552 (Ibidem, p. 579), it is quite likely that the David Rocciolo/Rosciolo cited in both is a close relative of the David Ram *alias* Rosciolo del fu Samuele included in the tolerance of 1577 (DC, r. 377, cc. 6v-8v). Not by chance, the Jewish moneylenders of Rome twice designate him, in 1540 (Stow 1999, doc. 486) and in 1542 (Ibidem, doc. 735), as their deputy, charging him with protecting their interests in the dispute which at that time had the group of "old" Jewish bankers of Rome in opposition to the "new" (Cooperman 2015).

20 DC, r. 377, cc. 6v-8v.

21 DC, r. 388, c. 147v.

22 Procaccia 2012, with particular reference to the table on p. 135.

inside informant, useful for reflecting on the social dynamics at work, between rises and falls, in the heart of the group enclosed in the ghetto. As the case of this dynasty demonstrates, those dynamics were not always nor were they necessarily determined by what happened within the ghetto itself: the origins of the Ram family's misfortunes, as we have seen, were found far from *rione S. Angelo*, and involved Christians, converts, and Jews who all resided elsewhere.

Salomone's testimony in 1594 offers a snapshot of the profession of Jewish banking at the end of the century. When asked what his business was, he replied by saying "my work is to do a little banking, lend against pledges, and also to buy and sell things however as a used goods dealer."[23] Salomone presented himself as a businessman with many investments, from the money trade to actual trade. His complaints to the judges about his bad fortunes are not surprising, and seem to be part of a typical attempt at *captatio benevolentiae*. Claiming that business had been bad could offer some sort of justification for the decision to turn to crime. The rhetoric of financial troubles was astutely deployed to this end. The bankruptcy of his brother Abramo in Ancona had reduced the family fortunes to a few *scudi*, so it had been necessary to take some initiative to refill the drained family coffers:

> My family is worth little money because almost two months before I went to prison (October – November 1593) I took stock of my holdings after the death of my father who had died a short time before (summer 1593) and I found that all my holdings and those of my brothers (Giuseppe in Venezia and Abramo in Ancona) were worth only approximately nine hundred *scudi* counting the dowry of my stepmother who is named Donna, which is worth four hundred and ninety *scudi*.[24]

---

23 *Processi*, r. 251, f. 3, c. 1r.
24 "Il mio val pochi soldi perche circa due mesi innanti che io venisse prigione [*ottobre-novembre 1593*] io feci bilancio dello stato della robba mia per la morte de mio padre che poco tempo prima era stata [*estate 1593*] et trovai che tutta la robba mia et di miei fratelli [*Giuseppe a Venezia e Abramo ad Ancona*] valeva solo novecento scudi incirca computatoci la dote de mia madregna chiamata Donna la quale è di scudi quattrocentonovanta." Among many, Salomone explicitly cites only one loan of 600 *scudi* extended to his father Casciano "by two bankers of the Offizio Company at ten *pavoli* per *scudo* by one who I don't know his name but is in the Pescheria and from another who still holds this money and is paying the interest" (*Processi*, r. 251, f. 3, c. 4r). Regarding bankruptcy regulation, see the entry on *Fallimento* by Pecorella and Gualazzini (1967); and Steele 1991. It is never easy to orient oneself in establishing the effective value of the old money; one measure could be offered by a comparison with average salaries: in this sense it is useful to recall that one *scudo* was worth 100 *baiocchi*, and that the working day for a laborer was valued at 16 *baiocchi*; see Martini 1976 and Friz 1980. A further point of comparison can be identified

Arriving in Venice after the amnesty and close to the divorce from his wife,[25] Salomone immediately committed to participating in the fabric trade and brokering business together with his brother. However, they only managed to put together what he called miserable earnings of 200 *scudi*.[26] The prospect of a business trip to Mantua, even if questionable, raised his hopes. Salomone accepted the offer, boarded a boat that had been made available by the Duke personally, and after three days of travel he reached the city to begin carrying out his assignments.[27] Right away it should be noted how the reconstruction of his movements over the arc of a just a few years reveals the image of an expert traveler: at Pesaro during the vacant office of Gregory XIII, between Ancona, Pesaro, Rome and Venice during the years of Sixtus V, a stop at the baths of Viterbo to cure scabies, in Florence at the moment of UrbanVII's death, another fifteen month stay in Venice, interspersed with expeditions in the province of Mantua, via Padua, and then the return to Rome to be called to account for his movements and business to the Governor.[28]

Pawn lending, the sale of clothing, brokerage of various types, and in the end, even the sale of fake currency, while always moving about central and northern Italy: this summarizes three years in the life of Salomone Ram. Two aspects that emerge from this story are useful in the reconstruction of the profile of a typical Roman Jewish banker in the early years of the ghetto. The

---

in the sums related to personal assets, valued differently according to the conditions of the owner, reported by Renata Ago and, based on which, Salomone Ram would turn out to be at a medium-low income level, small for a banker but perhaps a lot for a Jew recovering from financial disasters (Ago 1998, pp. 81–89). Based on dowries estimated at 50 *scudi* for poor unmarried girls, however, Donna's dowry, at 450 *scudi*, seems fairly huge (Van Boxel 1998), and this too can be a parameter of the economic standards of the Ram family. Based on a statistical analysis of Jewish women proposed on the Duchy of Milan, instead, the sum of 490 *scudi* would place the Ram dowry in a sample of "average" matrimonial appropriations (Meron 1998). Finally, for a general quantification of the dowries of young Jewish women, Livi 1920, p. 168 remains a valid source.

25   *Processi*, r. 251, f. 3, c. 6r.
26   *Processi*, r. 251, f. 3, c. 4r.
27   The particulars of this journey emerge in the interrogation of May 10, 1594, when, despite having denied any stay in Mantua in the preceding examinations, Salomone admits to having been in the city, officially to go and see a barrier under construction on the grounds of the Ducal Palace from which was sent, as has been mentioned, the boat made available for the trip gratis (*Processi*, r. 251, f. 3, c. 7r-v). Things being what they are in this affair, the role of the Gonzagas is intriguing, as they are known for their favorable attitudes towards the Jews (Simonsohn 1982–1986). In the absence of other documents, however, it is not legitimate to postulate any special interest or direct involvement of the Duke in these events.
28   *Processi*, r. 251. f. 4, cc. 5r-8v.

extraordinary whirlwind of cities and occupations was not the exclusive prerogative of the defendant, and this constitutes an important point in correctly understanding the troubled process of social development which the Jews of the city would encounter during this period.

Remaining within the limited sphere of this trial, Leone Sgrizzaro (one of the witnesses cited) can also be counted among the ranks of travelling Jews, though undoubtedly at a level much inferior to that in which the Ram family operated, further disproving the stereotype of the Roman Jews' lack of mobility: in fact, the reason he gave for his delayed response to the Governor's summons was that he had been on an expedition to the Pistoia Fair with his father. Their turnover was not very high; 12 *scudi* in linens at Pistoia, a hop over to Florence for a batch of spices, a quick visit to Pisa for similar sums, and then the satisfied return to Rome to oversee the family bank.[29] Another one of the witnesses in the Ram trial was Simone delli Panzieri, a former associate of Alessandro Angelo di Montefiascone, who at the time of the search and summons to appear at the hearing was away in Venice, where he was reached by a letter from his alarmed mother. Simone, like many of his colleagues, was a habitual traveler, because apart from pawn lending he made ends meet by selling clothing from Rome and Ferrara, and acquiring merchandise in Venice to sell in the capital marketplace. On this most recent expedition he had purchased a batch of rugs.[30]

The practice of multiple occupations, the diversification of investments, and the high degree of mobility, elements which are well beyond the traditional commitments of a bank job, were all common characteristics of the professional activity of the Jewish bankers of Rome. The words Salomone Ram used to present himself to those who were judging him – "my job is that of banker and I also do a little used goods selling"[31] – describe a professional universe in which buying and selling, without particular interest for the type of merchandise, was common practice. Salomone and the others applied themselves to the most promising businesses, dealing with all kinds of trade at one time or another. They were more merchants than bankers. And they acted like expert merchants, spreading out their risks through an astute diversification of interests, and employing their capital for the opportunities which they saw as most advantageous.

The category of merchant-banker was certainly not unusual. For the Jewish bankers of Rome, however, full entry into this group was something new, and

---

29 *Processi*, r. 251, f. 3, cc. 60r-66v.
30 *Processi*, r. 251, f. 3, cc. 84r-89v.
31 *Processi*, r. 251, f. 3, c. 3r.

a profound contradiction of the rules that they had imposed on themselves during the 1540s, with the ratification of commitments that had been formally stipulated in front of the city's Jewish notaries. The rules promulgated at that time followed intense negotiations between licensed bankers on one side, and converts who wanted to enter the market on the other, and imposed an impermeable boundary between banking activity and commercial activity: moneylenders had to stay away from ordinary commerce.[32] However, fifty years after that decision the world had changed, the ghetto had been instituted, and bankers too had to adapt to the new conditions. Both in the private spaces of the institutional management of the *Universitas* – where the importance of roles given to rabbis was a significant innovation – as well as in the public spaces of contact with Christians – where a tangible transformation of professions was underway – for the Jews of Rome, the process of reshaping a ruling class that was capable of keeping the group strong and united in the face of economic restrictions and pressures to convert produced an unexpected result: a society that was stubbornly structured around its own otherness, and was the scene of extraordinary social mobility.

3 The Regulation of the Jewish Banks (1590)

As demonstrated by the affairs of Salomone Ram and his colleagues, the open acceptance of the double role of merchant and banker was the group's response to new legal limitations placed on Jewish moneylending, which in the second half of the century had become progressively more restrictive. Important elements have already emerged from the reconstruction of a profile of the Jewish ruling class in the early years of the ghetto: the centrality of the rabbinate, the consolidation of community institutions, and the transformation of the banking profession, as exemplified by Salomone Ram and his family's epic undertakings. Considering the adventures of the Ram family, it becomes essential to reconstruct the legal framework and working conditions offered to Jewish moneylenders in this period. In fact, this is the only way we can balance our reflection on the evolution that was underway internally with an equally clear consideration of the Jewish ruling class' position in the outside world, and of its real or presumed marginality in the urban context.

The first point to examine regards the ruling issued in 1590, *Motu proprio della Conferma e Riforma istituita per li Banchi degli Ebrei*. This measure was a

---

32 Stow 1999, docs. 28, 80, 415, 486, 735; Cooperman 2015.

major intervention by Pope Sixtus V into the arena of Jewish banking, proposing a series of legislative measures which were generally meant to disadvantage the Jewish banker in his relationship with the customers he financed. In the first place it confirmed the two percentage point reduction of the allowable interest rate already established in the *Tolerantia pro hebraeis bancheriis in Urbe* of 1577[33] (from 20% to 18%);[34] then the deposit period granted for pawn items before they could be sold at auction was extended (growing from twelve months, as first called for by Leo X to sixteen months, established by Julius III, and then to eighteen months, decreed by Sixtus V); finally, the law introduced a series of minor measures aimed at overturning the lender's position of advantage over the borrower.

A comparison between the laws prior to the institution of the ghetto (which in large part date back to the pontificate of Leo X) and those issued in the ghetto to regulate unredeemed and lost pawn items allows us to reconstruct the changed environment for bankers in a phase of such powerful contrasts: on the one hand, the marginalization of the Jewish bankers in the city credit market, on the other, however, their survival as a class of professionals. Here too a few examples can help us to follow the reasoning.

We begin with unredeemed pawns. Based on the *Capitoli* issued by Leo X and an established tradition, these objects had always become entirely the property of the bankers, regardless of their resale value.[35] The new rules, instead, addressed the possibility that the sale price of an item at auction might end up being higher than the value of the loan when bankers included the costs of accumulated interest and the expenses of organizing the exhibit and sale in the price. In such circumstances the new law declared that bankers were only permitted to keep the sum needed to cover their investment, and that any surplus was to be sent to the defaulting owner:

> And before they sell the pawns they must put them to auction in the presence of the official who we have deputized to have authority over this, executing the aforementioned sale they can retain of the price the sum of their credit and the rest if there should be any they are required to restore to the owners, taken from the receipts of the aforementioned notary, who had to make notes in the margins each part of the sale, otherwise we will

---

[33] DC, r. 377, cc. 6v-8r.
[34] The interest rate progressively fell until reaching the 12 percent granted under Clement X (Poliakov 1956).
[35] The document is published in the appendix of Esposito 2002, p. 557.

not trust him, or we will turn him in to the aforementioned official, or to another person to be deputized by us; it is declared that the expenses will be at the cost of the manager of the pawn.[36]

In the case of theft or loss, the old regulations provided forms of protection for both parties which guaranteed lenders at least a minimal profit margin.[37] Now this possibility was swept away, and instead it was established that in cases like this the estimate of damages suffered and money to be refunded to the owner of the pledge would be based exclusively on the statements of the Christian, without any form of compensation for the banker/investor:

> Furthermore, if the pawn was stolen, or if it was lost the Jew giving sufficient indication of the loss, or of the theft he has to pay the established value of the piece, or rather if it is preferred by the Christian two thirds more than that sum of money that he had loaned against it, and in case, that for the aforementioned indications the theft or loss cannot be adequately proven he will pay what the Christian swears the value of the sum to be and the auditing notary will record this and if the pawn was of gold or silver it will be enough to pay based on its weight, and the Christian will swear to its manufacture which the notary will record in the same fashion as the sum.[38]

To the further detriment of the Jews, it should be recalled that based on the *Capitoli e convenzioni per l'Università dei bancherotti ossia cambiatori di moneta,*

---

36 The announcement is preserved in ASR, *Camerale II, Ebrei*, b. 2. "E prima che li pegni si vendino e si debbano mettere all'incanto in presenza dell'officiale da essere sopra di ciò deputato da noi, eseguendo la detta vendita si possino del prezzo ritenere la somma del loro credito ed il resto se ci sarà siano tenuti restituirlo alli padroni, pigliandone ricevuta dal detto notaro, la quale si abbia da notare in margine di detta vendita in ciascheduna partita, altrimenti non le si dia fede, o deponerla nelle mani del sopraddetto officiale, o di altra persona da deputarsi da noi; dichiarandosi che le spese vadino a danno del padrone del pegno."

37 Cited from Esposito 2002, p. 577.

38 ASR, *Camerale II, Ebrei*, b. 2. "Item, che se il pegno fosse rubato, o si perdesse dando l'ebreo sufficiente indizio della perdita, o del furto l'abbia a pagare quanto fosse provato che valesse, ovvero se più piacerà al cristiano due terzi più di quella somma di danari, che gli aveva imprestata sopra, et in caso, che per li suddetti indizii non si provasse sufficientemente il detto furto ovvero perdita che paghi quello che il cristiano giurerà che valesse della somma che il notaro uditore testerà in giù e se il pegno fosse di oro o di argento basti pagare il suo peso, e per la sua manifattura quello giurerà il cristiano similmente dalla somma che il notaro uditore tasserà in giù."

drawn up in Rome in 1587, Christian moneylenders were subject to a different set of rules for managing precisely these circumstances:

> If it happens that some of the aforementioned bankers should buy any sort of gold, silver or jewels in public for any price, or hold them for display and then find that they had been stolen, in such cases the aforementioned bankers should be reimbursed for their expenses, justifying these with trustworthy witnesses.[39]

Therefore by the last quarter of the 1500s, thanks largely to the efforts of Sixtus V, in the world of moneylending only a Christian was considered to be a "trustworthy witness," whose statements had to be accepted on strength of the person's certain good faith.[40] This progressive growth of mistrust in dealings with the Jews cannot be underestimated. Notwithstanding the fact that the question of the Jews' good faith was actually an ancient problem, the immediate effect of this provision in the professional arena took the terms of the issue even further.[41] The Papal legislation, whose consequences for Jewish banking activity did not escape the notice of their contemporaries,[42] reveals the backdrop of profound ideological changes to which the figure and the work of the Jew would be subjected during the years of the militant Counter-Reformation. In this sense, the most disruptive decision made by the Pope was not the definitive ratification of a lowered interest rate, but rather his indication that the word of a Jew was not equivalent to that of a Christian regarding an incident in which it would doubtlessly have been right to take account of both sides. Unfair competition wasn't restrained even when dealing with thefts. The Jewish banker, unlike his Christian colleague, was required to prove that he was the victim of a thief or a distraction, and that he was not trying to cheat the poor Christian. Jewish moneylending, and in the final

---

39   ASR, *Biblioteca, Collezione degli statuti*, 644/1, 1587, *Capitoli e convenzioni per l'Università dei bancherotti ossia cambiatori di moneta in Roma*. "Che occorrendo che alcuni di detti banchieri comprasse alcuna sorte d'oro, d'argento, o gioie per qualsivoglia prezzo in publico, o lo tenessi in mostra e poi si trovasse che fussero state robbate, in tal caso alli detti banchieri si debba restituir quel tanto havran speso, giustificandolo per testimoni degni di fede."
40   Ago 1998, pp. 66–75.
41   Regarding the untrustworthiness of the Jews and converts from Judaism, Todeschini 2007.
42   An anonymous memo about the precarious condition of the Jewish banks, probably written in the middle of the 1600s, points to the reduction in interest rates as the cause for two of the main Jewish bankers in Rome to abandon the activity of moneylending – unfortunately without mentioning the names (Procaccia 1994–1997, p. 134, n. 33).

analysis the very presence of the Jews in the heart of Christianity, constituted a necessary evil according to the theological assumptions related to the witness of the passion of Christ and to the mass conversion of the stubborn Jews as the essential condition for his return to Earth.[43] Thus their marginal condition had to be made even more recognizable when, as in the case of the unequal relationship between a lender-creditor and a payee-debtor, it would have logically been the Jew that found himself in a position of strength – a position that was incompatible with the aura of submission that still and always had to surround him.[44]

A final note: the fact that it was Sixtus V, an example of a "good Pope" according to some historians,[45] who addressed the issue in these terms – in a form where the dialectic between inclusion and exclusion, which is by definition typical of the age of the ghettos, acts insidiously to bring about the decline of the public role of the Jew[46] – invites further consideration. Felice Peretti's ambiguous policy proves to be a notable example of the distance between an explicitly discriminatory theory, accepted by all, and a practice of inevitable daily coexistence in which can be recognized the sum of relations between Jews and Christians in this period and for all of the modern age. Classic historiography, in fact, has found signs of benevolence towards the Jews in the career of Sixtus V which explicitly conflict with the ideology elaborated in the banking reform just examined. Sixtus V was the last pontiff to use the services of a Jewish chief physician (Meir Magino di Gabriello),[47] he surrounded himself with counselors of dubious origin, among whom stood out a *converso* financial advisor (Giovanni Lopez),[48] he ordered the general readmission of the

---

43   Stefani 2004
44   On the ridicule of Jews, see Toaff 1996c, in particular pp. 101–133, and more recently, for the 1700s and regarding the giudiate, see Caffiero 2012, pp. 362–367.
45   Berliner 1992; Milano 1984, pp. 79–83; Segre 1996a, pp. 734–736. On Sixtus V and his papacy in general, see Pastor 1910–1934 vol. 10, pp. 2–502; Caravale, Caracciolo 1963, pp. 375–406.
46   The consequences of the Jew's word losing its worth, because it is spoken by a Jew, will be vividly felt later on, during the pontificate of Benedetto XIV, another Inquisitor Pope, in a completely different area, that of the legitimacy of the offering of Jewish children to the Christian faith (Caffiero 2004).
47   Magino, a Venetian Jew, also found fame in Rome as an inventor, creating a new procedure both for the fabrication of clear glass and for the production of silk, to which he reserved a treatise dedicated to his protector Sixtus V (Gabrielli 1585); later nominated as consul of the nascent community, he was among the protagonists of the fate of the newly formed *Nazione degli Ebrei di Livorno*, about which cfr. Frattarelli Fischer 2000; Filippini 1997; Toaff 2010; Liscia Bemporad 2010.
48   Milano 1984, p. 82.

Jews to the lands of the Papal States with the bull *Christiana Pietas*,[49] and he granted privileges for the Levantine Jews of Ancona.[50]

The synthesis between two such irreconcilable positions should be looked for in the different contexts in which they were proposed and practiced. In his personal and private meetings with Jews (his doctor and his advisors), and in decisions made to promote the prosperity of the State, the Pope evidently acted in favor of the group. On the other hand, those same strategic choices, while undoubtedly aimed at bettering their objective quality of life, were animated by the stereotypical consideration of the Jews as one monolithic body, made up of useful bankers and capable doctors whose services were worth using. He did not lose, however, his sense of suspicion and mistrust in dealings with Jews, which was inevitably fed precisely because he was dealing with Jews. After all, even the prologue to the famous constitution *Christiana pietas* – with which the Jews were provisionally readmitted to the entire territory of the Papal States after the expulsion from small towns ordered by Pius V in 1569, and authorized to undertake a wide range of mercantile occupations – followed the classic scheme of tolerance as a means to win conversion, reaffirming the traditional Manichean vision juxtaposing the darkness of error with the light of salvation, and unhappiness with merciful tolerance:

> Christiana pietas, infelicem hebraeorum statum commiserans, illos apud se patitur diversari, ac etiam singulari complectitur humanitate, ut crebro illorum intuitu Passionis Domini memoria fidelium oculi frequentius obversetur, ipsique hebraei, huiusmodi pietate compuncti, suos agnoscant errores, ad verum lumen, quod est Iesu Christus, perveniant clavitatis [...].[51]

The inclination to support Jewish entrepreneurship, which was considered the key to reviving local microcredit, and thus offered ancillary benefits to the State economy, was an indication of the pragmatic and utilitarian vision that the Sienese Pope (and many others with him) held of the Jewish population

---

49   This readmission, ordered with a specific confirmation of privileges on October 6, 1586 (ASR, *Camerale II, Ebrei*, b. 2) brought a mass influx of Jews in the State, mainly headed for the small cities of Umbria, the Marche and Ancona, amply documented by a long list of licenses for *Introitus cum habitatione* granted to Jews and released between 1587 and 1590 (DC, r. 394, cc. 60r-73v).

50   The privileges of the Levantine Jews at Ancona guaranteed them an unquestionably favorable situation (*Privilegi d'hebrei levantini*, in ASR, *Collezione dei Bandi*, b. 366, d. 65). On the Jews of Ancona in general, see Angelini 1989; Andreoni 2013 and 2019.

51   *Christiana pietas*.

of the Papal States. For the Jews it was not a reassuring approach: they could be useful if they were able to provide some benefit to the Christians, but they were never considered indispensable.

4   The Jewish Banks

Well before the Sixtine measures, the management of a lending bank had become an increasingly difficult undertaking for the Jews of Rome, and the moneylenders accordingly began to turn to other sectors. Opportunities for Jews in the field of commerce, however, had been further restricted since the papacy of Paul IV, limiting them essentially to only the buying and selling of used fabric and clothing, despite the ups and downs of this business. In other words, the same occupation of second hand dealer that was ascribed to Salomone Ram, practiced alongside the more noble occupation of pure moneylending. It should be recalled that the business of the second hand dealer, as Carlo Maria Travaglini has demonstrated, met fundamental needs of the city's economy during the old regime, where putting used goods back in circulation took on a positive, and by no means humiliating connotation.[52]

Salomone's testimony gives us an idea of how much business could be done in sixteen months working in this environment. By his own accounting, Salomone valued the earnings from his work in Venice at less than 200 *scudi*. This was a period, moreover, in which business was bad due to his entanglement in the turmoil between Rome and Ancona, and his capital, once his debts had been paid, and not counting the dowries to be returned, didn't even amount to 500 *scudi*. That sum could certainly not be called minimal when compared, for example, to the total sum of some 12 *scudi* spent during that profitable tour of Tuscany which had delayed Leone Sgrizzaro's appearance in front of the judge. Before addressing the central issue of the diversification of investments, however, it is important to draw the most precise portrait possible of the main profession, and that is the occupation of banker. How did the Jewish lenders of Rome work? And what relations linked them with their Christian colleagues? Why, at a certain point, did these families turn away from banking to engage in other fields?

Another trial for counterfeit money discovered in Rome in 1572 offers preliminary responses to these questions. While this case lacks the presence of Jewish hands organizing cross-border distribution, and does not raise suspicions

---

52   Travaglini 1992.

about the trustworthiness of the mint, it does allow us to hear precise information from the voices of Jewish and Christian moneylenders. The recurring questions asked of the different witnesses concerned their volume of business, their years of experience and the name of the banker's source of cash. These are their highly summarized answers: Leone Ascarelli, a Jewish banker in the *via degli ebrei*, reported keeping the *quattrini* in *scartocci* of one *scudo*, that he was accustomed to having the money audited by Giovanni Pugliese and by Fiorenzuolo for fear of running into any errors, that he had been working in the profession only three months, and changed from 20 to 30 *scartocci* a week. Benedetto del *fu* Giovanni Auria from Bologna, a banker at *Monti*, changed 5, 6 *scudi* a week and had practiced for 9 years. Lorenzo del *fu* Blasi *alias* Fiorentino, a banker at *Banchi*, had practiced for 20 years, changed from 20 to 30 *scudi* a week, and got money from Francesco Musia, a banker at *Paradiso*. Nicola del *fu* Hieronimo de Turris, Sienese, with a bank in *Contrada Judeorum*, had worked for six years and changed from 20 to 30 *scudi* a week; Andrea del *fu* Francesco Lisurano from Perugia, a banker in *Campo de' Fiori*, had worked for eighteen years and changed a minimum of four *cartocci* a week. Stefano di Severo from Perugia, a banker in *Campo de' Fiori*, changed 15 or 16 *scudi* per week; Giuseppe del *fu* Mosè Calabrese, a Jewish banker in the *giudaria*, was an associate of his nephew Giuseppe and, since he had only been working a short time, declared that he was not yet able to report his weekly volume of business.[53]

The citation of these testimonies could continue at length, but what is interesting to note here is how, in the daily practice of their profession, Jewish and Christian lenders worked in a similar manner, often also helping one another, despite being, as we've seen, held to a different set of rules. The credit market followed practices and customs of its own, notwithstanding the prohibitions known to all. The Jewish banks worked like all the others, with the high value pawns placed in locked crates, available cash of different values and origins stored in *cartocci* valued at one *scudo*, and the account books ready to note all executed transactions.

The differences between Jews and Christians were felt in the rules. Indeed, the issuance of loans against pawns made by Jews had to be recorded in a public document drafted by the *Notaio dei pegni dei banchieri ebrei*.[54] This notary

---

53   *Processi*, r. 140, f. 4, cc. 295r-315v). For more on these aspects see Ago 1998, pp. 50–57. Regarding the *Contrada Judeorum* as a marketplace for goods, food and money, cfr. Esposito 1995; Modigliani 1998

54   From 1584 on this position was held under license of the *Cardinal Camerlengo* by notary Berladino Pascasio, who succeeded Zerbino Sperandeo, with whom he was also a collaborator (DC, r. 388, c. 25r-v). The documentation produced by this office, called for in the same capitoli that deal with Jewish bankers (ASR, *Camerale II*, *Ebrei*, b. 2, *Motu proprio*

was required to precisely indicate the amount of money loaned, the particulars of the agreement reached between the parties, the characteristics of the object offered as a guarantee and, finally, the item's stated value. This expert evaluation was considered the authoritative record in the case of the deposit being lost, stolen, or put up for public auction. Auction sales were held monthly, and were announced in advance by the posting of a special edict from the *Cardinal Vicario* in *Piazza Giudea* and *Campo de' Fiori*.[55] Taken together, this series of administrative measures would in the long run complicate the occupation for Jewish moneylenders. Destined to lose in a market in which unfair competition from their Christian colleagues had been enshrined in law, a powerful sense of urgency about expanding the range of their businesses took hold among Jewish bankers, to the detriment of their main occupation.

Whatever the amount of money might have been that actually moved through Jewish hands, it seems evident that the number was never particularly high. All the active banks together reported a business volume of no more than 150,000 *scudi* annually.[56] This total is far lower than that invested by Christian bankers in the public debt of the *monti* alone, valued by Fausto Piola Caselli at no less than 8,200,000 *scudi* for the period 1526–1605.[57] In fact, the financial resources available to the Christian lenders who were active in the Roman market allowed them to allocate considerable sums in just one sector, public debt. For example, in 1588, under the papacy of Sixtus V – one of the most important papacies in this arena as well – the Pinelli, Lopez and Giustiniani banks spent 400,000 *scudi* in only one year for the acquisition of unredeemed debt (*vacabili*) from the *Monte San Bonaventura v*.[58]

In the absence of a study dedicated to tracking down Jewish investors in *montis* among the owners of public debt securities, which were divided up into hundreds of different shares, it is still legitimate to speculate about the possible

---

       della Conferma e Riforma istituita per li Banchi degli Ebrei), apart from the registries of individual notaries that worked for them, is conserved in AC, *Archivio Urbano, Sezione III, Notai dei banchieri ebrei*. Belardino Pascasio, however, was one of the Roman notaries particularly dedicated to the drafting of documentation for Jews, even outside the responsibilities entrusted to him as the *Notaio dei banchiere*, and clear traces of this activity remain in his registries; thanks to Prof. Anna Esposito for pointing this out to me.

55   ASR, *Camerale II, Ebrei*, b. 2, *Motu proprio della Conferma e Riforma istituita per li Banchi degli Ebrei*.

56   Procaccia C. 2012

57   Piola Caselli 1991. On the locations of the monte in general, Ibid., 1993 and Lodolini 1956; for the 19th century, Laudanna 1989, in particular pp. 104–105.

58   Piola Caselli 1991, table on p. 478. Given the last name, we cannot exclude the possibility that the Lopez cited is an Iberian convert.

existence of a specifically Jewish interest in this sector, in which the middle class often concentrated its savings and in which the House of Catechumens, among others, invested the funds paid to converts by the *Universitas Iudaeorum*.[59] On the other hand, the role of Jewish lending in Rome and the Papal States was to provide consumer credit, working both at the city scale as well as across a much greater territory through the system of letters of exchange.[60] It was certainly not meant for the financing of a costly state apparatus, a role already occupied by other businesses in possession of assets so great that they could take on the profitable but onerous purchase of offices in the provincial treasuries and the *depositeria generale*.[61] Then there is the fact that it would never have been ideologically possible for the Church and its State to imagine entrusting the ordinary and extraordinary support of its public debt to Jewish bankers. However, if this specific sector represented the true heart of banking activity in the Papal States, then to what extent could the Jewish businessmen who worked at buying and selling money – and those who, for one reason or another, kept it cautiously at a distance – continue to be called bankers?

5   Still Bankers?

Ghetto or no ghetto, between one limitation and another and overcoming walls, barriers and boundaries, the Jews of Rome continued to practice the business of pawn lending until its suppression in 1682. During the long period that runs from the release of the first licenses in 1521 to the date of abolition, the moneylending business of the Roman Jews changed, adapting to both the general conditions of the city marketplace and, on the other hand, to the fluctuation in the laws that targeted Jews and their professions. The condition of constant uncertainty brought about by the strategy of the ghetto and the attempt to close off every outlet for Jewish entrepreneurship was at the heart of the transformation of the social and professional profile of the Jewish moneylenders. Capable of cautiously navigating contradictions in the laws, while doing their best to exploit the web of rivalries between the magistracies responsible for their oversight, Jews broadened the scope of their business activities in every sector conceded to them. This expansion, through the inclusion of

---

59   The only investment of this type that I encountered was found in a deed in Hebrew by notary Isacco delle Piattelle.
60   Procaccia C. 2012; Poliakov 1956, pp. 106–109.
61   On the management of provincial treasuries, Caravale 1974. Regarding the *depositeria generale*, Pastura Ruggiero 1987, pp. 192–202.

men with different career histories in the *élite* group of bankers, encouraged important dynamics of social mobility which were developed along a path of successive stages. A banker's career was built through associations with preexisting companies, occasional and prestigious assignments, and the diversification of investments, culminating with the granting of official recognitions and formal authorizations to manage their own bank, which in turn favored the rise to public and administrative roles in the *Universitas*. Complex plots and intertwined interests.

Acquiring all the authorizations required to start up a lending bank (*tolleranze*, protections, privileges) was a complex and risky business. As a result, the incorporation of moneylending partnerships was remarkably frequent. The management of a bank took place, as much as possible, within established familial structures which were part of networks that were at least national in scale, into which sons and nephews were gradually incorporated. The youth were called upon to assume different responsibilities based on their age, training, experience and on their individual skills.[62]

The formation of partnerships was on the agenda, and could involve setting up different types of relationships between the partners, from contracts for professional training to business investments, up to the assembling of companies with a more or less equal division of shares. Other than distributing the risks associated with the moneylending business and providing instruction for the youngest workers, the system, with all its variables, also allowed the inclusion of those who could not be called genuine bankers because they did not yet hold an individual license – and they were the majority – in the workplace. This practice was legitimate, and was part of a very large spectrum of agreements between private parties that were formalized by notarial deeds. As much as possible, the notary recorded any modifications in structure which a company might undergo, removing a contract that was no longer valid, or indicating the presence of a preceding deed. A concrete example will help orient us among the multitude of possible options, as demonstrated by the case

---

62   The testimony of Giuseppe del *fu* Mosè Calabrese in the 1572 trial for fake money was, from this point of view, completely reliable. Declaring himself unable to express a judgement on the volume of money being traded and the general progress of the business, Giuseppe simply revealed his subordinate role in a partnership where he still worked under the strict oversight of one of his uncles, who shared the same name, as an apprentice or little more. Without direct responsibility and lacking prior skills, the youth moved through the first steps in a sector where competition was fierce and mistakes were not allowed (*Processi*, r. 140, f. 4, cc. 295r-315v). For a general description of the familial structure at the base of Italian Jewish banks, see Luzzati 1996. For the evolution in 15th and 16th centuries, see Todeschini 2016

of Abramo Abbina and Sabbato di Ceprano, who in less than a year managed to try many of the possible solutions available regarding the organization of a business partnership. It should be noted that the entire transaction took place after the legal innovations introduced by Sixtus V, and precisely because of this it offers a reliable portrait of the management of these relationships and the training of Jewish moneylenders.

On June 22, 1589, Abramo loaned Sabbato 155 *scudi* to start an exchange bank, gave him part of his shop (in which he sold hats) where he could work in peace, and established that he would collect, as interest, a *giulio* more than Sabbato on each *scudo* earned by the store. The agreement meticulously regulated Sabbato's activities, which were subjected to very strict controls by the generous backer. The young man's job was set up like a true limited liability investment arrangement, in which one of the parties supplies the necessary money and workplace and the other the labor – and the willingness to turn over the account books at every request.[63] Things went well and trust developed. On the following December 27 the first contract was cancelled with the consensus of both parties, who then set up a new partnership "to practice the business of exchange," in which Abramo again put up the capital (100 *scudi*) and Sabbato the labor. With this second contract, however, the terms of control over the keys and the account book, which had been expressed so clearly in the earlier agreement, were relaxed, and Sabbato's career took a concrete step forward.[64] On May 15, 1590 Abramo declared that Sabbato had now cleared all of his debts,[65] and that from that date until the dissolution of the company (which happened on March 31, 1592)[66] the two partners would manage it with equal rights and responsibilities.

The two years spent under guardianship allowed Sabbato di Ceprano to learn the profession with the guidance of an expert moneylender. Abramo Abbina came from a family of licensed bankers[67] who were ready to seize the opportunity to expand their business beyond the traditional areas of interest and, more to the point, outside their circle of relatives. Furthermore, the Abbina family were holders of an *inhibitio in Curia ratione foenoris*, granted in 1588

---

63 NE, f. 14, l. 1, c. 130 r-v. Regarding limited liability financing in the formation of a partnership in Rome in the modern era, see Ago 1998, pp. 25–27. On the practice of using a single store for multiple purposes, see Modigliani 1998.
64 NE, f. 14, l. 1, c. 178r-v.
65 NE, f. 6, l. 2, c. 44r.
66 The dissolution is registered through a deed of cassation of the prior contract of December 1589 (NE, f. 14, l. 1, c. 178r-v).
67 DC, r. 377, c. 8r.

(and so a year before establishing the relationship with Sabbato). This *inhibitio* also included an unusual protection from the *Presidente delle Strade* and his officers, who maintained roads and collected fees, for practicing the business of *stracceria*.[68] Thanks to the hats, Sabbato's shop was already partially dedicated to this kind of business. In short, they were no longer only bankers.

Beyond the accounts and the particular facts, what is interesting to note is how all evidence shows that by the last quarter of the 16th century, profits from the money business were judged to be insufficient, and families tried, as much as possible, to supplement these falling profits by adding secondary businesses. This diversification of investments was necessarily limited only to trades that were legal for Jews. As we will see, this essentially meant managing the procurement of *fardelli* from the city hospitals and the administration of market stalls. While they may appear marginal, both of these activities were promising branches of business that also offered young men protected opportunities to test themselves. The figure and the work of Leone Sgrizzaro and his father – who, as we've seen, were among the witnesses in the trial of Salomone Ram in 1594 – can be taken as a model of these new professional paths.

Abramo Asriglio (Sgrizzaro was his nickname) was the son of Leone and grandson of the late Abramo. Among the notary Pompeo del Borgo's first clients, in the 1580s he worked alongside his father in his business ventures. Over the years Sgrizzaro managed to establish his professional profile, starting with buying and leasing market spaces,[69] as well as brokering the trade of quotas for the companies that specialized in monopoly hospital sector contracts,[70] and eventually obtained a position managing a bank that belonged to the convert Giuseppe Menasci (*alias* Coppolaro).[71] Menasci, in fact, having become a Christian with the new name Prospero da Santa Crevere, found himself subject to limitations in the practice of lending for interest that were related to his new religious condition. This was all to the benefit of Sgrizzaro and family, who were eager to take over his already signed contracts. The economic and social rise of the skilled Asriglio was soon validated by the assignment of an

---

68   DC, r. 392, c. 114v.
69   So, for example, on June 10, 1584, Leone Asriglio rented a market space that he owned, at the price of 16 *scudi* for two years (NE, f. 11, l. 6, c. 106r), to Manuele de Lattes and Isacco Capitano; Abramo leased another market space to David Roccas and Angelo di San Lorenzo on July 7, 1588 (NE, f. 14, l. 1, c. 51r).
70   So, for example, on December 28, 1583, Leone Asriglio, with Mosè di Bologna, and on a commission from Zio Lavo and Mosè Grande, sent, in all their names, the balance for the purchase of Salamone di Mazzone's shares in the *compre* of the *Ospedale del Santo Spirito*, of the *Consolazione* and of the *San Giacomo degli Incurabili* (NE, f. 11, l. 6, cc. 71v-72r).
71   DC, r. 392, c. 113v.

inhibitio in Curia ratione foenoris, obtained in 1585[72] and renewed in 1589.[73] The achievement of the pontifical license was in this case nothing less than a return to old glories, being that an Abraham Asriglio, likely the grandfather of our subject, was among the beneficiaries of licenses granted by Julius III in 1552.[74] The temporary disappearance of the family from the small group of license holders listed in 1577[75] did not, therefore, drive the family's members out of the profession; while waiting for better times Leone had simply continued to ply the traditional trade on a smaller scale, aimed at a clientele composed almost exclusively of fellow Jews, to whom he issued loans for small amounts and short durations, all of which were precisely recorded in the registries of the Jewish notaries.

There is one final aspect to mention. The fact that Sgrizzaro's return to the top coincided with the sudden conversion of a competitor is evidence of the incongruities of the ghetto as a strategy for proselytizing, and of the unquestionable Jewish capacity for survival and resistance. The commitment and talent invested by Asriglio (and by many of his colleagues) were paradoxically rewarded in the wake of another Jew's baptism, which in a sense seems to almost repudiate the convert's choice. Exemplary careers were advanced with great effort and tenacity during years in which ascents of this nature should not have been possible. Instead, the continuous dialectic woven between the Jews and the surrounding world was one of the main drivers of this advancement, through the progressive definition of paths of social establishment and advancement which took place simultaneously both inside and outside the Jewish world. The affairs of the Ram, Abbina, Ceprano and Asriglio families offer examples of some of the many possible itineraries.

Thus, closed in the ghetto though they were, the Jewish bankers did not lose heart. Instead they experimented with every alternative available, however difficult or unfamiliar. Driven by the exigencies of daily life, the Jewish moneylenders had no other choice but to add to their current businesses in order to make ends meet. Alongside banking they took up the kinds of mercantile and commercial businesses which their Christian colleagues were at the same time progressively abandoning, having become attracted by and occupied solely with purely financial investments.[76] The growing disconnect between the figure and work of the Jewish merchant-banker and that of the Christian banker,

---

72   DC, r. 389, cc. 91v-92r.
73   DC, r. 392, c. 113v.
74   Esposito 2002
75   DC, r. 377, c. 8r-v.
76   On these subjects cfr. Delumeau 1979; Piola Caselli 1991.

one increasingly a merchant, the other increasingly a banker (and increasingly ready to definitively enter the financial and bureaucratic oligarchy, grabbing jobs, offices, and even cardinal's *berrettas* in a State, that of the Church, where financial experience was regularly sought after at the top levels of the administration)[77] was, therefore, a part of the long process of adaptation and resistance experienced by the Roman community in the centuries of the ghetto. For precisely this reason it is worth looking at the social, cultural and economic consequences of this adjustment, and the extent of these consequences, focusing on the professional dynamics and changes that the Jewish ruling class would encounter a few years after the institution of the *serraglio* of the Jews.

77   Regarding the bureaucratization of ecclesiastical careers, see Prodi 1982.

CHAPTER 5

Unexpected Opportunities

The stories of Salomone Ram and his colleagues sketch a profile of Jewish banking activity in Rome after the institution of the ghetto. What emerges is a portrait of an economic and professional group that was fully part of the city marketplace, and capable of expanding its interests across central-northern Italy through networks of kinship and acquaintance among coreligionists. The marginal position imposed by law in 1555 and exacerbated by successive provisions – among which figures the *Motu proprio* of Sixtus V, examined above – contributed to separating the fate of the Jewish moneylenders from that of their Christian colleagues, but it did not succeed in wiping out Jewish entrepreneurship. The capacity for reaction and survival relied on the inclusion of new members in the ruling class, identified by the prestige of a rabbinic title and by successes achieved in the professional world. In both cases, people's good reputations established trust in individuals and their families, facilitating progress up the social ladder. The acquisition of credit developed simultaneously both inside and outside the ghetto, via mixed and complex paths that always, however, unfolded along the restricted range of professional choices permitted to the Jews.

Social mobility and institutional flexibility were the two essential elements in the Jewish minority's struggle for survival in the modern age. In this context, the shrewd and intelligent exploitation of every opportunity and every opening offered by the innumerable conflicts between the Christian magistrates was a key factor. We have looked at the shift in criteria for the selection of representatives of the *Universitas*. We have reconstructed the transformations that affected moneylending, and have seen how this was increasingly linked to the world of commerce. Now it is important to examine the sectors, mechanisms, rules, and criteria with which the Jews applied themselves to the only trade they were allowed to practice, *stracceria*. In this case as well, if we look closely the results present unexpected novelties; even old clothes (*stracci*) can hold surprises. Some *stracci* were of much higher value than others – such as the bundles of clothing from the hospitals (*fardelli*) – and the places and methods of selling these *stracci* could become a system of accumulating capital, just like the management of spaces in the city markets. Outside the walls of Rome, travel of short, medium and long range presented other business opportunities. Journeys to participate in textile fairs and meetings with partners and relatives were commonplace and, just like the *stracci*, served to expand the range of options available to the Jews of the ghetto.

1   Valuable *stracci* from the Hospitals

"*Judaei praefati sola arte strazzarie seu cenciariae, ut vulgo dicitur, contenti.*"[1] With these words in 1555, Paul IV defined the range of work specializations permitted to the Jews in the Papal States. Over the course of the three centuries that ran from the promulgation of *Cum nimis absurdum* to the breaching of the *Porta Pia*, different men would rise to the papal throne, driven by different priorities and political intentions regarding the Jewish minority. All of them, however, from time to time confirmed, mitigated or aggravated the scope of these provisions.[2] Thus for a long period, starting in 1555, the Jews of Rome found themselves constrained to making their living through the sale and recycling of used clothing.[3] The monopoly on management of the hospital *fardelli* was the means via which Jewish businessmen found a way to extricate themselves from the web of such unfavorable regulations. It is thanks precisely to this business that Jews built successful economic careers, even inside the ghetto.

In Rome, like everywhere else, the biggest producers of second hand clothing were the hospitals. The Jews, eager to stock up on raw materials, negotiated with the hospitals to acquire, at the best possible price, most of the clothing left behind by the deceased at the various institutions, which was gathered up in packages called *fardelli*.[4] These contracts were not an entirely new phenomenon, and it is possible to trace them back to the 1400s. However, it was

---

[1] The citation is from the Bull *Cum nimis absurdum*.
[2] A quick *excursus* of the legislation released by different pontiffs and their attitudes towards the Jews is found in Milano 1984, pp. 71–127.
[3] Even if, in truth, more or less successful attempts to continue trade in new merchandise continued until at least the 1700s, among the vigorous protests from the corporation of tailors (Groppi 1999). For a general description of the poor art of *stracceria* practiced by the Jews, Berliner 1992 and Milano 1984. Regarding the diffusion of this profession in the Italian ghettos, Siegmund 1996.
[4] The other side of the same coin is represented by the clothing of those condemned to death. These too were regularly sold to the Jews, and these transactions were recorded in the books of the Brotherhood of *San Giovanni Decollato*, in which, however, at the moment I have not found evidence of genuine contractual agreements. About the Roman hospitals in general, while lacking a study that examines the details of their organization as well as financial and administrative operations, Morichini 1892; Canezza 1933; Petrocchi 1970, pp. 107–108; and more recently for the 18th Century, Cormano 2001–2002. For a general picture of health in Rome, Piccialuti 2005.

only in the second half of the 16th century that they gradually became more numerous, and progressively assumed a more formal structure until they were set up like genuine monopoly contracts.[5]

The cornerstones of the contract, established by mutual agreement between the parties, observed a model which defined the responsibilities of each party, albeit with some variations. The contract specified the following elements: the unit price established for the entire duration of the contract, the obligation for the monthly collection of the *fardelli,* a requirement that the bundles be composed exclusively of fabrics (thus weapons, precious objects and money were excluded), the obligatory charitable donation of clothes to the hospital, and a prohibition on stealing parcels or selling them to others without the agreement of the contract holders. The oldest contract found so far in the registries of the Roman hospitals already presents the structure which gradually inspired those that followed. As such this document is worth examining in detail. The contract was stipulated on January 2 1564, between the Custodians and the Chamberlain of the *Ospedale della Consolazione di Roma* and Angelo Sacerdote, with Samuele Scazzocchio, regarding the *fardelli* from the men and women who would die in the hospital's care that year. On that occasion it was established that:

> Primarily the aforementioned Angelo and Samuelo are held and obligated and each of them first and foremost are to guarantee with their own money and to take all the aforementioned *fardelli* of the said people who die in the aforementioned hospital from men and women alike without any exception starting from the first of the coming month of January and to finish at the following price and named price of *iuli* 11 and *baiocchi* 7 for one of the *fardelli* from men and from women mentioned above. It has also been agreed and stipulated that the said *fardelli* will not include gold nor silver coins or money in other forms nor swords breastplates of armor and daggers and other sorts of weapons as well the said *fardelli* will be free and absent from these aforementioned items as they are not intended to be part of the said *fardello* but only fabrics of linen and wool and similar items. It has also been agreed and stipulated that the said Jews are obligated as above to give and fully pay to the said *Camerlengo* twenty *scudi* with a rate of 10 *giuli* per *scudo* in advance as a deposit for the said *fardelli* which twenty *scudi* shall remain with the said *Camerlengo* to credit to the said Jews for said *fardelli* that they took the previous

---

5 Thanks to Prof. Anna Esposito for pointing this out.

month of the stated year and not otherwise. Also that the said Jews are held and obligated as above to take the said *fardelli* month to month and when they collect them immediately and at the same time they must pay the price of these meaning however that they have not claimed the above mentioned deposit of twenty *scudi* by paying for the previous month as has been stated above. It has also been agreed and stipulated that the said Jews are held as above to leave five shirts per one hundred and this to aid the injured who come to this hospital. It has also been agreed and stipulated that none of the said signori *Guardiani* can or should remove any *fardello* without the prior agreement of the aforementioned Jews. Also that the aforementioned Jews can and each of them can come one time per week to see the *fardelli* and to put them in a *Camera* for which they have a key and the hospital official will be given the other. Also that the *fardelli* from men and women alike should be made immediately when the patient arrives and that they were not bundled without the presence of the said Jews, and the *spedaniera* [manager of the women's side of the hospital] of the women should immediately be sent to the *spedaniero* [manager of the men's side] of the men all the items of the patient with all that are listed fabrics such as shirts frocks socks clothing and the rest. Also that if any fraud is found in all of that committed by the *spedaniero* or *spedaniera* the said Jews can legitimately force them to pay it and the said *signori Guardiani* can keep their salary to satisfy the bill.[6]

---

6 ASR, *Consolazione, Istrumenti*, r. 37, cc. 177r-178r; this is the oldest contract found during a systematic research of these contracts that was carried out in the hospital sources believed to be the most important in this sector, based on the data that emerged from the examination of the registries of the Jewish Notaries; the hospitals in question are the *San Giacomo* (ASR, *S. Giacomo: Libro Mastro, Libri di entrata e uscita del camerlengo, Libro del Mastro di casa e Istrumenti*), the *Consolazione* (ASR, *Consolazione: Libro mastro generale e Istrumenti*), the *San Rocco*, (ASR, *S. Rocco, Istrumenti*) and the *Santo Spirito* (ASR, *Santo Spirito, Instrumenta*). "In primis che li sopradetti Angelo et Samuelo siano tenuti et obligati et ciascheduno di loro come principalmente et in solido sia tenuto et obligato ha pigliare tutti li sopradetti fardelli delle ditte persone che moriranno nel sopra detto hospitale tanto delli homini quanto delle donne senza alcuna excaptione cominciando dal primo del presente mese di gennaro et finire come seguita per prezzo et nome di prezzo di iuli 11 et baiocchi 7 l'uno delli fardelli tanto del 'huomo quanto delle donne predetti. Item cum pacto et conditione che li detti fardelli non ce s'intesa ne oro ne argento monetato et non monetato et quattrini ne spada giacco maniche et pugnale et altre sorte d'arme quale predette cose siano libere et assenti da dicti fardelli adeoche da detto fardello non s'intenda si non panno di lino et de lana et cose simili. Item con patto et conditione che detti hebrei siano obligati come di sopra ha dare et effectualmente paghare al detto S. Camerlengo scudi vinti di moneta a ragione di giuli 10 per scudo avanti tratto quali siano per arra di detti fardelli quali scudi vinti ristino sempre in mano del detto Camerlengo da scontarseli ha detti ebrei in detti fardelli che piglieranno

In the years that followed, the system put in to practice at the *Consolazione* became the norm at many of the city's hospitals – *Santo Spirito, San Rocco, San Giacomo degli Incurabili*, and *Fatebenefratelli*. Through a series of improvements and adjustments made from renewal to renewal, the duration of a single contract was gradually extended from being valid for one year, such as in the contract just cited, up to nine years, a term which was typical for rental contracts of that era, as specified in a contract dated May 20, 1594 between azio Celso and Francesco Parisi, custodians and administrators of the *Ospedale della Consolazione*, and Giuseppe dell'Aquila.[7]

The cost of the contract itself grew in the same fashion, to the point of calling for a donation of 150 *scudi* to the *Cardinal Vicario* in 1571,[8] as well as donations and gifts for almost dizzying sums in the agreements reached with the *Commissario* of the *Santo Spirito*. The detailed reconstruction of the contractual renewals negotiated by this institution in the 1580s – which I include here at the end of this chapter – clarifies the importance and the gradual evolution

---

l'ultimo mese del detto anno e non altimente. Item che detti hebrei siano tenuti et obligati come di sopra a pigliare detti fardelli a mese per mese et quando li piglieranno subito et incontinente habbino a paghare il prezzo da esse intendendo pero che non habbino mai a scomputare li sopra detti venti scudi se non l'ultimo mese come ha detto di sopra. Item con pacto et conditione che detti hebrei siano tenuti come di sopra ha lassare cinque camisie per cento et questo per medicare li feriti che venghino ha detto hospitale. Item con pacto et conditione che detti signori Guardiani ne ciascuno di loro possa ne debbia levare nissun fardello se prima non e d'accordo con li sopra detti hebrei. Item che li sopra detti hebrei possino et ciascuno di loro possa venire una volta la settimana ha vedere detti fardelli et metterli in una Camera della quale loro habbia una chiave et il maestro spedaviero l'altra. Item che li fardelli tanto de homini quanto de donne s'habbino da fare subito che sara venuto l'infermo et non s'habbino affardellare senza presentia de detti hebrei, et la spedaniera delle donne debbia subito consegnarli al spedaniero delli huomini tutta la robba della inferma con tutto quello che sara de panni listati camisie zenali calze veste et il resto. Item che se lo spedaniero o la spedaniera saranno trovati in alcuna fraude che de tutto quello che detti hebrei proveranno legittimamnte possino astungerli a pagharli et li detti signori Guardiani possino ritenere il loro salario et satisfarli per detto conto."

7   ASR, *Consolazione, Istrumenti*, r. 38, cc. 230r-231r. The price of a *fardello* was fixed at 1 *scudo*, at 10 *giuli* per *scudo*, and that of the contract itself was set at 100 *scudi*, to be paid in two installments to *Camerlengo* Giovanni Battista Alberini (the first payment was recorded on August 8, 1594, cfr. c. 231r); the contract went into effect beginning in 1597, and on April 14 of that year Giuseppe's sons, along with Salomone Silaus and Giacobbe Rosciello collected the first *fardelli* (c. 262r-v). On the *Ospedale di Santa Maria della Consolazione*, Belli 1834; Pericoli 1879.

8   ASR, *Consolazione, Istrumenti*, r. 37, cc. 266r-267r. The contract was stipulated between Giovanni d'Aurelio de Mattheis, guardian of the Ospedale della Consolazione, and Nissim Moro, Leone Mancino and Emanuele Sacerdote, and provided for the sale of all of the hospital's *fardelli* for four years, at the price of 9 and a half *giuli* each, and specified the payment of a deposit of 100 *scudi* (25 *scudi* per year) and an offering of 150 *scudi* to the Vicar of Rome.

of these monopoly agreements. Interpreted from this perspective, these contracts contributed to a significant redrawing of the Jewish economic and entrepreneurial outlook in Rome during this period.

On October 13, 1578 the *commissario* of the *Santo Spirito*, Monsignor Theseo Aldovrando, sold all of the *fardelli* of the *Ospedale Grande degli Infermi* (but not from the hospital reserved for nobility) to Emanuele Sacerdote and Prospero Menasse for a term of four years. The agreed upon price was 6 *giuli* for each *fardello*, and it was decided that the Jews would provide a donation of 500 *scudi* to the *ospedale*, to be paid in installments of 125 *scudi* at the beginning of January for each year of the contract. To that sum was further added 80 blankets of fine white wool, to be delivered in batches of twenty, also at the beginning of January each year.[9] On December 23, 1580 the next contract was recorded, valid for another six years, and awarded to a company of converts. This company would subsequently be joined by Emanuele Sacerdote *alias* Sciaquatello, with the permission of Theseo Aldovrando – and against all legal criteria, according to which any association between Jews and converts had never been and would never be legitimate. In this contract the price of a single *fardello* and the number of blankets to be donated remained the same, but the amount of the initial offering was doubled, now fixed at 1,000 *scudi*.[10] In 1583 a new agreement was signed for a six year term (until April 30, 1589) with Cascian Moresco, Samuele Scazzocchio, Salomone di Matthatia and Leone Mancino, to which a sixth quota was added for Sciaquatello, again by the express request of the *commissario*. This contract saw the price of *fardelli* rise to nine *giuli* each, the number of blankets (to be made of fine white wool and weigh at least eight pounds each) to be donated reduced to ten, and the deposit reduced to only 100 *scudi*.[11]

To summarize, in ten years the value of the contract had grown so much as to induce a clergyman to use his powers to circumvent the rules regarding the separation of Jews and converts. Such anomalous behavior indicates the

---

9   ASR, *Santo Spirito, Instrumenta*, r. 252, cc. 65v-66v.
10   ASR, *Santo Spirito, Instrumenta*, r. 254, cc. 79v-81r. The converts were Angelo di Anguillara, Benedetto dell'Arpa, Paolo Ghisello, Giuseppe dell'Arpa and Aron de Cathecuminis; on January 10, 1581, Emanuele Sciaquatello purchased the sixth share of the contract on the same terms accepted by the converts on Mary 8, 1581, and the convert Ieronimo Orsini (formerly Rabbi Aron di Benedetto) ratified the agreement.
11   ASR, *Santo Spirito, Instrumenta*, r. 255, cc. 136v-138v. In reality, the latter agreement is signed as a replacement for a prior accord reached on April 22, 1583 with the company of converts that had owned the contract since 1580, and this led to a misunderstanding the following July, when the number of blankets called for was already agreed upon as nine but the unit cost of the *fardelli* was higher, equal to one *scudo* (Ibid., cc. 110v-112r).

importance of this business for all involved: for the hospitals it represented the opportunity to quickly and conveniently resolve the problem of disposing of unwanted goods and to bring in cash for the institution's coffers. For the Jews, obviously, it was an extraordinarily productive sector for investment, in an age in which most other sectors were explicitly forbidden to them – other than worthless *stracci*.

However, it should be noted that if on one hand this business – buying merchandise to resell at retail, in bulk and at favorable prices for large quantities, with supplies for restocking always assured – was certainly profitable and very reliable, on the other hand it remained mired in negative connotations. Reselling the clothing of those who had died from illness or condemnation to death was not a neutral transaction. In the case of the hospital *fardelli*, therefore, the price trends seem to have been governed by several factors beyond just inflation. Apart from strictly financial factors, the symbolism connected to the fear of deadly contagions that inevitably accompanied the clothing of people who had died from disease also played a role. In this sense, then, the case of the *Ospedale del Santo Spirito* and its continuously renewed contracts is paradigmatic. Following the group of converts' decision to withdraw from the business, the Jews brought home a negotiated contract that was much more favorable than the one that was expiring. Jews were chosen for these contracts for lack of other candidates, and likewise the Jews sought out these contracts for lack of better options. Even if they would have preferred to avoid possible contamination from death and illness, real or imagined, the Jews did not have many options. Thus the professional specialization imposed by Paul IV implied subjection to a dangerous logic, which, even in cases involving the movement of large amounts of money, never eliminated the difficult and precarious position of the minority. Survival had a cost.

The price of the *fardelli* depended on the quality of the clothes that were included. While money, weapons and jewelry were always excluded from the *fardelli*, the types of merchandise that Jews ended up buying could vary, and might have included shoes and shirts, thus affecting the total cost of a single package. For example, *fardelli* from San Giacomo degli Incurabili were particularly "affordable" at only eight *giuli* each. The *San Giacomo* sold at a low price because their *fardelli* included "neither shirts nor towels nor handkerchiefs nor weapons nor money nor gold nor silver nor shoes as such things go to the hospital."[12] Beyond the listing of individual articles, though, on occasion items

---

12   ASR, *S. Giacomo, Istrumenti*, r. 43, c. 184v. With this *venidtio fardilllorum* on July 11, 1585, Giovanni Battista Garonetti, *Camerlengo* of the *San Giacomo degli Incurabili*, contracted to sell all the hospital's *fardelli* for four years (starting with February 12, 1586) to Sabbato

would be combined in a special sale. One such sale involved some clothing belonging to *signora* Agata Flandet, who died at the *Ospedale della Consolazione*. The group of items was purchased by Angelo Zarut for 33 *scudi*. This was a special package, of very stylish, higher than average quality clothing made of velvet, satin, gold, silver, and other precious fabrics, and therefore worthy of an exception.

Collection of the merchandise according to regular established deadlines is another point we find reiterated in the various contracts. The *fardelli* had to be collected every three months, and paid for, in one or more installments, prior to the date of the next distribution. The payments had to be punctual, and, on paper, it was not possible to request reductions of the agreed upon price.[13] Faced with actual needs, though, discounts in price and delays in payment became customary and accepted. So, in 1591 the hospital Custodians and *Camerlengo* raised no objection when Sabbato di Serena, with Giacobbe and Isacco Rosciello, asked several times for reductions in their payments for over 700 *fardelli*. This extraordinary number of *fardelli* had accumulated due to an unusually high number of deaths at the *Ospedale della Consolazione*. The hospital granted Sabbato and his partners payment extensions through the following spring,[14] when the extension was further prolonged. The final balance of 210 *scudi* was only sent on December 24, 1594, three years after the first extension.[15]

Mazzone, Angelo di Cave, Crescienzo Simonetti and Angelo Mazzone, at the price of 8 *giuli* each, an offering of 25 *scudi* to the hospital, and the commitment to pay for and collect the *fardelli* in three month intervals. On the *Ospedale di San Giacomo*, Vanti 1938; De Angelis 1952 and 1955; Lupo 2004–2005.

13   An exception is the contract stipulated on November 2, 1567 between the *Guardiani della Società* of the *Ospedale della Consolazione* and Leone Mancino Romano and Emanuele Sacerdote *alias* Sciaquatello, in which the collection of the *fardelli* is specified as having to be within one day of the patient's death, but, since a similar clause does not repeat in following documents, it is legitimate to suppose that the parties, given the practical difficulties of this arrangement, would have then agreed to return to the previous system of consignments each trimester (ASR, *Consolazione, Istrumenti*, r. 37, cc. 222v-223r).

una fadriglia di raso rosso con li borsoni di velluto crenesino, una ciamarra di velluto negro fatto a opera, una traversa con il suo busto di velluto negro la metà stampata con tune di oro e di argento, un'altra traversa con il suo busto di raso turchino tessuto un cappello di armesino con perne grantatune et medaglia de oro con un cameo et pennacchio roscio et bianco

14   ASR, *Consolazione, Istrumenti*, r. 38, cc. 190r-192v.
15   ASR, *Consolazione, Istrumenti*, r. 38, c. 236r-v.

The *capitoli* governing these contracts expressly prohibited procedures of this type, going as far as sanctioning any requests related to the subject with the imposition of heavy fines, up to ten *scudi* per attempt.[16] Despite this, the administrators charged with the good governance of the institutions entrusted to them were, if necessary, inclined to turn a blind eye in order to protect those interests. In some instances it was the chamberlains themselves who granted the sale of *fardelli* on credit to debtors whom they trusted completely.

As the case just cited demonstrates, the two Rosciellos, and especially Sabbato di Serena, were men with excellent reputations, whose credibility mitigated the risk of the hospital being exposed to financial disasters. Since the 1580s Sabbato di Serena had stood out as one of the most active acquirers of hospital contracts, buying up majority shares in purchases at the *Consolazione*, *San Rocco*[17] and the *Fatebenefratelli*.[18] Crowning a brilliant career in *robbe d'ospitale*,[19] on September 9, 1591 Sabbato and his brother Leone were rewarded with the granting of an *inhibitio in Curia ratione foenoris*. Although he did not hold a proper license for moneylending, thanks to the *inhibito* Sabbato could be said to have finally joined the group of Jewish bankers of Rome. The two Rosciellos, instead, were Sabbato's regular assistants; thus, while not expressly listed among the contractors for the *fardelli* of the *Ospedale della Consolazione*, over the years they were able to build a relationship of trust with the administrators, to the extent that they were included in this concession.

Sabbato di Serena's career followed a typical path whose progress sheds light on milestones that were common to other successful careers as well. Combining subsidiary businesses with the principal occupation of moneylending at interest was an established practice, imposed by prevailing

---

16 This was the amount specified in the quadrennial contract stipulated by Monsignor Theseo Aldovrandi, Emanuele Sacerdote alias Sciaquatello and Prospero Menasse for the *fardelli* of the *Santo Spirito* in 1578 (ASR, Santo Spirito, Instrumenta, r. 252, cc. 65v-66v).

17 On the *Ospedale di San Rocco delle Partorienti*, De Angelis 1952; Cormano 2001–2002.

18 Regarding the *Ospedale di San Giovanni di Dio Calibita*, called "Fatebenefratelli," from the founder's motto, Martire 1934; Russotto 1966.

19 In 1586, for example, he sold two quotas of the *Ospedali della Consolazione* and *San Giacomo* to Vito Moresco, Angelo Zarut, Cascian Tripolese and Mosè Negri (NE, f. 6, l. 1, c. 87r-v); then in 1589 he gave the option for the contract with the *Ospedale San Rocco*, which at that point had begun to be negotiated, to Samuele Scazzocchio and David di Salomone di Pellegrino (Ibid., f. 14, l. 1, cc. 172v-173r); later, in 1590 he appears as the new contractor with the Fatebenefratelli, for which he first paid 80 *scudi* to take over the current contract, and then a sum that is not clear to obtain the renewal; his partners David Sacerdote and Angelo Muccinello contribute with payments of 25 and 17 *scudi* respectively for the first contract and different monthly rates starting at 30 *scudi* (arriving at the sum of 150 *scudi*) for the second (Ibidem, f. 6, l. 2, c. 40r-v).

conditions. Privileged relations with the hospitals could accompany or prefigure official recognition of one's inclusion in the world of legitimate moneylenders. Sabbato di Serena was not the only one to obtain public proof of his inclusion in this circle after a long rise in the ranks conducted between hospital *fardelli* and market spaces. Similar paths were taken by Vito and Angelo Moresco, sons of Amadio: the first was known for all of the 1580s as a tireless promoter of business partnerships formed for acquiring *fardelli*,[20] while the second, after a long apprenticeship in the world of brokering and trade in market spaces,[21] saw his and his family's efforts rewarded with the issuance of a coveted *inhibitio*, at first valid for only four years, and thus granted, so to speak, *sub iudicio*.[22]

Investments in the hospital sector could offer ideal steps towards an entrepreneurial career, from the experience of apprenticeship alongside established professionals to the training acquired through first person management of a small business. However, interest in this sector also involved men who had long claimed quite respectable *curricula*. This was the case, for example, with Giacobbe d'Aversa, a banker who was licensed under the tolerance of February 1, 1577,[23] and the descendent of a line of license holding moneylenders that extended back to the concessions granted by Julius III.[24] Giacobbe had no disdain at all for the hospital contracts, and rather participated in them in order to provide some schooling for his sons.[25] The experience of Emanuele

---

20   Remaining only in 1586, for example, in partnership with Samuele Scazzocchio, Mosè Negri and Angelo Zarut, he purchased Giacobbe di Menasci's quota in the triennial contract of the *Santo Spirito* (NE, f. 6, l. 1, c. 75r-v), purchased Leone Deloro's quota in the contracts with the *Consolazione* and *San Giacomo* (Ibidem, f. 6, l. 1, c. 83r-v) and sold one of the ten quotas for the *Santo Spirito* to Cascian Tripolese (Ibid., f. 6, l. 1, c. 103r-v) and, for the same year the list could go on at length.

21   After years spent leasing and then subletting market spaces belonging to others (cfr. for example NE, f. 14, l. 1, c. 6r-v e c. 9r), in 1588 he finally begins to buy them himself (Ibid., f. 14, l. 1, c. 6r-v).

22   DC, r. 410, c. 53v. Furthermore, in the case of the Moresco brothers it is still possible that this was a later reconfirmation, there being, however, a Marzoccho Moresco among the bankers licensed by Julius III, whose lineage is unfortunately unknown to me; still, cfr. Esposito 2002, p. 580.

23   DC, r. 377, c. 8v.

24   Cfr. Esposito 2002, p. 580.

25   His sons Leone and Giuseppe, in fact, begin to get experience in this very sector: in 1586 Leone, as the guardian and caregiver for his brother's children, resolved all outstanding balances between Samuele Scazzocchio and the deceased Giuseppe concerning the hospital contracts (NE, f. 6, l. 1, cc. 113r-114r); some years later, in 1590, he released all his rights to the current contract at San Giacomo to Mosè Soschin Tedesco, Angelo di Cave, Giacobbe Rosciello and Abramo Scazzocchio (NE, f. 6, l. 2, c. 40r).

Sacerdote *alias* Sciaquatello was no different. Among the fortunate owners of a banking license,[26] he enjoyed excellent relations with the *Commissario* of the *Santo Spirito*, who took care to ensure that he received regular quotas in the contracts.[27]

An analysis of the *fardelli* contracts, conducted along the dual tracks of reconstructing the relations that developed with the hospitals and of identifying the *curricula* of those who were engaged in the trade, brings to light salient and until now little known aspects of the economic vitality of the Roman Jews in the second half of the 16th century. A *fardelli* monopoly was at times seen as an obligatory rite of passage and training towards an outstanding career, or a first step in social climbing. There is another aspect, however, also little known until now, which is worth lingering over for a moment. This regards the criteria by which the Jewish monopolists were chosen by their Christian counterparts. The volume of business was valued in the hundreds, and at times in the thousands of *scudi* annually; thus the hospital administrators preferred entrusting their contracts to people whose solvency, and thus ability to pay punctually, presented no cause for concern. The Jewish contract holders were, as we've seen, well-known figures in the Roman commercial market. At times the trust relationship could produce incredible outcomes. The case of Sciaquatello and his inclusion in the contract between the *Santo Spirito* and the partnership of converts, with him being allocated a one-sixth quota at the request of the hospital,[28] raises the suspicion that the *Commissario* sought guarantees through the Jew that these unknown converts, who by dint of their status as

---

26 ASR, *Camerale I, Diversorum del camerlengo*, r. 377, c. 8v.
27 Sciaquatello's interests, though, also push beyond privileged relations with the *Santo Spirito*. In 1567, with Leone Mancino he bought all the *fardelli* of the *Consolazione* for the following year (ASR, *Consolazione, Istrumenti*, r. 37, cc. 222v-223r), the contract again stipulated along with Leone Mancino, Salomone Mazzone and Mosè di Simonetto for the two year period 1570–1572 (Ibid., r. 37, cc. 266r-267r). In 1578 he takes a four year contract with Giacobbe Menasse for the *fardelli* of the *Santo Spirito* (ASR, *Santo Spirito, Instrumenta*, r. 255, cc. 136v-138r), and in 1581 he negotiated his rights in the purchase of a shed for the *compra* of the *Santo Spirito*, first by taking over Giacobbe's share (NE, f. 11, l. 5, c. 85r-v e c. 86r) and then also that of Salomone *alias* Zio Lavo, with the clear intention of qualifying as the sole owner of the useful storage space (Ibid., f. 11, l. 5, c. 90v). In the meantime, from 1580, Leone Mancino's company, in which Sciaquatello was also a partner, obtained a four year contract with the *Consolazione* (ASR, *Consolazione, Libro Mastro Generale*, r. 1291, c. 328) and, again in 1585, could offer credits of 5 *scudi* to Leone Mancino for "the part of Leon de Levi debtor to the *Santo Spirito* for the year he bought" (NE, f. 6, l. 1, cc. 41r-42r).
28 ASR, *Santo Spirito, Instrumenta*, r. 254, cc. 79v-81r.

new Christians had rights to all kinds of privileges and benefits,[29] were perhaps unable to offer.

The experience of the convert Paolo Ghisello and his associates under this contract could not have been particularly positive. In 1583, well in advance of the fixed expiration date, it fell to the new *Commissario*, Monsignor Giovanni Battista Ruini, to negotiate the terms of the contract's renewal. To further safeguard against unpleasant contingencies, a new clause was inserted in the contract that expressly prohibited the buyer from "giving company shares to a person, neither a Christian nor a Jew, without the express authorization of the aforementioned *Monsignor Commissario*."[30] The redistribution of company shares to a secondary market was a common practice in which the hospital curators normally took no interest. The prohibition recorded in this case is exceptional, both because it was accompanied by the hospital's renunciation of many previously agreed to fees and gifts, and also because it demonstrates the hospital's involvement in such secondary business.[31] The hospital's decision to renounce the agreed upon benefits three years before the end of the contract, which was still valid (therefore there was time available to find new buyers), would seem to be an explicit signal of the preference shown to the Jews (or really, to certain Jews). As in the case of the *Consolazione* and its excess dead, sufficient sentiments of esteem and trust had grown to allow the acceptance of a verbal agreement to postpone the payment of the balance due, in violation of the provisions of the law.[32]

The Jew who held the contract with the hospital negotiated the conditions of the monopoly contract for *fardelli* produced in a specific time period, during which packages that had accumulated since the previous consignment would be picked up according to a predetermined frequency, and the bill for the last consignment would be paid. After their initial stipulation these contracts had a second life in the ghetto where, in the office of a Jewish notary, the transactions from the quota of the monopoly contracts were recorded, and proper companies were set up for their management. The Jewish companies, for their part, contended for shares in partnerships and for property rights of the storage sheds for the *fardelli* themselves. These sheds were within the walls, or close to the institution in question. Trade in the quotas was a daily business,

---

29 Regarding the many privileges reserved for converts in the area of work, cfr. Caffiero 1997 and 2012; Groppi 1999.
30 ASR, *Santo Spirito, Instrumenta*, r. 255, cc. 110v-112r. A few months later, as we've seen, the converts withdraw from the contract and the new contract is given to a company of Jews.
31 ASR, *Santo Spirito, Instrumenta*, r. 255, cc. 136v-138r.
32 ASR, *Consolazione, Istrumenti*, r. 38, cc. 190r-192v, 194r-v, 201v-202r, 212r-v.

but only involved a limited number of investors. The high cost of the securities further limited the circle of buyers. The records of transactions from the monopoly contracts with the *Consolazione* over the course of twenty years – between cross-selling, new contracts and subdivisions – clearly illustrate these practices. The transactions for these contracts are summarized in a table to facilitate reading at the end of this chapter.

An analysis of recurring names found in the analytical reconstruction of the *fardelli* contracts issued by the *Ospedale della Consolazione* over a twenty year period reveals how although a contract was awarded to a few individuals, in reality it ended up being split up and managed by their clients; contracts were divided into at least twenty three different shares, which were exchanged for rights in partnerships that worked with other hospitals (particularly the *San Giacomo degli Incurabili*). The management of the contract involved a restricted group of wholesalers who were intent on using this business as another means of reinforcing their position in Jewish society. The ghetto was small, and the available investment opportunities for Jewish businessmen were very few indeed; thus, in order to avoid a surge of serious conflicts that were destined to be resolved in long and costly arbitrations, the same alliances that competed for pieces of different monopoly contracts decided to give themselves a set of common rules and a neutral place for discussion through the creation of a special *Compagnia degli Ospedali*.

At a meeting of its leaders in 1583, a group of Jewish monopoly holders gathered in this new institution – until now unknown – where they agreed to a series of *capitoli* that were recorded by the notary Pompeo del Borgo. These *capitoli* established that anyone who wanted to sell their quota of a contract would be required to report it to the company or, if the company was not interested, to sell it to one of the partners with the consent of the others. In a case where the company subsequently changed its mind and decided that it wanted to buy the quota, the partner who had acquired it would be required to resell it within a month, without any increase in the originally negotiated price. Finally, it was explicitly forbidden to buy, or have someone as a proxy buy goods without permission from the company. For goods that were inventoried before the drafting of the *capitoli* but not yet paid for, the purchasing partner would be required to inform the company, which, for its part, had the authority to take over the negotiations and pay the agreed sum.[33]

---

33 The founding partners were Leone Mancino, Giacobbe Di Menasci, Leone Scazzocchio, Samuele Scazzocchio, Salon del fu Diodato, Vito Di Lanciano, Leone Deloro, Mosè Grande, Angelo Zarut e Cascian Tripolese (NE, f. 11, l. 6, cc. 80v-81r).

How well the *Compagnia degli Ospedali* actually fared is hard to say. It certainly helped to reduce tensions and conflicts, and some negotiations were conducted according to the rules it prescribed. Thus in January of 1584, backed by the *Compagnia*'s approval, Samuele Scazzocchio sold his personal quotas of *fardelli* from the *San Giacomo* and the *Consolazione* to Mosè Grande and Leone Deloro.[34] Shortly afterwards, Vito Moresco's company negotiated with Leone Mancino to divide up the *compre* of the *Santo Spirito* and of the *Fatebenefratelli*, which until then had been held in common.[35] It should be recalled, moreover, that the *Compagnia degli Ospedali*'s essential task was to provide a private and extrajudicial forum to the Jews of Rome for the resolution of conflicts between competitors. In this sense, certainly, it worked.

The *Compagnia* was an institution of self-governance that was envisaged and legitimized not by the rules of the *Universitas* but by those who made use of it. Five years after its creation, by which time the institution's failure would have been confirmed by its abandonment, the *Compagnia* once again demonstrated its usefulness. In fact, Salomone di Diodato, Samuele Scazzocchio and Sabbato Patello decided to resolve litigation over their reciprocal debts and credits with a rival business by appealing to mediation by the *Compagnia* rather than taking the ordinary route. It was thus established that they would each pay 25 *giuli* to the *Compagnia degli Ospedali*, only after Vito Moresco collected the 40 *scudi* of credit from Leone Deloro, Angelo Zarut, Mosè Negri and Cascian Tripolese, and delivered the amount owed to Emanele Sacerdote *alias* Sciaquatello.[36]

The stories of the *fardelli* and their contracts played out both inside and outside the ghetto, and consequently took on different meanings. For the

---

34   NE, f. 11, l. 6, cc. 83v-84r.
35   The partners in Vito Moresco's company were Giacobbe di Prospero, Leone Scazzocchio, Samuele Scazzocchio e Salomone di Diodato; the partners in Leone Mancino's company were Leone Deloro, Cascian Tripolese, Angelo Zarut and his brother Mosè. The terms of division were these: 1) Vito Moresco's company, declared owner of the *San Giovanni*, is to "give the part" to Michele Gabriele and Angelo Di Piperno alias Dobelei; 2) Leone Mancino's company, which has the *Santo Spirito* contract, is to pay the other company 40 *scudi*, or 14 *scudi* and 10 *baiocchi* per partner; 3) at the end of the agreed upon year the common company would be reconstituted and the balances of both the contracts would have to at least be near equal; 4) the purchase of merchandise of a total value less than five *scudi* is prohibited, each transaction has to be reported to the company, and the partners may not compete with the other (NE, f. 11, l. 6, cc. 100r-101v).
36   NE, f. 1 4, l. 1, c. 56v.

Jewish world they represented a useful business opportunity in a context that had precious few to offer, while in the eyes of the Christians they once again highlighted the minority's ambiguous utility, so typical of the choices regarding Jews in the age of the Counter-reformation. The sick died and their clothing had to be disposed of; to get this done they turned to the Jews (those who were rich, to be precise), who quickly resolved the problem; the clothing was then sold at retail by the Jewish *rigattieri* in Rome and so put back in circulation. This procedure, however, was far from neutral. Rather it took place under a cloud of ambivalence that hovered over the brokering of items that were contaminated with serious and sometimes scandalous illnesses (such as syphilis, the cure for which was a specialty at the *San Giacomo*, and stab wounds, a specialty of the *Consolazione*).[37] This revived, once again, in superstitious forms and perhaps even unconsciously, the stereotype of the disease carrying Jew who profited from Christian blood, which was certainly not new.[38] For the Jews, on the other hand, it was not possible to give up one of the few permitted lines of business, especially trade which fell within one of the occupations traditionally reserved for them. Instead, the skill and the "capitalist" spirit demonstrated in this business led to promotions and confirmations of social roles. The decline of the figure of the Jewish banker, who was increasingly a merchant, continued to widen the gap between Jews and the ideals and businesses of their Christian colleagues, who were ready to quit dealing in clothing that smelled like a shop and invest in real estate, with a view to obtaining other positions.[39] This reality had to be accepted, if not even rewarded with the recognition of profits that led to professional advancement, which for Christians was only possible after the abandonment of the same businesses.

---

37 Cfr. Piccialuti 1994.
38 On this, see Caffiero 2012, pp. 296–329. On the disease-carrying Jew, cfr. Ginzburg 1989, pp. 36–61; Foa 1984. On the Jew as exploiter of Christian blood, Taradel 2002. In other ways, even the reiterated (and regularly violated) prohibition on Jews and converts entering into purchase agreements for buying items at the public auctions of the *Monte di Pietà* should be taken as an attempt to prevent Jews from being enriched by the misfortunes of poor Christians who are forced to part with their dearest possessions in order to make ends meet; regarding this prohibition, from time to time re-posted in public announcements, cfr. for example ASR, *Collezione dei bandi*, b. 366, *Bando contra gli Hebrei (e anco i Neofiti) che impegnano al Sacro Monte della Pietà*. There is also a brief discussion in Poliakov 1956, pp. 110–112.
39 Piola Caselli 1991.

2   Market Spaces: the Jews, Public Space and Real Estate Ownership

Signing a monopoly contract for a hospital's *fardelli*, or buying quotas from companies already doing business in that sector represented one of the possible paths for sustaining the people and professions that had been thrown into crisis by the anti-Jewish laws of this period. Equally important was the ability to skillfully manage the only form of real estate ownership granted to the Jews: *gazaga*, which was a lease on a property at a fixed cost, with a term of at least nine years. Much like with the complex business of *stracci* and *stracciaroli*, a thorough examination of the *gazagot* also reveals hidden stories that take place far from the ghetto walls, but which are managed within them. These transactions were as important as investments with the principal Roman hospitals; we will see how through some concrete examples.

In 1592, the *Cardinal Camerlengo*, Enrico Caetani, granted an *inhibitione in Curia per viam accessum* (and thus not *ratione foenoris*) to Mosè Sacerdoti. Sacerdoti requested and obtained a special protection from the surveillance and impediments placed by the *Presidenza delle Strade* on the free use of his space in the *Piazza Navona* market.[40]

The spaces reserved for commerce in Rome included areas on public land as well as actual stores. In these areas, which were sometimes sheltered by arcades, the vendors would put up whatever structures they needed to ply their trade. In some cases, such as with the marble stones at the *Portico d'Ottavia*, which served perfectly as workbenches for the fish sellers, it wasn't even necessary to build such installations. The city's daily life was organized around these areas, which were scattered around the entire city. Whether there were stores, loggias, stones, display tables or even bare spaces, portions of the wide variety of retail trades came together in the different city markets, according to the day of the week. *Piazza Navona* was the central market, largely dedicated to the buying and selling of foods.[41] Therefore, the fact that Mosè worked (or was owner of a site in which someone else worked) at the *Piazza Navona* market is the first piece of information to highlight, though we remain ignorant of what type of merchandise his business offered (probably not food, considering the laws of the time concerning Jewish commerce).[42] Mosè's case was not an

---

40   DC, r. 406, c. 157r-v. On the *Piazza Navona* market in this period, see Di Nepi 2014.
41   For all of these aspects of the organization of the city's commerce, see Modigliani 1998.
42   However, even this prohibition was regularly violated. Particularly interesting, in this sense, is the *Tracta grani regnicoli* with which on December 21, 1592, the *Camerlengo*, Cardinal Enrico Caetani authorized Salomone Corcos to import *"milla riva"* of grain from the Kingdom of Naples to Castro San Benedetto and in general to the countryside of Ascoli, taking advantage of the bank coupons offered in the Kingdom by Francesco and

exception, and the management of market spaces was actually one of the common businesses conducted by the Roman Jews.

Much like the well-known *gazagot* for housing,[43] these titles of ownership could be subdivided into quotas,[44] rented,[45] put up for sale,[46] included in an inheritance,[47] or be made part of a dowry.[48] They were a genuine asset, an integral part of a person's or a family's capital, and were considered as such.

Nicola de Capitanis. The Jews continue to handle foodstuffs and still in 1827 Jewish bakers were found in *rione Sant' Angelo* that, naturally, also sold bread to Christians (Caffiero 2000a, pp. 273-292).

43 *Jus gazagà* was the special right of tenancy given to the Jews who were forced to live in the ghettos; Milano 1984, pp. 199-200; Colorni 1961; Laras 1968; and now Gasperoni, Groppi 2018.

44 So, for example, in 1585 Samuele Scazzocchio, having just received 12 and a half *scudi* owed to him, returns to Vito Moresco the half of the market space he owns; Vito, in fact, had previously completely turned over that space to Samuele and Israele Sacerdote in exchange for the payment the two of them made in his name for his share of 25 *scudi* for a loan of 75 *scudi* total made to all three of them (NE, f. 6, l. 1, cc. 11v-12r).

45 The list of market spaces rented or sublet, partially or entirely, is very long; so for example in 1585 Isacco Capuano renewed the rental of his half of a market space to Abramo Di Modigliano and Giuseppe Di Reggio for two years, at the price of 12 *scudi* paid in advance (NE, f. 6, l. 1, c. 65r-v); in 1586, Leone Di Cammeo rented half his market space for two years to Consiglio di Limentani at the rate of six and a half *scudi* (NE, f. 6, l. 1, c. 94r) and, in the same year, David Corcos sublet a market space belonging to Giuseppe Polidoro to Isaac Moro for a year and a half, at the price of 12 *scudi* (NE, f. 6, l. 1, c. 117v); or, again, in 1588, Benedetto di Segni rents a market space to brothers Sabbato and Giuseppe Di Serena for two years, at the annual rate of 10 *scudi* (NE, f. 14, l. 1, c. 14v).

46 As further proof of the value and importance attributed to the ownership of a market space as compared to rental contracts, there are not many deeds for the sale of a space; however, I cite a few as examples. In 1581 Angelo Scazzocchio sold a market space to Daniele di Tivoli for 60 *scudi*, which was actually rented to David Galante, and bordered on the market space which Angelo had rented to Sabato di Tivoli (NE, f. 11, l. 5, cc. 74v-75r), and this sale was completed in a few months thanks to the balance paid by Daniele (NE, f. 11, l. 5, cc. 96v-97v); or, in 1588, Bonafossa and his wife Preziosa sold Angelo Moresco a market space in the women's quarter belonging to Preziosa at the price of 30 *scudi*, of which 25 were paid immediately in cash and the rest at the next Passover when then license was issued (NE, f. 14, l. 1, c. 6r-v).

47 This is the case of the market space inherited by Isacco Perugia's sons, sold by the mother Gemma Bondi to brothers Benedetto and Mosè Fiorentino, who needed, however, to proceed with the alienation of consent of the paternal uncle Abramo Perugia and David del Borgo, who was present for the transaction and, probably, was another of the boys' guardians (NE, f. 9, l. 1, cc. 37v-38r).

48 This is clearly the case of the market space sold to Angelo Moresco by Bonafossa and Preziosa in 1588, cited supra, n. 49; the space, in fact, was owned by Preziosa who, therefore, being a subject in the negotiation of an asset she owned, was explicitly present at the moment of the sale.

Reaching an agreement about the division of a market space was difficult, and arguments over this subject cropped up regularly, just as with housing. In fact, disputes about this subject seem to have been, if possible, even more heated than the many other arguments that took place. While, by all accounts, dividing up an apartment to add more people, however tight the space, was difficult but not unworkable, the common ownership of a workplace meant the continual reprise of discussions about one subject; money spent and money earned. These disputes, with all their implications related to livelihood and social opportunities for an individual or a family could become even more explosive then those over stairs, beds and windows put together. Conflict could be triggered both by unresolved differences between partners who co-owned one space, as well as by the more frequent controversies between owners of neighboring spaces trying to agree on a precise definition of the borders between one space and the other.[49] The question of accurate locations remains open for us since it was not possible to retrace the placement of these Jewish market spaces with any certainty, as the registries of licensing letters and tax documents from the magistracy that was officially responsible for this subject are unfortunately missing for this time period.[50]

Though we lack specific documentary discoveries, some evidence suggests that although the majority of these spaces were certainly located inside the *Contrada Iudeaorum*, they were also found elsewhere, particularly in *Piazza Navona*, as indicated by Mosè Sacerdoti. Some years later, in February 1619, two Jews, David de Lustro and Iacob de Scela, were cited in an *Editto con elenco dei luoghi da devolversi e residuo di altri luoghi in Piazza Navona abbondonati o non curati dai precedenti titolari* as owners who had defaulted on their market spaces.[51] This again offers proof of a commercial presence that was perhaps small but which remained active over time. Almost two centuries later, at

---

49 For example, both elements figure in the long dispute that broke out in 1576 between Giacobbe Delopiglio, his son Benedetto, and Angelo Scazzocchio on one side and Aron Passapiera and Michele di Gabriele on the other regarding "the ownership and borders of the market and butcher spaces near those of Giacobbe, Benedetto and Angelo." To resolve this it was necessary to turn to two different arbitrators (NE, f. 9, l. 1, cc. 3v-7r).

50 In the source *Presidenza delle Strade,* preserved at the State Archive of Rome, in fact, the registries for these years are also missing for the *Taxae Viarum* (payments, for which there exists a list of paying residents in the ghetto in 1569 which, however, naturally does not report the merchants), and for the *Lettere patenti* issued by the *Maestri delle Strade* with the seal of the President, of which for the earliest, which was compiled starting in 1692, (that is, after the legitimization of the partial autonomy of this presidency sanctioned by the Bull *Sacerdotali et Reginae Urbis* by Innocent XII), there is an index attached to the inventory, published in Sinisi, Verdi 1995.

51 ASR, *Collezione dei Bandi,* b. 366.

the moment of the introduction of free trade decreed by Pio VII immediately after his consecration,[52] Roman Jews were among those who applied to the *Cardinal Camerlengo* with claims for compensation for the liberalization of commerce in *Piazza Navona*, attaching their centuries-old lease contracts as proof of ownership.[53] Again in 1758, in a catalog in which the Consultors of the Holy Office periodically collected and organized the cases currently under consideration in the Congregation's daily work, a heading appears concerning "Jews regarding keeping shops and storage spaces outside the ghetto of Rome, dispute between them and the *fondacali* merchants (the authorized Christian vendors) remains outstanding."[54]

In general the market spaces could be found inside the Jewish quarter or immediately close by, grouped together.[55] The notary records concerning these spaces – whether they involved partial or complete leases, property sales or disputes – confirm this proximity, normally identifying the space under negotiation by a precise listing of the owners of the bordering spaces, almost always Jews. The intended use of the different sections of the space was also determined based on these demarcations.

At times the indication is more accurate, citing specific areas of Rome – an otherwise unidentified *Osteria del Muletto*,[56] a *via dei Cappellari*,[57] an obscure "women's quarter,"[58] the "shirt-makers' quarter,"[59] and "the neighborhood of the hat makers found at the beginning of the street."[60] In these cases it is easy to presume that the contract dealt with a place that was located in an unusual area where there were traditionally few Jewish merchants present. These were often identified by the particular craft that was a specialty in the area, which the Jew mentioned would also have practiced.[61] What emerges is a toponymy

---

52   Caravale, Caracciolo 1963, pp.576 et seq.
53   ASR, *Camerale III, Roma città e comune*, b. 1934.
54   Archivio della Congregazione della Dottrina della Fede, S. Offizio, St. St. I-2, *sub voce Hebraeis*.
55   It would seem to indicate a position at the limit of the zone of the ghetto proper, and actually define the borders of the market space rented to David Lattes by Giuseppe di Polidoro, sited immediately after that of Benedetto Del Presto and opposite the gate of "cavaliere Sancti" (NE, f. 11, l. 5, c. 110r-v).
56   NE, f. 11, l. 6, cc. 57v-58r.
57   NE, f. 14, l. 1, c. 1v.
58   NE, f. 14, l. 1, c. 6r-v.
59   NE, f. 14, l. 1, c. 9r.
60   NE, f. 14, l. 1, c. 154r.
61   Rome, moreover, was a city that since the late Middle Ages had become characterized and structured more for professional specialization than for being based on ethnic or national membership; cfr. Esposito 2001, pp. 3-47; and for a general overview, see now Formica 2019.

shaped by market spaces, an evident sign of a city that was lived in and imagined through spaces for commerce and socializing. These spaces were part of the daily parlance, in the form of references and symbols that were understandable to all, and which drew a map of the real Rome, built on work as well as its monuments.[62] From a Jewish bastion in the heart of the Rome of the Popes, a position outside the segregated space was made possible only by the contiguous presence of coreligionists. For example, in 1585, when Angelo Delopiglio sold part of his market space to Isacco Rosciello for a term of two years, as interest for the 60 *scudi* he had received as a loan *gratis e pro amore*, it was defined in these terms:

> That is he gives a space towards that of Salomone Di Scantriglia and beyond that 4 *palmi di loco* of the façade in front of that used by the said Agnilo with the capacity to be able to hold two crates from the space of Agnelo Moreso and the crates of Angili Delopiglio must stay from the space from the side behind Mosè Cappellaro and two crates of Isacco from the façade of the corner where the said Isach is about to expand and it is legitimate for Isach to be able to keep two poles towards the part of Agnilo Moresco and two of the parts of Mosè Cappellaro to cover the aforementioned [...] if they agree that the expense of transporting the poles and paying the *maestri de Strada* is shared by both of them [...].[63]

Once again the perception of the city (that is of the life that was experienced there) must be looked for in the words chosen to describe it. The detailed list of the borders and neighboring spaces translates to a realm other than economic and social. Created as a physical and real description of a well-known world, it leads us to imagine the appropriation of essential urban spaces in a city of

---

62 Regarding the words used to define the city see Marin 2007 and Topalov, Marin, Depaule, Coudroy de Lille 2010.

63 NE, f. 6, l. 1, cc. 22v-23v. The practice of defining the negotiated position of a market space by its borders was naturally common among Christians as well (Modigliani 1998); "Cioè li dà una banda verso il loco di Salomone Di Scantriglia et oltre di quello 4 palmi di loco dalla facciata dinanzi dove gode detto Agnilo con facultà di potere tenere doi casse dalla banda de Agnelo Moresco e li cassi de Agnili Delopiglio debbi stare dalla banda de dietro canto Mosè Cappellaro et doi cassi se Isacco dalla facciata del cantone dove sta a espandere detto Isach et sia licito a Isach de potere tenere doi pertiche verso la parte de Agnilo Moresco e doi dalle parte di Mosè Cappellaro a covrire da di sopra [...] pur se. convengono che la spesa di portare le pertiche e pagare li maestri de Strada sia comune a tutti e due [...]."

which the Jews considered themselves to be an integral part, but which instead ideologically rejected and marginalized them.[64]

The use of a market space, even for a limited time, had a value of its own which was suitable for covering the interest and securities for the issuing of loans. The buying and selling of these real estate titles for cash was a common practice. So, for example, Giuseppe Polidoro leased one of his market spaces in rapid succession, first in 1583 to Abramo Ambron in exchange for a loan of 60 *scudi di moneta*,[65] then in 1585 to David Corcos, who paid 45 *scudi* and agreed to pay this sum two more times as annual rent.[66] The appeal of this market space rested wholly on its position between those of Giacobbe d'Aversa[67] and Salomone di Segni,[68] which is to say that it was in a strategic location for those interested in the banking business, something which David Corcos and Abramo Ambron had much in common; they were partners in a company dedicated to that trade, and both were close relatives of skilled professionals in the field.[69]

In 1584 David and Abramo liquidated the business by mutual agreement,[70] and David, who still held the market space and the credit, quickly worked to take advantage of them. First he formed a new company with his brother Salomone, investing the first 119 *scudi* in merchandise and cash, plus the market space. Salamone was provided with a shop, as well as his son Isacco's labor as an unpaid apprentice (the boy was actually required to pay a *giulio* per day to the company should he decide to go work for someone else).[71] He then proceeded to renew his contract with Giuseppe Polidoro,[72] and finally, in 1586, he sublet the site in question to Isaaco Moro for 12 *scudi*.[73] While this figure wasn't

---

64 On borders within a city, see *Les divisions de la ville*, a collection of studies directed by Christian Topalov (2007); see in particular the essays by Brigitte Marin and Samuel Fettah. And see even Topalov, Marin, Depaule, Coudroy de Lille 2010.
65 NE, f. 11, l. 6, cc. 5v-6r.
66 NE, f. 6, l. 1, cc. 54v-55r.
67 About Giacobbe d'Aversa, a banker licensed in the tolerance of 1577 (DC, r. 377, c. 8v), see above in the section on hospital contracts.
68 He was also member of a family of bankers, in which the owner of the license was the paternal uncle Giuseppe del *fu* Angelo (DC, r. 377, c. 8v).
69 Both of them, in fact, could boast of brothers among the owners of the moneylending licenses of 1577 (DC, r. 377, c. 8v).
70 NE, f. 11, l. 6, c. 96r-v.
71 NE, f. 11, l. 6, cc. 98v-99r.
72 Giuseppe's debt, moreover, was cancelled at the end of the contract. (NE, f. 11, l. 6, cc. 15v-16v).
73 NE, f. 6, l. 1, c. 117v. Isacco Moro was also an active acquirer of market spaces and hospital contracts.

particularly high – the rates for rentals went from 6 to 12 *scudi* and the sale prices were around 40 to 60 *scudi* – the investment was generally recognized as having a higher value than its actual price. Thus people like Isacco Rosciello, one of the two brothers who were among Sabbato di Serena's best clients,[74] not only managed their market spaces personally but also willingly offered their services as brokers and mediators of negotiations and loans, activities in which ownership of these spaces functioned like a security and replaced the collection of an interest rate in cash.

The emerging class of Rome's Jewish community was predisposed to holding multiple investments, whether they were mercantile or financial in nature, dealing in luxury goods as well as consumer goods and used clothing. This also included an interest in market spaces, which, as was done with *fardelli*, they would buy up wherever possible, either to deal with personally or to temporarily lease to others. The ownership of a loan *gazagà*, moreover, offered a prestige that was closer to the granting of and participation in the hospital monopolies than the ownership of an apartment, and not only for its role in a profitable business. Like with housing, this type of ownership was the only real estate asset available to Jews, and it is no accident that terminology from the institution of *jus gazagà* which governed the rental of residences was taken as the formal norm and regulation for these commercial spaces as well. The difference was that the housing market was ultimately aimed only at the inhabitants of the ghetto, while ownership of a market space meant that the owner had a direct presence in the urban fabric, limited by daylight hours though it may have been.

The market space, embedded in the daily life of the city, became the only fixed point of the strenuous peregrinations through the city streets to collect the *fardelli* from the hospitals, which would, at a later time, then be resold on those same market stands. The intrinsic impermanence of these commercial spaces, spread out among the *piazze* of Rome, was moderated by the erection of poles and tents to protect the seller and his goods from bad weather. Raising such tents could, but did not always or even regularly require paying a tax to the *Maestri di Strada*. The creation of these structures, which, between the covering and the sales counters could at least appear permanent, provided a defined space for exchanges between Jews and Christians. Most of all, though, these structures also symbolically offered the Jews, theoretically hidden away in the dark, narrow lanes of the ghetto, a visible place and role in the daily

---

74   Regarding Sabbato di Serena and the Rosciello brothers, cfr. above in the section on hospital contracts.

urban scene that was even more significant because it continued over time and was not an exception.[75]

3 Business Travel

The life of the Jews of Rome took place on the streets of the city, in its *piazze* and in its markets, maneuvering amongst the small openings that could be found in the mesh of laws meant to discriminate against them. No longer fully bankers and not only merchants, Jews kept on moving to survive. At whatever level one operated, the retail trade required travel, going to fairs, and seeking out new buyers and suppliers. Business travel, necessary as it was, could present a problem for Jews, in particular if they were headed to an area that did not have a ghetto where they could stay. *Cum nimis absurdum* offered only a legislative void on this subject. In fact, though the bull mandated the creation of ghettos in every city and castle in the Papal States, ordered Jews to remain inside them during night hours, and permitted Jews to only trade in second hand textiles, it never addressed the problem of regulating their travels. It did not prohibit them, nor did it authorize them; it simply remained silent on the subject.

Precisely because of this silence the subject of Jewish mobility became a source of conflict among ecclesiastical institutions, each with their own claims of authority in the matter: the Apostolic Chamber, the Holy Office, and the local magistrates, all of whom were sometimes favorable to, and sometimes against the presence of Jews. In 1751, counselor Pier Girolamo Guglielmi drafted a memorandum for the cardinals of the Roman Inquisition, spelling out the terms of the problem: on the one hand, there was the initiative of those who, in various roles, authorized the Jews' travels; on the other hand there were the ongoing attempts by Jews to take advantage of the travel permits and establish themselves permanently outside the ghetto; and finally there were the reactions of the local authorities, balanced, according to each case, between encouragement and repression. Overseeing it all, with few successes even in the middle of the 18th century, was the Sant'Uffizio, which, for its part, reiterated its jurisdiction over any instance of illicit contact between Jews and Christians.[76]

---

75 This is the case of the possession ceremony, about which see Prosperi 1996b; Caffiero 2000a; Di Castro 2010 and the documents presented in the appendix of the exhibition catalog, edited by myself. In general on ceremonies in Rome, see Visceglia 2002.
76 On this memorandum its context, see Di Nepi 2008. Regarding the Inquisition's purview over the Jews, see Caffiero 2004 and 2012.

The issuing of safe conducts for Jewish travel was the responsibility of the *Cardinal Camerlengo* of the Apostolic Chamber. That same Chamber, however, had a direct interest in some of these travels: Rome collected money across all of central and northern Italy to cover numerous taxes, which its sister cities in the Papal States, Romagna and Lombardia were also required to pay. The collection of the *Agone e Testaccio* taxes in these regions, contracted yearly to different vendors by the *Fattori* of the Roman Jewish community, required the release of a *condotta di viaggio* signed by the *Camerlengo*.[77] While this onerous tax was sent to the Camera Capitolina, the authorization for travel was the prerogative of the central magistracy, the Apostolic Chamber, which was in turn a creditor of the local Chamber.[78] Because of this the safe conducts included a long series of privileges that were meant to facilitate the mission of the Roman envoys. The collection of the agreed upon sums was always a long and complex operation, and a display of Cameral authorizations in the face of rebellious taxpayers could be a winning card to play. Protection from high places, granted for the management of a public mission, also remained in effect in cases where the holder stopped to take care of personal business during the expedition. This, then, was its added value. Combining public and private interests on these journeys was an established practice. However, we will return to this later. For now it is interesting to highlight another fact: the widespread mobility among the Jews of Rome, during a phase in which they have too often been envisioned as being completely enclosed in the seraglio, and the direct line connecting that mobility to both the Camera Apostolica and the daily work of the Jews of the ghetto. Once again, a concrete example helps to define the issue.

In August of 1590, upon accepting Dattilo Scazzocchio as a 50 percent partner in the contract for the coming year's tax collection, Sabbato di Veroli explicitly provided for the contingency that one of the two of them would stop along the way to deal with personal interests. In fact, in drawing up the *capitoli* that defined the obligations and reciprocal duties concerning the expenses to be incurred for purchasing the journal necessary to carry out the job, payment for the "*lettera della Comunità*," and for the grant of the license and *condotta di viaggio* from the *Camerlengo*, a clause was added to address this issue:

> While they agree that if God forbid he should cause one of them to be sick on this trip that the other companion cannot abandon him in any

---

[77] On the tax of *Agone e Testaccio*, Toaff 1996b. On the Agone and Testaccio games, Ademollo 1891; Boiteux 1976; Caffiero 2012, pp. 362–369.
[78] Francescanegli 2012.

way until he is healed, rather he must take care of him and see to all of his needs; in this situation all the expenses that accrue for the one who has fallen ill go to the expense of the sick one [...] While the subject parties consent to agree that it is not permissible for any of the said company to abandon each other until they have returned to Rome and rescue with the help of God. And they further consent to the agreement that upon their return if some of them want to spend money on merchandise it is up to each one of them to buy that which they like and a companion cannot force another to buy merchandise that they themselves want. And they agree that if something from his relatives in Castellanza and in Florence is donated to mastro Dattilo it is only for the said mastro Dattolo and that Sabbato should not have any part.[79]

Work easily took Jews outside the ghetto, some of them bound for distant locations, others remaining within the limits of the district of Rome.[80] Jews came and went from Rome for a wide range of reasons, from business to study, from answering legal summons to visiting relatives. The experience of Salomone Ram (the banker who was tried for dealing in fake money) is an example of this aspect too. At home in many different cities, Salomone's regular travels pivoted between Rome, where his parents had a home in the ghetto, and Venice and Ancona, where his brothers lived. This convergence of family and professional networks fully corresponded with the characterization of Jewish entrepreneurship shaped by the figure and the choices of the merchant-bankers, who for centuries had built their fortunes on precisely these overlaps between private life and public business. The roles of Venice and Ancona were in turn defined in relation to Rome: there was a dialog between the offices of a single parent company, whose center had to be identified

---

[79] NE, f. 6, l. 2, c. 70r-v. "Pur si convengono che se campando Idio sia ammalasse alcun di loro per detto viaggio che l'altro compagno non lo possi abbandonare in alcun modo sin che sia guarito, anzi debbi haver cura di lui et governarlo di tutto quello li farrà bisogno; imperò tutte le spese che si farranno per quello che si ammalasse vadi alle spese del malato [...] Pur si convengono d'accordo le parti suddetti che non sia lecito a nessuno di detti compagni abandonarsi l'un l'altro sin che siano tornati a Roma a salvamento con laguito de Dio. Et di più si convengono d'accordo che al ritorno loro volendo alcun di loro spendersi dinari in mercantia stia arbitrio d'ognun di loro a comprarsi quel che alloro piacerà et non possi compagno sforzar all'altro che compra mercantia al voler suo. Et si convengono che essendo donati a mastro Dattilo cosa alcuna da soi parenti in Castellazzana e in Firenza siano de detto mastro Dattolo et Sabbato non debbi haver parte."

[80] For example, Durante del Sestier to Nice (DC, r. 389, c. 118r) and Leone Serena to Safed (NE, f. 9, l. 1, c. 72v).

in Rome and not elsewhere, because in the Urbe lived the *pater familias*, who by all evidence was the point man for the entire operation. Rome's inclusion in a quartet of merchant cities, along with Venice, Ancona, and Livorno,[81] where families of Iberian origin operated in the 1600s has already been highlighted by Claudio Procaccia, based on data that emerged from a systematic analysis of letters of exchange issued by the Jewish bankers of Rome.[82] What is interesting to note here is that these extra-urban connections involved not only financial transactions related to lending at interest and the groups that specialized in that sector, but they also included the sale of merchandise of many different types and values, a fact that until now has been completely overlooked for the 1500s.

Therefore – and this is the new and interesting fact – the paradigm of mobility was not only a central aspect of the professional initiative of the richest and most fortunate Jews, but turns out to have been more generally valid, gradually moving down the social scale, where Jewish mobility happened over shorter distances and with lower value transactions. It was not just bankers travelling to and from Rome, as was personally demonstrated to the Governor's deputy by the witnesses who were called to appear in the case of Salomone Ram and his illegitimate commerce. While the Governor's police searched stalls and stores, recording detailed inventories of what was discovered and issuing citations, none of the parties concerned was in Rome. Leone Sgrizzaro was on a tour of the Tuscan fairs, Simone delli Panzieri was in Venice to handle the sale of a consignment of rugs and Angelo di Montefiascone, who actually was in the city at that moment, was careful not to be found, and having gotten wind of the justice system's interest in him, prepared a quick departure from Rome, prevented only by the calming intervention of a trusted friend.[83]

---

81 Naturally, at the end of the 16th Century, Livorno is not yet one of the sides of this quadrilateral; the Jewish Nation of the Tuscan port, in fact, obtained the privileges that were destined to transform it into one of the principal Jewish communities in Europe only in the 1590s, which then established it as a privileged location for exchanges and meetings among coreligionists during the following century; on this subject, Trivellato 2010; the excellent and rich works of Lucia Frattarelli Fischer 2003, 2000 and 2008. For the 18th Century, see Bregoli 2011 and 2014. For an investigation of relations of this type in the Tuscan community in the modern age, see Galasso 2002. For an analysis of the community understood from the perspective of the historiographic concept of "Port Jew," see Lehman 2005.

82 Procaccia 2012, p. 139.

83 *Processi*, r. 258, caso 4, cc. 84r-87v.

Roman Jewish society was in continuous movement. Their travels involved a large number of destinations – among which Ancona and Venice certainly stood out – had different purposes, and involved both inbound and outbound journeys.[84] The list of safe conducts granted by the *Camerlengo* over a limited period of time – the year 1577 – presents a cross-section of Jewish travel to and from Rome during this phase. Abramo di Sabbato Moscato, a resident of Fossombrone in the Duchy of Urbino, obtained a *littera passus* that was valid for three months to undertake a journey to the city. This trip included a stop at Camerino to collect documentation that was to be presented at a trial underway in Rome.[85] Mosè Abbina di Siena instead requested a safe conduct for business travel to Rome and Benevento.[86] Another conduct was registered to Isacco del *fu* Bonaventura da Viterbo, allowing him to accompany his daughter to Castel Sant'Agnolo, in the Duchy of Urbino.[87] A safe conduct was also issued to Isacco Crescas and Abramo di Vitale, who were preparing to return to Avignon,[88] and another was granted to David and Giaccobe Pellegrino for travel to and from Venice, where one of their brothers had just died.[89]

Common elements in the safe conducts issued to Jews were a validity limited to three months, an obligation to carry a bill of health from the city of provenance, and an exemption from exhibiting the sign of recognition for the safe conduct holder and his traveling companions. In general these companions were partners and servants, and more rarely wives and young children, an indication that these were mostly short-term, solitary trips. In some particular cases the duration of the travel pass could be extended,[90]

84   The Papal State and its capital, in fact, remained attractive to foreign Jews, and when Sixtus V decreed the readmission to cities other than Rome, Ancona and Avignon, many accepted the invitation. Cfr. the long list of *introhitu cum habitatione* permissions granted to Jews in DC, r. 394, cc. 60r-73v, regarding which see below in this chapter. On the problems this raised, Di Nepi 2008. On the mobility of the Italian Jews, see Luzzati 1996 and 1985. For a brief description of travels and travelers in the age of the ghettos, identified, however, only with the wealthiest Jews, Siegmund 1996.
85   DC, r. 377, c. 28v. The argument evidently must have gone on for a long time, and Abramo Moscato obtained a second safe conduct the following year for the same reasons (Ibid., r. 377, c. 179v), and he was granted a third one in 1579, thanks to which, moreover, he would have been able to stop at Camerino and also at Fabriano (Ibid., r. 379, c. 159v).
86   DC, r. 377, c. 31v.
87   DC, r. 377, c. 34r-v.
88   DC, r. 377, c. 46r.
89   DC, r. 377, c. 123v.
90   So, for example, in 1580 the Chamberlain grants to Abramo Moscato, who lives in Fossombrone, and Isacco Perugia, a resident of Gioello and his uncle and companion, a safe conduct good for a year, and including the privilege of exemption from wearing the mark while they did business in the lands of the ecclesiastic State (DC, r. 382, c. 79r).

allowing the possibility of a brief stay in another city, and, in the case of Ancona,[91] of acquiring the privileges granted to the Levantine Jews there, even if one belonged to another nation. Sometimes this mobility also materialized in the acquisition of a store in another city, for example in Florence, which would then be managed from afar in Rome with the help of local agents.[92] Furthermore, the expedient of taking advantage of a temporary permit for travel and layovers in order to try and set up commercial activities and settlements in parts of the State where Jewish residence was prohibited was typical of the whole modern age, and occurred equally in large and small cities.[93] The dangers of travel, always feared at the beginning of a journey, justified the permission for temporary anonymity that the unusual exemption from wearing the badge offered the Jews. Occasionally a Jew could even be granted the right to travel armed, as provided for in the passport granted to Samuele Corcos, who was headed to Venice and equipped with an arquebus at the wheel.[94]

The *compre* of the *Ospedale della Consolazione* (1564–1592)

January 2 1564	Custodians and *Camerlengo*	Angelo Sacerdote and Samuele Scazzocchio	Annual contract at the price of 10 *giuli* per *fardello* + a deposit of 20 *scudi*
November 2 1567	Guardians of the Company	Leone Mancino and Emanuele Sacerdote *alias* Sciaquatello	Annual contract for 1568 at the price of 10 *giuli* per *fardello* + a deposit of 50 *scudi*

---

91 On May 2, 1585, the *Camerlengo* grants to Samuele Corcos an *Indultum gaudendi privilegiis hebreorum levantinorum* for the period in which the Jewish banker and his family would be staying in Ancona (DC, r. 389, c. 82r).

92 NE, f. 9, l. 1, c. 19r.

93 In these cases, naturally, the local merchants rose up against the new and scarcely welcome competition, petitioning Holy Office to put an end to these scandals; cfr. Kertzer 2006, and Di Nepi 2008.

94 DC, r. 384, c. 122v. Samuele Corcos was the son of Salvatore, who was the owner of a moneylending license granted in 1552, (Esposito 2002, p. 580), and obtained his own license with the tolerance of 1577 (DC, r. 377, c. 8v).

UNEXPECTED OPPORTUNITIES   187

The *compre* of the *Ospedale della Consolazione* (1564–1592) (*cont.*)

September 19 1569	Vincentino Zilera de Laude (majordomo of the Company)	Emanuele Sacerdote *alias* Sciaquatello, Leone Mancino Salomone Mazzone Mosè di Simonetto	Two year contract for 1570 and 1571 at the price of 9 *giuli* each + a deposit of 25 *scudi*
September 18 1571	Giovanni d'Aurelio de Mattheis (guardian)	Nissim Moro, Leone Mancino and Emanuele Sacerdote *alias* Sciaquatello	Four year contract at the price of 9 *giuli* per *fardello* + a deposit of 100 *scudi di moneta* + and a donation of 150 *scudi* to the *cardinal vicario*
1572–1574	Mancino and company + Giacobbe d'Aversa and company	Vincenzo (House master at the Hospital)	Payment of 531.23 *scudi* at the agreed upon price of 92 and a half *baiocchi* per *fardello*
1572–1576	Giacobbe d'Aversa and company	Niccolò (Prior of the Hospital)	Payment of 1485.25 and 50 *baiocchi* at the price of 92 *scudi* and 50 *baiocchi* for the purchase of the four year contract
July 30 1576	Hospital	Crisca Sacerdoti, Leone Pelato, Vito de Amodio Moresco, Israele Sacerdote e Mosè Sabatini	Debt of 39 *scudi* and 65 *baiocchi* to repay by September 15
1578–1580	Unidentified Jews	Hospital	Payment of 895.55 *scudi* for the purchase of *fardelli*
1581–1583	The company of Leone Mancino, Emanuele Sacerdote + a company of Christians	Hospital	Payment of 1922.96 *scudi* and a half for the purchase of *fardelli*

The *compre* of the *Ospedale della Consolazione* (1564–1592) (*cont.*)

November 22 1583	Leone Mancino	Samuele Scazzocchio	Sale of half of the quota both from the present contract for the *compra* of the *Ospedale del San Giacomo* and from the *compra* of the *Ospedale della Consolazione* for 25 *scudi di moneta*
Idem	Cascian Tripolese	Leone Mancino	Loan *gratis et pro amore* of 30 *scudi di moneta* to be repaid by the transfer of half of Leone's quota of the *compra* of the *Ospedale della Consolazione* (the contract for which was good for another seven and a half years) and in the *compra* of the *Ospedale del San Giacomo degli Incurabli* (this with three years remaining)
November 27 1583	Salomone Mazzone	"Zio Lavo" and Mosè Grande	Sale of quotas in the *compre* of the *Ospedale del Santo Spirito*, the *Consolazione* and the *San Giacomo degli Incurabili* at the price of 45 *scudi di moneta*
January 20 1584	Samuele Scazzocchio	Mosè Grande and Leone Deloro	Sale of quotas in *compre* of the *San Giacomo* and the *Consolazione* (purchased by Leone Mancino) for 25 *scudi*

The *compre* of the *Ospedale della Consolazione* (1564–1592) (*cont.*)

February 23 1586	Giacobbe del fu Prospero	Vito Moresco, Mosè Negri, Angelo Zarut and Cascian Tripolese	Sale of all the rights in the contracts with the *San Giacomo* and the *Consolazione* at the price of 20 *scudi di moneta* in cash (*contanti*) + settlement of the debt of 4 *scudi* and 2 *giuli* in the contract with the *Ospedale della Consolazione*
Idem	Leone Deloro	*Idem*	Sale of all the rights in the contracts with the *San Giacomo* and the *Consolazione* at the price of 20 *scudi di moneta* in cash (contanti) + settlement of the debt of 42 *giuli* in the contract with the *Ospedale della Consolazione*
March 6 1586	Sabbato di Serena	*Idem*	Sale of two quotas of the *Ospedale della Consolazione* and the *San Giacomo* at the price of 30 *scudi di moneta in contanti*
March 11 1586	Isacco Moro	*Idem*	Sale of all the rights in the contracts with the *Ospedale della Consolazione* and the *San Giacomo* at the price of 14 *scudi di moneta* in cash (*contanti*)
March 16 1586	Siman Tov Moro	*Idem*	Sale of quotas in the contracts with the *Ospedale della Consolazione* and the *San Giacomo* at the price of 14 *scudi di moneta in contanti*

The *compre* of the *Ospedale della Consolazione* (1564–1592) (*cont.*)

March 18 1586	Israele Sacerdote	Michele del fu Gabriele	Sale of quotas in the contracts with the *Ospedale del San Giacomo* and the *Consolazione* for 18 *scudi di moneta in contanti*
March 20 1586	"Zio Lavo"	Vito Moresco, Mosè Negri, Angelo Zarut and Cascian Tripolese	Sale of quotas in the contracts with the *Ospedale della Consolazione* and the *San Giacomo* at the price of 22 *scudi di moneta in contanti* and 40 *baiocchi*
Idem	Leone Scazzocchio	Idem	Sale of quotas in the contracts with the *Ospedale della Consolazione* and the *San Giacomo* at the price of 22 *scudi di moneta in contanti*
May 3 1586	Nissim Moro	Idem	Sale of quotas in the contracts with the *Ospedale del San Giacomo* and the *Consolazione* at the price of 18 *scudi di moneta in contanti*
May 16 1586	Angelo Moresco	Idem	Sale of quotas in the contracts with the *Ospedale della Consolazione* and the *San Giacomo* at the price of 18 *scudi di moneta in contanti*
September 16 1586	Pietro Paolo de Fabiis (Procurator)	Michele di Perugia	Stipulation of contract: 10 *giuli* per *fardello* for every package produced from December 20, 1589 to December 20, 1596 + 200 *scudi* for the purchase of the contract

UNEXPECTED OPPORTUNITIES 191

The *compre* of the *Ospedale della Consolazione* (1564–1592) (*cont.*)

December 26 1586	Giacobbe Rosciello	Vito Moresco, Cascian Tripolese, Angelo Zarut and his brother Mosè Piperno	Sale of the quota of the late Giuseppe d'Aversa (one of the 23 hospital contractors) at the price of 14 *scudi di moneta in contanti*
October 18 1588	Ottavio Muti (*camerlengo*)	Angelo Zarut, Vito Moresco, Mosè Grande, Cascian Tripolese	Consignment of 70 *fardelli*, of which 10 are at no charge, to be paid for within three months
Februrary 25 1589	Ottavio Muti (*camerlengo*)	Vito Moresco, Mosè Grande, Angelo Zarut	Consignment of 72 *fardelli* to be paid for within three months
June 15 1589	Hospital	Vito Moresco, Angelo Zarut, Giacobbe Rosciello	Consignment of 73 *fardelli* to be paid for within three months
October 19 1589	Vito Moresco	Vito Moresco sells to Angel Negri Napolitano and to Abramo de Bonadonna	Sale of a quota in the contract underway with the *Ospedale della Consolazione* which expires next Christmas as the price of 4 and a half *scudi di moneta* and for the payment of 12 *scudi* in debt contracted with this quota
January 4 1590	Giovanni Battista (collection agent)	Angelo Zarut	Consignment of 38 *fardelli* to be paid for within three months
March 22 1590	Giovanni Battista (collection agent)	Michele di Perugia	Consignment of 67 *fardelli* to be paid for within three months

The *compre* of the *Ospedale della Consolazione* (1564–1592) (*cont.*)

December 21 1591	Valerio de Valle, Ottavio Gabriello, Paolo Maggio (custodian) and Marco Antonio Rotolanti (*camerlengo*)	Sabbato di Serena Giacobbe and Isacco Rosciello	Credit for 700 *fardelli*; the Jews will be forgiven a further 81 *fardelli* and the remaining 161 are to be paid for by the middle of March 1592
January 4 1591	Hospital	Angelo Zarut	Consignment of some clothing of the late Agata Flandet at the price of 33 *scudi di moneta* to be paid by the month of April 1592
July 4 1591	Marco Antonio Rotolanti (*camerlengo*)	Sabbato di Serena, Giacobbe and Isacco Rossciello + Michele Di Perugia guarantor	Consignment of 142 *fardelli* to be paid for in three installments by September 1592
October 17 1591	Valerio de Valle (custodian)	Sabbato di Serena, Giacobbe and Isacco Rossciello	Consignment of 159 *fardelli* to be paid for in two installments by September 1
December 18 1591	Marco Antonio Rotolanti (*camerlengo*)	Sabbato di Serena, Giacobbe and Isacco Rossciello	Consignment of 244 *fardelli* to be paid for in two installments by the middle of September 1592
December 5 1592	Valerio de Valle, Statilio Pacifico, Hieronimus Ruis (custodian) and Marco Antonio Rotolanti (*camerlengo*)	Sabbato di Serena Isacco dello Strologo and Giacobbe Rosciello	Receipt for 250 *fardelli* just consigned + 160 of debt to be paid by the middle of March 1594

CHAPTER 6

The *Camerlengo*, a Protector in the Curia

The reconstruction of the careers of the moneylenders and the profiles of the *Fattori*, rabbis, and other distinguished exponents of the Roman Jewish community has brought the role of the Cardinal Chamberlain of the Apostolic Chamber to the foreground: in addition to the concession of a key provision – the *inhibitio in Curia ratione foenoris*, coveted by all and repeatedly cited in the preceding pages – and the signing of safe conducts for travel, the law dictated that this high magistrate should have control over the work of Jewish bankers. It was Leone X who saw the office of the *Camerlengo* as the magistracy most suited to this role. From that moment, and perhaps even from earlier on, relations between the ecclesiastics who occupied this office and the Jewish ruling class were inevitably drawn together in an inextricable tangle. For Jews, professional success was established and guaranteed by public roles and representation in the Jewish institutions. Cooptation into the ruling class was based on the family of origin's social position, on specifically Jewish skills gained from rabbinic studies, and on the authority earned in the Christian world, which was certified by the concession of privileges reserved for bankers and their associates. It was a closed circuit, whose movements were controlled by the Chamberlain, and which facilitated the building of privileged relations between this Cardinal and the Jewish moneylenders. Jewish society was molded by, and even mirrored Christian society through the interweaving of relations between the exponents of the Jewish emerging classes and the most important magistracies of the Papal States which exclusive jurisdiction over them. This rapport became entwined thanks to the concession of privileges and safe conducts, granted to individuals for the conduct of their own private business or to the *Universitas* in the exercise of its prerogatives. This chapter is dedicated to an analysis of the mechanisms via which this dialectic continued to be interwoven in the first decades of life in the ghetto.

1   The *inhibitiones ratione foenoris*

The *inhibitiones ratione foenoris* represented the principal instrument through which the relationship between the Jewish emerging classes and the Camera Apostolica was set up in this period (and in following centuries). There are copious examples of them, some more detailed than others. On March 1, 1577

Isacco Gioioso, rabbi and son of Giacobbe, received one of the moneylending licenses that Cardinal Luigi Cornaro, the *Camerlengo* of the Apostolic Chamber granted to fifty-five Jewish bankers in Rome.[1] On May 28, 1584 the same banker, this time accompanied by Sallustio Betarbò, obtained a genuine *inhibitio in Curia ratione foenoris* from that cardinal's successor, Filippo Guastavillani, reaffirming and reinforcing his privileges as a licensed moneylender.[2] On December 15, 1587, the Gioioso-Betarbò partnership obtained an audience with the new *Camerlengo*, Cardinal Caetani, where they were granted the same document, the *inhibitio in Curia ratione foenoris*, thanks to which the two Jews were once again assured of the Camera's protection.[3]

Isacco and Sallustio were not the only ones to return to the Curia after being granted licenses. In the early months of 1577, some before and some after, many of their colleagues knocked on the door of Cardinal Cornaro, the signatory of these documents, asking for an *inhibitio*. The names of Durante del Sestier[4] and Mosè Menasci with his son Giuseppe are just a few among the many who were granted privileges at the time.[5]

This list of names could go on at length, but from the first lines alone it becomes clear that a special relationship existed between these professionals and the *Camerlengo* of the Holy Roman Church. It was not by chance that between the end of 1584 and the beginning of the following year, directly after the death of Cardinal Cornaro, numerous Jews presented themselves in rapid succession at the office of his newly named replacement, Cardinal Filippo Guastavillani, hoping to obtain the release of a new *inhibitio*.[6] The same scene was repeated

---

1   DC, r. 377 c. 8v. On Luigi Cornaro (1517–1584), *Camerlengo* from 1570 until his death and active promoter of the anti-Turk struggle, see Cardella 1793. t. V, pp. 330–331; Chacón 1630.

2   DC, r. 388, cc. 25v-26r. On Filippo Guastavillani (1541–1587), *Camerlengo* from 1584 until his death, Cardella 1793, t. V, pp.154–155; Chacón 1630; Weber 1994 pp. 115, 280, 386, 718.

3   DC, r. 392, c. 113v. On Enrico Caetani (1550–1599), *Camerlengo* from 1587 until his death and the first to rise to the magistracy by purchasing it (for 50,000 *scudi*), tied to France between 1589 and 1590 with the task of guaranteeing the rise to the throne of another Catholic King after the death of Henry III, Cardella 1793, t. V, pp. 228–230; Chacón 1630; Weber 1994, pp. 151, 535.

4   The moneylender, already included in the list of licensed bankers of February 1577, obtained an inhibition the following July (DC, r. 377, c. 62r-v), which would be renewed on May 28, 1584 by the new *Camerlengo*, Filippo Guastavillani (Ibid., r. 388, cc. 21v-22v) and then later entitled by Enrico Caetani to his sons Salomone and Sancton (Ibid., r. 391, c.113v) after his death (Ibid., r. 392, c. 114v).

5   Both were bankers licensed in February 1577 (Ibid., r. 377, c. 8v) and holders of an *inhibitio* starting from the following June, nominally granted only to Mosè because, according to the text, the exclusive jurisdiction privilege would automatically extend to the owner's sons (Ibid., r. 377, c. 90r-v).

6   DC, rr. 388 e 389.

when the office again changed hands during the winter of early 1587, and the job was entrusted to Cardinal Enrico Caetani.[7] This mutual interest was supported by solid roots and motivations. The Jewish bankers who lined up at the office of the *Camerlengo* were all aiming to receive the precious *inihibitiones* signed by the powerful cleric, and this objective was regularly achieved. With each change at the top of the Camera Apostolica, in fact, the registries reserved for the Cardinal's decrees punctually record, line after line in rapid succession, the granting of these types of privileges to the Jewish moneylenders of the city.

The *inhibitio in Curia ratione foenoris* was a document of exceptional value and importance. It involved a very broad legal privilege, which reserved exclusive jurisdiction over the holders of the document for the *Camerlengo* and his court. This privilege was extended to partners, employees and to family members of the beneficiary. The scope of the *inhibitio* curtailed the authority of all (or almost all) the Roman magistracies that, with their powers, could and should have kept an eye on the activities of Jewish moneylenders. The interdict covered the Governor of Rome,[8] the *Auditor Camerae*,[9] the *Vicario* and his vice-regent,[10] the Senators and the Conservators of Rome, the capital Curia, the *bargello* (Captain of the Court Police), the officials, judges and notaries of the Courts of *Ripa, Ripetta, Borgo, Tor di Nona* and *Savelli*, and the *Gabellario maggiore*, (the City tax collector). Furthermore, the protection was automatically extended to all the employees and staff of the aforementioned institutions.[11]

Subjection of Jewish bankers to any form of control or jurisdiction by the entities that performed these functions in the territory of Rome and the surrounding districts carried a penalty of one thousand gold *scudi*. This provided the bankers with powerful protection that could defend them from many different sources of interference, from the tax authorities to rulings by local and outlying courts, up to the powers represented by the central authorities of the Apostolic Chamber itself. Although the reorganization of the Roman courts was not yet on the horizon in the 1500s,[12] it was actually then that the

---

7   DC, r. 392, cc. 113v-114v.
8   Regarding the Criminal Court of the Cardinal Governor of Rome, see Barrovecchio San Martini 1981; Ruggiero 1987, pp. 211–219; Fosi 2007.
9   Regarding the *Auditor Camerae* and on his tribunal, Ruggiero 1987, pp. 211–219.
10 On the *Tribunale del Vicario di Roma*, cfr. Cuggiò 2004. On the *Vicario*'s viceregent, cfr. Del Re 1972.
11 For a quick summary of the various attributions and areas of competence of the magistrates cited, cfr. Ruggiero 1987; Pompeo 1991; Fosi 2002.
12 On the reorganization of the Roman tribunals, started in 1612 under Paul V, see Fosi 1997 and 2002.

diverse ambitions of the many different institutions active in the local judiciary were becoming increasingly clear.[13] The prominent role of the Governor as the highest legal authority at the time for criminal cases in the city, district, and occasionally the entire State, much like the Uditore di Camera for civil cases, imposed itself on tasks traditionally assigned to different municipal bodies. The scope of these offices' work, now limited only to people legally defined as Roman citizens, found little space in the lively and cosmopolitan city that was the capital of the Papal States.[14] Judicial functions were not, in fact, extraneous to the long battle engaged by the Popes and their bureaucracy, since the definitive re-entry of Martin V to Rome, to assure that the central magistracies at all orders and levels had pre-eminence over all areas of public management (from food supplies to roads and city maintenance),[15] over and above the municipal agencies. Thus, through the progressive strengthening of State authorities – the Governor and the *Auditor Camerae* – the magistracies of the capital city saw their powers and privileges hollowed out over the course of the 15th and 16th centuries. From this point of view at least, it appears that the *inhibitio* was not a significant innovation, and that it only formalized on paper prerogatives already established in practice.

The inclusion of the *Vicario* and his court in the list of institutions relegated to the margins by the *inhibitio* – at first glance forced – was connected to the involved subjects' status as Jews; precisely because they were Jews they traditionally fell within a vast range of cases under his jurisdiction. The episcopal magistracy, unlike the municipal magistracies, was not in direct competition with the central institutions, and was concerned with aspects that, by their nature, did not interest the administrators charged with the day-to-day management of the State's affairs.[16] The fact that the Jews were among the subjects pertinent to episcopal law was nothing new. Rather, the relationship between the *Universitas Iudaeorum de Urbe* and the Cardinal was so close that it was not unusual for the community to request his intervention regarding a wide variety of internal conflicts.[17] Later, in the 1600s, the division of boundaries and assignments between the Roman magistracies would confirm this tradition,

---

13   Regarding these aspects, above on the subject of the *Tribunale Criminale del Governatore di Roma* and its action against the judicial activity assigned to the Senate, see Del Re 1972.
14   On the population and demographic characteristics of the city of Rome in general between the Renaissance and the Modern Age, Sonnino 1998, 2000.
15   In general on the so-called "bi-frontal" magistracies (*Annona, Strade, Acque* and *Grascia*, that is supply of wheat, streets, waters and meat), Pastura Ruggiero 1987, pp.75–99.
16   Caffiero 2003a, 2005.
17   See, for example, Schwarzfuchs 1970.

reserving many aspects of authority over the Jews and their institutions for the *Vicario*, a choice which was certainly considered natural by all those involved.[18] After all, while they too engaged in the custom of navigating among the large number of available tribunals and their irremediably entwined jurisdictions in search of the most favorable judgement, a widespread practice among the Pope's subjects, the Jewish world never sought to cast doubt on the pre-eminent role of the *Vicario's* court as such. Put more simply, in the search for benevolent sentences in the most delicate and controversial cases, Jews sought the involvement of the ecclesiastical court more than the ordinary courts that were active in the city.[19]

The Holy Office, moreover, when confronted with issues that were strictly economic in nature – such as the permanent presence of Jewish merchants outside Rome and Ancona – always heard cases that were brought to its attention by dint of the mixed nature of this type of crime, committed by Jews who were conducting legitimate business but in places that were explicitly prohibited to them.[20] The case of the Jewish bankers could open a variety of scenarios, both because their work entered the slippery realm of usury – although legitimized by licenses and rules, and because this business – useful, but by its very nature morally reprehensible[21] – was further complicated because it happened in the holy city of Rome and was practiced by Jews, regarding whose good faith, especially in matters of money, Christian society had always harbored strong doubts.[22] An ideological tangle such as this, steeped in reciprocal

---

18   Stow 2001.
19   Caffiero 2004, pp. 29–34. Also, for solving conflicts that were apparently strictly financial in nature, however, this tribunal's authority was not questioned (Di Nepi 2008; Canonici 1998).
20   Di Nepi 2008.
21   The words of Abbott Moroni about usury, a subject that not by chance is not given its own entry and is included under the heading *Monte di Pietà*, leave no room for doubt on the subject: "The excess of usury, *Foenus Mutuum* that will bring about the foundation of the *monti di pietà*, has always been seen as reprehensible by natural law, sacred canon, pontifical edicts, canonical and civic law, and has always been severely condemned and punished; if for the judges of the old law usury with foreigners was at times permitted, that was for a special divine dispensation. Thus although the Jews still practice is, this does not mean they have absolute permission for usury; rather we must say with S. Tommaso that they are tolerated only to avoid greater evils [...]. The usurers of the Church are detested more than thieves" (Moroni 1840–1861, pp. 255–257).
22   Regarding this subject Giacomo Todeschini rightly recalls how, since the centuries of the early medieval period, Jewish specialization in the consumer credit sector "happened against the background of an established Christian perception of Jewish wealth gained from usury, and thus fraudulently, as well as from the common acquisition of the stereotype of Jewish greed, the prototype of which would have been represented by Judah

suspicions and fears, would have been fertile ground for the intervention of the *Vicario* of Rome, the magistrate who was charged with maintaining urban morality.[23] Thus in the granting of *inhibitiones* it was deemed necessary to add the office of the *Vicario* to the list of agencies which, due to the matters entrusted to them, could have interfered with the work of the Jewish bankers even more than the *Vicario*, such as the Governor of Rome and the presidents of the *Dogane*.

Jewish bankers' activity in the Roman marketplace had many implications. In the world of medieval and Renaissance Italy, small Jewish communities flourished around the figure and work of one banker who held a moneylending permit.[24] Rome, however, would have to wait until 1521 and the papacy of a Medici, Leone X, to see the first formal grants of authorization for this type of work.[25] From then on, until the suppression of the Jewish banks decreed by Innocent XI in 1682, these licenses continued to be issued, while the number of licensees, the permitted rate of interest, and the rules governing relations between debtor and creditor varied over time.[26] Therefore, as much as Jewish moneylenders were well protected by the *capitoli*, the legitimacy of their operations was not always safe from challenges. Not by chance, contemporary legal scholars saw recourse to the *inhibitio* as a useful legal tool for dealing with the inevitable problems connected with engaging in the money business in territories that were subject to the temporal, and not only the spiritual authority of the pontiff.[27] Once again, the formal acceptance of Jews in a socially prestigious occupation such as banking was an example of unresolved issues, where the symbolic and theoretical levels pointed in a much different direction than the one taken in the city's daily practices, remained difficult for the intellectuals of the age to reconcile with their prejudices. What the consequences of the persistence of these ambiguities over a long period of time might have been, and their role in the formation of widespread ideologies concerning Jews – still and always perceived to be a foreign body, tolerated only on the basis of needs

---

the seller of Christ" (Todeschini 2002). On these subjects also see Toaff 1996a and more recently, Todeschini 2007, 2016 and 2018.
23   Cfr. Cuggiò 2004.
24   Luzzati 1985; Veronese 1998. For Umbria, Toaff 1989. For the Marche, Bonazzoli 1990, and more recently, Andreoni 2019. In general, cfr. the essays collected in the special issue of *Zakhor* focused on Jews merchants and money lenders (1997), and the syntheses in Luzzati 1991, 1996.
25   Esposito 2002 and 2008.
26   Procaccia C. 1994–1997.
27   A very interesting analysis in this sense is proposed in Stow 1977.

that were to be identified and confirmed from time to time – is a subject that would be worth considering beyond the case examined here.

The *inhibitio* represented an important professional tool which granted its holders the right to exclusive jurisdiction. There is another aspect of the *inhibitio*, though, which is perhaps even more important; holders of this privilege had the power to invoke the name and authority of one of the most important State institutions when collecting from their debtors, some of whom, naturally, were also Christians, and against whom they could issue a demand for payment in the name of the *Camerlengo*. The Jews did not fail to take advantage of the wide range of possibilities this presented. For example, it was by dint of the special protection guaranteed to him by an *inhibitio* that Salomone Corcos obtained a *sequestrum in Curia* for goods belonging to two merchants who owed him more than 700 gold *scudi*.[28] In another example, in November of 1577 Cardinal Cornaro issued a *Mandatum de restituendo cum inhibitione* to "Curio del Schiavo (*alias* Rubeis)," ordering him to return to Mosè Solon *alias* Romano everything that had been fraudulently taken from him without any right, and inflicting serious damage; particularly books, gold rings and chains, and furniture.[29] Again, on a completely different occasion in 1590, Cardinal Caetani allowed Giacobbe Marvano, who had contracted debts outside of Rome, to defer payment until the expiration of his safe conduct, forbidding the relevant authorities from acting against him.[30]

The main role of the *inhibitio* remained that of offering protection against interference from any authorities other than the *Camerlengo* himself. Thus "Onorio Trincha *gabellario maiore di Roma*" was instructed to return to "Sabbato Tyburtinus," who had just sworn to his innocence, goods which had been sequestered from the Jew on suspicion of fraud.[31] Again in 1583, pressure was put on the president of the *Carceri* to promptly return to Angelo di Sonnino the property that had been confiscated from him at the request of two Christians.[32] In 1588, on the strength of an *inhibitio* granted just a few days earlier,[33] Judge Hersilio De Montibus was removed from a case involving Jewish banker Salvatore Corcos.[34]

---

28 DC, r. 377, cc. 8v-9r.
29 DC, r. 377, cc. 119v-120r.
30 DC, r. 399, cc. 101v-102r.
31 DC, r. 382, cc. 4v-5r.
32 DC, r. 386, c. 95r.
33 DC, r. 388, c. 51r-v.
34 DC, r. 388, cc. 78v-79r.

The scope of the *inhibitio* was inherently that of solutions to economic problems related to debts and debtors. As the cases quickly cited here demonstrate, the intervention of the *Cardinal Camerlengo* was frequently and willingly requested by Jews who were having trouble protecting their personal wealth. These were the individual assets that frequently, through a binding contract *personaliter et in solido,* offered guarantees for loans and Jewish lenders reciprocally among Jews, as well as with their Christian counterparts. These assets also constituted, as they did for Salomone Ram (banker and fence for fake *baiocchelle*), the liquid cash that, invested and divided up, was the foundation of the banking business. The intervention of the Roman Cardinal could also be requested for unforeseen occurrences outside the Urbe, such as in the case of Giacobbe Marvano and the temporary difficulties he encountered outside Rome in an unidentified locality – to reach this place he once again had to knock on the door of the *Camerlengo*.

As we saw in the previous chapter, travel permits were signed by the powerful Cardinal for those who traveled on their own business as well as for those who traveled in the name of the *Universitas Judaeorum de Urbe*. All this, along with the moneylending licenses, the *inhibitiones*, the permits to study and pursue a degree, and numerous other provisions, created continuous occasions for encounter between the Roman Jews and the magistrate who exercised the greatest power over the protection and control of their ruling class. As a result this legal tool remained in favor, even after the abolition of the Jewish banks. In the mid-1700s Church leaders still granted an *inhibitiones ratione auri* to goldsmiths, silversmiths and antique dealers – the new occupations of wealth and prestige in the Jewish community of Rome.[35]

2   In the Name and on Behalf of the *Camerlengo*

Collection of the taxes that were owed to the Treasury, among them the triennial *Sussidio* and the contributions for road maintenance, was one of the principal tasks assigned to the Apostolic Chamber.[36] Jewish communities had been required since the beginning of the 1300s to send a specific payment to the *Camera Capitolina*, the *Agone e Testaccio* tax, created to finance the organization of games for the Roman carnival, and at first imposed solely on the city's Jewish community. Then, in 1418, due to the group's endemic and growing

---

35   Di Castro 2012.
36   Caravale 1998; Bauer 1927; Piola Caselli 1991; Strangio 2001.

financial troubles, the tax was extended to include the other *Universitates* of the Papal States.[37] The payment of 1130 *fiorini* each year was a heavy burden for the Jews, but it was not the only one. To this already excessive tax were added levies claimed directly by the Apostolic Chamber (primarily the triennial *Sussidio* and the *Vigesima* taxes on the Jews), which were also collected in part outside Rome.

Every year the community would certify the guidelines for the collection of the entire tax burden,[38] adjusting the sums imposed on individual families based on their income and on the number of relatives in their care. Just like in any community structure found across the region, the central body – in this case the Roman community – entrusted the task of managing collections to local leaders. In the meantime, not having received the money, they waited to send the required payment to the Chamber.[39] It was not an easy business. Rome's sister communities were perennially late with their payments, and the envoys sent from Rome to collect the money were opposed in every way, running the risk of returning home with next to nothing. The *Universitas Iudaeorum de Urbe* often found itself weighed down by heavy debts in its dealings with the Chamber, in good part due to its own problems and delays. As a result, they just as often found themselves negotiating with the *Camerlengo* over the extension, if not elimination, of payments.

According to Attilio Milano's calculations, the community's tax obligations reached around 10,000 *scudi* annually, to which was occasionally added the unpaid interest that had accrued from the last payment. Among delays, extensions, and petitions, and on top of the unfavorable conditions to which the Jewish economy had been condemned by the politics of conversion, the situation was difficult to remedy.[40] It should be said, though, that in a system of taxation in which the control and collection of predetermined, centrally imposed

---

37   Toaff 1996b, pp. 125–126, 142–147. On the Jews of Rome and the city's Carnival, cfr. Boiteux 1976; Caffiero 2005 and 2012 (pp. 362-269).
38   An example of the criteria used in the division of taxes for 1554 is in NE, f. 2, l.2, c. 91r-v; a summary of the document is in Stow 1999, docs. 1544–1545.
39   In fact, even with the peculiarities of the recognized specificities of the Jewish community with respect to the *jus gentium* of their members (about which see the still excellent work of Colorni 1945 and 1956), the general legal condition and the administrative structure of these was not so different from that found in the communities across the territory, and it is precisely the management of their tax burdens that clearly testifies to this; on this subject, Claudio Canonici is doing comparative work, and I thank him for the substantial exchange of ideas related to the issue. On the regulation of the territorial communities, see Tocci 1989, 1998.
40   Milano 1984.

taxes was entrusted to local leaders, it was not only the Jewish community of Rome that found itself significantly indebted to the administration.[41] In the absence of a specific study on the conditions of accrued local tax debts in the relationship between the center and the periphery, it is difficult to establish to what extent the poverty that the *Universitas Judaeorum de Urbe* complained of continually – for some aspects, while excepting issues strictly related to religious diversity, the management of its relations with the State, and its autonomies, similar to those of a regional community – was at least in part a façade, or represented something exceptional, or could be ascribed, perhaps for larger than average sums, to a more general panorama.[42] The fact remains that, whatever the Jewish community's specific tax obligations, over the centuries the Popes attempted, though among a thousand contradictions, to offer some remedy. In the effort to amortize this debt they repeatedly turned to different tools, all equally ineffective: from the tax on bread to the ill-fated monopoly on soldiers' bedding.[43]

At least for the period at the center of this research, during which, due to the chronological proximity to the institution of the ghetto, the *Universitas* navigated in calmer waters,[44] the Roman community worked hard to compel the rebellious Italian communities to send the agreed upon sums. To achieve that goal, delegates of the Roman *Universitas* learned to travel with certain essential documents. Along with the travel permit, these tax collectors also carried *de iure sommario* letters, orders for payment and an *inhibitiones extra Curiam*. This last document gave the collectors the right to demand the complete support of local governors and Jews in the carrying out of their mission. All of these legal documents bore the signature of the *Cardinal Camerlengo* on the bottom line, and in case of problems it was to him that the Jews appealed. Thus, in order to solve a problem that arose in 1577 between Rome and Ancona, it was the *Camerlengo* who issued the order for payment against the *marchigiani*. In that instance, which concerned the collection of Ancona's share of the tax for 1030 gold *fiorini* (or really 535 *scudi* and 3 *giuli*), the Cardinal ordered

---

41 *Communitates immediate subiectae* means the lands and communities owned by the Papal States, directly under the temporal authority of the Pope-King and, because of this, subjected to a taxation and legal regime different than that of the territorial lordships (or *terrae mediate subiectae*); about these issues see Caravale 1988; Calasso 1965; Tocci 1998.

42 Lattes forthcoming.

43 Milano 1984.

44 Cfr. for example, the schedule presented in 1575 by the *Fattori* Angelo Capuano, Samuele "Il Pagliano" and Consiglio Tedesco, with which they pledged to pay off a prior debt with payments of 900 *scudi* per year for five years (Archivio Storico della Comunità Ebraica di Roma, *1Tc (parte II)*, f. 9).

the *Università* of Ancona, and with it the community of the Marche, to send the customary contribution of 77 gold *scudi* to their Roman counterparts; that sum increased due to the late payments that had accumulated over the years, reaching a total of 196 gold *scudi*. It should be noted that it was only thanks to this intervention from a high official that the *marchigiani* finally agreed to pay what they owed.[45]

The problems in Rome also stemmed from the issue of internal taxation. In the same year that the Jews of the Marche appealed to the *Camerlengo* against the demands of their Roman coreligionists, Gregory XIII found himself forced to issue a brief on that subject in which, in response to a petition presented to the *Camerlengo* by some Jewish citizens, he declared "that the *Fattori* can collect the duties and that nobody can refuse to pay them." The Pope made a clear pronouncement on this subject in a printed document – destined, therefore, for a large public – which unequivocally established that everyone (and that really meant everyone, including the privileged *camerali*) was obliged to punctually pay their taxes. The *Fattori*, who were leaders *in solido* (that is, backed by personal assets), had recourse to declaring excommunication *more hebraeorum* against those who continued to offer resistance, by dint of their authority to act against tax defaulters with full Papal support by sending letters and demands that were of "appropriate tone," as is reaffirmed in this provision.[46] It fell to the Pope to personally resolve a dispute that arose when several Jews thought it was a good idea to call on the *Camerlengo* to seek exemption from their tax burdens, in the effort bypassing both ordinary law as well as pontifical authority. While the brief by Gregory XIII does not explicitly record the names of the privileged aspirants, but rather encapsulates them in the vague definition of "wealthy," it is not so difficult to put forward some idea about the subjects in question. In all probability, they should be looked for among those who had frequent encounters with the *Camerlengo*, the magistrate to whom the request for tax exemption was addressed in the first place.[47]

In this sense, the collection of taxes itself offered an opportunity. The winners of the annual contract for the collection of taxes imposed outside Rome could not pursue their task without first obtaining authorization to leave the

---

45   DC, r. 376, c. 113r-v.
46   ASR, *Camerale II, Ebrei*, b. 2.
47   After all, despite the fact that the pontifical edict openly prohibited it, it could happen that the high prelate would intervene in disputes over internal taxation; in 1590, for example, it was precisely this magistrate to release an *inhibitio* to Giacobbe Tarmi, against the claims of the *bargello* and the *Fattori* of the Jewish Community of Rome about a dispute over the payment of the custom duties of *Ripa* (DC, r. 398, cc. 54v-55r).

city, which, as with every other safe conduct, had to be approved by the Cardinal.[48] Indeed, given the practical difficulties connected with the nature of their mission, the community delegates traveled directly under the *Camerlengo's* protection. The cardinal's main interest was seeing the operation successfully completed, with full tax payments deposited in the Chamber's coffers. To this end he issued decrees in support of the Jewish tax collectors, thanks to which local authorities were required to offer their maximum support to these "envoys."

The Jews, who were formally traveling solely on behalf of the *Universitas*, did their best to take advantage of the opportunity this offered, and during their official journeys they always made time for personal business. They strove to keep their public obligations separate from their private interests by including specific clauses to address this issue in their *ad hoc* partnership contracts. To clarify these situations, the "delegates" concerned themselves with setting up rules for such circumstances, establishing the partners' reciprocal obligations and defining the specific rights they could claim in negotiations being conducted for personal business.[49] The collection of taxes in the regions of Romagna, Toscana and Lombardia, specifically the *Agone e Testaccio* tax, the tax for the *Fanciulle Vergini* and the funds for ransoming Jewish prisoners who had been captured by pirates, doubtlessly represented an opportunity from many points of view. Not by chance, the position of tax collector was used almost as though it was a degree to be earned, both by socially climbing families – such the notary Pompeo del Borgo's family[50] – as well as by those that were already established, whose young men were searching for a practical internship in which they could prove their abilities and skills.

So, as an example, for two consecutive years two members of the di Sicilia family[51] could be counted among those who started out on this *Grand Tour* of Jewish Italy. Among this family's members could be found, naturally, merchants engaged in the sale of fabrics and market spaces,[52] and a licensed

---

48   Cfr., for example, NE, f. 6, l. 2, c. 70r-v.
49   One thinks, for example, of the case of Dattilo Scazzocchio and Sabbato di Veroli (NE, f. 6, l. 2, c. 70r-v), cited earlier in Chapter 4.
50   The Del Borgo family claimed the contract in 1579 (NE, f. 9, l. 1, c. 72r).
51   Isacco in 1578 (DC, r. 377, cc. 150v-151r) and David the following year (Ibid., r. 382, cc. 17v-18r).
52   For example, on August 7, 1589 an Abramo di Sicilia son of David received, along with Mosè di Rignano da Salomone di Scantriglia, a parcel of old and new fabric with a total value of 290 *scudi* to hold outside of Rome on behalf of Salomone himself (NE, f. 14, l. 1, c. 144r-v). The activity of David son of Prospero instead covers various branches of business typical of Roman Jewish families: from the already cited tax collection to the rental

banker.[53] The di Marino family also invested in this extremely sensitive sector, sending Leuccio out on the roads of the peninsula in 1593.[54]

The collection of taxes outside Rome was a world that was in large part reserved for the sons of the ruling class, who made the most of the opportunity this apprenticeship offered them.[55] Travel allowed them to get to know coreligionists who lived elsewhere, and offered clear advantages in establishing business relations with the Christian merchants and authorities of the localities they visited. These Jews, in fact, were empowered by the endorsement of authority and prestige that came with formally traveling in the name and on behalf of not only the Jewish community of Rome, but of the *Camerlengo* of the Apostolic Chamber.

The toponymy with which notary Isacco delle Piatelle indicated the regions involved in the tax collection, in a list written in Hebrew, provides insights about the geographical universe of the Roman Jews. The list explicitly cites the regions of Romagna, Toscana and Lombardia, while curiously leaving out the areas that were closest to Rome, such as Umbria. Even more conspicuously absent are the Marche and the wealthy community of Jews in Ancona, with whom controversies over the subject of taxes were, as we have seen, quite frequent. The presence of Romagna on the list seems to exclude the possibility that the list referred exclusively to foreign regions. The fact that Umbria is excluded is easily explained – due to the expulsions, the region was at the time frequented solely by traveling Jews. The omission of the community of Ancona is more difficult to account for. Relations with the *marchigiano* port, in fact, were very frequent and cordial between families – consider the case of the Ram family – and extremely tense on the institutional level, most likely due to the many privileges granted to the Levantine Jews who lived there. It is certain, though, that while their absence from the geographical map referred to by the Jews of Rome can raise questions in terms of the history of mentalities, the residents of Ancona were nevertheless regularly, albeit reluctantly, forced to pay their obligations.

---

of a market space (NE, f. 14, l. 1, cc. 174v-175r and f. 6, l. 2, c. 66v), and the trade of merchandise with Christian merchants (Ibid., f. 6, l. 2, cc. 18v-19r).

53   The official banker of the family was Laudadio son of David, who is present in the list of 1577 (DC, r. 377, c. 8v).

54   DC, r. 410, cc. 22r-23r.

55   The supposed young age of the travelers in question, in fact, is inferred from the fact that the holders of these conducts and the parties in the contract cited up to now have, normally, the father still alive – and thus not labeled *quondam* – when the documents is issued. Regarding this, see Di Nepi 2007b.

The types of taxes that were collected deserve some specific consideration. The function and logic of the *Agone e Testaccio* tax is well known,[56] and the need to provide dowries for poor, unmarried girls is consistent with the view of charity and support that was typical of the age.[57] However, we still lack a specific study on the methods used to ransom Jews who were captured by pirates, for whom, as clearly emerges from the notarial documentation in question, funds were collected regularly. A trial in 1617 for the controversial ransoming of a false Jew reveals something of the inner workings of this procedure. Simon di Basilea, a Jewish mediator from Mantua, freed, at the expense of the Roman community, a man who was at oars on a Neapolitan *galere*. This case is unusual because the freed man turned out to actually be a Muslim. Once released from captivity he went underground, fearing that the Jews would discover his deception and denounce him. Though this case is quite particular, it still demonstrates the efficacy and pervasiveness of the Jewish network, so well-known and reliable that even a Muslim was willing to pass as a Jew in hopes of obtaining an otherwise impossible emancipation.[58] Traces of this activity also come up in grants of travel permits, though only sporadically. One such example is the safe conduct issued to "Leo, a Levantine Jew," who was leaving for Malta on a commission from the Jews of Ancona, in hopes of liberating some Jews who were being held as slaves.[59]

3   The Story of a Special Relationship

The special protection granted by the *Cardinal Camerlengo* to the Jewish ruling class of the city of Rome included the entrepreneurial activities of individuals, carried out in the city market (but also beyond its walls), as much as it did the interests of the *Universitas Iudaeorum di Urbe*, which, as we have seen, frequently coincided with those of the Camera itself. In one case after another, whether it concerned private or public business interests, in actuality the Cardinal negotiated with the same people.

The *Fattori*, the tax collectors, the auditors, the chamberlains, and the delegates of the *Scole* generally belonged to a single social group. It is certainly true that not all bankers could claim the same volume of business; neither could all rabbis claim the same degree of skill and authority, nor did all doctors

---

56   Milano 1984, pp. 130–131; Toaff 1996b, pp. 125–126.
57   Van Boxel 1998.
58   *Processi*, r. 139, cc. 355–362. This case is discussed in Di Nepi 2012.
59   DC, r. 388, c. 127r-v.

earn their title at a prestigious university. Nevertheless, it remains the case that it was generally people who came from those worlds who were called upon when it came to filling roles in governance. Thus, the *Fattori* who usually went to the *Camerlengo* to request protection for the Jewish Community of Rome had in a different capacity already made the same petition for themselves and their own interests. This dynamic fostered personal relationships between the Christian authorities and the Jewish leaders.

So, in a brief period of time between 1577 and 1578, Salomone Corcos, rabbi and son of the late Salvatore, obtained an order for the seizure of merchandise belonging to his debtors, Tiberio and Geronimo de Cecchis,[60] and also got his lending license renewed; at the same time he carried out his functions as *Fattore,* and in that capacity also assumed the role of judge-arbitrator in a difficult to resolve dispute.[61] During this time span the Corcos family – holders of banking licenses since the first concessions[62] – obtained a second lending license issued to Salvatore del *fu* Salamone. This license would also go on to be reinforced by subsequent *inhibitiones*.[63]

Another example is the very industrious Durante Del Sestier, who moved in the same direction. An envoy of the Community of Rome,[64] for which he served as a *Fattore*,[65] he was a licensed banker,[66] a traveler,[67] and holder of not just one but two *inibitiones* (the first granted in 1577[68] and the second in 1584).[69] His sons did just as well: in 1587 Salomone received a concession that was valid for only four years,[70] and shortly thereafter in 1588, Sancton managed to get one issued to him with unlimited duration.[71] The same path was followed by Mosè Menasci – the last example – who was also a *Fattore*,[72] licensed banker,[73] and holder of an *inhibitio*.[74]

---

60   DC, r. 377, cc. 8v-9r.
61   NE, f. 9, l. 1, cc. 73v e 93v-r.
62   Esposito 2002.
63   DC, r. 377, cc. 8r-v, 324 e 330.
64   NE, f. 9, l. 1, c. 58v.
65   NE, f. 9, l. 1, c. 26r.
66   DC, r. 377, c. 8r.
67   DC, r. 389, c. 118r.
68   DC, r. 377, c. 62r-v.
69   DC, r. 388, cc. 21v-22v.
70   DC, r. 391, c. 113v.
71   DC, r. 392, c. 114v.
72   NE, f. 3, l. 2, c. 91v.
73   DC, r. 377, cc. 8r.
74   DC, r. 377, c. 90r-v.

These connections were the norm, not the exception, and are the result of a clearly structured social pyramid which is not at all specifically Jewish. At the top of the pyramid, the *élites* in power – of whom, as we have seen, rabbis were an integral part – were chosen from among the emerging classes that were the most dynamic socially and culturally. The case of the Ram family, which is paradigmatic for this investigation, is once again useful in helping us summarize. The Ram family was among the prominent members of the Jewish ruling class in Rome for all of the 1500s. However, once struck by financial misfortune, they found themselves pushed out of prestigious and public roles. By the 1600s the family did not appear among the operators of the banks being abolished, nor were they listed among the current *Fattori*, proof of the family's progressive decline in status both inside and outside the ghetto.[75]

At the end of the 1500s, almost fifty years after the raising of the ghetto walls, Jewish society proved to be vital, endowed with an able ruling class, capable of making changes, and of managing generational and social exchange (i.e. reacting positively to external stimuli in an era that was undoubtedly difficult for the group). The question remains, however, as to just how long this vitality was destined to last. Recent studies by Monica Calzolari demonstrate that in the revolutionary years at the end of the 1700s – when the ghetto was abolished and its inhabitants freed, though for only a short time – some of Rome's Jews were prepared to seize the opportunities that a city without a Pope and without restrictions could offer them. They immediately identified the real estate market as a promising sector for business, almost like taking revenge by moving in to a sector that up to then had been prohibited to them.[76] The last names of these Jews – Ambron, Moro, Modigliani, Sestieri – could be the late offshoots of the line of leadership that had been so clearly articulated three centuries earlier.[77] This long arc of time, however, saw the suppression of the Jewish banks, the impoverishment of the community,[78] and the progressive

---

75 Regarding the Ram family and its vicissitudes, see above, Chap. 4.
76 On this subject, see Calzolari 2012.
77 From this point of view, for example, the rise of Tranquillo Vita Corcos in the 1600 would also have developed along a traditional line of identification of the ruling class, a path that could, like few others, bring the extraordinary personality of this scholar to light (Caffiero 2019).
78 In the absence of new and comprehensive studies on the socio-economic conditions of the Jews of Rome during the long era of the ghetto, the only possible references are those present in the classic bibliography (Milano 1984; Berliner 1992), all of which touch on the subject of general impoverishment. Some of the more recent research, focused on single aspects and on shorter time periods (bankers between 16th and 17th centuries, art clients in the 18th century, real estate investments in the revolutionary years) would seem, however, to see for the entire modern age the existence of a strong social stratification in

strengthening of the strict policy of conversion, with all the accompanying pressures and implications.[79] While we lack specific studies, including biographical and genealogical, on social dynamics among the Jews of Rome for the entire modern age, there are still suggestions prompted by the frequent and repeated appearance in the limelight of certain last names, and therefore perhaps certain families. While these suggestions are naturally destined to remain pure hypothesis in anticipation of precise and documented analyses, it remains valid to inquire about the processes that were underway in the ghetto, about their movements, their causes, and the degree of their coincidence with processes underway contemporaneously on the outside.

The *Cardinal Camerlengo* was a central protagonist in Jewish social representation, holding the power to confirm and sanction the positions they achieved. These positions were symbolically represented by the granting of privileges to individuals and their companies, and, in their name and on their behalf, to the institutions of the *Universitas*. The protection granted to the Jews of Rome by the succession of Cardinals who held this office had a very strong influence on members of Jewish society. The protection of the Camera, in fact, opened up an extraordinary range of possibilities for its beneficiaries. This information is of particular interest if we recall how, on one hand, the *Camerlengo* was one of the highest ranking clergymen of the State, while on the other hand, the Jews, at least in theory, were supposed to remain confined to the margins of social and economic life of that same State. This relationship took the form, therefore, of a special connection, at the limits of paradox and a clear symptom of the porosity of the world in the modern age, where practice and rules could easily be short circuited.

The activity of the *Camerlengo* extended into the intimate spaces of the homes and families of some of his beneficiaries. Thus Servideo Crocolo, heir to a dynasty of bankers,[80] was issued an *indultum ducendi alia uxore viventi prima*, which was apparently superfluous, being, as the text itself explicitly records, a divorce, normally adjudicated and regulated by Jews through their ancient traditions.[81] Cardinal Caetani's motivations, however, were hardly an unprecedented interference in the rights of a Jewish family. On the contrary, he

---

which different situations lived together, from the majority's extreme poverty to a situation of being relatively "well-off" enjoyed by a privileged few, in the end not unlike the general condition of the city (see Caffiero, Esposito 2012).

79   Caffiero 2004.
80   The licensed banker was, from 1577, Settimo del *fu* Dattilo (DC, r. 377, c. 8*v*).
81   DC, r. 406, c. 166*r-v*. For an analysis of this particular type of *inhibitio* and of its possible significances, cfr. Procaccia M. 2007a. Regarding the partial autonomy granted to the Jews in matters of family law, see Colorni 1945. The possibility for Jews to divorce, a practice that was legal in some Italian States and banned in others, proved to be a problem at the

was instead concerned with much more prosaic business. Thanks to the *indultum ducendi*, in fact, Dulcetta, the ex-wife who had been repudiated after six months of an unhappy union that produced no children, would never be able to lay claim to any of the husband's possessions; included among these assets were Servideo's shares in the Croccolo family bank, the good health of which was of great concern to the Cardinal.

The elective associations between the *Camerlengo* and the Jews of Rome, on the other hand, take on a different significance when examined from the perspective of Church history. From this point of view, these relations can be seen as part of the more general regulation of relations between the Christian world and the Jewish minority. On the other hand, they also contributed to defining the boundaries of competence and reciprocal forces within the Apostolic Chamber, the institution led by the *Camerlengo*.

We will examine the first aspect, focusing on a specific moment: the months following the promulgation of *Christiana Pietas* by Sixtus V. The widespread diffusion of Jewish settlements in central and northern Italy was thrown into crisis by the invention of the ghetto and the enactment of the restrictive rules that followed. The sense of insecurity brought about by the new condition – and constantly fueled by insistent voices that called on the Pope to proceed with the definitive expulsion of the Jews from his lands – found confirmation in 1569, when Pius V decreed that the ghettos in the cities of Rome and Ancona were the only places where Jews were permitted to reside. The rise of Sixtus V to the Papal throne reversed this policy, and in 1586 Jews were readmitted to many of the places from which they had been expelled only a few years earlier, provided that they maintain a system of clear physical separation. Many Jews, even foreigners, took advantage of the opportunity that was being offered to them. For the favorable price of ten *giuli* per person they obtained conducts of entry and residence permits from the *Cardinal Camerlengo,* with which they could start a new life and begin new businesses in the provinces of the Papal States. With the death of Pope Peretti, though, all of this was once again called into question. While the Papal office was vacant, it fell to the sitting *Camerlengo,* as the magistrate responsible for managing current affairs while awaiting the white smoke, to handle the doubts and problems connected with so many uncertainties.

Many Jews applied to Cardinal Enrico Caetani for permission to live and work in Fano, Perugia, the City of Castello and many other cities, small and

---

moment of the Unification; on this aspect, cfr. Capuzzo 1999 and Ferrara degli Uberti 2017 2011.

not so small, leaving a mass of supplications and requests on the cleric's desk. The positive responses to these petitions were recorded in a long list by notary Andrea Martini, and collected in a special registry entitled *Diversorum sedis vacantis*, a volume that is full of these kinds of documents (and which would be extremely useful, moreover, in an effort to draw a map of the Jewish resettlements in the Papal States at the end of the 16th century). Only one Roman Jew, Daniele de Tibure, appears on this list receiving the grant of an *inhibitio*,[82] with no intention whatsoever of seeking confirmation of his right of residence. For de Tibure and his Roman coreligionists, this right was never in question. This was a reversal of the previous system in which, as was the case before the tolerance of 1521, an authorization for moneylending in the provincial markets represented a means for circumventing the prohibition on practicing this profession in Rome.[83] Now, after the most recent regulations, it was moneylending in Rome and the concession of travel permits useful for running a bank that offered Jews unassailable grounds for leaving the ghetto, despite the continued rebukes from local competitors, and sometimes from the Holy Office itself.[84] Thus the *Camerlengo's* exclusive jurisdiction over the Jewish bankers of Rome was an important fact which had direct influence on the lives of these and many other Jews, even if they were residents elsewhere.[85]

Now we come to the second aspect, which relates to the real significance that the Jewish question had within the institutional evolution encountered by the magistracies charged with the temporal management of the Papal States. Jurisdiction over the Jews was part of the broader powers of the Apostolic Chamber, or really of its executive body, the *Piena Camera*, and the cleric-functionaries who constituted its membership, and it played a role here as well. In the middle of the 16th century, the clerics of the Chamber found themselves, along with their president, the *Camerlengo,* and the General Treasurer, who had the ultimate responsibility for papal finances, involved in a process of significant transformation that was destined to reshape the very structure of the State.[86]

---

82   DC, r. 403, c. 124r-v.
83   Esposito 2008.
84   Di Nepi 2008.
85   See, for example, the moneylending licenses for the Piedmont (DC, r. 388, cc. 131v- 136v) or registry 395 of the *Diversorum del camerlengo*, which, being entirely dedicated to the Jews (1587–1594), contains tolerances valid for many communities of the ecclesiastical State, and at the end of the papers there are safe-conducts and authorizations for entry into the State's lands. Obviously only a small percentage of documentation involving Rome can be found in this registry and is comprised exclusively of the moneylending licenses granted in excess of the 55 of 1577.
86   Prodi 1982.

Through the identification and regrouping of precise and well-defined areas of intervention in the *mare magnum* of governing tasks assigned to the Apostolic Chamber, they progressively experimented with more centralized and modern forms of administration. The responsibilities ranged from traffic to archives, from mountain regions to galleys, and the provisioning of basic necessities.[87] All of these issues raised the eternal question of the procurement and management of resources, and ended up conflicting with the necessity and the ambitions of the spiritual mission Rome attributed to itself.[88]

This process went on for a long time, driven by diverse goals that did not always coincide: on the one hand there was the need to establish an efficient government, capable of best managing the resources which the territorial principality made available. To this end there was a need to create the most uniform possible centers of operation within the Presidencies, through scrupulous delegations that were clearly distinct from one another.[89] On the other hand, all of this conflicted with the personal ambitions and personalities of individuals who were occasionally called to the clergy after having paid out large sums. It also conflicted with the tradition and laws desired by the *Camerlengo*, as well as their fate as determining factors in the daily division of duties and practices. Although this is certainly not the forum for discussing the modes and duration of the institutional evolution experienced by the Chamber, slowly and among many contradictions, between the 16th and 17th centuries, the fact remains that at this end of this path the figure and the work of the *Camerlengo*, a figure so important to the Jews, emerged drastically reduced, in favor of increased power for the office of the Treasurer.[90]

The granting of licenses to the Jews remained the purview of the *Camerlengo,* and was reconfirmed as such from time to time. Thus we find this power explicitly included in the long list of prerogatives reserved for this Cardinal compiled by Pope Paul V in 1621. Intent on sending a solid set of regulations to the Chamber, Paul V clearly defined the exclusive powers of the cleric-presidents.[91] As it happens, the emerging magistracies do not seem to have claimed relevance in matters concerning the Jews. Intent on establishing autonomy in decision-making, they concentrated instead on sectors held to be

---

87   Pastura Ruggiero 1987.
88   Prodi 1982; On the "internal" politics of the Papal States, see Caracciolo, Caravale 1963.
89   Pastura Ruggiero 1987.
90   Regarding these aspects, see Caravale, Caracciolo 1963; Prodi 1982; Pastura Ruggiero 1987, pp.63–71; on the use of careers in the Curia, see Ago 1990.
91   The list of these powers is summarized, along with a detailed analysis of the evolution of the office of *Camerlengo*, in Pastura Ruggiero 1987, pp. 66–68.

more vital: first and foremost roads, food supply and finances, but, evidently, not including Jews.[92] The fact that the privileged relationship between the *Camerlengo* and the Jews was not changed the way others were was one of the reasons that this relationship grew progressively stronger, and was seen as increasingly crucial by those who were directly involved, that is, individual Jews. On the other hand, the scant attention paid to them by their counterpart demonstrates how this relationship was, in the end, a marginal phenomenon. Oversight of the Jews could provide profit and some power to its holder, but it was not among the major responsibilities entrusted to the Apostolic Chamber that were worth fighting for.

The Jews, enclosed in the ghettos, were a secondary consideration among the many interests of the territorial principality. Thus on the material level they never equaled the central role reserved for them in theology and canon. This lack of consideration also included the Jewish bankers who represented the élite of their communities. Notwithstanding their many efforts and the numerous different businesses they invented, in the end these Jewish leaders remained an integral part of a very restricted group in an isolated position, and therefore had little influence. Many years later in the 18th century, during a time when Pope Benedict XIV was actively concerned with Jews and strategies for dealing with them on the spiritual front, he failed to record oversight of the Jews among the powers of the *Camerlengo* in the *motu proprio* of 1742, in which document the Pope definitively established the assignments of the Treasurer and the aforementioned *Camerlengo* – whose office was no longer defined as supervisor of the Camera's every action. This omission says a great deal about the actual influence of the Jewish community. The fact that this role was so easily overlooked reveals with absolute clarity just how great a distance there was between reality and perception. In spite of everything, however, these perceptions – and the dangers that could result – continued to be fueled on the representational and symbolic level.[93]

92 Ibid., p. 68.
93 The Letters with which Benedict XIV will revolutionize the conditions under which baptisms of Jewish children and the quarantine of adults in the House of Catechumens were held to be legitimate are from these years; Caffiero 2004, pp. 73–110. Also on these issues, see Rosa 1989.

CHAPTER 7

Separate at Home

The ability to maintain lively relations with the Christian world was central to Jewish business, as demonstrated by the catalog of professions practiced by the Jews and the ways in which these businessmen managed to bend and exploit the discriminatory laws. The ambiguous sharing of the social and economic spaces in the city of Rome fostered the habit of daily exchanges and contacts. The Jews spent their workdays outside the gates of the ghetto, applying themselves to all sorts of businesses and trade on the streets and plazas of Rome. There were rich moneylenders seated behind the family's bank counter, assessing pawns and paying out money, skilled wholesalers of used clothing looking to negotiate purchases and payments with the administrators of the city hospitals, strolling vendors with their merchandise in tow, going house to house selling fabric and clothing at retail, or, finally, merchants who owned fixed spaces and sales counters in the marketplaces, some of whom enjoyed the protection of the *Camerlengo*. All of them, without exception, found themselves working shoulder to shoulder with Christians on a daily basis – and vice versa.

The community's entrenchment in the city was the result of the choice not to proceed with the definitive expulsion of the group, sanctioned in 1555. The change in the rules of tolerance, though, had a profound effect on the social practices that defined relations between Jews and Christians. The time period and ways in which this shift took place are documented among the lines of the deeds entrusted to Jewish notaries, where Christians continue to appear even after the publication of *Cum nimis absurdum*. The presence of Christians and converts in these "strange" registries closes this reflection on Jewish society and the tools it was able to develop for surviving the ghetto and remaining faithful to itself. If contacts with Christians were naturally inevitable living in a Christian society, then an examination of the relationships recorded by an internal source such as notarial records is of great interest, and allows us to consider, from a lateral perspective, how each party interpreted the inevitability of these relations.

1   Christians at the Jewish Notary

The presence of Christians inside a very private Jewish space, as reported in the registries of the Jewish notaries, is an indication of the progress of relations between majority and minority. We may take the idea of Jews and Christians sharing spaces, events, and cultures in the age of the ghettos for granted – this is clear in every type of source. That said, Christian acceptance of the special rules that restricted these Jewish contracts is itself an important point which, if properly illustrated, allows us to illuminate in concrete terms how such a complex and partially illicit interaction came about in a precise place and time: Rome in the second half of the 16th century.[1]

The first step to take, however, leads in the opposite direction: before we can ask why Christians freely entrusted the care of their personal interests to contracts written by Jews, we must first look at the official Christian notaries and inquire about the nature and extent of their dealings with Jews.

The dense network of relations between the two groups is abundantly and variously attested to in the documentation available to us for the end of the 16th century (as well as for the preceding and following periods). The multiplicity of these relations has left traces of evidence in the trial and administrative records produced by the Roman magistrates (which were examined in earlier chapters), and likewise in the notarial registries. Jews and Christians, ready to negotiate business contracts, appeared both as principals and witnesses in agreements, pacts, loans, arbitrations, extensions and every other kind of legal negotiation that was recorded in notarial deeds.[2] All the richness of these personal relations, whether occasional or long term, situated inside or outside the ghetto, between Jews and Jews or Jews and Christians, was formally transposed into written text by the notaries of the city. Notaries were called upon at various times to guarantee the legitimacy and publication of agreements stipulated between individuals and for commercial transactions, grants of small to medium level credit, the formation of partnerships, as well as prenuptial agreements and wills.

Private contracts involving both Jews and Christians as parties with equal rights and obligations are found consistently in the Roman documentation from the Modern Age. This phenomenon deserves highlighting. Considering the large number of professionals at work in the city contemporaneously, it is not simple to identify, from among the thirty notaries in the capital offices, along with the notary secretaries and clerks of the *Camera*, the *Vicario*, and of

---

[1] Caffiero 2012.
[2] Particularly important in this area are the studies of Anna Esposito collected in Esposito 1995. For an example of the use of notarial sources for the economic and social history of Rome between the 17th and 18th Century, see Groppi 2000; and now also Gasperoni, Groppi 2018. For a theoretical systemization of the use of these sources for the modern age, see Ago 2000.

the other magistrates, those who served more Jewish clients than others. Given the fact that the choice to make use of a notary could be based on a variety of considerations – such as the proximity of his office to the Jewish quarter or to the market plazas, or a Christian counterpart's preferences, or even the specific skills of a notary who was particularly well-versed in certain subjects – it becomes difficult, if not impossible, to select which notaries to include in the investigation and which to discard *a priori*. For the historian this situation means two things: on one hand, the theoretical possibility of digging up useful information, even if fragmentary, from the documents of all the active notaries from a specific time period, and on the other, the concrete necessity of identifying which professional services were most often and most regularly chosen by Jews (although this discussion would hold true for any other group being researched).

This is the case with the notary Berardino Pascasio, who kept an office in *Regio Arenula*. In 1584 he was appointed *Notary of the Pawns of the Jewish Bankers* with Cameral privileges. However, at the time of this assignment, perhaps due to the convenient location of his studio, he was already quite accustomed to working with Jews. So, on January 21, 1583, before his nomination to that role, he drew up a deed for Dattilo di Benafri which released the convert Ludovico and his brothers from their debt of 20 *scudi*.[3] Several days later Pascasio would draft the deed formalizing the loan of 39 *scudi* which Federico and Filippo "de Fabia Vaccinari in Regio Arenula" received from Salomone Roccas.[4] Or again, on February 2, 1586, he edited the contract with which a certain Andrea Milanese made an agreement with Salomone Corcos, who, acting as a *Fattore*, represented Giacobbe di Mursia in arranging the rental of a home "*in reclaustro hebreorum*" to Giacobbe.[5] Shortly thereafter, the following May, he was employed to draw up the receipt cancelling the debt issued by Jewish banker Mosè Menasci, *alias* Coppolaro, to Camillo de Rubeis.[6]

It is interesting to note how the relationship between this specific notary office and the Jews of Rome was in all probability further consolidated with the passing of the years, to the point that in the early decades of the 1700s it was one of Pascasio's later successors, Bernardino De Sanctis, who was among the notaries most frequently used by the Jews of Rome for dowries, trade, business and wills.[7]

---

3   ASR, *Notai Capitolini*, uff. 16, a. 1583, cc. 41v-42v (notary Berardino Pascasio).
4   Ibid., c. 48r-v.
5   ASR, *Notai Capitolini*, uff. 16, a. 1586, c. 136r (notary Berardino Pascasio).
6   Ibid., c. 405r-v.
7   ASR, *Trenta Notai Capitolini*, uff. 16, 1722–1756; a survey of this notary's papers is in Di Nepi 2015.

So far none of this is new. However, we find that the opposite situation also arose, although more sporadically; that is, Christians appearing in documents drawn up by a Jewish notary. For example, on October 18, 1583 it fell to Pompeo del Borgo to record the details of an agreement in which Samuele and Stella Di Ceprano, after formally declaring their debt of 15 *scudi* and 80 *baiocchi*, loaned to them by Roberto Roberti for the purchase of "a gold *fronzetta* and a pair of earrings with pearls" from Roman Scazzocchio, committed to pay down the debt at the monthly rate of 2 *scudi* each.[8] In another case, Giovanni di Cordova made several appearances in Pompeo's office in February of the preceding year. His first visit was to hand over 3.77 *scudi* to Vito Moresco,[9] who wanted to purchase a pound and half of saffron. The next visit, a few days after the meeting with Vito, was to receive from Asierico, a Jew, the 8 *scudi* which he needed to stock up on fabric; the loan was guaranteed by Conci di Meluccio.[10]

The involvement of a notary was an essential aspect of every business transaction; only through his added legal authority, in fact, did the clauses of a negotiation take on certain contours and the bargaining could be said to be concluded. This task could be entrusted to "public and authentic" Christian notaries, or to Jewish notaries. The pacts between Jews and Christians were more easily formalized before the first; a sample of the available documents in Latin, Hebrew and Italian reveals this with irrefutable clarity. However, though it happened rarely, there were times when Christians were themselves willing, as in the examples just cited, to place their trust in the notaries of the ghetto. While the discovery of Jews appearing as principals or witnesses in the registries of Roman notaries does not constitute an exceptional finding, (the opposite idea would, naturally, carry a much different meaning), the discovery of Christian contractors in the registries of Jewish notaries reveals unknown aspects of the relations between the first and the second and, as such, is significant for the purpose of this research. For a Christian, the choice to make use of a Jewish notary, though not uncommon, represented an unusual option that was exercised in special situations where, for one reason or the other, the guarantee offered by the Jewish notary was felt to be stronger and more inviolable than others.

Jewish notaries met the need that community institutions and Jewish individuals both had for public documents that were valid not only if produced in a civil court, but that were particularly coercive for Jews, also being based on *halakha*. Thus the penalty for contract violations, for example, called for

---

8   NE, f. 11, l. 6, cc. 61*v*-62*r*.
9   NE, f. 11, l. 5, c. 114*r*.
10 NE, f. 11, l. 5, c. 116*r-v*.

a rebuke involving special spiritual sanctions alongside the normal material penalties. The existence of this double guarantee may have been an attraction for outsiders who did business with Jews in situations where, for one reason or another, these assurances were seen as valuable protection.

For a Christian, the decision to employ the professional services of a Jewish notary, however good their motivations were, could not and would not have been a choice that was made lightly. This was the only circumstance, in fact, where a Christian found himself in a subordinate position to his Jewish counterpart, and in the exceptional position of gaining advantage from knowledge of the subtleties of the system of law and the alphabet in use. In this one instance, when standing before a Jewish notary, the traditional roles were overturned by mutual agreement, the majority in the role of minority and the minority as majority. Here the Christians were the different, the others, and the weight of the usual unbalanced interactions could have tilted against them. So, why would a Christian have ever had to submit to so great an abuse of power?

The answer to this question lies within the documents themselves. Carefully examining the papers compiled in the registries of the Jewish notaries, it is notable how the Christian parties were always assigned an ambiguous, secondary role, even in cases where they should have appeared as principals in the negotiations. This is because the role of a minority could only be marginal, even once the perspective was inverted, and the negotiation between a minority and a majority, both suspicious of their dealings with the opposite party, led to a fictitious equilibrium. An analysis of the concrete examples just presented allows us to reconstruct in concrete and tangible terms the fluctuating progress of this very ambiguous dialectic.

Although it was the Christian who actually disbursed the funds in the aforementioned loan negotiated between Roberto Roberti and the di Ceprano spouses, it was the Jew Romano Scazzocchio who conducted the negotiation, and the exchange of money for merchandise ultimately involved only coreligionists. In the same fashion Giovanni di Cordova, as a debtor, was only able to obtain the loan he wanted thanks to the intervention of another Jew, Conci di Meluccio, who made himself available to provide the needed *"sicurtà"* to the counterpart. Apparently the fact that the recipient of the payout was himself in a position to grant loans did not seem to provide sufficient guarantee to the lender.

Roberto Roberti and Giovanni di Cordova both found themselves participating in business that remained private among Jews and was conducted as such. It was this quality that also made these transactions advantageous for Christians who, precisely because of the undisputed Jewishness of the business, accepted having documents drawn up by a member of that group; or, they agreed to go to a Jewish notary because there was one readily available. As much for the first as for the second case, it was only the recommendation of a third party, esteemed by all involved – respectively Romano Scazzocchio and Conci di Meluccio – that made it possible for the negotiations to succeed.

The intervention of a mediator was the norm in negotiations between Jews and Christians. Although the relationships between individuals of different faiths that were woven into the city's daily life could actually lead to the development of confidence and friendship between the one and the other, this familiarity remained limited to the individual Jew (and the individual Christian), and did not automatically extend to the rest of the group. Indeed, when Andrea Milanese was eager to rent out a home in the ghetto, not knowing the prospective tenant personally and not wanting to run unnecessary risks, he took the precaution asking one of the *Fattori* – that is, a formal representative of the *Università* – to take part in the agreement, in a sense wanting his participation to guarantee the good faith and seriousness of the other party.

It was precisely on the basis of these strictly individual encounters, and therefore the occasional overcoming of mistrust and prejudices, that relations which were dubious and ambiguous on the ideological level could temporarily come together at the practical level. Failing this, the issue would be handled according to other practices, as in the case of the hospital *fardelli*, where Jewish individuals held private agreements with Christian individuals. Once these were formalized with the appropriate notarial contract, the Jewish contract holder, via a second deed drawn up by a Jewish notary, reported the results of these negotiations to the other Jews who were involved in the business. On such occasions the subsequent redistribution of the goods to the community's secondary market held little interest for the Christian party, who was disposed to put his trust exclusively in (and thus to negotiate with) the Jew responsible for the agreement.

This same individual/group dialectic was also at work in the stipulation of lower value contracts. Thus, on December 4, 1578 Leone Treves sent a receipt of debt cancellation to Sabato del *fu* Mosè, a Jewish innkeeper, for the "cost of two barrels of wine as well as certain tables" which had been purchased in partnership with the "associates of Fabian Crapano in *Trastevere*," and for which Leone had advanced the money, as witnessed "in an instrument drawn up by Il Caldino in *piazza de banco*." Also included was the cost of another batch of wine bought by Sabato together with Venturicchio, who was an innkeeper. This purchase was also made possible by a loan from Leone, which was recorded in another document, once again by Pompeo del Borgo.[11] In this case the negotiations between

---

11   Another interesting aspect of this deed is related to the information regarding the religious practices and observances of the Jews, who are clearly not too concerned about

Jews and Christians, conducted with the mediation of banker Leone Treves, also had a trail back to the ghetto of which the "associates of Fabian Crapano" had not been informed; in the Jewish notary's record of the event, the specific contract having been drafted by others, the Christians only appear in passing.

Or in February of 1583, again before Pompeo del Borgo, David de Gaiosa Sacerdote committed to honoring the guarantee of 35 *scudi* offered to him by Angelo di Muccinello for a deal with merchant Giovanni Battista Cosmedo towards the delivery of various merchandise. Massimo Gugnetta, the notary for the *Vicario*, had already drafted a special deed for this sale. For his part, David de Gaiosa gave assurances that he would honor his obligation to Angelo di Muccinello, promising to cede his shares in the contract for the *fardelli* of the Hospital of *San Giovanni di Dio* should there be delays.[12]

Sabato di Marino and Beniamino di Rignano made a similar choice. After they secured a joint loan from a Christian merchant for 20 *scudi*, leaving various personal objects with the merchant as a deposit, they turned to a Jewish notary to distinguish one person's goods from the other. In this second contract the two Jews also agreed that if at least one of the two decided it was time to retrieve his personal property, they would go together to the Christian lender and assure him that the balance of the debt would be paid within a month's time, and thus obtain the restitution of the items in question.[13]

Women also participated in these types of business, using the assets from their dowry. Samuele di Fiorentino's wife Diana agreed, with their consent, to "*rilevare in danno*" (that is to counter-sign) the guarantee Abramo Asriglio offered to her husband Samuele towards both "*mastro* Gianbattista Porti and company" for the sum of 107 *scudi* and "*mastro* Jacomo *parigino*" for 102 *scudi*.[14] Diana's role was limited to providing financial backing for her husband's activities. Ester di Segni, instead, appears as a genuine businesswoman, purchasing sheets on credit from "Geronimo Rusticucci *neofita romano*" for 16 *scudi* in 1588. She too was backed by her husband Prospero's approval, and ready to promise repayment of the debt in a few months.[15]

---

checking the *kashrut* of the wine served by their coreligionist hosts. Regarding the respect for Jewish dietary laws about wine in the medieval and modern ages, cfr. Toaff 1989 and, with some quick annotations to demonstrate how the question of wine was not of particular interest to the Roman community until recent years, see Toaff 2000, pp. 47–50.

12   NE, f. 11, l. 6, cc. 4v-5r.
13   NE, f. 111, l. 6, c. 55r-v.
14   NE, f. 6, l. 2, c. 23v.
15   And in fact, the following September 21, little more than two months after the stipulation of this contract, the debt was paid off and the deed cancelled with the consent of both

In the case of women's entrepreneurship the possibility of recourse to a dual legal system showed all of its advantages. Jewish women, in contrast with Christian women, owned their own assets, and therefore they needed no more than permission from their spouse to make use of them.[16] While for Diana in the end this meant simply completing business among Jews that had originated outside the group, Ester's story presents different characteristics: with this contract, in fact, the woman (or perhaps Geronimo himself, a convert who was aware of Jewish practices and customs) wanted to state unequivocally that she was exercising her legitimate spending power granted by Jewish law, based upon which the agreement itself was formalized and reviewed. Indeed, in a situation where assets were held in common by a married couple, it could wind up being the woman (on the strength of the dowry she held) who gave her blessing to her husband's proposals: such was the case with Brunetta di Collevecchio, who declared that she had no objection to the rental of a market space she co-owned with her husband to Vito Treves.[17]

What this series of deeds has in common is the ways in which the parties knew how to make use of the opportunities as much as the penalties that a minority's persistent and ambiguous presence in the social body brought with it. These different worlds were forced to come together and coexist in compliance with unequal rules. Paradoxically, at times an impromptu recourse to an incomprehensible law could serve to protect the interests of those already protected by the laws in force. The divorce ordained by Pope Paul IV and his ghettos turned out to be impossible, only resulting in the crystallization of the relationship in a consensual separation.

2 The Business of Converts

There remains one further aspect to investigate; conversions. The reconstruction of the dynamics of changes set in motion as a strategy for surviving the aggressive evangelization in the ghetto cannot overlook apostasies. Baptisms had undesirable effects that contributed to stirring up the already troubled waters

---

parties (NE, f. 14, l. 1, c. 60r-v). The convert Geronimo Rusticucci, however, was not new to giving out money, always, at least nominally *"gratis et pro amore,"* to his former coreligionists, and some time later, in 1590, he gave 50 *scudi* to Giacobbe Rosciello on credit (NE, f. 6, l. 2, c. 12v).

16   On Roman Jewish women's ownership of their own dowries, see Stow, De Benedetti, Stow 1986, and more recently, Di Nepi 2007b.
17   NE, f. 6, l. 1, cc. 40v-41r.

of Jewish life: it is to these collateral effects, observed from a very particular point of view, from the inside, to which we must turn in order to sum up this story. In the real life of a family or a company of Jews, where the maze of money and sentiments, business and relatives was never perfectly definable, what happened after a conversion?

The law granted a long series of privileges to converts, and at the same time it prohibited any kind of contact between them and their former coreligionists.[18] On the material level, achieving an abrupt severance of these ties was a complex operation which required time and notarial contracts in order to succeed. To whatever degree they disavowed the Jewish religion and however much they broke old bonds of solidarity and familiarity, in the end converts still had relatives, acquaintances and business partners who remained Jews. Complete cessation of all contacts and economic interests with these Jews was never really possible.[19]

Accordingly, it could be a good idea to address these issues with the mediation of an accredited professional who was considered trustworthy by all the involved parties, and who was naturally familiar with the claims and the personalities of each of the parties – after all, until recently they had all lived in the same quarter, sharing the same lifestyle, friends, relatives and habits. Notwithstanding the many privileges granted to converts by law, a fundamental mistrust emerged and became problematic precisely during the resolution of the economic problems that resulted from the religious choice, as the new Christian negotiated with someone who had remained Jewish, and now found himself defending his personal interests from the designs of a convert.

The same conversionist strategy that was behind the ghettoization of the Jews would also condemn those who switched sides. Converts left outstanding accounts behind that needed to be settled, despite their new privileges and protections. Ideology, however, was not sufficient for resolving every dispute. As much as the law favored the baptized, at a certain point it came down to finding agreements between parties and getting the shared and quantified resolutions to disputes recorded in black and white. Here again the Jewish notaries came into play. Thus when Tommaso and Prudentia Livoletta, both converts, decided to meet with Prudentia's recently remarried mother Stella

---

18 Caffiero 2005.
19 Regarding the continuing familiarity between Jews and converts, and on the resulting role of converts as mediators, see Luzzati, Olivari, Veronese 1988. For the Roman situation see Esposito 1995; Procaccia M. 1998; Canonici 1998; Foa, Stow 2000; Stow 1993; Caffiero 2005, pp. 299–327. And now on this topic, see the detailed reconstruction of the life and adventures of a convert in Renaissance Italy by Tamar Herzig (2019).

to give her and other heirs the receipt for Prudentia's dowry, they met in the offices of Pompeo del Borgo.[20] Prudentia and Stella would meet there again a few days later, on January 23, 1583, to negotiate the sale of a sheet worth 15 *scudi* to the Jewish woman. It is no surprise that a Jewish notary was called upon to certify the terms of both agreements, reached by a family that was torn apart by conversions and mourning.[21]

Despite the dictates of canonical rules, which called for the maximum and most complete separation between new Christians and old Jews, cutting off all relations was not possible. There were co-owned market spaces, banking licenses and titles to *gazagà* to be divided up, taking into account, however, that certain types of assets – such as inheritances, moneylending authorizations or the *gazagot* for living spaces in the Jewish quarter – which were no longer accessible to the Christian in his new condition. For example, in 1589 Leone Asriglio was able to obtain the lending license formerly owned by Giuseppe Menasci *alias* Coppolaro, who, now with the new name of Prospero da Santa Creve, was forced to look for a new job. It is possible, among other things, that Prospero *alias* Giuseppe may have even tried to keep the bank as a Christian; the *inhibitio* granted to his successor Leone Asriglio was actually accompanied by an *instantia definitiva* awarded by the *Camerlengo* at the request of the *Auditor Camerae* in response to an earlier dispute.[22]

The problems did not end here. Viewed with suspicion by both their new and former coreligionists, building a new professional career was not easy for converts, who would often continue practicing their previous occupations. Such was the situation in the case described in an earlier chapter, concerning the consortium of converts who for a short time obtained the exclusive contract for the *fardelli* of the *Santo Spirito*, though they did not manage to secure its renewal in subsequent years. One of those converts, Michelangelo, son of the late Giacobbe di Capua, a Jewish used clothing dealer who had lived in *Campo Marzio*, remained in the used clothing business himself. Later on, when he was being questioned about the purchase of "certain items" that turned out to have been stolen from "Cocchino di Cocchio," he explained that he had not had any suspicions about the provenance of the package of clothes, and, after describing his daily business and commitments, stated that he had probably resold them to an otherwise unidentified "Jew."[23] In this case, then, the change

---

20 The dowry was paid thanks to the repayment of an outstanding balance of 8 *scudi* made by Abramo di Pontecorvo, the renter of their market space (NE, f. 11, l. 6, c. 3v).
21 NE, f. 11, l. 6, c. 4v.
22 DC, r. 396, c. 146r-v.
23 ASR, *Tribunale Criminale del Governatore, Costituti*, r. 232, cc. 95v-97r.

of identity did not have a significant effect on the professional life of the convert. Despite his baptism, Michelangelo continued to spend his working hours going house to house and store to store buying and selling fabric and other used objects at retail, just as did many of his Jewish colleagues, with whom he maintained at least professional contact.

Converts conducted their business under the protective wing of the House of Catechumens. Following the events surrounding a market space and its recently converted owners clearly illustrates how intricate the mesh of these relationships was, and to what degree an intervention from above could succeed in undoing them. So it was that in November 1587, thanks to the high protection guaranteed to her by conversion and the presence of a Jewish notary, Maddalena Ghisella, the widow of Costantino Ongarino, collected the 30 *scudi* owed to her for some time from Leone di Pontecorvo, by order of the *Congregazione dei Catecumeni*. With the mutual consent of her daughter Veronica, to whom the money was simultaneously being donated, Maddalena graciously approved the cancellation of the Jew's promissory note.

The point – and this is the fact that I am interested in highlighting – is that Leone di Pontecorvo's debt was not incurred during the years when both he and his creditor shared a common existence as Jews. Rather it was initiated in transactions with former coreligionists, with the rental and then the sale of the market space that the married couple had not given up after conversion. In October of 1584 Maddalena and Costantino rented that space to Abramo di Pontecorvo and his son Leone. Perhaps conscious of the possible irregularity of this interfaith agreement, they took the precaution of asking two Christians with stores in the area to serve as witnesses.[24] The following November 29 Leone di Pontecorvo received a loan of 30 *scudi* from Costantino, obviously "*gratis et pro amore*" as Christians were not allowed to loan to Jews or charge interest, with a guarantee from his parents, Abramo and Donna di Pontecorvo, and a promise to repay the sum within a year.[25] As we have seen, Leone did not keep his word. Three years later the situation reached the point that the House of Catechumens had to order him to pay the balance as soon as possible.[26]

---

24 The witnesses, in fact, were "*mastro* Cotardo di Giampietro Baretti da Bresaglia *oste alli Savelli e mastro* Oliviero di Gianmaria Di Montepulciano, *macellaro al ponte Quattro Capi*" (NE, f. 11, l. 6, c. 134v).

25 NE, f. 11, l. 6, cc. 140v-141r.

26 Also on this occasion, when the debt contract was cancelled and the receipt of payment drawn up, Christian witnesses would be used, turning to "Antonio *alias* Tentator Di Gennazzano *facchino e* Sperandio Di Norcia *pescivendolo nella pescheria di Sant'Angelo di Roma*" (NE, f. 11, l. 6, cc. 140v-141r).

Maddalena and Veronica were driven to solicit this help by their own business obligations with another convert, who was, respectively, their son-in-law and brother-in-law. He had guaranteed a loan of 25 *scudi* which the two women had received from Ceriaco Matteo in March of 1586, and he now asked to be relieved of his obligations in light of the collection against Leone di Pontecorvo's debt.[27]

The Grisella/Ongarino family was not the only family of converts that continued to frequent the ghetto for business reasons. There were also some, like the convert Pietro Spada, who seemed to unable to do without it. On November 15, 1585 he declared that he had been loaned the sum of 16 *scudi* by another convert, Ambrogio di Giambattista. As a guarantor for the loan Pietro offered his Jewish son Giacobbe, who was quick to help his father, while "knowing that he is not obliged to be held as such until repayment is complete."[28] The following summer Pietro received another 4 *scudi* from Ambrogio, this time without involving his son. This contract, probably to protect Giacobbe's interests, was signed by Jewish witnesses in front of a Jewish notary.[29] At the end of October, with the first installments of the debt paid off, Pietro and Giacobbe received another joint loan of 50 *scudi* from Ambrogio, with the guarantee of Mosè Napolitano.[30] Relations between father and son evidently grew stronger over the years, because in 1588 we find Giacobbe once again involved in Pietro's business dealings. Pietro, in fact, in debt to Mosè Negri for 25 *scudi* for the third party sale of various quantities of coal, decided to settle the issue without requesting money from the partnership until Mosè had been fully repaid for the capital he had invested. As part of the conditions of this arrangement, they established that, working alongside him in something of a supervisory role, would be one of Mosè's apprentices and, as usual, Giacobbe, once again in the role of a guarantor in business involving his father's coreligionists.[31]

The convert Ambrogio, son of the late Giambattista of Rome, also a convert – Pietro Spada's first creditor – was accustomed to negotiating money matters with his Jewish acquaintances. Apart from his dealings with Pietro, he could offer guarantees, for sums of various amounts, to two Jews who had

---

27   There were Christian witnesses in this case as well, "Matteo Caffi *calzolaio* and Marcantonio Est" (NE, f. 6, l. 1, cc. 92v-93r).
28   The payment, however, arrived on time and the contract was cancelled on October 28, 1586 at the request of Ambrogio and in the presence of Abramo di Modigliano, Mele di Nepi, and Angelo di Ventura representative of the Jewish Community of Rome, "*mandataro della Comunità Santa di Roma*" (NE, f. 6, l. 1, cc. 61v-62r).
29   NE, f. 6, l. 1, c. 120r.
30   NE, f. 6, l. 1, cc. 135v-136r.
31   NE, f. 14, l. 1, cc. 59v-60r.

remained Jews, Graziano Tripolese[32] and Graziano Sed.[33] And one wonders if Mosè Negri was motivated to show such patience in his dealings with Pietro Spada because he was aware of how unpleasant it was to find oneself with a convert in the family. When Mosè died, in fact, Cascian Tripolese, the administrator of Mosè's assets, in order to close out some unresolved business had to seek out the deceased's relatives, who were themselves converts, and obtained from them the receipt for an old debt of 20 *scudi* to Mosè's relative Olimpia. Olimpia was a widow and daughter of the late convert Giambattista Capo di Bove of Rome[34] – and perhaps, considering the surname, the sister of the moneylender Ambrogio mentioned above. At this point Olimpia resumed contact with her former coreligionists, deciding at that time, much as many others in her position had done, to hand out sums of money to some of them *gratis et pro amore*. Her first beneficiary was one of the witnesses she got to know at the meeting with Cascian Tripolese, Crescienzo di Frascati, along with one of the woman's recently found cousins, Isacco Negri.[35] It is easy to suspect that hiding behind all these handouts were unauthorized loans, contracted in the grey and falsely friendly realm of the prohibited (but inevitable) ties between Jews and converts.

It was a business network whose protagonists were inextricably intertwined with each other by personal relationships, family origins, or casual acquaintance. Though it endured over time, it was destined to involve only a small number people (Pietro Spada, for example, had no choice but to turn to his son), and remained confined to the workplace. The authorities focused their attention on these kinds of relationships, which by nature involved strong emotions that had been seriously compromised on both sides by the irreversible choice of conversion, a cause of bitterness and hatred that were difficult to heal. The Fathers of the House of Catechumens, on the word of a convert, could burst in on the quiet lives of families, forcing offerings and oblations of women, minors and relatives who were unaware of who had come for them, provoking suffering, pain and fear.[36] However, from the Jewish point of view, well beyond the bitterness of the moment, conversion took on the connotation of an incomprehensible surrender, and came to be

---

32 This concerned nine *scudi* advanced for the purchase of a tablecloth (NE, f. 14, l. 1, c. 3r).
33 In this case as well Ambrogio had advanced the needed sum for the purchase of goods for resale and Graziano, with the consent of his wife Piacentia, committed to pay it back within a month (NE, f. 14, l. 1. c. 60v).
34 NE, f. 14, l. 1, c. 133v.
35 NE, f. 14, l. 1, c. 145r.
36 Regarding these aspects see Caffiero 2005.

marked by a symbolic period of mourning in the name of the relatives who had converted.

As difficult as it was for converts to earn the respect of Jews (and Christians), they represented an unbreakable link between the two worlds. Once a convert's first approaches to his old community turned out well, whatever the motivation may have been, it became easier for these newly established ties, which remained limited to very specific subjects, to lead to new encounters, even involving people who until that moment had remained distant. So it was in the case of Olimpia but also, naturally, in those of Ambrogio, of Pietro Spada and, in other ways, for the family of Abramo and Leone di Pontecorvo, who leased property from converts. On the other hand, there are Leuccio and Stella Delopiglio, who went to a convert for a loan well before their daughter Prudentia chose the path of baptism. The lender, Giovanni Angelo dell'Anguillara, was called Mosè when still a Jew, and earned his living trading in used clothing. Now, as a Christian, he continued to do business in the same places which had always been familiar.[37]

At the end of the 16th century, conversion did not succeed in bringing about a complete break with the convert's former life. It did, however, signal the crossing of a threshold, after which relationships that had been born and raised among the families and neighbors of the quarter changed their tone from that of close friend or relation to that of useful acquaintance. Most often converts continued to practice the trades they already knew, working the plazas, markets, and fairs shoulder to shoulder with colleagues who had remained Jewish. It was thus impossible to prevent these encounters, unwelcome to all, from taking place. When such interactions verged on becoming dangerous due to the nature of the profession, as was the case with butchers, and more generally the handling of food, with the many risks of contamination that all priests and rabbis feared (although for different reasons), then, and only then, would authorities intervene directly. Thus in 1590, Jewish butchers Abramo Di Campo Fallone, Mosè del *fu* Livoletta, and Graziadio *alias* Veneziano committed to not working as butchers with the convert Salvatore Marsaino, and to not help him or serve him in any way for a period of one year. The agreement called for a penalty of 20 *scudi* each, half of which would go to the Apostolic Chamber

---

37   NE, f. 11, l. 5, c. 130r. As a Jew Giovanni Angelo dell'Anguillara was called Angelo di Mosè dell'Anguillara and became mixed up in a story of thefts and illegal nocturnal exits from the ghetto (about which see below in this chapter); as a Christian, instead, he was one of the partners in the company of converts that took the contract for the *fardelli* of the Santo Spirito (ASR, *Santo Spirito, Instrumenti*, r. 254, cc. 79v-81r).

and the other half to Giacomo Lanciano, himself also a convert.[38] The fact that this agreement was signed for a term of only one year indicates without question that the authorities judged the game to be lost before it started. Thus with pragmatic realism they concerned themselves with assuring for the convert a window of time that was evidently considered sufficient for the strengthening of his new religious convictions. Once this time-out expired, and the souls involved had made use of the time to fortify not only their faith, but their feelings of mutual hostility, there was no reason to forbid reunions that were bound to happen in such a restricted urban space.[39]

It could certainly happen at times that business agreements could cross tacitly established boundaries and involve issues of ritual. Such was the case in the arrangement made between Mosè Del Presto and Giuseppe Franchi, a convert, in August of 1583, shortly before the fall season of Jewish holidays got underway. The pair formed a company to purchase, at the expense of the Jew and with the labor of the Christian, palms and citrons to sell to Jews as they left synagogue after services for Hoshana Rabba. They promised to divide the profits equally.[40] Deals of this type, though, exposed the convert to the accusation of Judaizing, and perhaps because of this were executed privately in front of a Jewish notary with Jewish witnesses. Such cases ultimately remained isolated occurrences.

In daily practice, converts and conversions could be counted among the wide range of engines of social change. For the convert this meant a transformation of identity and a better quality of life. For those left behind, forced to heal the emotional (but also economic and professional) void left by the new Christian, it meant both drawbacks and opportunity. It was a problem to be resolved,

---

38 NE, f. 6, l. 2, c. 49r-v. To guarantee the deed, almost in the role of counterpart, two Christians were called as witnesses (Gian Gregorio di Ascoli and Massimiliano della Camerata) and a Jewish butcher (Conci di Meluccio). The document has already been cited by Kenneth Stow in 1993, p. 271, within a long list of deeds meant to demonstrate the continuity of working relationships even after conversion. On the significance of food and the *kashrut* of foodstuffs in the relations between Jews, Christians and converts in Rome during this period, see Di Nepi 2006.

39 Among other things, at that point, the Jews would have had to face serious problems using meat handled by a Christian; but this would not have caused any sleepless nights for those who wanted to convert them and who certainly did not discount recourse to one of the oldest methods used to complicate the daily life of the Jews. On these aspects, see Bonfil 1991; Toaff 1989; Foa 1992. For a specific treatment of the case cited as an example and the question of Jewish butchery in Rome, see Di Nepi 2006. Regarding the society of Jewish butchers and the ethnic conflict they encountered in the period spanning the 15th and 16th centuries, refer to Esposito 2006.

40 NE, f. 11, l. 6, cc. 53v-54r.

overcoming the sense of defeat that a premature and tragic loss always brings with it (recall that on the ritual level, the baptism of a relative called for formal mourning). The conversion of a loved one should and could have caused an incurable wound, leading to capitulation by others, as happened in many cases. However, alongside the expansion of businesses and the capacity to profit from networks of institutional and professional contacts, even the apostasy of neighboring Jews could present an opportunity for starting over and getting back in the game for those remaining in the ghetto. Read this way, the history of the Jews of Rome takes on a new appearance, going beyond images of persecution, marginalization and a silent resignation to misfortune. Instead it becomes an important example of the expedients that a group under tremendous divisive pressures can bring to bear in order to successfully defend their identity, and with it, their chances of survival. The Jews of Rome at the end of the 16th century were not passive spectators to a sinister fate. To the contrary, from their stories they unexpectedly emerge as unstoppable builders of their own fortunes. Among the paths they took there was business of all types, travels, contacts and contracts, and sometimes, conversions. It is a story of life, not the end of the story.

Conclusions

The social history approach that underpins this study has allowed us to sketch a profile of Roman Jewish society in the 16th century, a key period in its history. The principal elements are well known: the difficult process of absorbing the Sephardic minority, the terrible tragedy of the Sack of Rome, the gradual deployment of an unprecedented evangelical campaign in the midst of the Italian Wars, and, with the establishment of the ghettos, the opening of a new phase in the long history of turbulent coexistence between Jews and Christians.

The revolution set down in writing by Paul IV in 1555 sought to encourage the conversion of Jews via physical and economic marginalization of the group, implemented in a context of powerful social and cultural pressure. On the ideological plane, a well-balanced system underpinned this project of inclusive exclusion. On the one hand, a revival of the classic tools of proselytism was needed to persuade Jews of the ease of conversion and of the many advantages that came with it. On the other hand, the isolation of the Jews was meant to demonstrate the severe and definitive defeat of the people of Israel. The marginalization of the group within the heart of Christian society was the keystone of this project; thus, in a clearly delimited time and place, notwithstanding the efforts of many, the complete expulsion of the Jews from society was not possible, nor was this end even fully pursued.

A variety of factors prevented the achievement of a definitive result in this direction. The contradictory formulation of the Catholic theological conception of the place and role of the Jews in the heart of the Christian world – which was the foundation for theorizing about segregation – played an important role. It's no accident that the redefinition of the rules of coexistence imposed by *Cum nimis absurdum* did not sever relations between Jews and Christians. The documentation unequivocally demonstrates how the system of daily exchanges in the realms of both individual and institutional conduct was changed, but not diminished. The exclusion of the Jews from the normal social fabric, as sanctioned by law, did however transform relations between Jews and Christians into a precarious system of personal encounters, the legitimacy of which could be called into question at any moment.

The reshaping of the community was the result of the group's conscious management of the interaction between internal and external social and cultural dynamics. In the context of an endless negotiation over the conditions of the Jews' presence, economic and professional success, as contract agreements and disputes tell us, became a litmus test in the unbalanced relationship between the privileged group and the segregated group. The special relations with the *Camerlengo* and the Curia that were individually cultivated by members of the ghetto elite, involving a continual mixing of private business and community interests, demonstrate how extraordinarily permeable the walls of the ghetto were. The makeup of the internal social leadership, in fact, reflected successes achieved outside the private space of the Jewish nucleus, both as businessmen and as representatives of the *Universitas*. The stories of families engaged in loan banking and the sale of used clothing, such as the Ram family (who figure prominently in the 1594 trial examined as a case study in this volume), break down the stereotype of the Jewish rag seller and reveal how dynamic Roman Jewish society was in the second half of the 16th century. The mechanisms that made adaptation to the new regime possible cover a very broad range of possibilities: the monopoly contracts for used clothing from the hospitals, the constant short, medium and long range travel, the prudent use of market stalls, and the interplay between internal agreements and external ratifications sanctioned from the granting of *inhibitiones ratione foenoris*. The result was to preserve the viability of a ruling class which was credible even outside the group, was generally considered trustworthy and that, on paper, *Cum nimis absurdum* should have eliminated.

In the decades following the promulgation of the bull, the Jews of Rome were subjected to a rapid process of transformation that affected the structure of their institutions of self-governance as much as it did the professional life and economic capacity of individuals and families. Without abandoning its traditions and without compromising its religious otherness, Jewish society managed to reshape itself, tenaciously confronting three centuries of humiliating segregation and relentless proselytizing while remaining faithful to its identity. It was a difficult course to follow, in which multiple factors came into play: the growing role of religion in the institutions, very strong social mobility and the interweaving of ambiguous relations with the most important magistracies of the Papal States. The strengthening of the community leadership and the legitimization of its representative and intermediary role in dealings with both the Jewish community and with the external world was the most evident outcome of this phase. The main criteria that favored such leadership were, on the one hand, individual study and the advantages connected with earning rabbinic titles, and on the other hand the building of new assets and reinforcement of old means of income via the aggressive use of every available space.

The growing role of the *maskilim/rabbis* was not part of a careful strategy, and it was even less an attempt to gain some form of legal autonomy to support cultural diversity. Rather, this process was the manifestation in daily social practices of the responses that Jews knowingly offered to the challenge directed against them. The publication of the *Capitoli di Daniel da Pisa* in 1524 laid down the base upon which this institutional consolidation would later be constructed. The statute was drawn up to solve conflicts resulting from the difficult inclusion of non-Italian Jews within the nucleus of Roman Jewry, and the attendant social and cultural changes this meant. Jewish institutions would gradually become a generally accepted point of reference, and their authority found confirmation in the type of people who were chosen to manage them. Relocation to the ghetto would accelerate the process of identifying Jews by the community they belonged to, a process that played out according to a dynamic that is of great interest. The stability of the *Universitas* was, once again, dependent on those chosen to represent it: the *Fattori* (political leaders), the *Tassatori* (tax collectors), members of the Congregation and the arbitrators who from time to time were engaged to settle disputes. In this context, when it came to the defense of the right to religious difference, public trust in the rabbis – who were also merchants and bankers of some prestige – began to grow significantly, leading to ever more frequent calls for them to assume direct responsibility.

The initial questions asked by this research regarding the Jews' actions in reaction to the process of social and cultural restructuring in the 16th Century have brought to light some important elements. The comparison of material obtained from diverse sources has provided completely new information about the Jewish ruling class in Rome; their institutional organization, their choices of professions, and the inevitable interplay between events and business inside and outside the ghetto. What has emerged is a detailed image of the experiences lived by this community in the 16th Century. Thanks to these details it was possible to go beyond simple case studies, while thoroughly retracing events in the lives of individuals. Documentation that was produced both inside and outside the Jewish enclave refutes traditional conceptions about the marginalization of the Jews and their passive acceptance of a condition of absolute imprisonment during the years of the ghetto. Within the ghetto lived a multifaceted, stratified and contentious community. They were fully a part of the Rome of the Counterreformation, and, precisely because of this, capable of remaining strong even in these very difficult years.

The 16th century was a dire period for Jews. The burning of the Talmud in 1553 represented a declaration of war against the Jews' otherness and their religious roots, and it was immediately recognized as such by Italian Jews. The paradoxical case of the imaginary blood libel in 1555 is a clear sign of how the Jews interpreted, after the fact, in the story by Josef ha-Cohen a few years later, the ongoing process. The mechanisms employed in Rome to manage the changes brought about by the ghetto correspond to the same logic of fear and worry for Jews that is embodied in the narrative of the real infanticide that happened the same year. The assumption that events could veer towards a different path is ever-present: the fear of another turn to expulsion or pogrom – which did not occur – is evoked in this exemplary tale. It is a story that revolves around the protections that the Church of Rome continued to give the Jews, even at this juncture. Also fundamental to the story, though in different terms, are the institutional affairs which I have reconstructed, beginning with the avoidance of reforms to the *Capitoli*. Faced with a powerful attack, the choice was made to embrace the roots of the group's identity and its traditions. Such apparent immobility, exemplified well by the stability of the statute's text even in an era a great changes, did not, however, impede the reorganization of the society and its institutions. It did even less to affect the condition of general uncertainty, a fact attested to by the confusion between the two cases argued in 1555.

The period of the ghettos was, as has often happened in Jewish history, an example of strenuous cultural resistance by a minority against a multitude of pressures aimed at convincing them to renounce their identity. Writing Jewish history means reflecting on the painful and varied experiences of a community that survived, kept strong by an extremely durable identity. This identity remained durable even though it was composite, contentious and itself a product of the (often hostile and unwilling) interaction that continuously took place with the unfriendly majority who, more often than not, wanted to eliminate that identity. The examination of the social practices which facilitated this survival has put the mechanisms of self-governance and the relations between these and the emerging classes at the center of this research.

The history of Jewish institutions is the complex story of their evolution, and of the changes that occurred regarding who was called upon to manage them, carried out in strict adherence with the processes in progress outside the walls of the ghetto. These are parallel phenomena, but obviously not identical. The signs of dialog between inside and outside are numerous: Pompeo del Borgo's choice to write up his protocols in Italian although he was able to write in Hebrew is one example of this, just as are the adventures of Salomone Ram and of his false *baiocchelle*, the granting of the *inhibitiones*, and the intra-Jewish management of the business of new converts.

Conflicts between the Jews themselves are also a part of the picture. The construction of the ghetto only amplified them, mainly due to the limited availability of living space and a job market that was shackled to a very restricted spectrum of options for occupations. Arguments were the order of the day, and involved relatives, associates, neighbors and even synagogues, in disagreement over bordering stairs, doors and windows. The capacity to resolve these disputes was, in my view, one of the essential mechanisms of the survival strategy attempted in the ghetto of Rome. Disputes easily bled over to the outside, involving the Christian magistrate in their solutions and thus threatening the authority of Jewish institutions. The attention of the ordinary courts could be aroused by a conversion (as in the case of the Sforno trial), by the decision of one of the parties to appeal to gentile courts, or even by an investigation ordered by the judges themselves (as with the affair of the thefts in the middle of Shabbat). The examples are potentially infinite but, while extraordinary in their frequency, they did not lead to an unravelling of Jewish society (in the broad meaning that I have indicated).

My theory is that the gradual inclusion of the "rabbis" in the most important Jewish institutions represented a winning move for these institutions without, however, turning the ghetto into a theocracy. The appeal to the arbitration entrusted to the rabbis and *Fattori* served to tamp down controversies before they exploded irreparably. The sentences handed down by the groups of three arbitrators managed only occasionally to settle the litigants' disputes, perhaps even rarely. However, the very fact that such a system existed and operated regularly represented an important factor in the ghetto. Before going to knock on the door of the Christian magistrate, the unwritten rule called for appeal to the Jewish system of arbitration first, contributing to the cohesion of the group. The opportunity to submit to the decisions of Jewish arbitrators did a great deal to legitimize the community institutions, as well as the authority of those who represented them. In the end it was of little importance if a ruling was rejected: every rejection implied a prior effort in defense of the autonomy of identity that segregation sought to disrupt. The system of formalizing economic agreements in two phases – the first by a Christian notary with a Christian counterpart and the second between Jews, by a Jewish notary in compliance with a law managed by Jews – is a part of this context. There was an inside and there was an outside, separated by boundaries which were easily crossed. Both spaces represented familiar places, governed by well-known rules. The Jews of the ghetto found themselves at the center of system of overlapping pressures: on the one hand, the very familiar world of peers, on the other, the continuous prospect of change toward a better and finally normal life that was not subject to an alternate set of rules and customs – a change achievable only through conversion. The boundaries, as porous as they were, ultimately separated the two societies, and it was clear to all that once they had been crossed, it was not possible to turn back. They were separate lives, close and interwoven, but above all different.

The study of the tools that in different times and places have allowed Jews to remain Jews, yet still able to contribute to the development of the society of which they were a part, invites reflection on the cultural, national and religious affiliations which make up the world in which we live. Rome, with its ghetto and the travails of the "Counter-Reformation", represents a specific case which is, however, part of a much wider panorama. The histories of identities recount multifaceted and widely varying events, which include moments of dialogue as well as periods of mutually accepted silence, crises and processes of cultural redefinition, forms of collaboration, inclusion, and also exclusion. The stories of events in the life of this 16th century community restore elements of one of these histories, and in doing so, offer important points for understanding the workings of a society that was rich with contrasts and committed to the attempt to validate and limit their differences, just as was that of the modern age.

Bibliography and Reference Works

Archival Sources

Rome, Archivio Storico Capitolino, Archivio Urbano, *Sezione III "Notai Ebrei"*.
Notary Isacco delle Piattelle:
Fascicolo 9, libro 1: marzo 1576-luglio 1580 (Hebrew).
Fascicolo 3, libro 2: December 1580- December 1583 (Hebrew); *Fascicolo 9, libro 2*: January 1584-January 1591 (Hebrew).
Notary Pompeo del Borgo:
Fascicolo 3, libro 1: 1578–1579 (Italian) *Fascicolo 11, libro 5*: 1580–1582 (Italian) *Fascicolo 11, libro 6*: 1583–1584 (Italian) *Fascicolo 6, libro 1*: 1585–1587 (Italian) *Fascicolo 14, libro 1*: 1588–1589 (Italian) *Fascicolo 6, libro 2*: 1590–1591 (Italian).
Rome, Archivio Storico della Congregazione della Fede *S. Offizio*, St. St. I-2.
Rome, Archivio di Stato di Roma.
Camerale I:
Diversorum del camerlengo, rr. 295, 376, 377, 379, 382, 383, 384, 385, 386, 388, 389, 390, 391, 392, 393, 394, 396, 397, 398, 399, 400, 402, 403, 405, 406, 407, 410 *Diversorum del tesoriere*, r. 715.
Decreti della Camera, r. 297.
Taxae Maleficiorum, bb. 1747, 1749, 1750.
Camerale II, *Ebrei*, bb. 2–3.
Camerale III, *Roma città e comune*, b. 1934 Collezione dei Bandi, bb. 2, 5, 6, 7, 354, 366.
Consolazione:
Istrumenti, rr. 37, 38.
Libro mastro generale, r. 1291.
Notai Capitolini:
Ufficio 7, notaio Aristotele Tuscolani.
Ufficio 16, notai Berardino Pascasio e Berardo Rocco De Sanctis *Ufficio 23*, notaio Evangelista Ceccarelli.
Ufficio 33, notaio Simone Gugnetta.
S. Giacomo:
Istrumenti, r. 43.
Libri di entrata e uscita del camerlengo, rr. 1246, 1247, 1248, 1350 *Libro del mastro di caso*, r. 1395.
Libro mastro generale, r. 1459.
S. Giovanni Decollato, *Testamenti*, b. 15.
S. Rocco, r. 9.
S. Spirito, *Instrumenta*, rr. 253, 254, 255, 658 Statuti, 170, 327.

Tribunale Criminale del Governatore:
Costituti, rr. 49, 232, 233, 234.
Processi, rr. 20, 21, 140, 158, 160, 193, 232, 233, 234, 237, 238, 258 *Registrazioni d'atti*, r. 69.
Università, b. 61.
Rome, Archivio Storico della Comunità Ebraica di Roma, Archivio Medievale e moderno, *1Tc* (*parte II*).
Jerusalem, National Archives for the History of the Jewish People IT/An 96.

Primary Sources

Ademollo 1891: Ademollo, Alessandro. *Il Carnevale di Roma al tempo di Alessandro VI, Giulio II e Leone X (1499- 1529)* (Florence: Carlo Ademollo fu Gio. Editore).

Bullarium: Bullarium *privilegiorum ac diplomatum Romanorum Pontificum amplissima collectio cui accessere Pontificum omnium Vitae, Notae, et Indices opportuni. Opera et studio, Caroli Coquelinies, Tomus Quartus, Pars Quarta* (Rome: Typis, et Sumptibus Hieronymi Mainardi, 1747).

Bando contra gli Hebrei (e anco i Neofiti) che impegnano al Sacro Monte della Pietà;; contra gli offerenti alle vendite de' pegni in detto Monte et in Piazza Giudea, che s'accordano insieme di fare à parte e à mezzo (Rome: appresso agli Stampatori della Reverenda Camera Apostolica, 1605).

Belli 1834: Belli, Andrea. *Della origine del Ven. Arcispedale di S. Maria della Consolazione, già chiamata della vita eterna con censo ed appendice* (Rome: Tipografia Marini).

Berliner 1992: Berliner, Abraham. *Storia degli ebrei di Roma: dall'antichità allo smantellamento del ghetto* (Milan: Rusconi).

Cardella 1793: Cardella, Lorenzo. *Memorie storiche de' cardinali della Santa Romana Chiesa* (Rome: Stamperia Pagliarini).

Chacón, 1630: Chacón, Alfonoso. *Vitæ, et res gestæ Pontificvm Romanorum et S. R. E. Cardinalivm ab initio nascentis Ecclesiæ vsque ad Urbanvm VIII. Pont. Max.*, 2 voll. (Rome: Stamperia Vaticana).

Che li Fattori possano riscuotere le tasse e che nessuno possa ricusare di pagarli (Rome: Antonio Blado Stampatore Camerale, 1577).

Cuggiò 2004: Cuggiò, Niccolò Antonio. *Della giurisdittione e prerogative del vicario di Roma*. Edited by Domenico Rocciolo (Rome: Carocci, 2004).

de' Giudici, 1987 = de'Giudici, Battista. *Apologia Iudaeorum. Invectiva contra Platinam. Propaganda antiebraica e polemiche di Curia durante il pontificato di Sisto IV*. Edited by Diego Quaglioni (Rome: Roma nel Rinascimento).

D'Azeglio 1848: D'Azeglio, Massimo. *Sull'emancipazione degli israeliti* (Firenze: s.n.).

Delicado 1998: Delicado, Francisco. *Ritratto della Lozana Andalusa*. Edited by Teresa Cirillo Sirri (Rome: Roma nel Rinascimento).

De Luca 1673: De Luca, Giovanni Battista. *Il dottor volgare, overo, Il compendio di tutta la legge civile, canonica, feudale e municipale, nelle cose più ricevute in pratica* (Rome: Giuseppe Corvo, 1673).

Francois 1886: Francois, Achille. *Elenco di Notari che rogarono atti in Roma dal XIV sec. all'anno 1860* (Rome: Tipografia della Pace di Filippo Cuggiani).

Garzoni 1617: Garzoni, Tommaso. *La piazza universale di tutte le professioni del mondo* (Venice: Olivier Alberti).

Gabrielli 1585: Gabrielli, Maggino di. *Dialoghi sopra l'utilissime invenzioni circa la seta* (Rome: gli eredi di Giovanni Gigliotti).

Innovationis costitutionum Pauli Quarti e Pii Quinti, contra Medicos Hebreos, et illarum exstensionins ad eos qui Medicos Haebreos, vel infideles ad Christianorum curam vocant, admittunt, vel eisdem medendi licentiam concedunt (Rome: Paolo Blado, 1581).

Infessura, Stefano. *Diario della città di Roma.* Edited by Oreste Tommasini (Rome: Forzani & C. Tipografi del Senato, 1890).

Ioly Zorattini, 1980–1999: Ioly Zorattini, Pier Cesare, ed. *Processi del S. Uffizio di Venezia contro ebrei e giudaizzanti,* 16 vols (Florence: Olshki).

Giustiniani, Quirini 1995: Giustiniani, Paolo; Quirini, Pietro, *Lettera al Papa. Paolo Giustiniani e Pietro Quirini a Leone X.* Edited by Germiano Bianchini (Modena: Artioli).

Liscia Bemporad, 2010: Liscia Bemporad, Dora, ed. *Maggino di Gabriello hebreo venetiano. I Dialoghi sopra l'utili sue inventioni circa la seta* (Firenze: Edifir).

Lutero 2000: Lutero, Martin. *Degli ebrei e delle loro menzogne.* Edited by Adelisa Malena (Turin: Einaudi).

Marini 1784: Marini, Gaetano. *Degli archiatri pontifici* (Rome: Stamperia Pagliarini).

Morichini 1892: Morichini, Carlo Luigi. *Degli istituti di carità per la sussistenza e l'educazione dei poveri e dei prigionieri di Roma* (Rome: Marini e compagno).

Moroni 1840–1861: Moroni, Gaetano. *Dizionario di erudizione storico-ecclesiastica da S. Pietro ai giorni nostri* (Venice: Tipografia Emiliana).

Ordini da osservarsi sopra le scommesse de Maschio ò Femina emanati dal camerlengo (Rome: Paolo Blado, 1589).

von Pastor 1910–1934: von Pastor, Ludwig. *Storia dei papi dalla fine del Medioevo.* Italian edition edited by Pio Cenci and Andrea Mercati, 16 vols (Rome: Desclèe).

Pericoli 1879: Pericoli, Pietro. *L'Ospedale di S. Maria della Consolazione di Roma dalle sue origini ai giorni nostri* (Imola: Ignazio Galeati e figlio).

Privilegi d'hebrei levantini, d'ordine dell'Ill.mo e Rev.mo Monsignor Cardinal Camerlengo per special commissione di N.S. PP. Clemente VIII che si osservi quanto da Sisto Papa V di felice memoria per sue lettere fu concesso à detti Hebrei, Turchi, Greci e altri Mercanti Levantini nella città di Ancona, con altre concessioni di novo. A suppli- catione di Esaya Pernica e Mosè Carcassuni Mercanti e Ambasciatori della Natione Levantina. Tradotto di Latino in Volgare per più facile intelligenza (Rome: Paolo Blado, 1593).

Regesti di bandi editti notificazioni e provvedimenti diversi relativi alla città di Roma ed allo Stato Pontificio, 7 voll. (Rome: Tipografia Cuggiani, 1920–1958).

Rodocanachi 1891: Rodocanachi, Emmanuel Pierre. *Le Saint-Siège et les Juifs: le ghetto à Rome* (Paris: Firmin-Didot).

Simonsohn 1980–1991: Simonsohn, Shlomo. *The Apostolic See and the Jews*, 9 vols (Toronto: Pontifical Institute of Medieval Studies).

Simonsohn 1982–1986: Simonsohn, Shlomo. *The Jews in the Duchy of Mantua*, 4 voll. (Jerusalem: Makhon Ben-Tsevi 'al-yede Ḳiryat Sefer).

Vogelstein, Rieger 1895–1896: Vogelstein, Hermann, Rieger, Paul. *Geschichte der Juden in Rom*, 2 voll. (Berlin: Mayer & Muller).

Studies and Reference Works

Akman 2013: Akman, Dogan Davit Akman. "A scholarly blind spot: The term *marrano*". *Sephardic Horizons* 3, n. 1: https://www.sephardichorizons.org/Volume3/Issue1/Akman.html.

Ago 1990: Ago, Renata. *Carriere e clientele nella Roma barocca* (Rome-Bari: Laterza).

Ago 1998: Ago, Renata. *Economia barocca. Mercato e istituzioni nella Roma del Seicento* (Rome: Donzelli).

Ago 2000: Ago, Renata. "Le fonti notarili del XVII secolo: alcune istruzioni per l'uso". *Mélanges de l'École française de Rome. Italie et Méditerranée* 1: 31–44.

Allegra 1996: Allegra, Luciano. *Identità in bilico. Il ghetto ebraico di Torino nel Settecento* (Turin: Zamorani).

Andreoni 2013, Andreoni, Luca. " 'Perché non se habbia più a tribulare.' Gli ebrei della Marca fra spazi economici e conflitti giudiziari alla metà del XVI secolo." In Caffiero, Esposito 2012b: 109–47.

Andreoni 2019: Andreoni, Luca. *"Una nazione in commercio". Ebrei di Ancona, traffici adriatici e pratiche mercantili in età moderna* (Milano: Unicopli).

Andretta 1995: Andretta, Stefano. "Alessandro Farnese". *Dizionario biografico degli Italiani*, vol. 45 (Rome: Istituto per l'Enciclopedia Italiana): http://www.treccani.it/enciclopedia/alessandro-farnese_(Dizionario-Biografico)/.

Angelini 1989: Angelini, Walter. "Tra Cinquecento e tardo Settecento: preparazione e maturità dell'attività mercantile degli ebrei ad Ancona". In *The Mediterranean and the Jews: Banking, Finance and International Trade (16th – 18th Centuries)*. Edited by Aariel Toaff, Simon Schwarzfuchs (Tel Aviv: Bar Ilan University): 12–38.

Ascarelli, Di Castro, Migliau, Toscano 2004: Ascarelli, Gianni, Daniela Di Castro, Bice Migliau, Mario Toscano eds. *Il Tempio Maggiore di Roma nel centenario dell'inaugurazione della sinagola (1904–2004)* (Turin: U. Allemandi).

Baron 1952–1983: Baron, Salo Wittmayer. *A social and religious history of the Jews*, 18 voll. (New York: Comubia University Press).

Barrovecchio San Martini 1981: Barrovecchio San Martini, Maria Luisa. *Il Tribunale criminale del Governatore di Roma (1512-1809)* (Rome: Ufficio Centrale per i Beni Archivistici).

Bartolucci 2017: Bartolucci, Guido. *Vera religio. Marsilio Ficino e la tradizione ebraica* (Turin: Paideia).

Bauer 1927: Bauer, Clemente. "Studi per la storia delle finanze papali durante il pontificato di Sisto IV". *Archivio della Società Romana di Storia Patria* L: 319–400.

Beinart 2005: Beinart, Haim. *The Expulsion of the Jews from Spain*. Translated by Jefrrey M. Green (Oxford, Portland (Or): The Littman Library of Jewish Civilization).

Berengo 1999: Berengo, Marino. *L'Europa delle città. Il volto della società urbana europea tra Medioevo ed età moderna* (Turin: Einaudi).

Bellabarba 2008: Bellabarba, Marco. *La giustizia nell'Italia moderna (XVI-XVIII sec.)* (Roma: Bari, Laterza)

Bidussa 2008: Bidussa, David. "Macchina mitologica e indagine storica. A proposito di Pasque di sangue e del «mestiere di storico»". In *Vero e falso. L'uso politico della storia*, edited by Marina Caffiero and Micaela Procaccia (Rome: Donzelli): 139–72.

Bloch 2004: Bloch, Marc. *La guerra e le false notizie: Ricordi (1914–1915) e Riflessioni (1921)* (Rome: Donzelli).

Boesh Gajano 1983: Boesh Gajano, Sofia (ed.). *Aspetti e problemi della presenza ebraica nell'Italia centro-settentrionale (secc. XIV-XV)* (Rome: Tipografia Ripoli).

Boiteux 1976: Boiteux, Martine. "Les Juifs dans le Carnaval de Rome (XVe-XVIIe siècles)". *Mélanges de l'École français de Rome. Moyen Âge-Temps Modernes* 88, 2: 745–787.

Bonazzoli 1990: Bonazzoli, Viviana. *Il prestito ebraico nelle economie cittadine delle Marche fra '200 e '400* (Ancona: Istituto di storia economica e sociologia).

Bonfil 1990: Bonfil, Roberto. *Rabbis and Jewish Communities in Renaissance Italy* (Oxford: Oxford University Press) [Italian edition: Naples, Liguori 2012].

Bonfil 1991: Bonfil, Roberto, *Gli Ebrei in Italia all'epoca del Rinascimento* (Florence: Sansoni).

Bonfil 1996: Bonfil, Roberto. "Lo spazio culturale degli ebrei d'Italia fra Rinascimento ed età barocca". In *Storia d'Italia, Annali* 11, *Gli ebrei in Italia*. Edited by Corrado Vivanti, t. 1, *Dall'alto medioevo all'età dei ghetti* (Turin: Einaudi): 413–73.

Bonfil 2000: Bonfil, Roberto. *Cultural Change Among the Jews of Early Modern Italy* (Farnham: Ashgate).

Bonfil 2012: Bonfil, Roberto. "Due documenti sul banco di Massa Fiscaglia (Ferrara) dalla raccolta di Aron Leoni". In *Studi sul mondo sefardita. In memoria di Aron Leoni*. Edited by Pier Cesare Ioly Zorattini, Michele Luzzati and Michel Sarfatti (Florence: Olshki): 101–6.

Bonora 2001: Bonora, Elena. *La Controriforma* (Rome-Bari: Laterza).

Bonora 2011: Bonora, Elena. *Roma 1564. La congiura contro il papa* (Rome-Bari: Laterza).

Bonora 2014: Bonora, Elena. *Aspettando l'imperatore. I prinicipi italiani tra il papa e Carlo V* (Turin: Einaudi).

Botticini, Eckstein 2012: Botticini, Maristella, Eckstein, Zvi. *I pochi eletti. Il ruolo dell'istruzione nella storia degli ebrei (70- 1492)*(Milan: Università Bocconi).

Bregoli 2011: Bregoli, Francesca. "The Port of Livorno and its "Nazione Ebrea" in the Eighteenth Century: Economic Utility and Political Reforms". *Quest. Issues in Contemporary Jewish History* 2 http://www.quest-cdecjournal.it/focus.php?id=227.

Bregoli 2014: Bregoli, Francesca. *Mediterranean Enlightment. Livornese Jews, Tuscan culture and Eighteenth-century reform* (Standford: Standford University Press).

Bruckner 1996: Bruckner, Wolfgand. "La riorganizzazione delle fedi nello Stato confessionale post-tridentino". In *Il Concilio di Trento e il moderno*. Edited by Paolo Prodi (Bologna: Il Mulino): 187:223.

Brunelli 2011: Brunelli, Giampiero. *Il sacro consiglio di Paolo IV* (Rome: Viella).

Caffiero 1997: Caffiero, Marina. "Tra Chiesa e Stato. Gli ebrei in Italia dall'età dei Lumi agli anni della Restaurazione". In Vivanti 1997, 1089–132.

Caffiero 2000a: Caffiero, Marina. *Religione e modernità in Italia (secoli XVII-XIX)* (Pisa, Roma: Istituti editoriali e poligrafici internazionali).

Caffiero 2000b: Caffiero, Marina. "«Il pianto di Rachele». Ebrei, neofiti e giudaizzanti a Roma in età moderna". In *L'Inquisizione e gli storici: un cantiere aperto* (Rome: Accademia nazionale dei Lincei, 2000): 307–328.

Caffiero 2003a: Caffiero, Marina. "«La caccia agli ebrei». Inquisizione, Casa dei Catecumeni e battesimi forzati nella Roma moderna". In *Le inquisizioni cristiane e gli ebrei. Tavola rotonda nell'ambito della Conferenza annuale della Ricerca* (Rome: Accademia Nazionale dei Lincei): 503–37.

Caffiero 2003b: Caffiero, Marina. "Alle origini dell'antisemitismo politico. L'accusa di omicidio rituale nel Sei- Settecento tra autodifesa degli ebrei e pronunciamenti papali". In *Les racines chrétiennes de l'antisémitisme politique (fin XIXe-XXe siècle)*. Edited by Catherine Brice and Giovanni Miccoli (Rome: École française de Rome): 25–59.

Caffiero 2004: Caffiero, Marina. *Battesimi forzati. Storie di ebrei, cristiani e convertiti nella Roma dei papi* (Rome: Viella) [English edition translated by Lydia G. Cochrane, Los Angeles: University of California Press, 2011].

Caffiero 2005: Caffiero, Marina. "1789: il cahier des doléances degli ebrei romani alla vigilia dell'emancipazione". In *Chiesa, laicità e vita civile. Studi in onore di Guido Verucci*, a cura di Lucia Ceci, Laura Demofonti (Rome: Carocci, 2005): 225–45.

Caffiero 2007: Caffiero, Marina. "Gli ebrei sono eretici? L'Inquisizione romana e gli ebrei tra Cinque e Ottocento". In *I tribunali della fede: continuità e discontinuità dal medioevo all'età moderna*. Edited by Susanna Peyronel Rambaldi (Turin: Claudiana): 245–64.

Caffiero 2008: Caffiero, Marina, ed. *Rubare le anime. Il diario del rapimento di Anna Del Monte, ebrea romana* (Rome: Viella).

Caffiero 2011: Caffiero, Marina, ed. "Ebrei: scambi e conflitti tra XV e XX secolo". Monographic Issue, *Roma moderna e contemporanea* 1.

Caffiero 2012: Caffiero, Marina. *Legami pericolosi. Ebrei e cristiani tra eresia, libri proibiti e stregoneria* (Turin: Einaudi).

Caffiero 2014: Caffiero, Marina. *Storia degli ebrei nell'Italia moderna. Dal Rinascimento alla Restaurazione* (Rome: Carocci).

Caffiero 2019: Caffiero, Marina. *Il grande mediatore. Tranquillo Vita Corcos, un rabbino nella Roma dei papi* (Rome: Carocci).

Caffiero, Di Nepi, 2017: Caffiero, Marina; Di Nepi, Serena. "The Relationship between Jews and Christians. Toward a Redefinition of the Ghetto. Introduction to Special issue". *Rivista di Storia del Cristianesimo* 14, no. 1: 3–10.

Caffiero, Esposito 2012a: Caffiero, Marina; Esposito, Anna, eds. *Judei de Urbe. Roma e i suoi ebrei: una storia secolare* (Rome: Ministero per i Beni e le Attività Culturali).

Caffiero, Esposito 2012b: Caffiero, Marina; Esposito, Anna, eds. *Gli ebrei nello Stato della Chiesa. Insediamenti e mobilità (secoli XIV–XVIII)* (Padua: Esedra Editrice).

Calabi 2016: Calabi, Donatella. *Venezia e il ghetto. Cinquecento anni del recinto degli ebrei* (Turin: Bollati Boringhieri).

Calasso 1965: Calasso, Giuseppe. *Gli ordinamenti giuridici del Rinascimento medievale* (Milan: Giuffrè).

Calimani 2001: Calimani, Riccardo. *Storia del ghetto di Venezia* (Milano: Mondadori).

Calzolari 2001: Calzolari, Monica. "Delitti e castighi". *Rivista storica del Lazio IX*, 4: 39–75.

Calzolari 2012: Calzolari, Monica. "Ricerche sul patrimonio immobiliare degli ebrei romani tra prima emancipazione e Restaurazione". In Caffiero, Esposito 2012a, 181–95.

Calzolari, Di Sivo, Grantaliano 2001: Calzolari, Monica; Di Sivo, Michele; Grantaliano, Elvira, eds. "Giustizia e criminalità nello Stato pontificio: ne delicta remaneant impunita". Monographic Issue, *Rivista storica del Lazio IX*, 4.

Canezza 1933: Canezza, Alessandra. *Gli arcispedali di Roma nella vita cittadina, nella storia e nell'arte* (Sancasciano Pesa: Tipografia Fratelli Stianti).

Cantù 2007: Cantù, Francesca. *La Conquista spirituale. Studi sull'evangelizzazione del Nuovo Mondo* (Rome: Viella).

Cantù, Visceglia 2003: Cantù, Francesca; Visceglia, Maria Antonietta. *L'Italia di Carlo V. Guerra, religione e politica nel primo Cinquecento* (Rome: Viella).

Canonici 1998: Canonici, Claudio. "Condizioni ambientali e battesimo degli ebrei romani nel Seicento e nel Settecento". *Ricerche per la storia religiosa di Roma* 10: 237–72.

Canonici 2012: Canonici, Claudio. *La presenza ebraica nel Patrimonio di San Pietro fra XVI e XVIII secolo: fonti e problemi*. In Caffiero, Esposito 2012b, 88–108.

Cappelli 1969: Cappelli, Adriano. *Cronologia, cronografia e calendario perpetuo* (Milan: Hoepli).

Capuzzo 1999: Capuzzo, Ester. *Gli ebrei nella società italiana. Comunità e istituzioni tra Ottocento e Novecento* (Rome: Carocci).

Caravale 1974: Caravale, Mario. *La finanza pontificia nel Cinquecento: le province del Lazio* (Camerino: Jovene).

Caravale 1988: Caravale, Mario. *Ordinamenti giuridici dell'Europa medievale* (Bologna: il Mulino).

Caravale, Caracciolo 1963: Caravale, Mario. Caracciolo, Andrea. *Lo Stato pontificio da Martino V a Pio IX* (Turin: Utet).

Cassen 2014: Cassen, Flora. "The Last Spanish Expulsion in Europe: Milan 1565–1597". *AJS Review, 38* (1): 59–88.

Cassen 2017: Cassen, Flora. *Marking the Jews in Renaissance Italy. Politics, religion and the power of symbols* (Cambridge: Cambrige University Press).

Cassese 2002: Cassese, Michele. *Girolamo Seripando e i vescovi meridionali (1535–1563)* (Napoli: ESI).

Castaldini 2005: Castaldini, Alberto. "Reti creditizie, reti culturali. Sabato da Lodi a Villafranca veronese nella seconda metà del Quattrocento". *Reti medievali. Rivista* VI, 1: http://www.storia.unifi.it/_RM/rivista/dwnl/Ebrei.

Cipolla 1998: Cipolla, Carlo M. *Le tre rivoluzioni e altri saggi di storia economica* (Bologna: Il Mulino): 263–77.

Concina, Camerino, Calabi 1991: Concinna, Ennio, Camerino, Ugo, Calabi, Donatella, eds. *La città degli ebrei. Il ghetto di Venezia: architettura e urbanistica* (Venice: Albizzi).

Cohen 1999: Cohen, Abraham. *Il Talmud* (Rome-Bari: Laterza).

Cohen E. 1991: Cohen, Elizabeth. "Camilla la magra, prostituta romana". In *Rinascimento al femminile*. Edited by Niccoli, Ottavia (Rome-Bari, Laterza): 163–96.

Colorni 1945: Colorni, Vittore. *Legge ebraica e leggi locali. Ricerche sull'ambito di applicazione del diritto ebraico in Italia dall'epoca romana al secolo XIX* (Milan: Giuffrè).

Colorni 1956: Colorni, Vittore. "Gli ebrei nel sistema del diritto comune fino alla prima emancipazione" (Milan: Giuffré).

Colorni 1961: Colorni, Vittore. "Gazagà". In *Novissimo Digesto Italiano*, vol. 7 (Turin: Unione Tipografico Torinese): 770–771.

Cooperman 2004: Cooperman, Bernard Dov. "Theorizing Jewish self-Government in Early Modern Italy". In *Una manna buona per Mantova. Man Tov le-Man Tovah. Studi in onore di Vittore Colorni per il suo 92° compleanno*. Edited by Mauro Perani (Florence: Olschki): 365–80.

Cooperman 2006: Cooperman, Bernard Dov. "Ethnicity and institution building among Jews in Early Modern Rome". *AJS Review* 30: 119–45.

Cooperman 2015: Cooperman, Bernard Dov. "Licenses, Cartels, and Kehila. Jewish Moneylending and the Struggle against Restraint of Trade in Early Modern Rome." In *Purchasing Power. The Economics of Modern Jewish History*. Edited by Rebecca Kobrin and Adam Teller (Philadephia: University of Pennsylvania Press): 27–45.

Cooperman 2018: Cooperman, Bernard Dov. "The Early Modern Ghetto. A study in Urban Real Estate". In *The ghetto in global history. 1500 to present*. Edited by Wendy Z. Goldman and Joe W. Trotter Jr (London, New York: Routledge): 57–73.

Cooperman 2019: Cooperman, Bernard Dov. "Defining Deviance, Negotiating Norms: Raphael Meldola in Livorno, Pisa, and Bayonne". In Kaplan 2019, 157–194.

Cormano 2001–2002: Cormano, Natascia. "Maternità e salute femminile nella Roma del '700: l'Ospedale di S. Rocco", MA dissertetion (Sapienza University of Rome).

Cozzi 1986: Cozzi, Gaetano, ed. *Gli ebrei a Venezia (secoli XIV-XVIII)* (Milan: Comunità).

Davanzo Poli, Melasecchi, Spagnoletto 2016: Davanzo Poli, Doretta; Melasecchi, Olga; Spagnoletto, Amedeo. *Antique Roman Mappot. The precious textile archive of the Jewish Museum of Rome* (Rome: Campisano Editore).

Davis, Ravid 2001: Davis, Robert C; Ravid, Benjamin. *The Jews of Early Modern Venice* (Baltimore: Johns Hopkins University Press).

De Angelis 1952: De Angelis, Pietro. *Il cardinale Antonio Maria Salviati (1536–1602) benefattore insigne degli ospedali di S. Giacomo in Augusta e di S. Rocco delle Partorienti* (Rome: s.n.).

De Angelis 1955: De Angelis, Pietro. *L'arcispedale di S. Giacomo in Augusta* (Rome: Tipografia Editrice Italia).

De Caro 1973: De Caro, Gaspare. "Caetani Enrico". In *Dizionario Biografico degli Italiani*, vol. XVI (Roma: Istituto della Enciclopedia Italiana): 149–154.

De Caro Balbi, Londei 1984: De Caro, Silvana, Londei, Luigi. *Moneta pontificia da Innocenzo XI a Gregorio XVI* (Rome: Quasar).

Del Col 2006: Del Col, Andrea. *L'Inquisizione in Italia dal XII al XXI secolo* (Milan: Mondadori).

Del Re 1972: Del Re, Niccolò. *Monsignor Governatore di Roma* (Roma: Istituto di studi romani)

Delumeau 1979: Delumeau, Jean. *Vita economica e sociale di Roma nel Cinquecento* (Florence: Sansoni).

Di Nepi 2004: Di Nepi, Serena. "I registri notarili ebraici come fonte storica". *Materia Giudaica* 9, 1–2 (2004): 53–64.

Di Castro 1994: Di Castro, Daniela. *Arte ebraica a Roma e nel Lazio* (Roma: F.lli Palombi)

Di Castro 2010: Di Castro, Daniela, ed. *Et ecce gaudium. Gli ebrei romani e la cerimonia di insediamento dei pontefici* (Rome: Araldo De Luca).

Di Castro 2012: Di Castro, Daniela. "Committenza ebraica e oggetti d'arte a Roma: il caso Baraffael". In Caffiero, Esposito 2012a, 204–12.

Di Nepi 2006: Di Nepi, Serena. "Aronitto, Monteritoni, Muccinello e gli altri. I macellai e la carne nella comunità ebraica di Roma della seconda metà del Cinquecento". *Zakhor* IX: 79–92.

Di Nepi 2007a: Di Nepi, Serena. "«Io come madre cercava ogni strada». Una madre ebrea e un figlio nei guai nella Roma del Cinquecento". *Storia delle Donne* 3: 99–121.

Di Nepi 2007b: Di Nepi, Serena. "Sapere e saper fare: la formazione dei professionisti ebrei nel ghetto di Roma". In *Scuola e itinerari formativi dallo Stato pontificio a Roma capitale. L'istruzione primaria*. Edited by Carmela Covato, Manola Ida Venzo (Milan: Unicopli): 207–21.

Di Nepi 2008: Di Nepi, Serena "Gli ebrei di Roma fuori di Roma: mobilità ebraica verso il territorio e conflitti giurisdizionali in età moderna. Prime note su una ricerca in corso". *Archivi e cultura* XL: 143–71.

Di Nepi 2009: Di Nepi, Serena. "Dall'astrologia agli Astrologo: ebrei e superstizioni nella Roma della Controriforma". In *Le radici storiche dell'antisemitismo. Nuove fonti e nuove ricerche*. Edited by Marina Caffiero (Rome: Viella): 41–70.

Di Nepi 2010: Di Nepi, Serena. "Neofiti". In *Dizionario storico dell'Inquisizione Romana*. Directed by Adriano Prosperi with Vincenzo Lavenia and John Tedeschi (Pisa: Edizioni della Normale): II, 1112–3.

Di Nepi 2012: Di Nepi, Serena. "I "professionisti": notai, medici e banchieri nella seconda metà del Cinquecento". In Caffiero, Esposito 2012a, 131–54.

Di Nepi 2015: Di Nepi, Serena. "I turchi in sinagoga? Una riflessione sull'identità e sugli strumenti dell'autorappresentazione sociale nel ghetto di Roma (XVIII-XIX secolo)". In *Storie intrecciate. Cristiani, ebrei e musulmani tra scritture, oggetti e narrazioni (Mediterraneo, secc. XVI-XIX secolo)*. Edited by Serena Di Nepi (Rome: Edizioni di Storia e Letteratura, 2015): 169–94.

Di Nepi 2017: Di Nepi, Serena. "Relazioni oltre le mura. Un processo ad Ancona all'epoca dei ghetti (1555–1563)." *Rivista di Storia del Cristianesimo* 14, no. 1: 27–48.

Di Nepi 2018: Di Nepi, Serena. "Autobiografie di minoranza. Prospettive individuali tra scritture personali e racconti di vita di ebrei e musulmani a Roma in età moderna". *Società e storia* 160, 289–313.

Di Nepi 2019: Di Nepi, Serena. "Jews in the Papal States between Western Sephardi Diasporas and Ghettos. A Trial in Ancona as a Case Study (1555–1562)". In Kaplan 2019: 291–322.

Dimant 2019: Dimant, Mauricio. "The Sephardic Community and Social Practices in the Circuit of Money: Social Implications of Payment Networks in the Context of the Livorninas". In Kaplan 2019: 323–345.

Di Sivo 2000: Di Sivo, Michele. "Il fondo della Confraternita di S. Giovanni Decollato nell'Archivio di Stato di Roma (1497–1870). Inventario". *Rivista storica del Lazio* XII (2000): 181–225.

Di Sivo 2001: Di Sivo, Michele. "Per via di giustizia. Sul processo penale a Roma tra XVI e XIX secolo". *Rivista storica del Lazio* IX, 4 (2001): 13–35.

Di Sivo 2012: Di Sivo, Michele. "Giudicare gli ebrei: i tribunali romani nei secoli XVI-XVIII". In Caffiero, Esposito 2012a: 81–102.

Dweck 2011: Dweck, Yaacob. *The Scandal of Kabbalah. Leon Modena, Jewish Mysticism, Early Modern Venice* (Princeton: Princeton University Press).

Esposito 1995: Esposito, Anna. *Un'altra Roma. Minoranze nazionali e comunità ebraiche tra Medioevo e Rinascimento* (Rome: Il calamo).

Esposito 2001: Esposito, Anna. "La città e i suoi abitanti". In *Roma del Rinascimento*. Edited by Andrea Pinelli, (Rome-Bari: Laterza): 3–47.

Esposito 2002: Esposito, Anna. "Credito, ebrei, Monte di Pietà a Roma tra Quattro e Cinquecento". *Roma moderna e contemporanea* x, 3: 559–75.

Esposito 2004: Esposito, Anna. "Ebrei sefarditi a Corneto-Tarquinia nel 1493". In *Una manna buona per Mantova. Man Tov le-Man Tovah. Studi in onore di Vittore Colorni per il suo 92° compleanno*. Edited by Mauro Perani (Florence: Olschki): 281–296.

Esposito 2005: Esposito, Anna. "Ebrei siciliani a Roma tra Quattro e Cinquecento". In *Hebraica hereditas. Studi in onore di Cesare Colafemmina*. Edited by Giancarlo Lacerenza (Naples: L'Orientale, 2005): 59–66.

Esposito 2006: Esposito, Anna. "Macellai e macellazione ebraica a Roma tra fine Quattrocento e inizi Cinquecento: accordi e conflitti". *Zakhor* IX: 45–77.

Esposito 2007: Esposito, Anna. "The Sephardic Communities in Rome in the Early Sixteenth Century". *Imago temporis. Medium Aevum* I: 177–85.

Esposito 2008: Esposito, Anna. "Gli ebrei di Roma prima del ghetto: nuovi spunti". In *Monaci, ebrei, santi. Studi per Sofia Boesch Gajano*. Edited by Andrea Volpato (Rome: Viella): 377–94.

Esposito 2012: Esposito, Anna. "Conflitti interni alla Comunità ebraica di Roma tra Quattro e Cinquecento". In Caffiero, Esposito 2012a, 69–80.

Esposito, Procaccia, 2011: Esposito, Anna; Procaccia, Micaela. "Ebrei in giudizio. Centro e periferia dello Stato pontificio nella documentazione processuale (secc. XV-XVI)". *Roma moderna e contemporanea* XIX, 1: 11–29.

Facchini 2007: Facchini, Cristiana, ed. "Omicidi rituali. Morte della storia?". Monographic Issue, *Storicamente*, 3: http://www.storicamente.org/02facchini.htm.

Feci 1998: Feci, Simona. "Tra il tribunale e il ghetto: le magistrature, la comunità e gli individui di fronte ai reati degli ebrei romani nel Seicento". *Quaderni storici* 99, 3: 575–99.

Ferrara 2011: Ferrara, Pierina. "La struttura edilizia del «serraglio» degli ebrei romani". *Roma moderna e contemporanea* 1: 83–102.

Ferrara 2015: Ferrara, Micol. *Dentro e fuori dal ghetto. I luoghi della presenza ebraica a Roma tra XVI e XIX secolo* (Milan: Mondadori).

Ferrara degli Uberti 2011: Ferrara degli Uberti, Carlotta. *Fare gli ebrei italiani. Autorappresentazione di una minoranza (1861–1918)* (Bologna: Il Mulino, 2011) (English Edition, New York: Palgrave Macmillan, 2017).

Ferrara degli Uberti 2017: Ferrara degli Uberti, Carlotta. *Making Italian Jews. Family, Gender, Religion and the Nation, 1861–1918* (New York: Palgrave Macmillan) (Italian Edtion: Bologna: il Mulino, 2011)

Fettah 2007, Fettah, Samuel. "Nommer et diviser la ville portuaire: la lexique politico-administratif toscan et Livourne (XVIIIe-XIXe siècle)". In *Les divisions de la ville*. Edited by Christian Topalov (Paris: Editions Unesco): 81–100.

Filippini 1997: Filippini, Jeanne Pierre. "La nazione ebrea di Livorno". In Vivanti 1997: 1045–66.

Finkelstein 1924: Filippini, Louis. *Jewish Self-Government in the Middle Ages* (New York: 1924).

Foa 1988: Foa, Anna. "Il gioco del proselitismo: politica delle conversioni e controllo della violenza nella Roma della Cinquecento". In Luzzatti, Olivari, Veronese 1988 (Rome: Carucci): 155–169.

Foa 1984: Foa, Anna, "Il nuovo e il vecchio: l'insorgere della sifilide (1494–1530)". *Quaderni storici* 19, 55: 11–34.

Foa 1992: Foa, Anna. *Ebrei in Europa dalla peste nera all'emancipazione* (Rome-Bari: Laterza).

Foa 1998: Foa, Anna. "Un vescovo marrano: il processo a Pedro de Aranda". *Quaderni storici* 99: 533–55.

Foa 2003: Foa, Anna, "La prospettiva spagnola: il Papa e gli ebrei nell'età di Carlo V". In *L'Italia di Carlo V. Guerra, religione e politica nel primo Cinquecento*. Edited by Francesca Cantù, Maria Antonietta Visceglia (Rome: Viella): 509–22.

Foa, Stow, 2000: Foa, Anna; Stow, Kenneth. "Gli ebrei di Roma. Potere, rituale e società in età moderna". In *Storia d'Italia, Annali* 16, *Roma, la città del papa*. Edited by Luca Fiorani, Adriano Prosperi (Turin: Einaudi): 557–81.

Formica 2019: *Roma. Romae. Una capitale in età moderna* (Rome: Bari, Laterza).

Fosi 1985: Fosi, Irene. *La società violenta. Il banditismo dello Stato pontificio nella seconda metà del Cinquecento* (Rome: Edizioni dell'Ateneo).

Fosi 1997: Fosi, Irene, ed. "Tribunali, giustizia e società nella Roma del Cinque e del Seicento". Monographic Issue, *Roma moderna e contemporanea* v.

Fosi 1998: Fosi, Irene. "Criminalità ebraica a Roma fra Cinquecento e Seicento: autorappresentazione e realtà", *Quaderni storici* 99, 3: 553–573.

Fosi 2002: Fosi, Irene. "Il governo della giustizia". In *Roma moderna*. Edited by Giorgio Ciucci (Rome-Bari: Laterza): 115–142.

Fosi 2007: Fosi, Irene. *La giustizia del papa. Sudditi e tribunali nello Stato Pontificio in età moderna* (Rome-Bari: Laterza) [English edition translated by Thomas V. Cohen: Washington DC: Catholic University of America Press, 2011].

Fragnito 2011, Fragnito, Gigliola. "Gli spirituali e la crisi religiosa del Cinquecento italiano". In *Cinquecento italiano. Religione, cultura e potere dal Rinascimento alla Controriforma*. Edited by Elena Bonora, Miguel Gotor (Bologna: Il Mulino): 141–230.

Francescangeli 2012: Francescangeli, Laura. "Scritture notarili e atti del Comune. Un percorso nelle fonti documentarie dell'Archivio capitolino". In Caffiero, Esposito 2012a, 259–285.

Frattarelli Fischer 2000: Frattarelli Fisher, Lucia. "Cristiani nuovi e nuovi ebrei in Toscana fra Cinque e Seicento. Legittimazioni e percorsi individuali". In *L'identità dissimulata. Giudaizzanti iberici nell'Europa cristiana dell'età moderna*. Edited by Pier Cesare Ioly Zorattini (Florence: Olshki, 2000): 99–149.

Frattarelli Fisher 2003: Frattarelli Fisher, Lucia, "Reti toscane e reti internazionali degli ebrei di Livorno nel Seicento". *Zakhor* VI, 93–116.

Frattarelli Fisher 2008: Frattarelli Fisher, Lucia, *Vivere fuori dal ghetto: ebrei a Pisa e Livorno (secc. XVI-XVIII)* (Turin: Zamorani).

Friz 1980: Friz, Giuliano. *Consumi, tenore di vita e prezzi a Roma dal 1770 al 1900* (Rome: Edindustria).

Galasso 2002: Galasso, Cristina. *Alle origini di una comunità. Ebree ed ebrei a Livorno nel Seicento* (Florence: Olschki).

Garin 1996: Garin, Eugenio. "L'Umanesimo italiano e la cultura ebraica". In Vivanti 1996, 361–383.

Gasperoni, Groppi 2018: Gasperoni, Michael, Groppi, Angela. "Négocier ses droits dans les ghettos des États de l'Église, xvie-xixe siècle". *Annales. Histoire, Sciences Sociales*, 73(3): 553–557.

Giordano 2000: Giordano, Silvano. "Sisto V". In *Enciclopedia dei papi*, t. III (Rome: Istituto dell'Enciclopedia italiani): 202–222.

Ginzburg 1989: Ginzburg, Carlo. *Storia notturna. Una decifrazione del sabba* (Turin: Einaudi).

Golan 1985: Golan, Shoshanna. "Le vie des juifs de Rome de la moitié du XVIe siècle à la deuxième moitié du XVIIe siècle (d'après des documents tirées des Archives Historiques du Capitole à Rome)". «*Revue des études juives*» CXLIV: 169–179.

Grendi 2004: Grendi, Edoardo. "Falsa moneta e strutture monetarie degli scambi tra Cinquecento e Seicento". In Id., *In altri termini. Etnografia e storia di una società di Antico Regime*. Edited Osvaldo Raggio, Angelo Torre (Milan: Feltrinelli, 2004): 167–200.

Groppi 1999: Groppi, Angela. "Ebrei, donne, soldati e neofiti: l'esercizio del mestiere tra esclusioni e privilegi (Roma, XVII-XVIII secolo)", in *Corporazioni e gruppi professionali nell'Italia moderna*. Edited by Alberto Guenzi, Paola Massa, Angelo Moioli (Milan: Franco Angeli): 533–59.

Groppi 2000: Groppi, Angela. "Fili notarili e tracce corporative: la ricomposizione di un mosaico". *Mélanges de l'École française de Rome. Italie et Méditerranée* 1: 61–78.

Guetta 2014: Guetta, Alessandro. *Italian Jewry in the Early Modern Era. Essays in Intellectual History*.

Iannuzzi 2009: Iannuzzi, Isabella. "Processi di esclusione e contaminazione alla fine del Quattrocento spagnolo. Il caso del Niño de La Guardia". *Dimensioni e problemi della ricerca storica* 1: 145–171.

Heyberger, García-Arenal, Colombo, Vismara 2009: Heyberger, Bernard; García-Arenal, Mercedes; Colombo, Emanuele; Vismara, Paola, eds. *L'Islam visto da Occidente. Cultura e religione del Seicento europeo di fronte all'Islam* (Genova: Marietti).

Herzig 2019: Herzig, Tamar. *A Convert's Tale. Art, Crime, and Jewish Apostasy in Renaissance Italy* (Cambridge (Mass.): Harvard University Press).

Idel 2007: Idel, Moshe. *La Cabbalà in Italia* (Firenze: Giuntina).

Israel 1991: Israel, Jonathan. *Gli ebrei d'Europa in età moderna: 1550–1750* (Bologna: il Mulino)[Original Edition: Oxford, Clarendon Press 1985].

Kaplan 2007: Kaplan, B. Yosef. *Divided by faith. Religious conflict and the practice of toleration in early modern Europe* (Cambridge, Mass: Harvard University Press)

Kaplan 2019, Kaplan, Yosef ed. *Religious changes and cultural transformations in the Early Modern Western Sephardic Communities* (Boston, Leiden: Brill).

Katz 1993: Katz, Jacob. *Tradition and Crisis. Jewish Society at the end of the Middle Ages* (New York: New York University Press).

Kellenbez, Prodi 1989: Kellenbez, Hermann; Prodi, Paolo, eds. *Fisco, religione e Stato nell'età confessionale* (Bologna: Il Mulino).

Kertzer 1996: Kertzer, David I. *Prigioniero del papa re* (Milano: Rizzoli).

Kertzer 2006: Kertzer, David I. *Antisemitismo popolare e Inquisizione negli Stati pontifici, 1815–1848* (Rome: Tipografia della Pace).

Laudanna 1989: Laudanna, Luigi. "Le grandi ricchezze private di Roma agli inizi dell'Ottocento". *Dimensioni e problemi della ricerca storica* 2: 104–21.

Laras 1968: Laras, Giuseppe. "Intorno al «ius cazacà» nella storia del ghetto di Ancona". *Quaderni storici delle Marche* 7: 27–55.

Lattes 1998: Lattes, Andrea Y. "Aspetti politici e istituzionali delle comunità ebraiche in Italia nel Cinque- Seicento". *Zakhor* 11: 21–37.

Lattes *forthcoming*: Lattes, Andrea Y. *Una società dentro le mura. Gli ebrei a Roma nel Seicento* (Rome: Gangemi, in press).

Lehman 2005: Lehman, Mathias B. "A Livornese "Port Jew" and the Sephardim of the Ottoman Empire". *Jewish Social Studies. History, Culture, Society* 11, 2: 51–71.

Ligorio 2017: Ligorio, Benedetto. "Ragusa, il secondo ghetto. Una comunità di mercanti nel-l'Adriatico orientale(1546–1667)". *Rivista di Storia del Cristianesimo* 14, no. 1: 53–70.

Livi 1920: Livi, Livio. *Gli ebrei alla luce della statistica, vol. II,* (Florence: Libreria della Voce, 1920).

Lodolini 1956: Lodolini, Armando. "I «Monti camerali» nel sistema della finanza pontificia»". *Archivi storici delle aziende di credito* 1: 263–278.

Lolli 2019: Lolli, Elena. "Il *Pinqas ha-niftarim* della comunità ebraica di Lugo di Romagna per gli anni 1658–1825 (Ms. New York, JTS, n. 3960)". PhD dissertation (Alma Mater Studiorum, University of Bologna).

Londei 1987: Londei, Luigi. "La Presidenza della Zecca e le Magistrature proposte alla monetazione". In Pastura Ruggiero, Maria Grazia. *La Reverenda Camera Apostolica e i suoi archivi (secc. XV-XVIII)* (Rome: Ministero per i Beni e le Attività Culturali, 1987): 149–166.

Lori Sanfilippo 1990: Lori San Filippo, Isa. "Appunti sui notai medievali a Roma e sulla conservazione dei loro atti". *Archivi per la storia* III, 1: 21–39.

Luzzati 1985: Luzzati, Michele. *La casa dell'ebreo. Saggi sugli ebrei a Pisa e in Toscana nel Medioevo e nel Rinascimento* (Pisa: Nistri Lischi).

Luzzati 1991: Luzzati, Michele. "Ruolo e funzione dei banchi ebraici nell'Italia centro-settentrionale nei secoli XV e XVI". In *Banchi pubblici, banchi privati e Monti di Pietà nell'Europa preindustriale. Amministrazione, tecniche operative e ruoli economici,* Atti del Convegno, Genova, 1–6 ottobre 1990, 2 vols (Genoa: Società Ligure di Storia Patria): 733–50.

Luzzati 1996: Luzzati, Michele. "Banchi e insediamenti ebraici nell'Italia centro-settentrionale fra tardo Medioevo e inizi dell'Età moderna". In Vivanti 1996, 175-35.

Luzzati 2004: Luzzati, Michele. "«Satis est quod tecum dormivit». Vero, verosimile e falso nelle incriminazioni di ebrei: un caso di presunta sodomia (Lucca, 1471–1472)". In *Una manna buona per Mantova. Man Tov le-Man Tovah. Studi in onore di Vittore Colorni per il suo 92° compleanno.* Edited by Mauro Perani (Florence: Olschki): 261–280.

Luzzati, Olivari, Veronese 1988: Luzzati, Michele, Olivari, Michele, Veronese, Alessandra, eds. *Ebrei e Cristiani nell'Italia medievale e moderna: conversioni, scambi* (Rome: Carucci).

Luzzatto Voghera 2008: Luzzatto Voghera, Gadi. "I rabbini nell'Italia medievale e moderna". In *Le religioni e il mondo moderno* II, *Ebraismo.* Edited by David Bidussa (Turin: Einaudi): 532–56.

Luzzatto Voghera 2011: Luzzatto Voghera, Gadi. *Rabbini* (Rome-Bari: Laterza).

Maifreda 2019: Maifreda, Germano. *The Business of the Roman Inquisition* (London and New York: Routledge)

Malkiel 2005: Malkiel, David. "Ebraismo, tradizione e società: Isacco Lampronti e l'identità ebraica nella Ferrara del XVIII secolo". *Zakhor* VIII: 9–42.

Malkiel 2014: Malkiel, David. *Stones speak Hebrew. Hebrew Tombstones from Padua (1529–1862)* (Boston, Leiden: Brill).

Mampieri 2020: Mampieri, Martina. *Living under the Evil Pope. The Hebrew* Chronicle of Pope Paul IV *by Benjamin Nehemiah ben Elnathan from Civitanova Marche (16th century)* (Boston, Leiden: Brill).

Marin 2007: Marin, Brigitte. "Lexiques et découpages territoriaux dans quelques villes italienne (XVIe-XIXe siècle)". In *Les divisions de la ville.* Edited by Christian Topalov (Paris: Editions Unesco): 8–45.

Marconcini 2016. Marconcini, Samuela. *Per amor del cielo. Farsi cristiani a Firenze tra Seicento e Settecento* (Firenze: Firenze University Press).

Martini 1976: Martini, Angelo. *Manuale di metrologia ossia misure, pesi e monete in uso attualmente e anticamente presso tutti i popoli* (Rome: ERA).

Martire 1934: Martire, Egilberto. *L'isola della salute. Dal tempio di Esculapio all'Ospedale di S. Giovanni di Dio* (Rome: Rassegna romana).

Martone 1984: Martone, Luciano. *Arbiter-Arbitrator. Forme di giustizia privata nell'età del diritto comune* (Naples: Jovene).

Massa 2005: Massa, Eugenio. *Una cristianità nell'alba del Rinascimento. Paolo Giustiniani e il «Libellus ad Leonem X» (1513)* (Genoa: Marietti).

Melcer Padon 2019: Melcer Padon, Nurit. "Charity begins at home. Reflections on the Dowry Society of Livorno". In Kaplan 2019, 346–380.

Meron 1998: Meron, Orly. "The dowries of Jewish women in the Duchy of Milan (1535–1597). Economic and social aspects". *Zakhor* 11: 127–137.

Miccoli 1974: Miccoli, Giovanni. "La storia religiosa". In *Storia d'Italia*, II, *Dalla caduta dell'Impero romano al secolo XVIII*, t. 1 (Turin: Einaudi): 431–1079.

Milano 1935–1936: Milano, Attilio "I Capitoli di Daniel da Pisa e la comunità di Roma". *Rassegna Mensile di Israel* x, 7-8: 324–38; and x, 9–10: 409–26.

Milano 1963: Milano, Attilio. *Storia degli ebrei in Italia* (Turin: Einaudi).

Milano 1984: Milano, Attilio. *Il ghetto di Roma. Illustrazioni storiche* (Rome: Carucci) [Original edition: Rome, Staderini 1964].

Modigliani 1998: Modigliani, Anna. *Mercati, botteghe e spazi di commercio a Roma tra medioevo ed età moderna*, (Rome: Roma nel Rinascimento).

Moretti 2011: Moretti, Massimo. "«Glauci coloris». Gli ebrei nell'iconografia sacra di età moderna". *Roma moderna e contemporanea* 1: 29–64.

Muzzarelli 1991: Muzzarelli, Maria Giuseppina. "Beatrice de Luna, vedova Mendes, alias Donna Gracia Nasi: un'ebrea influente (1510–1569 ca)". In *Rinascimento al femminile*. Edited by Ottavia Niccoli (Rome-Bari: Laterza): 83–116.

Novoa 2014: Novoa, James N. *Being the Nação in the Eternal City: new christian lives in Sixteenth century Rome* (Peterborough (Ontario): Baywolf).

Parente 1996: Parente, Fausto. "La Chiesa e il Talmud". In Vivanti 1996 (Turin: Einaudi): 524–637.

Pittella 2012: Pittella, Raffaele. "«A guisa di un civile arsenale». Carte giudiziarie e archivi notarili a Roma nel Settecento". In *La documentazione degli organi giudiziari nell'Italia tardo-medievale e moderna*. Edited by Andrea Giorgi, Stefano Moscadelli e Carla Zarrilli (Rome: Ministero per i Beni e le Attività Culturali): 669–768.

Pastura Ruggiero 1987: Pastura Ruggiero, Maria Grazia. *La Reverenda Camera Apostolica e i suoi archivi (secc. XV-XVIII)* (Rome: Ministero per i Beni e le Attività Culturali).

Pecorella, Gualazzini 1967: Percorella, Corrado, Gualazzini, Ugo. "Fallimento". In *Enciclopedia del diritto*, vol. XVI (Milano: Giuffrè): 221–33.

Perani 2017: Perani, Mauro ed. *Nuovi studi su Isacco Lampronti. Storia, poesia, scienza, halakah* (Firenze: Giuntina).

Perani 2020: Perani, Mauro. "Il documento ebraico. I Registri delle comunità e delle confraternite come fonte storica interna". Seminar paper (Ravenna, May 4, 2020: https://www.academia.edu/43050977/I_registri_delle_comunità_e_delle_confraternite_ebraiche_come_fonte_storica_interna.

Petrocchi 1970: Petrocchi, Massimo. *Roma nel Seicento* (Bologna: Cappelli).

Piano Mortari 1958: Piano Mortari, Vincenzo. "Arbitrato – Diritto intermedio". In *Enciclopedia del diritto*, tomo III (Milan: Giuffrè): 895–9.

Piccialuti Caprioli 1994: Piccialuti Caprioli, Maura. *La carità come metodo di governo. Istituzioni caritative a Roma dal pontificato di Innocenzo XII a quello di Benedetto XIV* (Turin: Giappichelli).

Piola Caselli 1991: Piola Caselli, Fausto. "Banchi privati e debito pubblico pontificio a Roma tra Cinquecento e Seicento". In *Banchi pubblici, banchi privati e Monti di Pietà nell'Europa preindustriale. Amministrazione, tecniche operative e ruoli economici*, Atti del Convegno, Genova, 1–6 ottobre 1990, 2 vols (Genoa: Società Ligure di Storia Patria): 463–495.

Piola Caselli 1993: Piola Caselli, Fausto. "Una montagna di debiti. I monti baronali e l'aristocrazia romana nel Seicento". *Roma moderna e contemporanea* 1: 21–56.

Piola Caselli 1997: Piola Caselli, Fausto. *Il buon governo: storia della finanza pubblica nell'Europa preindustriale* (Turin: Giappichelli).

Po-chia Hsia 2001: Po-chia Hsia, Ronnie. *La Controriforma. Il mondo del rinnovamento cattolico* (Bologna: Il Mulino).

Poliakov 1956: Poliakov, Léon. *Le banquiers juifs et le Saint-Siège du XIIIe au XVIIe siècle* (Paris: Calmann: Levy) [English translation by Miriam Kochan. London: Routledge, 1977].

Pompeo 1991: Pompeo, Augusto. "Procedure usuali e «Jura specialia in criminalibus» nei tribunali romani di antico regime". *Archivi per la storia* IV: 111–24.

Pratesi 1999: Pratesi, Alessandro. *Genesi e forme del documento medievale* (Rome: Jouvence).

Procaccia C. 1994–1997: Procaccia, Claudio. "I banchieri ebrei nella seconda metà del XVII secolo". PhD Dissertation.

Procaccia C. 2003: Procaccia, Claudio. "Testimonianze sull'attività di cambio mediante lettera nella seconda metà del XVII secolo". *Zakhor* VI: 129–46.

Procaccia C. 2012: Procaccia, Claudio. "I banchieri ebrei nella seconda metà del Seicento: il prestito su pegno". In Caffiero, Esposito 2012a, 155–79.

Procaccia M. 1995: Procaccia, Micaela. "«Non dabarà»: gli ebrei di Roma nelle fonti giudiziarie della prima metà del Cinquecento". In *Italia Judaica VI, Gli ebrei nello Stato Pontificio fino al Ghetto (1555)* (Rome: Ministero per i Beni e le Attività Culturali): 80–93.

Procaccia M. 1998: Procaccia, Micaela. "«Bona voglia e modica coactio». Conversioni di ebrei a Roma nel secolo XVI". *Ricerche per la storia religiosa di Roma* 10: 207–34.

Procaccia M. 2007a: Procaccia, Micaela. "Allegrezza e Dolcetta, donne ebree romane nei documenti camerali della seconda metà del '500". In *Donne nella storia degli ebrei d'Italia*. Edited by Cristina Galasso, Michele Luzzatti (Florence: Giuntina): 137–150.

Procaccia M. 2007b: Procaccia, Micaela. "L'«ape ingegnosa». Debora Ascarelli, poetessa romana". *«Rivista di storia del cristianesimo»*, 2: 355–67.

Procaccia, Micaela; Spagnoletto, Amedeo. *Tutto l'oro e l'argento di Roma. L'immagine di Roma nella tradizione ebraica* (Bologna: Pàtron, 2000).

Prodi 1979: Prodi, Paolo. "Nuove dimensioni della Chiesa: il problema delle missioni e la «conquista spirituale» dell'America". In *Problemi di storia della Chiesa nei secoli XV-XVII* (Naples: Edizione Dehoniane): 267–93.

Prodi 1982: Prodi, Paolo. *Il sovrano pontefice. Un corpo e due anime: la monarchia papale nella prima età moderna* (Bologna: Il Mulino).

Prodi 1994: Prodi, Paolo, ed. *Disciplina dell'anima, disciplina del corpo e disciplina della società tra medioevo ed età moderna* (Bologna: Il Mulino).

Prosperi 1989: Prosperi, Adriano. "La Chiesa e gli ebrei nell'Italia del Cinquecento". In *Ebraismo e antiebraismo: immagine e pregiudizio*. Presented by Cesare Lupporini (Florence: Giuntina): 171–183.

Prosperi 1994a: Prosperi, Adriano. "L'Inquisizione romana e gli ebrei". In *L'inquisizione e gli ebrei in Italia*. Edited by Michele Luzzati (Rome-Bari: Laterza): 67–120.

Prosperi 1994b: Prosperi, Adriano. "Riforma cattolica, Controriforma, disciplinamento sociale". In *Storia dell'Italia religiosa, 2, L'età moderna*. Edited by Giuseppe De Rosa, Tullio Gregory, André Vauchez (Rome-Bari: Laterza).

Prosperi 1996a: Prosperi, Adriano. *Tribunali della coscienza: inquisitori, confessori, missionari* (Turin: Einaudi).

Prosperi 1996b: Prosperi, Adriano. "Incontri rituali: il papa e gli ebrei". In Vivanti 1996, 497–520.

Prosperi 1999: Prosperi, Adriano. *America e Apocalisse e altri saggi* (Pisa-Rome: Istituti editoriali e poligrafici internazionali).

Prosperi 2000: Prosperi, Adriano. *Introduzione*. In Lutero, Martin. *Degli ebrei e delle loro menzogne*. Edited by Adelisa Malena (Turin: Einaudi): VII–LXX.

Prosperi 2001: Prosperi, Adriano. *Il Concilio di Trento. Un'introduzione storica* (Turin: Einaudi).

Prosperi 2005: Prosperi, Adriano. *Dare l'anima. Storia di un infanticidio* (Turin: Einaudi).

Prosperi 2011: Prosperi, Adriano. *Il seme dell'intolleranza. Ebrei, eretici, selvaggi: Granada 1492* (Rome-Bari: Laterza).

Prosperi 2013: Prosperi, Adriano. *Delitto e perdono. La pena di morte nell'orizzonte mentale dell'Europa cristiana (XIV-XVIII secolo)* (Turin: Einaudi).

Prosperi 2010: Prosperi, Adriano, ed.; with Vincenzo Lavenia and John Tedeschi. *Dizionario storico dell'Inquisizione Romana*, 4 vols. (Pisa: Edizioni della Normale, 2010).

Quaglioni, Diego. "Fra tolleranza e persecuzione. Gli ebrei nella letteratura giuridica del tardo Medioevo". In Vivanti 1996, 646–76.

Reinhard 1989: Reinhard, Wolfgan. "Finanza pontificia, sistema beneficale e finanza statale nell'età confessionale". In *Fisco, religione e Stato nell'età confessionale*. Edited by Hermanna Kellenbenz, Paolo Prodi (Bologna: il Mulino): 459–503.

Reinhard 1994: Rehinard, Wolfgan. "Disciplinamento sociale, confessionalizzazione, modernizzazione. Un discorso storiografico". In *Disciplina dell'anima, disciplina del corpo e disciplina della società tra medioevo ed età moderna*. Edited by Paolo Prodi (Bologna: Il Mulino): 101–23.

Romeo 2004: Romeo, Giovanni. "L'inquisizione nell'Italia moderna" (Rome-Bari: Laterza).

Rosa 1989: Rosa, Mario. "Tra tolleranza e repressione: Roma e gli ebrei nel '700". In *Italia Judaica III, Gli ebrei in Italia dalla segregazione alla prima emancipazione* (Rome: Ministero per i Beni e le Attività Culturali): 81–98.

Roth 1935: Roth, Cecil. "Some Revolutionary Purims (1790–1801)". *Hebrew University College Annual* X: 451–82.

Ruderman 1981: Ruderman, David B. *The World of a Renaissance Jew. The Life and Thought of Avraham ben Mordechai Farissol* (Cincinnati: Hebrew Union College).

Ruderman 1992: Ruderman, David B., ed. *Preachers of the Italian Ghetto* (Berckley: University of California Press).

Ruderman 2010: Ruderman, David B. *Early Modern Jewry. A new Cultural History* (Princeton-Oxford: Princenton University Press).

Russotto 1966: Russotto, Gabriele. *L'origine del Fatebenefratelli di Roma* (Rome: Ospedale Fatebenefratelli).

Piccialuti 2005: Piccialuti, Maria. "La sanità a Roma in età moderna". Monographic Issue. *Roma moderna e contemporanea* XIII, 1.

Scarlata, Mariano 1967: Scarlata Fazio, Mariano. "Falsità e falso (Falso numerario)". In *Enciclopedia del diritto*, vol. XVI (Milan: Giuffrè): 512–513.

Schwarzfuchs 1970: Schwarzfuchs, Simon. "Controversie nella Comunità di Roma agli inizi del secolo XVI". In *Scritti in memoria di Enzo Sereni*. Edited by Daniel Carpi, Attilio Milano, Umberto Nahon (Jerusalem: Fondazione Sally Mayer): 95–100 (Italian part).

Schwartz 2008: Schwartz, Stuart B. *All can be saved: religious tolerance and salvation in the Iberian Atlantic world* (New Haven & London: Yale University press)

Segre 1985: Segre, Renata. "Nuovi documenti sui marrani d'Ancona (1555–1559)". *Michael* 9130–233.

Segre 1996a: Segre, Renata. "La Controriforma: espulsioni, conversioni, isolamento". In Vivanti 1996: 709–78.

Segre 1996b: Segre, Renata. "La formazione di una comunità marrana: i portoghesi a Ferrara". In Vivanti 1996: 779–841.

Schilling 1994: Schilling, Heinz. "Chiese confessionali e disciplinamento sociale. Un bilancio provvisorio della ricerca storica". In Disciplina dell'anima, disciplina del corpo e disciplina della società tra medioevo ed età moderna. Edited by Paolo Prodi (Bologna: il Mulino): 125–160.

Siegmund 1996: Siegmund, Stephanie. "La vita nei ghetto". In Vivanti 1996: 845–892.

Siegmund 2006: Siegmund, Stephanie. *The Medici State and the Ghetto of Florence. The construction of an Early Modern Jewish Community* (Stanford: Standford University Press).

Silvera 2012: Silvera, Myriam, ed. *Medici rabbini. Momenti di storia della medicina ebraica* (Rome: Carocci).

Simonsohn 1988: Simonsohn, Shlomo. "Alcuni noti convertiti ebrei del Rinascimento". In *Ebrei e Cristiani nell'Italia medievale e moderna: conversioni, scambi, contrasti*. In Luzzatti, Olivari, Veronese 1988: 93–104.

Simonsohn 1995: Simonsohn, Shlomo. "The Jews in the Papal State to the Ghetto". In *Italia Judaica VI, Gli ebrei nello Stato Pontificio fino al Ghetto (1555)* (Rome: Ministero per i Beni e le Attività Culturali): 11–29.

Simonsohn 1996: Simonsohn, Shlmo. "La condizione giuridica degli ebrei nell'Italia centrale e settentrionale (secoli XII-XVI)". In Vivanti 1996, 98–120

Simonsohn 1977: Simonsohn, Shlomo. *History of the Jews in the Duchy of Mantua* (Jerusalem: Kiryath Sepher)

Sinisi, Verdi 1995: Sinisi, Daniela; Verdi, Orietta. "I registri delle lettere patenti della Presidenza delle strade (1691–1701)". *Archivi e cultura* XXVIII:191–231.

Sonnino 1998: Sonnino, Eugenio, ed. *Popolazione e società a Roma dal medioevo all'età contemporanea* (Rome: Il calamo).

Sonnino 2000: Sonnino, Eugenio. "Le anime dei romani: fonti religiose e demografia storica". In *Storia d'Italia, Annali 16, Roma, la città del papa*. Edited by Luigi Fiorani, Adriano Prosperi (Turin: Einaudi): 329–364.

Spagnoletto 1999: Spagnoletto, Amedeo. "La notte degli orvietani o Purim Shenì di Pitigliano. Ricordi di un rituale a 200 anni dagli avvenimenti". *Rassegna Mensile di Israel* XLV, 1: 141–178.

Spagnoletto 2007: Spagnoletto, Amedeo. *Edizioni ebraiche del XVI secolo del Centro Bibliografico dell'Ebraismo Italiano dell'Unione delle Comunità Ebraiche Italiane. Catalogo* (Rome: Lithos).

Spagnoletto 2013: Spagnoletto, Amedeo. "Le tradizioni rituali degli ebrei di Roma e delle altre regioni italiane, in Storia religiosa degli ebrei d'Europa". Edited by Luciano Vaccaro (Milano: Centro Ambrosiano): 51–73.

Spizzichino 2008: Spizzichino, Giancarlo. "Il Mo'ed di piombo: storia di uno scampato pericolo" (Milan: Morasha).

Spizzichino 2011: Spizzichino, Giancarlo. *La scomparsa della sesta Scola. La sinagoga Portaleone* (Rome: Gangemi).

Steele 1991: Steele, Mark. "Bankruptcy and Insolvency: Bank Failure and its Control in Preindustrial Europe". In *Banchi pubblici, banchi privati e Monti di Pietà nell'Europa preindustriale. Amministrazione, tecniche operative e ruoli economici*, Atti del Convegno, Genova, 1–6 ottobre 1990, 2 vols (Genoa: Società Ligure di Storia Patria): 183–204.

Stefani 2004: Stefani, Pietro. *L'antigiudaismo. Storia di un'idea* (Rome-Bari: Laterza, 2004).

Stow 1972: Stow, Kenneth R. "The Burning of the Talmud in 1553, in the Light of Sixteenth Century Catholic Attitudes toward the Talmud". *Bibliothèque d'Humanisme et Renaissances* 34: 435–459.

Stow 1977: Stow, Kenneth R. *Catholic Thought and the Papa Jewry Policy* (New York: The Jewish Theological Seminar of America).

Stow 1985: Stow, Kenneth R. "Delitto e castigo nello Stato della Chiesa". In *Italia Judaica II, Gli ebrei in Italia tra Rinascimento ed Età barocca* (Rome: Ministero per i Beni e le Attività Culturali,): 173–92.

Stow 1992a: Stow, Kenneth R. "Ethnic Rivalry or Melting Pot: The «Edot» in the Roman Ghetto". *Judaism* 41: 286–296.

Stow 1992b: Stow, Kenneth R. "Prossimità o distanza: etnicità, sefarditi e assenza di conflitti etnici nella Roma del sedicesimo secolo". *Rassegna Mensile Israel* LVIII, 1–2 (1992): 61–74.

Stow 1992c: Stow, Kenneth R. *Consciousness of Closure: Roman Jews and Its "Ghet"*. In *Essential Papers on Jewish Culture in Renaissance and Baroque Italy*. Edited by David B Ruderman (New York: New York University Press): 386–400.

Stow 1993: Stow, Kenneth R. "A Tale of Uncertainties: Converts in the Roman Ghetto". In *Shlomo Simonsohn Jubilee Volume*. Edited by Moshe Gil, Daniel Carpi (Tel Aviv: Tel Aviv University, 1993): 259–81.

Stow 1999: Stow, Kenneth R., ed. *The Jews in Rome. 1536–1557*, 2 vols (Leiden: Brill).

Stow 2001: Stow, Kenneth R. *Theater of Acculturation. The Roman Ghetto in the Sixteenth Century* (Seattle-London: University of Washington Press, 2001) [Italian Edition. Rome: Viella, 2013].

Stow 2002: Stow, Kenneth R., "Abramo Ben Aron Scazzocchio: Another Kind of Rabbi,". In *The Mediterranean and the Jews. Society, Culture and Economy in Early Modern Times*, II (Ramat Gan: Bar Ilan University).

Stow, De Benedetti Stow 1986: Stow, Kenneth R; De Benedetti Stow, Sandra. "Donne ebree a Roma nell'età del ghetto: affetto, dipendenza, autonomia". *Rassegna Mensile di Israel* LII, 1: 63–116.

Strangio 2001: Strangio, Donatella. *Il debito pubblico pontificio. Cambiamento e continuità nella finanza pontificia dal periodo francese alla restaurazione romana, 1798–1820* (Padua: CEDAM).

Taradel 2002: Taradel, Ruggero. *L'accusa del sangue. Storia politica di un mito antisemita* (Rome: Editori Riuniti).

Terstra 2015: Terpstra, Nicholas. *Religious refugees in the early modern world. An alternative history of the Reformation* (New York: Cambridge University Press)

Teter 2011: Teter, Magda. *Sinners on Trial. Jews and Sacrilege after the Reformation* (Cambridge (MA): Harvard University Press).

Toaff 1973: Toaff, Ariel. "Getto-ghetto". *The American Sephardi* 6, 1–2 (1973): 70–77.

Toaff 1974: Toaff, Ariel. "Nuova luce sui marrani di Ancona (1556)". In *Studi sull'ebraismo italiano in memoria di Cecil Roth*. Edited by Elio Toaff (Rome: Barulli).

Toaff 1979: Toaff, Ariel. "Lotte e fazioni tra gli ebrei di Roma nel Cinquecento". *Studi romani* 27 (1979): 25–32.

Toaff 1989: Toaff, Ariel. *Il vino e la carne, una comunità ebraica nel Medioevo* (Bologna: il Mulino, 1989).

Toaff 1996a: Toaff, Ariel. "«Banchieri» cristiani e «prestatori» ebrei?". In Vivanti 1996, 268–87.

Toaff, 1996b: Toaff, Ariel. "Gli ebrei a Roma". In Vivanti 1996, 123–52.

Toaff 1996c, Toaff, Ariel. *Mostri giudei. L'immaginario ebraico dal Medioevo alla prima età moderna* (Bologna: il Mulino).

Toaff 2000: Toaff, Ariel. *Mangiare alla giudia* (Bologna: il Mulino).

Toaff 2007: Toaff, Ariel. *Pasque di sangue. Ebrei d'Europa e omicidi rituali* (Bologna: il Mulino).

Toaff 2010: Toaff, Ariel. *Il prestigiatore di Dio. Avventure e miracoli di un alchimista ebreo nelle corti del Rinascimento* (Milan: Rizzoli).

Tocci 1989: Tocci, Giovanni, ed. *Le comunità negli Stati italiani di Antico Regime* (Bologna: Clueb).

Tocci 1998: Tocci, Giovanni. *Le comunità in età moderna: problemi storiografici e prospettive di ricerca* (Rome: Carocci).

Todeschini 2002: Todeschini, Giacomo. *I mercanti e il tempio. La società cristiana e il circolo virtuoso della ricchezza tra Medioevo ed Età moderna* (Bologna: il Mulino).

Todeschini 2007: Todeschini, Giacomo. *Visibilmente crudeli: malviventi, persone sospette e gente qualunque dal Medioevo all'età moderna* (Bologna: il Mulino).

Todeschini 2016: Todeschini, Giacomo. *La banca e il ghetto: una storia italiana* (Rome-Bari: Laterza).

Todeschini 2018: Todeschini, Giacomo. *Storia degli ebrei nell'Italia medievale* (Rome: Carocci).

Tonini Masella 2012, Tonini Masella, Ginevra. *Donne sole, modelle, prostitute. Marginalità femminili a Roma tra Sette e Ottocento* (Rome: Edizioni di Storia e Letteratura).

Tolan 2015: Tolan, John (ed.). *Expulsion and diaspora formation. Religious and ethnic identities in flux from antiquity to the seventeenth century* (Turnouht: Brepols)

Topalov 2007, Topalov, Christian, ed. *Les divisions de la ville* (Paris: Éditions Unesco).

Topalov, Marin, Depaule, Coudroy de Lille 2010: Topalov, Christian; Brigitte Marin; Jean-Charles Depaule; Laurent Coudroy de Lille eds. *L' aventure des mots de la ville à travers le temps, les langues, les sociétés* (Paris: R. Laffont).

Travagliani 1992: Travaglini, Carlo M. "Rigattieri e società romana nel Settecento". *Quaderni storici* 27: 415–48.

Travaglini 1998: Travaglini, Carlo M. "Dalla corporazione al gruppo professionale: i rigattieri nell'Ottocento Pontificio". *Roma moderna e contemporanea* VI, 3: 427–71.

Trivellato 2010: Trivellato, Francesca. *The familiarity of strangers: The Sephardic diaspora, Livorno, and cross- cultural trade in the early modern period* (New Haven: Yale University Press).

Urbani 1992: Urbani, Rossanna. "Indizi documentari sulla figura di Josef ha-Cohen e della sua famiglia nella Genova del XVI secolo". In *E andammo dove il vento ci spinse. La cacciata degli ebrei dalla Spagna*. Edited by Guido Nathan Zazzu (Genova: Marietti): 59–67.

Van Boxel 1998: Van Boxel, Peter. "Dowry and the conversion of the Jews in sixteenth century Rome: competition between the Church and the Jewish Community". In *Marriage in Italy, 1300–1650*. Edited by Trevor Dean, Kate J.P. Lowe (Cambridge: Cambridge University Press): 489–508.

Vanti 1938: Vanti, Mario. *S. Giacomo degli Incurabili di Roma nel Cinquecento* (Rome: Tipolitografia Rotatori).

Vaquero Piñeiro 1994: Vaquero Piñeiro, Manuel. "Una realtà nazionale composita: comunità e chiese "spagnole" a Roma". In *Roma Capitale: 1447–1527*. Edited by Sergio Gensini (Rome: Ministero per i Beni e le Attività Culturali): 473–91.

Veltri 2017: Veltri, Giuseppe. "Exchanging Cultural Space. The Jewish Ghetto and the Ita-lian Academies". *Rivista di Storia del Cristianesimo* 14, no. 1: 15–30.

Veltri, Chayes 2016: Veltri, Giuseppe; Chayes, Evelyne. *Oltre le mura del ghetto. Accademie, scetticismo e tolleranza nella Venezia barocca. Studi e documenti d'archivio* (Palermo: New Digital Press).

Veltri, Miletto 2012: Veltri, Giuseppe; Miletto, Gianfranco eds. *Rabbi Judah Moscato and the Jewish Intellectual World of Mantua in the 16th-17th Centuries* (Boston, Leiden: Brill).

Veronese 1998: Veronese, Alessandra. *Una famiglia di banchieri ebrei tra XIV e XVI secolo: i da Volterra. Reti di credito nell'Italia del Rinascimento* (Pisa: ETS, 1998).

Vivanti 1996: Vivanti, Corrado ed. *Storia d'Italia, Annali* 11, *Gli ebrei in Italia*. Vol. I, *Dall'alto Medioevo all'età dei ghetti* (Turin: Einaudi).

Vivanti 1997: Vivanti Corrado ed. *Storia d'Italia, Annali* 11, *Gli ebrei in Italia*. Vol. II, *Dall'emancipazione a oggi* (Turin: Einaudi).

Visceglia 2002: Visceglia, Maria Antonietta. *La città rituale. Roma e le sue cerimonie in età moderna* (Rome: Viella, 2002).

Visceglia 2013: Visceglia, Maria Antonietta, ed. *Papato e politica internazionale nella prima età moderna* (Rome: Viella).

Weber 1994: Weber, Cristoph. *Legati e governatori dello Stato della Chiesa (1550-1809)* (Roma: Ministero per i Beni e le Attività Culturali)

Yerushalmi 2010: Yerusahmi, Yosef H. *Assimilazione e antisemitismo razziale. I modelli iberico e tedesco*. Con un saggio introduttivo di David Bidussa (Florence: Giuntina).

Yerushami 2011: Yerushalmi, Yosef H. *Zakhor. Storia ebraica e memoria ebraica*. Con un saggio introduttivo di Harold Bloom (Florence: Giuntina).

Yates 1979: Yates, Frances Amelia. *The occult philosophy in the Elizabethan Age* (London: Routledge & K. Paul) (Italian Edition, Torino: Einaudi, 1982)

Index of Places

Ancona   14–15, 19–20, 50–51, 53, 93, 137, 141–142, 148–149, 183–185, 202–203, 205–206
Ascoli   174
Asti   79
Avignon   7, 19–20, 81–82, 185

Benevento   185
Bologna   61–62, 64, 150–151

Camerino   185
Castiglione di Gandolfo (now, delle Stiviere)   134, 137
Castro San Benedetto   174
Correggio   56

England   55–56

Fabriano   185
Ferrara   7–8, 44, 56, 143
Fossombrone   185
France   55–57
Florence   7, 135, 142, 185–186

Germany   13–14, 55–56, 58
Genoa   29, 56, 81–82

Livorno   7, 183–184
Lombardia   205

Madrid   13–14
Malta   206
Mantua   56, 137–138, 142, 206
Marca/Marche   127–128, 137, 203
Milan   56
Modena   56

Naples   55–56, 58–59, 206
Nice   183

Padua   7–8, 142
Parma   56
Perugia   150–151
Pesaro   135, 138, 142
Piacenza   32–33

Pisa   7
Piedmont   8
Pistoia   135–136, 143
Portugal   12, 26, 32–33, 41, 55, 57
Po Valley   138

Ragusa (Dubrovnik)   8–10, 55
Rimini   135–137
Romagna   205
Rome
   Botteghe Oscure   72–73
   Campo de'Fiori   42–43, 151–152
   Campidoglio   137
   Campo Santo   68, 70–71, 73–77
   Capo di Bove   27–28
   Contrada Judaeorum   150–151, 176–177
   Corte Savelli (Prison of)   63–64, 77–78
   Great Synagogue   1
   Jewish Museum   1
   Largo Cenci, C2.P42
   Monti   150–151
   Osteria del Muletto   177–178
   Paradiso   149–150
   Pescheria   141
   Piazza Giudia   77–78, 135, 137, 151–152
   Piazza Navona   174–177
   Portico d'Ottavia   174
   Regio Arenula   216
   Rione Sant'Angelo   93, 140–141, 174
   Rotonda (Pantheon)   72
   San Giacomo degli Spagnoli (Church and neighborhood)   66–67, 71–72
   San Geronimo, Church of   77–78
   Trastavere   219–220
   Via Appia   27–29
   via degli ebrei   150–151
   via dei Cappellari   177–178
   via di Passatore   114

Sardinia   56
Sicily   56
Siena   185
Spain   9, 12–13, 16–17, 26, 31–33, 41, 45, 49, 55–58, 77–79, 139

Toscana 205

Urbino 185
Umbria 127–128, 205

Venice 7–12, 45–46, 55–57, 135, 138, 141–143, 183–185

Warsaw 11–12

General Index

Abbina, family   155–157
   Abramo, moneylender   154–156
Abbina, Mosè, a Jew from Siena   185
Adel Kind, Cornelio   67–68n
Ademollo, Alessandro   182n
Ago, Renata   96n, 100–101n, 141n, 147–148n, 150–151n, 155n, 212n, 215n
Akman, Dogan Davit   28n
Alberini, Giovanni Battista, *camerlengo* of the *Consolazione*   163n
Aldovrandi/Aldovrando, Theseo, *commissario* of the *Santo Spirito*   164, 167n
Alexander VI (Rodrigo Borgia), pope   12–13, 28, 30–33, 56–57, 76
Allegra, Luciano   91–92n
Ambrogio di Giambattista, neophyte   225
Ambron, family   208–209
Ambrosini, Tranquillo, *luogotenente* of the Criminal Court of the Governor of Rome   132, 136–137
Amron/Ambron, Abramo, owner of a market place   179–180
Anav, Samuele, *rabbi*   116
Andreoni, Luca   50–51n, 54n, 148–149n, 198–199n
Andretta, Stefano   8ın
Angelini, Werther   148–149n
Angelis, Pietro de   165–167n
Angelo, owner of a *gazagà*   101n
Angelo, son in law of Salomone Scandriglia, indicted   128
Antonio, *alias Tentator di Gennazzano*, porter   224–225n
Antiqua Iudaeorum Improbitas (1581)   54–55
Antonius, maestro di casa of Ludovico de Mendoza   73–74
Arpa, Benedetto dell', neophyte   164n
Art collections in the *Scole*   21–22

Ascarelli, Debora, poetess   121n
Ascarelli, Leone, moneylender   150–151
Ascarelli, Gianni   1
Asriglio, family   156–157
   Abraham, moneylender   156–157
   Abramo di Leone   see Sgrizzaro
   Leone   99n, 135–136n, 156
Augustin, saint   5
Auria, Benedetto del fu Giovanni, moneylender   150–151
Avdon, Rubino, moneylender   87–88, 110–111, 116

Baretti da Bresaglia, Cotardo di Giampietro, innkeeper   224–225n
Baron, Salon W.   26n
Barrovecchio San Martini, Maria Luisa   135–136n, 195n
Bartholomeo, bancherotto in Roma   137
Bartolucci, Guido   26n
Bauer, Clemente   200–201n
Beinart, Haim   27–28n
Bellabarba, Marco   132n
Belli, Andrea   163
Benedict XIV (Prospero Lambertini), pope   21, 148–149n, 213
Benso, Camillo, count di Cavour   1
Berardini, Francesco, contractor of the mint of Castiglione delle Stiviere   134
Berengo, Marino   101–102n
Berliner, Abraham   16, 43n, 47–48n, 96–97n, 123n, 138n, 148–149n, 160n, 208–209n
Betarbò/di Viterbo, Sallustio, moneylender   193–194
Bidussa, David   80–81n
Blanis, Moisè da Pesaro, Jew of Ancona   137
Bloch, Marc   80
Boiteux, Martine   182n, 200–201n

Note: Personal names about which further information is not available are shown as they appear in the sources and italicized. Surnames consisting of the toponym preceded by "di" / "del" / "dell'" / "dello" etc., not yet definitively settled in 16th century sources have been indexed under the letter "d". In these instances the use of upper and lower case letters reflects the original forms.

Bonafossa 175–176n
Bonazzoli, Viviana 198–199n
Bondì, Gemma, widow of the late Isacco Perugia, owner of a market place 99–100n, 175–176n
Bonfil, Roberto 19, 19n, 26n, 29n, 43–44n, 50–51n, 75–76n, 82, 82–83n, 87–88n, 91–92n, 94–96n, 103–105n, 105n, 107n, 107–109n, 111–113n, 118, 227–228n
Bonora, Elena 13–14, 42–43n, 46–47n, 67n, 67–68n, 101–102n
Borgia, Cesare, the Duke Valentino 12–13n
Botticini, Maristella
Bregoli, Francesca 7–8n, 183–184n
Bruckner, Wolfgang 119n
Brunelli, Giampiero 14–15n

Caetani, Enrico, cardinal 174, 174–175n, 194–195, 199, 210–211
Caffi, Matteo, shoemaker 225n
Caffiero, Marina vii–, 6–7n, 11, 13–14n, 19–22n, 33n, 41n, 41n, 41–43n, 43, 53–55n, 55n, 65n, 69–70n, 83–84n, 91n, 135n, 138n, 147–149n, 169–170n, 172–175n, 180–182n, 196–197n, 200–201n, 208–209n, 213–215n, 222n, 226–227n
Calabi, Donatella 11, 134n
Calabrese, Giuseppe *del fu* Mosè, moneylender 150–151, 154n
  Giuseppe, nephew of Giuseppe *del fu* Mosè 150–151
Calasso, Francesco 201–202n
Caldino, Il, notary 219–220
Calimani, Riccardo 45–46n
Calzolari, Monica 138–139n, 208–209
Camerata, Massimiliano della 227–228n
Camerino, Ugo 134n
Camilla senese 77–78
Canezza, Alessandro 160–161n
Canonici, Claudio 201n, 222n
Cantù, Francesca 31n
Capellaro, Samuele, tenant 114n
Capitanis, Francesco de, Neapolitan 174–175n
  Nicola de, Neapolitan 174–175n
Capitoli of Daniel da Pisa (Statute of the Jewish Community of Rome) 17–19, 35, 40, 86–87, 103, 131

Capo di Bove, Giambattista, neophyte 225–226
  Olimpia, neofita 225–227
Cappellaro, Mosè, owner of a market place 178
Cappelli, Adriano 69–70n
Capuano, Angelo, *Fattore* 116, 202–203n
  Isacco, tenant 175–176n
Capuzzo, Ester 209–210n
Caracciolo, Alberto 44–45, 148–149n, 176–177n, 211–212n
Caravale, Mario 44–45n, 148–149n, 152–153n, 176–177n, 200–202n, 211–212n
Cardella, Lorenzo 193–194n
Carpianus Antonius, Florentine moneylender 132–133
Cassen, Flora 8n, 49–50n
Cassese, Michele 81n
Castaldini, Alberto 138–139n
Cathecuminis, Aron de, neophyte 164n
Cecchis, Geronimo de, merchant 207
  Tiberio de, merchant 207
Celso, Orazio, *custode* of the Consolazione 163
Cervini, Marcello see Marcello II, pope
Chacón, Alfonso 193–194n
Charles V, Holy Roman Emperor 11–15, 55–56
Charles VIII, King of France 12, 55–56
Chayes, Evelyn 11n
Chin, Katelyn vii–
Christiana Pietas (Bull, 1586) 210
Cipolla, Carlo Maria 96n
Clement VII (Giulio de' Medici), pope 19–20, 35–36, 40, 53
Clement VIII (Ippolito Aldobrandini), pope 20–21
Clement X (Emilio Bonaventura Altieri), pope 144–145
Clement XI (Giovanni Francesco Albani), pope 21
Coen di Viterbo see Sacerdoti di Viterbo
Cohen, Abraham
Cohen, Elisabeth 134–135n
Cohen, Abraham 107–109n
Colonna, Oddone see Martino V, pope
Colorni, Vittore 103–104n, 175–176n, 201n, 209–210n

GENERAL INDEX

Concina, Ennio   134n
Cooperman, Bernard D.   vii–, 7–8n, 10n, 17–18n, 36–38n, 87–88n, 90–92n, 96–97n, 108n, 111–112n, 116, 139–140n, 143–144n
Council of Trent   14–15, 44–47, 51–52n, 59, 84–85, 119–120
Corcos, Elia, *Fattore*   110–111n, 116–117n
   Salomone di Elia, moneylender   110–111n, 174–175n, 216
Corcos, family   114–115, 207
   David, merchant   175–176n, 179–180
   Salomone of Salvatore, *maskil* and moneylender   110–111, 114–117, 121, 179–180, 199, 207
   Salvatore, moneylender   110–111
   Salvatore di Salomone, moneylender   114–115, 185–186n, 199, 207
   Samuele di Salvatore moneylender   185–186
Corcos, Giacobbe, moneylender   116
Corcos, Tranquillo Vita, rabbi   19–21, 91, 124, 208–209n
Cordoba, Petro de, indicted   66–67
Cordova, Giovanni di   218–219
Cormano, Natascia   160–161n, 167n
Cornaro, Luigi, cardinal   193–195, 199
Corsetto, Sabbato del, *scortica cavalli*   125–126
Cosmedo, Giovanni Battista, merchant   220
Costadoni, Anselmo, monk   51–52n
Coudroy de Lille, Laurent   177–179n
Cozzi, Gaetano   134n
Cracolo/Crocolo, Servadio/Servideo, moneylender   110–111, 209–210
   Dulcetta   209–210
   Settimio del fu Dattilo, moneylender   209–210n
Crapano, Fabian, debtor   219–220
Cremonesi, Giovanni Maria, carpenter   114n
Crescas, Isacco, Jew of Avignon   185n
Criminal Court of the Governor of Rome
   Counterfeit money trial, 1572   150–151
   Cristophorus Robuster trial   74–75
   Petro de Cordoba trial   66–67
   Ram trial   132
   Salomone and Angelo di Scandriglia trial   128

Sforno trial   60–61, 79–80, 84, 86
Solis trial   60–61, 71–75, 84, 86
Vituccio di Lanciano trial   124
Cuggiò, Niccolò Antonio   197–198n
Cum nimis absurdum (Bull, 1555))   14, 18, 45–51, 53–55, 58–60, 83, 89–90, 93–94, 128–129, 131–132, 139, 160, 181, 214, 230
Cupientes Iudaeos (Bull, 1542)   41
Curio del Schiavo (*alias de Rubeis*)   199

da Pisa, Daniel, moneylender   17–18, 37–40, 86–88, 96–97n, 233
da Perugia, Stefano di Severo, moneylender   150–151
da San Martinello, Salomone, Jew   77–78
d'Aversa, Giacobbe, moneylender   168–169, 179, 186
   Giuseppe di Giacobbe, moneylender   168–169n
   Giuseppe, merchant   186
   Leone di Giacobbe, moneylender   168–169n
D'Azeglio, Massimo   1–3
David figliolo de Angelo de Nanna, Jew in Ancona   137
Davanzo Poli, Doretta   21n
Davis, Robert C.   45–46n
De Benedetti, Sandra   96–98n, 220n
de Bonadonna, Abramo, merchant   186
De Caro Balbi, Silvana   132–133n
de Fabia, Federico, *vaccinaro*   216
   Filippo, *vaccinaro*   216
del Borgo, family   99–100, 204
   David, merchant and brother of Pompeo   99–100, 175–176n
   Graziosa, sister of Pompeo   101
   Pompeo (Mosè del Borgo), notary   24, 94–103, 121, 128–129, 171, 204, 217, 219–220, 222–223, 233
   Prospero, merchant, father of Pompeo   99–100
Del Col, Andrea   42–43n, 47n, 138n
Delicado, Francisco   34–35
Dell'Anguillara, Giovanni Angelo (Angelo di Mosè), neophyte   164n, 227
dell'Aquila, Giuseppe, merchant   163
delle Piattelle, Leone, notary   99–100, 108–111, 114n, 128–129

delli Panzieri, Simone, merchant   135–136, 143, 184
dello Strologo, Isacco, merchant   186
Delopiglio, Angelo/Agnilo, owner of a market place   178
   Benedetto of Benedetto, prosecutor   175–176n
   Giacobbe, prosecutor   175–176n
   Leuccio   227
   Prudentia, neophyte see Livoletta, Prudentia
   Stella   222–223, 227
Deloro, Leone, merchant   171–172, 186
Del Presto, Benedetto, owner of a market place   177n
Del Presto, Mosè   228
Del Re, Niccolò   195–196n
del Sestier/delli Sestieri, Durante, moneylender   114–116, 194, 207
   Salomone di Durante, moneylender   207
   Sancton di Durante, moneylender   207
De Luca, Giovanni Battista   138–139n
Delumeau, Jean   157–158n
de Lustro, David, owner of a market place   176–177
Depaul, Jean-Charles   177–179n
de Scela, Iacob, owner of a market place   176–177
de Tibure, Daniele, merchant   210–211
de Turris, Nicola del fu Hieronimo, moneylender   150–151
di Ascoli, Giangregorio   227–228n
di Basilea, Simon, Jew in Mantua   206
di Bologna, Mosè, merchant   156–157n
di Campofallone, Abramo, buthcer   227–228
Di Cammeo, Leone   175–176n
di Capua, Vito, moneylender   109–110
Di Castro, Alessandra   vii
Di Castro, Daniela   1, 21–22, 180–181n, 200n
di Cave, Angelo   165–166n, 168–169n
di Ceprano, family   157
di Ceprano, Prospero, *Fattore*   89–90n, 109–110
Ceprano, Sabbato, merchant and moneylender   154–156
di Ceprano, Samuele   217
   Stella   217
di Collevecchio, Brunetta, owner of a market place   220
di Diodato, Salomone   172n

di Fiorentino, Samuele   220
   Diana, wife of Samuele   220
di Frascati, Crescienzo   225–226
di Imola, Giovanni Antonio, indicted   137
di Imola, Marco, indicted   137
di Lanciano, Vito, *detto* Vituccio, thief   124–128
di Lanciano, Vito, merchant   171n
di Lattes, Giacobbe   89–90n
di (de) Lattes, Manuele, merchant   156–157n
di Lattes, Samuele, *rabbi*   110–111
Dimant, Mauricio   7–8n
di Marino, Leuccio, contractor   204–205
di Marino, Sabato   220
di Mattathia, Salomone, merchant   164
di Meluccio, Conci, butcher   217–219
di Modigliano, Abramo   175–176n, 225n
di Montefiascone, Alessandro Angelo, moneylender   135–136, 143, 184
di Montepulciano, Oliviero di Gianmaria, butcher   224–225n
di Murcia, Leone, *Fattore*   89–90n, 109–110
di Murcia/Mursia, Giacobbe, tenant   216
di Mus, Leone, indicted   137
di Nepi, Mele   225n
Di Nepi, Serena   7–8n, 17–18n, 22n, 50–52n, 54–55n, 88n, 91–92n, 96–97n, 104–105n, 126n, 128n, 138n, 174n, 181n, 185n, 185–186n, 196–198n, 205–206n, 210–211n, 216n, 220n, 227–228n
di Palestrina, Michele, contractor   116
di Pellegrino/Pellegrino, David di Salomone, merchant   167n, 185
   Giacobbe   185
di Perugia, Isacco, husband of Gemma Bondì   99–100n
di Perugia, Michele, merchant   186
di Piperno, Angelo, *detto* Diobelei
di Pontecorvo, Abramo, tenant   222–225, 227
   Donna, wife of Abramo   224–225
   Leone di Abramo   224–225, 227
di Porto, Grandilio, notary   97–98n
di Reggio, Giuseppe   175–176n
di Rignano, Beniamino   220
di Rignano, Mosè   204–205n
di Scantriglia, Salomone, mercante   178, 204–205n
di Segni, Benedetto, tenant   175–176n
di Segni, Ester   220

GENERAL INDEX

di Segni, Giuseppe del fu Angelo, moneylender 179n
    Salomone, moneylender 179
di Serena, Giuseppe, merchant 175–176n
    Sabbato/Sabato, merchant 175–176n, 179–180, 186
di Sicilia, family 204–205
    Abramo di David, merchant 204–205n
    David di Prospero, merchant 204–205n
    Isacco, merchant 204–205n
    Laudadio di David, moneylender 204–205n
di Simonetto, Mosè, merchant 186
Di Sivo, Michele 51–53n, 73–74n, 126n, 135n, 135–136n
di Sonnino, Angelo, moneylender 199
di Tagliacozzo, Gabriele 116
di Tivoli, Daniele, merchant 175–176n
    Sabato, mercante
di Venafri Angelo, moneylender 109–111n
di Venafri/Benafri, Aron, moneylender
    Dattilo, moneylender 216
    Mosè, moneylender 216n
di Venafri, Mosè del fu Giacobbe, moneylender
di Ventura, Angelo, *mandatario* 225n
di Veroli, Sabbato, contractor 182–183, 204n
di Vitale, Abramo, Jew of Avignon 185n
di Viterbo, Isacco del fu Bonaventura 185
Dudum siquidem (Bull, 1493) 31
Dweck, Yaacob 26n

Edict of Nantes (1598) 15
Emanuele Filiberto, Duchy of Savoy 79
Errera (Herrera), Bartholomeo, neophyte 134–135, 137
Esposito, Anna vii–, 6n, 17, 17–18n, 27–29n, 34, 36–38n, 38–39n, 50–51n, 86–87n, 96–97n, 103–104n, 109–113n, 135n, 138–140n, 145–146n, 150–152n, 160–161n, 167–168n, 177–178n, 185–186n, 198–199n, 207–211n, 215n, 222n, 227–228n
Est, Marcantonio 225n
Eximiae Devotionis (Bull, 1493) 31

Fabiis, Pietro Paolo de, *procuratore* of the Consolazione 186
Facchini, Cristiana 80–81n
Farnese, Alessandro, cardinal 67–68, 77–78, 81–83
Feci, Simona 126n, 135n

Federici, Girolamo, Governor of Rome
Ferdinando I de'Medici, Grand Duke of Toscany 7
Ferdinand II of Aragon 16–17, 30
Ferrara, Pierina / Micol 50–51n
Ferrara degli Uberti, Carlotta 2, 111–112n, 209–210n
Fettah, Samuel 178–179n
Filippini, Jeann-Pierre 148–149n
Finkelstein, Louis 43n
Fiorentino, Benedetto, buyer of a market place 99–100n, 175–176n
    Mosè, buyer of a market place 99–100n, 175–176n
Fiorenzuolo, merchant 150–151
Flandet, Agata 165–166
Floruccia hebrea, witness 61–66, 84
Foa, Anna 6–7, 26n, 28n, 28–33n, 47–48n, 53–54n, 60, 65n, 67–69, 80–82n, 222n, 227–228n
Formica, Marina 177–178n
Fosi, Irene 69–70n, 84n, 126n, 135n, 135–136n, 172–173n, 195n, 195–196n
Fragnito, Gigliola 81n
Francescangeli, Laura 96–99n, 182n
Franceschi, Alessandro (Hananel da Foligno), neophyte 67–68, 76–77
Francesco di Silvestro, bancherotto in Piazza Giudea 135, 137
Francesco Portoghese, mastro 72
Franchi, Giuseppe, neophyte
Frattarelli Fisher, Lucia 7n, 148–149n, 183–184n
Fresco, Simon
Friz, Giuliano 141n

Gabrielli, Meir Magino 148–149
Gabriello, Ottavio, *custode* of the Consolazione 186
Galante, David 175–176n
Galasso, Cristina 103–104n, 183–184n
Garin, Eugenio 26n
Garonetti, Giovanni Battista, *camerlengo* of the San Giacomo degli Incurabili 166n13
Gasperoni, Michaël 113n, 175–176n, 215n
Gershom ben Yehuda, *rabbi* 113
Ghisella/Ghisello, Maddalena, neophyte, widow of the late Costantino Ongarino 224–225
    Paolo, neophyte 170

Giacobbe del fu Prospero, merchant 172n, 186
Giacobbe, di Ambrogio di Giambattista, neophyte 225–227
Ginzburg, Carlo 172–173n
Gioioso, Giacobbe, *rabbi* 114–116, 116–117n, 193–194
Gioioso, Isacco, *rabbi* and *moneylender* 110–111, 193–194
Gioseppe in Piazza Giudia 77–78
GiovanniPugliese 150–151
Giovanni Battista, collector agent of the *Consolazione* 186
Giudici, Battista dei, Apostolic Commissioner 51–52n
Giustiniani, bank 152
Giustiniani, Pietro, monk 51–52
Golan, Shoshanna 24n, 96–97n
Gonzaga, family 142n
Grande, Mosè 156–157, 172, 186
Graziadio, *detto* Veneziano, butcher 227–228
Graziano, Salomone 68, 74–76, 80–81, 86
Gregory I, the Great, pope 5
Gregory XIII (Ugo Boncompagni), pope 103–104, 139, 142, 203
Grendi, Edoardo 138–139n
Groppi, Angela 113n, 160n, 169–170n, 175–176n, 215n
Grunfeld, Isidor
Guastavillani, Filippo, cardinal 193–195
Gualazzini, Ugo 141n
Guetta, Alessandro vii, 19, 26n
Guglielmi, Pier Girolamo, *consultore* of the Holy Office 181
Gugnetta, Massimo, notary of the Vicar 220

Haro, Lopez de, Spanish ambassador 30–31, 56–57
Hebraerorum gens (Bull, 1569) 19–20
Herzig, Tamar 57n, 222n
Holy Office (Congregation of) 46–47, 54–55, 69–70, 138, 181, 197–198, 210–211
House of Catechumens 33, 41–42, 44–45, 47, 54–55, 65, 152–153, 224–227

Idel, Moshe 26n
Iannuzzi, Isabella 81–82n
Ibn Verga, Shelomoh 29, 76

Illius (Bull, 1543) 41, 54–55
Indrimi, Natalia vii
Infessura Stefano, diarist 27–28, 30, 30n
Innocent XI (Benedetto Odescalchi), pope 198–199
Innocent XII (Antonio Pignatelli), pope 198–199
Inter Coetera (Bull, 1493) 31
Isabella di Castiglia, Queen of Spain 26
Isacco, notary 24, 89–90n, 95–96, 99–100, 102, 112–116, 152–153n
Israel, Jonathan 26n, 26n, 55

Jacomo parigino, mastro 220
Josef ha-Cohen 67–68, 74–76, 79, 81–82, 86, 234
Julius III (Giovanni Maria Ciocchi del Monte), pope 66–67

Kaplan, Benjamin Yosef vii, 26n, 55
Katz, Jacob 123n
Kellenbenz, Hermann 119–120n
Kertzer, David 2, 22n, 185–186n

Lampronti, Isacco, rabbi 91
Lanciano, Giacomo, neophyte 227–228
Laras, Giuseppe 113n, 175–176n
Lattes, Andrea Yaakov 38–39n, 94n, 201–202n
Lattes, David, owner of a market place 177n
Lattes, Isacco, *rabbi* 61
Laudanna, Luigi 152n
Lehman, Mathias B. 183–184n
Leo, Levantine Jew 206
Leone, servant of the Sforno family 64
Leo X (Giovanni de' Medici), pope 34–37, 87–88, 139–140n, 144–146, 193, 198–199
Levi, Leon de, merchant 168–169n
Ligorio, Benedetto 9–10n
Limentani, Consiglio di, tenant 175–176n
Limentani, Giacomo, *detto* Lillo 108n
Lione ebreo sul cantone de' Chiavari 77–78
Liscia Bemporad, Dora 148–149n
Lisurano, Andrea del fu Francesco, moneylender 150–151
Livi, Livio 141n
Livoletta, Prudentia (Prudentia Delopiglio), neophyte 222–223, 227
Tommaso, neophyte 222–223
Lolli, Elena 110–111
Londei, Luigi 132–133n

GENERAL INDEX

Lopagio, Isach da Pesaro, Jew of Ancona   137
Lopez, bank   152
Lopez, Giovanni, *converso*   148–149
Lorenzo del fu Blasi, *detto* Fiorentino, moneylender   150–151
Lori Sanfilippo, Isa   96–97n
Ludovico, neophyte   216
Lupo, Alessandra   165–166n
Luzzati, Michele   51–52n, 82–83n, 91–92n, 125n, 154n, 185n, 198–199n, 222n
Luzzatto, Simone, rabbi   11
Luzzatto Voghera, Gadi   91n, 94n

Machiavelli, Niccolò   12–13n
Maggio, Paolo, *custode* of the Consolazione   186
Maimonide, Mosè, (Rambam)   42–43
Maifreda, Germano   vii–, 138n
Malena, Adelisa   51–52n
Malkiel, David   110–111n
Mancino, Leone, *detto* Romano, merchant   163–164, 166n, 168–169n, 168–169n, 172n, 186
Mandarino, Erika   vii
Manilio/Manlilio, Paolo, neophyte   61–63, 65–66
Mampieri, Martina   44–45n, 60n, 68n
Marcellus II (Marcello Cervini), pope   67–68, 71, 77–78
Marconcini, Samuela   7n
Margherita, *romana*   71–73
Marin, Brigitte   177–179n
Marini, Leone, owner of a market place   101n
Marrano's stake in Ancona (1556)   14–15, 50–51
Martini, Andrea, notary of the Chamber   210–211
Martini, Angelo   141n
Martin Luther   13–14, 41, 51–52
Martin V (Oddone Colonna), pope
Martire, Egilberto   167n
Martone, Luciano   105–106n
Marsaino, Salvatore, neophyte, butcher   227–228
Marvano, Giacobbe, moneylender   199–200
Mascetti, Jacopo   vii
Massa, Eugenio   51–52n
Matio, business partner of Bartholomeo Errera   137

Matteo, Ceriaco   224–225
Mattheis, Giovanni d'Aurelio de, *guardiano* of the Consolazione   163–164n, 186
Mazzone, Angelo, merchant   165–166n
Sabbato, merchant   165–166n
Salomone, merchant   156–157n, 168–169n, 186
Melasecchi, Olga   21n
Melcer Padon, Nurit   7–8n
Menasci, Giuseppe, *alias* Coppolaro see S. Crevere, Prospero da
Menasci, Mosè, moneylender   110–111, 194, 207
Menasse, Giacobbe, merchant   168–169n
Prospero, merchant   164, 167n
Mendoza, Ludovico de   73–74
Merizi, Benedetto   109–110
Meron, Orly   141n
Miccoli, Giovanni   119n
Michelangelo (del fu Giacobbe di Capua), neophyte   223–224
Michele, owner of a *gazagà*   101n
Michele di Gabriele/del fu Gabriele, merchant   172n, 175–176n, 186
Migliau, Bice   1
Milanese, Andrea   216, 219
Milano, Attilio   16–18n, 21–22n, 38n, 38–40n, 45–51n, 51n, 53n, 69–70n, 89–90n, 92n, 96–97n, 104n, 138n, 148–149n, 160n, 175–176n, 201–202, 206n, 208–209n
Miletto, Gianfranco   11
Mittarelli, Giovanni Benedetto, monk   51–52n
Modigliani, family   208–209
Modigliani, Anna   150–151n, 155n, 174–175n, 178n
Montibus, Hersilio de, judge   199
Moresco, Angelo, owner of a market place   175–176n, 178
Moresco, Angelo di Amadio, merchant   167–168, 186
Cascian, merchant   164
Vito di Amadio, merchant   167n, 167–168, 172, 175–176n, 186, 217
Moresco, Marzocco, moneylender
Moretti, Massimo   49–50n
Morichini, Carlo Luigi   160–161n
Moro, family   208–209
Moro, Isacco, merchant   175–176n, 179–180, 186

Moro, Nissim, merchant   163–164n, 186
Moro, Siman Tov, merchant   186
Moroni, Gaetano   197–198n
Mortara, Edgardo, neophyte   2
Mortari, Vincenzo   105n
Moscato, Abramo di Sabbato, Jew of Fossombrone   185, 185–186n
Moscato, Judah, rabbi   11
Mosè del fu Livoletta, butcher   227–228
Mosè ha Rofè *Fattore*   89–90
Muccinello, Angelo, merchant   167n, 220
Musia, Francesco, moneylender   150–151
Muti, Ottavio, *camerlengo* of the Consolazione   186
Muzzarelli, Giuseppina   54n

Napolitano, Mosè   225
Negri, Angelo, *napolitano*, merchant   186
Negri, Isacco   225–226
Negri, Mosè, merchant   167n, 172, 186, 225–226
Niccolò, priore of the *Consolazione*   186
Novoa, James Nelson   30n, 32–33n

Olivari, Michele   222n
Ongarino, Costantino   224–225
    Maddalena   see Ghisella, Maddalena
    Veronica   224
Orsini, Ieronimo (Aron di rabbì Bendetto), neophyte   164n

Pacifico, Statilio, *custode* of the Consolazione   186
Palombelli, Cecilia   vii
Paul III (Alessandro Farnese), pope   13–14, 17–18, 41–43, 46–47, 58, 67–68, 70–71
Paul IV (Gian Pietro Carafa), pope   3, 9–10, 14–15, 17–19, 21–22, 27, 44–54, 58–60, 66–70, 75, 77–80, 82–86, 88–89, 93–94, 150, 160, 165, 230
Paul V (Camillo Borghese), pope   195–196n
Parente, Fausto   42–43n, 47–48n
Parisi, Francesco, *custode* of the Consolazione   163
Pascasio, Belardino/Berardino, notary   96–97, 101, 151–152n, 216
Passapiera, Aron   175–176n
    Meir di Aron, *detto* Meluzzo
Pastor, Ludwig von   47–48n, 148–149n

Pastura Ruggiero, Maria Grazia   152–153n, 195n, 195–196n, 211–213n
Patello, Sabbato   172
Peace of Augusburg (1555)   15
Pelato, Leone, merchant   186
Pecorella, Corrado   141n
Petrapauli, Doralice, accuser in a trial   128
Perani, Mauro   vii, 24–25n, 91n
Pericoli, Pietro   163
Perugia, Abramo, guardian   175–176n
    Isacco, owner of a market place   175–176n
Perugia, Isacco, uncle of Abramo Moscato   185–186n
Petrocchi, Massimo   160–161n
Philip II, King of Spain   14–15
Piccialuti, Maura   160–161n, 172–173n
Pinelli, bank   152
Pittella, Raffaele Cosimo   90–91n, 101–102n
Pius V (Michele Ghislieri), pope   53n, 149, 210
Pius VII (Barnaba Chiaramonti), pope   19–20, 176–177
Pious IX (Giovanni Maria Mastai Ferretti), pope   2
Piola Caselli, Fausto   152, 157–158n, 172–173n, 200–201n
Piperno, Angelo, v. Zarut, Angelo
    Mosè, merchant and brother of Angelo Zarut   171, 186
Po-chia Hsia, Ronnie   46–47n
Poliakov, Léon   144–145, 152–153n, 172–173n
Polidoro/di Polidoro, Giuseppe, owner of a market place   175–177n, 179–180
Pompeo, Augusto   135–136n
Porti, Giambattista, *mastro*   220
Pratesi, Alessandro   104–105n
Preziosa, moglie di Bonafossa   175n47
Procaccia, Claudio   20–21n, 140–141n, 147–148n, 152n, 152–153n, 198–199n
Procaccia, Micaela   61–62n, 76n, 79–80n, 121n, 135n, 138–139n, 209–210n
Prodi, Paolo   31n, 119n, 119–120n, 157–158n, 211–212n
Prosperi, Adriano   31n, 51–52n, 74–75n, 84–85n, 138n, 180–181n
Provenzale, Israel, *rabbi*   116–117

Quaglioni, Diego   49n, 51–52n
Querini, Vincenzo, monk   51–52

GENERAL INDEX

Ram, family   139, 144, 157, 208, 230–231
   Abramo di Casciano, Jew of Ancona   141
   Casciano del fu Salomone (Donato), moneylender   114–115n, 135, 139–140
   David, *detto* Rosciolo (Rocciolo), del fu Samuele, moneylender   139–140
   Giuseppe di Casciano, Jew of Venise   141
   Salomone di Casciano, moneylender and indicted   131–132, 139, 144, 150, 159, 183–184, 200, 234
Ravid, Benjamin C   45–46n
Reinhardt, Wolfgang   119n
Reformation: 9–10, 13–14, 40–41, 119
Ricci, Diomedi, notary of the *Auditore della Camera in Banchi*   101
Rieger, Paul   96–97n
Roberti, Roberto   217–219
Robuster, Cristophorus, indicted for a killing   74–75
Roccas, David   156–157n
Roccas, Salomone, moneylender   216
Rodocanachi, Emmanuel   47–48n
Roman Jewish Library   25
Romeo, Giovanni   138n
Rosa, Mario   213n
Rosciello, Giacobbe, merchant   163n, 166–169n, 186, 220n
   Isacco, merchant   166–167, 179–180
Rosenberg, Paul M.   vii–
Rosso a larco de' Cenci, il   77–78
Roth, Cecil   69–70n
Rotolanti, Marco Antonio, *camerlengo* of the Consolazione   186
Rubeis, Camillo de   216
Ruderman, David B.   7–8n, 26n, 26n, 44n, 84n, 91n
Ruini, Giovanni Battista, *commissario* of the Santo Spirito   170
Ruis, Hieronimus, *custode* of the Consolazione   186
Russotto, Gabriele   167n
Rusticucci, Geronimo, neophyte   220

Santa Crevere, Prospero da (Giuseppe Menasci, *detto* Coppolaro), neophyte   156–157, 194, 216, 223
Sabatini, Mosè, merchant   186
Sabato del fu Mosè, innkeeper   219–220

Sacerdote, Angelo, merchant   161–162, 167n, 186
Sacerdote, Emanuele, v. Sciaquatello
Sacerdote, David di Gaiosa, merchant   220
Sacerdote, Israele, merchant   175–176n, 186
Sacerdoti, Crisca, merchant   186
Sacerdoti di Viterbo (Coen di Viterbo), Eliezer Prospero, *rabbi*   19, 114–117
   Iechiel del fu Mechallel, moneylender   110–111
Sacerdoti, Mosè, merchant   174, 176–177
Salomone del fu Diodato, merchant   171–172
Samuele "Il Pagliano", Fattore   202–203n
Sanctis, Bernandino de, notary   216
San Giovanni Decollato, confraternity of   73–74, 135–136n
Savelli Giacomo, cardinal
Savoia, Carlo Alberto, King of Sardinia   1
Savy, Pierre   vii
Scandriglia, Salomone, indicted   128
Scarlata-Fazio, Mariano   138–139n
Scazzocchio, Abramo, *lawyer*   109–110n
Scazzocchio, Abramo, merchant   168–169n
   Leone, merchant   171n, 186
   Samuele, merchant   161–162, 167n, 171–172, 175–176n, 186
Scazzocchio, Angelo, merchant   175–176n
Scazzocchio, Dattilo, contractor   182–183, 204n
Scazzocchio, Romano   218–219
Schilling, Heinz   119n
Schwarz, Stuart B.   31n
Schwarzfuchs, Simon   29n, 50–51n, 196–197n
Sciaquatello (Emanuele Sacerdote), merchant and moneylender   163–169, 172, 186
Sed, Graziano   225–226
   Piacentia, wife of Graziano   225–226n
Segre, Giacomo, captain   2
Segre, Renata   41–43n, 43n, 45–47n, 50n, 53n, 53–55n, 67n, 76n, 79n, 91–92n, 120n, 148–149n
Serena, Sabbato di Lustro   110–111, 166–168
Seripando, Girolamo, cardinal   8n
Sestieri, family   208–209
Settimezzo, Massimo, moneylender
Sforno, family   61–64, 79–80
   Benenata/Bononata, victim during the Sack   61–63

Sforno, family (cont.)
    Moyses di Servadio, victim during the
        Sack   61–62
    Servadio (*Ovadia*), rabbi   61–62
    Samuele, victim during the Sack   61–62
Sforno, trial   61, 66, 80, 83
Sgrizzaro (Abramo di Leone Asriglio),
    moneylender   135–136, 143, 150,
    156–157, 220, 223
Siegmund, Stephanie   7n, 91–92n, 160n, 185n
Silaus, Salomone, merchant   163n
Simone, business partner of Leone di
    Mus   137
Simonetti, Crescienzo, merchant   165–166n
Simonsohn, Shlomo   38–39n, 43n,
    67–68n, 142n
Sinisi, Daniela   175–176n
Sixtus v (Felice Peretti), pope   53, 132–133,
    142, 144–145, 148–150, 152, 154–155, 210
Solis, Domenico de (dottor Sulim), Spanish
    physician   66, 68, 71–75, 77–80, 84, 86
Solon, Mosè, *detto* Romano   199
Sonne, Isaiah   25
Sonnino, Eugenio   195–196n
Soschin, Mosè Tedesco, merchant
    168–169n
Spada, Pietro, neophyte   225–227
    Giacobbe di Pietro, Jew   225
Spagnoletto, Amedeo   21n, 69–70n, 76n,
    82–83n
Sperandeo, Zerbino, notary
Sperandio di Norcia, fishseller   224–225n
Spizzichino, Giancarlo   51n, 69–70n
Steele, Mark   141n
Stefani, Piero   32n, 49n, 51–52n, 147–148n
Stow, Kenneth   6–7, 23–24, 29n, 42–45n,
    47–48n, 51–52n, 55, 89–90n, 95–97n,
    97–99n, 99–101n, 106–108, 108–110n,
    112–113n, 119–120n, 139–140n, 143–144n,
    196–199n, 201n, 220n, 222n, 227–228n
Strangio, Donatella   200–201n
Subrahmanyam, Sanjay   7–8n
Sulim, dottor   see Solis, Domenico

Taradel, Ruggero   69–70n, 81–82, 172–173n
Tarmi, Giacobbe   203n
Tedesco, Consiglio, *Fattore*   202–203n
Terpstra, Nicholas   55

Teter, Magda   83n
Toaff, Ariel   6n, 29n, 37n, 54n, 61n, 80–82n,
    89–90n, 147–149n, 182n, 197–201n,
    206n, 219–220n, 227–228n
Tocci, Giovanni   201n
Todeschini, Giacomo   5–6n, 11, 55n, 66–67n,
    147–148n, 154n, 197–198n
Tolan, John   55
Topalov, Christian   177–179n
Torquemada, Tomás de   32–33
Toscano, Mario   1
Travaglini, Carlo Maria   150n
Treves, Leone, moneylender   219–220
Treves, Vito, moneylender   99n, 220
Trincha, Onorio, gabellario   199
Tripolese, Cascian, merchant   167n, 171–172,
    186, 225–226
Tripolese, Graziano   225–226
Trivellato, Francesca   7n, 7–8n, 26n,
    183–184n
Tyburtinus, Sabbato, moneylender   199

Urban vii (Giovanni Battista Castagna),
    pope   142
Urbani, Rossana   81–82n

Valle, Valerio de, *custode* of the
    Consolazione   186
Van Boxel, Piet   141n, 206n
Vanti, Mario   165–166n
Vaquero Piñeiro   87–88n
Veltri, Giuseppe   vii–, 11
Verdi, Orietta   175–176n
Veronese, Alessandra   198–199n, 222n
Villani, Stefano   vii
Vincenzo, maestro di casa of the
    Consolazione   186
Visceglia, Maria Antonietta   31n, 180–181n
Vito, owner of a *gazagà*   101n
Vittoria, in casa di Caterina senese   77–78
Vogelstein, Heinrich   96–97n

Wars in Italy (1494–1559)   11–14, 16–17,
    46–47, 55–56, 58
    Battle of Agnadello (1509)   13–14, 57
    Cateau-Cambresis (Peace of, 1559)
        56, 59
    Charles viii's invasion (1494)   55–56

GENERAL INDEX

Sack of Rome (1527)   13–14, 33–35, 39, 41, 44–45, 51, 61
Weber, Christoph   193–194n
Western Sephardi Diasporas   7–9, 12–13, 15–17, 26–27, 40, 76

Yates, Frances   26n
Yerushalmi, Yosef Haim   28, 82–83

Zadik, Beniamino, *rabbi*   116
Zarut, Angelo (Angelo Piperno), merchant   165–167n, 171–172, 186
Zilera de Laude, Vincentino, *maggiordomo* of the *Consolazione*   186
Zio Lavo (Salomone), merchant   156–157n, 168–169n, 186

Printed in the United States
By Bookmasters